5-1-44   (63-1991)

Philippe Halsman

MARSHALL FIELD III

Marshall Field III

A Biography by STEPHEN BECKER

SIMON AND SCHUSTER

NEW YORK, 1964

To my Mary with love

Marshall Field III

FOREWORD

M ARSHALL FIELD III was a liberal and a gentleman; his biographer is a liberal. Field would never have descended to my occasional surly truculence, but he would have excused it; more, enjoyed it. He would have seen very quickly that I was not really a biographer in any Boswellian sense, still less a scholar; he would probably have described me as a free-lance complainer, and would surely have cheered me on. For one thing, he believed in cheering people on; when men wanted to write or make speeches or swear mighty oaths or just think, he believed they ought to go to it, and he spent much of his life defending or advancing the kind of society in which they could. For another, my complaints are approximately his complaints.

This is, in short, a partisan biography, in which adverse criticism is restrained, though not silenced, by affinity. It is not impartial, detached, or objective. It is a discursive and sometimes waggish essay wrapped around the life of a good man, and its author has not tried to suppress his own libertarian convictions in favor of an austere, and to him insipid, neutrality. That will flaw the essay for the Olympian, improve it for the splenetic, and perhaps enliven it for both.

Mrs. Marshall Field III offered me full access to her late husband's papers; she also gave freely of her time and memories. For the personal aspects of Marshall Field's life I naturally relied upon his family and close friends. In return for truth I respected privacy. But my privacy too was respected: no one close to Field so much as hinted that I should alter or restrain my own view of American society or of Field's place in it; a respect for which I am grateful, the more so as Field himself would have abhorred any such polite censorship.

Further acknowledgments are at the back of the book. Also

at the back of the book are the reference notes, which are few and are not indicated in the text; reference noting has lately become licentious. A reader interested in references will surely want more than the usual library-card information; and the reader bored by references may legitimately hope to be spared such tedium. If my prose is marred by excess and barbarism, my page is not marred by superscripts.

—STEPHEN BECKER

There is properly no history; only biography.

—EMERSON

If, in the account of this interesting people, I have deviated from the strict and original line of my undertaking, the merit of the subject will hide my transgression or solicit my excuse.

—GIBBON

CHAPTER ONE

It takes a kind of genius to make a fortune, and especially a large fortune. It is neither goodness, nor wit, nor talent, nor strength, nor delicacy. I don't know precisely what it is: I am waiting for someone to tell me.

—JEAN DE LA BRUYÈRE,
Caractères, VI, 1688

W HEN MARSHALL FIELD III WAS BORN, on September 28, 1893, Chicago was "the crowning city, whose merchants are princes, whose traffickers are the honorable of the earth." The most princely and honorable of those merchants, the most perfect (or least flawed) expression of nineteenth-century capitalism, was the infant's grand-father, Marshall Field I; his life had paralleled, his career had epitomized, the most explosive burgeoning of technology and com-merce that mankind had yet seen. If 1893 was a year of severe panic, if Coxey's Army was recruiting, the one was a salutary adjustment and the other a trifling annoyance. In the twenty-eight years—not at all a long time—since the Civil War our population had doubled, and stood near 70,000,000; thirty-six states had become forty-four; railroads had spanned the continent; what was once the West had become the Middle West; the millionaire had replaced the frontiers-man as folk hero; and industrialization had transformed the coun-try's economy so energetically that the Sherman Antitrust Act had been judged necessary—though it was not seriously enforced until 1902. The three decades were a ceaseless moil of chaotic growth: immigration, a sprawling rush westward, capital leapfrogging wildly, patents by the thousands. Money flowed west from Boston, New York, and Washington, and returned on the next tide doubled and trebled. Politicians and capitalists, often indistinguishable, saw no end to it all; if the periodic panics were severe, they were also brief, and every recovery was a leap forward. Skeptics and trouble-makers like the Knights of Labor (whose ranks welcomed women and Negroes, and excluded bankers, lawyers, and liquor dealers) suggested that the country was only converting its moral capital to financial capital; esthetically inclined New Yorkers and Bostonians recoiled from the unparalleled ugliness of our industrial centers and the egregious tastelessness of our "better neighborhoods"; Euro-peans complained that we were barbarians (or worse, adolescents) blindly and purposelessly accumulating riches and power. But the age was not hospitable to fractious malcontents. America was on its way. No one knew where; only a few cared.

Henry Adams cared; he was disturbed and repelled by our ne-glect of tradition; but he was a snob. Walt Whitman cared, and tried to create a tradition for us; but he was a poet. Painters and archi-tects cared, but they were working in a vacuum; imitations of the past were sterile, the present was tawdry, and the future looked too much like Jay Gould in a silk hat riding on an immigrant worker. We had no Plantagenets, no Tudors, not even Four Georges to look back to; only Founding Fathers, but they were dead less than a century, some of them still attacked and defended in public debate, none of them yet venerated caricatures.

We were, in short, the first *new* country to industrialize, and also the first republic. With a loose class structure and an ill-defined elite we lacked standards and goals outside, independent of, our own rush to wealth and power, and anyone who publicly lamented the lack was regarded as a moony fellow or worse. What we did have was an ideology, the dominant ideology of the Anglo-Saxon world, and it flourished wildly in America precisely because it met no competition: not from royalty, or nobility, or a hierarchy of classes, or a firm and forbidding church; not even from the land, which fed it generously. The ideology was modern mercantile Cal-vinism.

The phrase must not be taken too literally; the United States was no Geneva. There was plenty of drinking, gambling, dancing in the streets, and sexual adventure. A glib statement of the ideology, for example that riches are a sign of moral superiority and God's favor, is a gross and unjustified oversimplification. Richard Baxter, a good Presbyterian, carried the doctrine to its extreme in 1673 when he wrote, "If God show you a way in which you may lawfully get more . . . (without wrong to your soul, or to any other) if you refuse this, and choose the less gainful way, you cross one of the ends of your Calling, and you refuse to be God's steward," but even he stressed that only *moral* gain was true gain: "It is not lawful to take up or keep up any oppressing monopoly or trade, which tends to enrich you by the loss of the Commonwealth or of many." Tawney discussed its real attraction: ". . . a creed which transformed the acquisition of wealth from a drudgery or a temptation into a moral duty was the milk of lions. It was not that religion was expelled from practical life, but that religion itself gave it a foundation of granite. . . . The good Christian was not wholly dissimilar from the economic man." Then, however, he went on to warn of the inevitable result: "But the quality in modern societies which is most sharply opposed to the teaching ascribed to the Founder of the Christian Faith lies deeper. . . . It consists in the assumption, accepted by most reformers with hardly less *naïveté* than by the defenders of the established order, that the attainment of material riches is the supreme object of human endeavor and the final criterion of human success."

But nineteenth-century Americans were not so sophisticated, and what Tawney and Parrington later spent a lifetime anatomizing was then too obvious, too implicit, too all-pervading for debate. There was consequently not as much hypocrisy in the prevailing American attitude as we now like to think; Marshall Field I cheated neither his customers nor his God, and Rockefeller's Baptist munificences were nothing so naïve as propitiation. Christianity was simply a Higher Good, and the happiness of the rich Christian proved it. America itself was a Higher Good, young and aggressive, creating the ultimate Eden. Lewis Mumford quotes a poet's diary:

Nov. 8, 1864. Stood two hours in the rain and voted for Old Abe. Realized on stocks and made $1375.

Nov. 9. Yesterday a great triumph for the National Cause. Thank God! The future of America is now secure.

Nov. 10. Fall in gold. I make on everything I manage for myself and lose on the operations of my agents.

"The dual motives that ran through the period," he writes, "could not be better expressed." But in a sense there was only one motive: affirmation that the United States was God's country. Civilization was near its zenith, and God was already the Great Silent Partner. There was consequently little friction between business and government, and no invidious distinction was drawn between fortunes made privately and those originating at the public trough. Mumford is accurate and sharp:

The people who had fought through the Civil War were chiefly conscious of the political issues that were decided, or temporarily silenced, by the conflict. Our recent histories have shown in detail all the industrial and financial transformations that were either brought on or hastened by the war: the growth of steel mills, the mechanization of agriculture, the substitution of petroleum for whale oil, the development of the trade union movement, and the concentration of great fortunes, built up by graft, speculation, war profits, or the outright donation of priceless lands to great railway corporations, *acquisitions which were not called theft, and doles which were not denounced as inimical to manhood and independence, only because the sums involved were so huge and the recipients so rich.* (Italics added.)

Sources made no difference; we were all washed in grace. *Laborare orare erat.* And the many dissidents—the labor unions, the artists, the anarchists, even the free silverites—were more than just misfits; they were heretics. In many respects they still are; the Deity is constantly quoted as sanctioning traditional economic theory and social custom; the United States remains as much a mystique, a practical theology, as a nation, and when patriotism is openly questioned the air is heady with brimstone. But mercantile Calvinism is an old ideology now, and losing its teeth, and our new heretics give the country much of its vigor. Marshall Field I would have abhorred them, as he abhorred the Haymarket anarchists. He would have been puzzled by his grandson, who liked heretics and fought for them, but he would have recognized that Marshall III, too, was a man of his times (a similarity that the grandson pointed out decades later), and he would have been relieved to hear that the younger man was essentially an old-fashioned liberal who believed in competition—not quite a heretic, but an American descendant of the best in traditional British Whiggery. The old gentleman might have consoled himself with Psalms XXXIX, 6: He heapeth up riches, and knoweth not who shall gather them.

2

The heaping up began modestly in Pittsfield, Massachusetts, in 1851. Born August 18, 1834, Field had grown up in Conway, on a patch of rich farmland—not the usual rocky soil of New England, but the fertile loam of the Berkshire foothills. The American branch of the family went back to Zechariah Field, come over from Yorkshire in 1629, and the Fields seemed notably lacking in that ancestor worship so common among early settlers anywhere; whether the name went back to an ancient Saxon invader, or was Anglicized from des Prés, or was corrupted from some throaty Boadicean war cry, was a matter of indifference. "I have nothing to say, nothing to give you," Marshall Field I answered a hopeful genealogist years later. "Why do *we* need a genealogy?" His father was John Field, his mother Fidelia Nash Field; their farmhouse stood on Field's Hill, a mile from Conway, in the Berkshires. There were nine children of whom six survived, four of them sons; Marshall was the third boy. Chandler Augustus, the oldest, was to take over the family farm. Joseph Nash, three years senior to Marshall, and Henry, seven years his junior, planned business careers. When Marshall went off to Pittsfield to clerk in a dry-goods store, Joseph and Henry came to visit often, and the three speculated—probably with dry Yankee restraint—on the future and on success.

Marshall had gone to school until he was seventeen, longer than most farmboys of the time, but he displayed no desire to go further, and no regret, ever, that he had missed out on a higher education. "The truth is," he wrote later, "that for most young men a college education means that just at the time when they should be having business principles instilled into them, and be getting themselves energetically pulled together for their life's work, they are sent to college. Then intervenes what many a young man looks back on as the jolliest time of his life. . . . Often when he comes out of college the young man is unfitted by this good time to buckle down to hard work, and the result is a failure to grasp opportunities that would have opened the way for a successful career."

He led a quiet life in Pittsfield. He was a principled young Presbyterian with a precocious singleness of mind, and it seems to have cost him no great effort to avoid the taverns and fleshpots—which could hardly have been spectacular in Pittsfield. He worked hard; he "studied storekeeping with the dry passion of a genius," and presumably earned the right to be pompous later on: "The trouble with most young men," he said, "is that they do not learn anything thoroughly and are apt to do the work committed to them in a careless manner; forgetting that what is worth doing at all is worth doing well, they become mere drones and rely upon chance to bring them success. The business world is full of just such men, content in simply putting in their time somehow and drawing their salaries; making no effort whatever to increase their efficiency and thereby enhance their own as well as their employers' interest." Field was no drone, and never relied upon chance. He studied the merchandise, and he studied his customers. He had a way—a very businesslike way—with women shoppers. "He seemed to know just what they wanted," a neighbor reported years later, "and if that was not in stock, he was able without deceit to sell them something else."

He was unassuming, ambitious, talented, and probably stuffy. We may assume that he carried himself well, and we know that his blue eyes were cold and level.* He had the supreme confidence of the man who has chosen virtue. He was hardworking, abstemious, and honest; and the folk wisdom and sermons of his time, not to mention the pronouncements of the successful, promised him a reward here on earth. He might have become a conniver, a manipulator; he had the requisite intelligence, alertness, and knowledge of human needs. But he had, more than any of these, principle. He was armored in a faith; not specifically a faith in God, but rather a conviction that the justice of God's universe, as set down by the generations, was immutable. The eternal verities were his weapons: the sweat of his brow, thrift, a sense of duty, an avoidance of frivolity, and a firm belief in victory through virtue. Working a farm through the long Berkshire winters had created a strong sense of responsibility and, we may assume, a confidence that what he chose to do

---

* "My uncle," Stanley Field said decades later, "had the coldest blue eyes you ever saw and they read you through and through."

in life he would do successfully. It also created a stern notion of the value of thrift, which he expressed forcefully when he was old: "The average young man of today, when he begins to earn is soon inclined to habits of extravagance and wastefulness; gets somehow imbued with the idea that irrespective of what he earns, he must indulge in habits corresponding to those of some other young man simply because he indulges, or imagines he cannot be manly without. The 5, 10, or 15 cents a day that is squandered, while a mere trifle apparently, if saved would in a few years amount to thousands of dollars and go far toward establishing the foundation of a future career." The statement is a reflection—and justification—of the five years he spent in Pittsfield clerking, observing, and setting aside that 5, 10, or 15 cents a day.

In 1855, when he was twenty-one, he made his first serious adult decision: he would go west to Chicago and put his talents to work. Chicago was only a year or two older than he; perhaps he felt that they would grow together. Pittsfield was small, old, and set in its ways; it offered little scope to ambition. His boss there offered him a partnership, in time, if he would stay; but Field had made up his mind. When he left he bore with him this letter of reference:

The bearer, Mr. Field, has been in my employ for nearly the past five years and now leaves me for the West. I can, without qualification, commend him as a young man of unusual business talent and worthy of the confidence of any who may employ him. His character and his principles, as well as his business qualifications, are such that I cannot doubt he will meet with that success in life which usually accompanies industry, perseverance, and integrity, when combined with strict integrity and energy of character.

He has my warmest wishes for success in whatever situation he may fill or business he shall engage in.

The letter is dated January 19, 1856. Franklin Pierce was President, soon to be supplanted by Buchanan, the last Democrat but one until Woodrow Wilson. Kansas was bleeding, and the Dred Scott decision was a year away. Chicago had produced its first crop of millionaires. Geology was still the work of Satan. Darwin was twenty years off the *Beagle,* but his *Origin of Species* was still three years away. The Crimean War was almost over. Two years before, Matthew Perry had pried a hazy sort of treaty out of an exotic island empire called Japan. Fort Sumter was only one of a thousand sleepy garrisons. Marx was sitting on his boils in the British Museum; his *Manifesto* was eight years old. The London *News Gazette* had just celebrated its 200th birthday; the San Francisco *Bulletin,* its first. Timothy Shay Arthur's *Ten Nights in a Barroom and What I Saw There* was a national best seller, but there was still hope: John Lothrop Motley's *Rise of the Dutch Republic* was on press, and while a queer sort of fish story called *Moby Dick,* published five years before, had not sold very well, a few unregenerate intellectuals kept telling one another how good it was. The whole world believed in God, and Protestant denominations in the United States were splitting like rotifers on the issue of slavery. In Freiberg, Moravia, the Freuds were hoping it would be a boy.

Marshall Field I left for Chicago.

3

The shoestring start is an essential ingredient of American success stories. It has consequently been hazarded that Field arrived in Chicago penniless—an asseveration contradicted by everything we know about the man and the times. Field was a saver, a prudent man; it is doubtful that he would have left for the West with anything under $500 in his kick, and more likely that he had a thousand or so. A thousand, in those deflated times, was a good, round, symbolic sum, a bridge-burning sum: travel money plus the first year's expenses—security against even the slowest start. Whatever he brought with him, it sufficed. His older brother, Joseph, persuaded Cooley, Wadsworth and Company, the city's largest drygoods house, to give the young man employment. Cooley noted that he seemed at first to lack confidence, but shortly began to display all the businessman's virtues.

He knew his job, surely, and was frugal; but the panic of 1857, a bad one, might have set him back sharply if not for a highly instructive detail: Cooley, Farwell (Cooley had taken on a new partner) did a cash business. When the panic came they owed no money, and were owed only a small amount. They simply retrenched and rode it out. "I learned what I consider my best lesson," Field recalled much later, "and that was to do a cash business."

The merchant's talent was so strong in Field that in less than four years he became a full partner in the firm. He was twenty-five, and getting ahead; he had saved half of his first year's salary of $400, "sleeping in the store, and buying no new clothes except a pair of overalls," and apparently saw little need to change his ways over the next few years. His life was far more interesting than in Pittsfield, of course; the sights and sounds and smells of a new universe were all about him. But he was not yet a participant. Chicago offered an infinity of temptations, but Field, armored in the old principles, was impervious. While he was never a miser in the classic sense, he must have delighted as his fortune grew and he became more obviously one of the elect. There were many fortunes in the city, and big ones, built entirely of dirty money. Chicago abounded in vulgarians, corrupt politicians, bunco artists, petty hoodlums; in speculators and sensualists; in railroad men and remittance men and real estate hustlers. But there were also many ex-New Englanders of unassailable rectitude. To Field these latter were the only people whose respect and good will mattered. Honest riches came a bit slower, but they endured, and their getting left a man's soul intact.

The Civil War, a cataclysm, affected him little personally. Surely he considered slavery immoral (and in the long run uneconomical), surely he was a staunch Union man (though Chicago was full of Copperheads and Field himself was occasionally a Democrat), and just as surely there was never any question of his joining up (though he was a bachelor of twenty-seven when the war began). For one thing Chicago was part of the old Northwest Territory, rambunctious and as distrustful of the East as it ever was of the South, and even if Lincoln was a good Illinois man, the war seemed an Eastern war, with Eastern money playing a prominent part. And for another, Field must have felt by then that he was rolling along on a foreordained course; that to leave his partners, his work, his very character, for anything as egregious and bawdy and impulsive and unprincipled as a war, would have approached blasphemy. But he understood certain aspects of the war, and professionally it had a great impact upon him. While it cut down on his volume, it did no harm to his prices, and later, when a Union victory was inevitable, a sense of coming expansion, of future boom, must have tingled in him like love. Which is not an empty simile; in 1863 he married, and it seems to have kept him away from the store only briefly.

The lucky girl was Nannie Douglas Scott, and he met her at a gathering in the home of a friend, on one of his rare nights in company. She was twenty-three, delicate and lovely, the daughter of a prosperous iron founder in Ironton, Ohio. Field fell in love quickly and hotly; when Miss Scott left Chicago he went to the train with her, hopped aboard, proposed, was accepted, and got off at the first stop to return to town. It was the one dashing act of his life, and it is admirable. Dressed to the nines, he swings aboard the train; quickly, fervently, he woos, dimly aware that he is in the grip of madness, that each passing second carries him farther from the gingham counter; breathless, rapturous, overwhelmed by his persistence, by his dash, by his swashbuckling, cavalier contempt for the proprieties, Miss Scott accepts. The wedding took place on January 3, 1863.

People said later that Nannie Field was never happy; that the promise was never fulfilled; that Field went back to work after the wedding (there is almost the implication that he glanced at his watch as he said "I do") and left his bride to live the life of a chattel. These are half-truths. The promise is rarely fulfilled, and only the naïve expect that a rich man's marriage is happier. And nineteenth-century marriages are said to have been bleaker than most, as though the period was an arid, stony track between the late medieval jungle of romantic love and the sanitary carnival of the twentieth century. It is reasonable to say that a man of Field's character—God-fearing, orderly, an accumulator—was no Lancelot. At any rate Nannie bore him three children, the first of whom, Lewis, born January 19, 1866, did not survive; she moved modestly and properly through the highest level of Chicago's society; she was surely no more put upon, no more tragic, than any other chatelaine of the time. Whatever else she was, she was Mrs. Marshall Field, and very soon after the wedding that became not so much a name as a title.

Cooley retired in 1864, and the organization became Farwell, Field, and Company. That same year Field left, taking with him a man named Levi Leiter. Farwell accepted their departure with more than equanimity; he lent each of them $100,000. Field had money of his own put away, and enjoyed a high credit rating; when he and Leiter joined forces with Potter Palmer in the ownership and management of Palmer's wholesale and retail dry-goods store on Lake Street, Field's capital investment was $260,000. (Leiter's was half that; Palmer and his brother Milton provided half a million.) In 1867 Palmer retired, and on January 1, 1869, formal partnership papers were signed in the firm of Field, Leiter and Company. Field's satisfaction was all the livelier because his brothers Joseph and Henry were junior partners, each putting up $100,000. Field and Leiter invested $400,000 each, and two others, Henry J. Willing and Lorenzo G. Woodhouse, came in for $100,000 each.

If Marshall Field was at all concerned about the risks of heavy capitalization, he displayed no nervousness in public, and by the end of 1867—even before Field, Leiter was formally established— he knew he had won his gamble. The firm grossed $9,000,000 that year, far more than any other in the city. (Only two of their rivals persisted into the twentieth century—Mandel Brothers and Carson, Pirie, Scott—and they were barely on their feet in 1867.) There would be troubles still—panics and fires and personal tragedy—but Field was henceforth an archon, a public figure, at times a folk hero. Even his penny-pinching was viewed with awful respect; Andrew MacLeish (the poet's father), who had worked for Field and who in 1867 took charge of Carson, Pirie's retail division, complimented Field on his wage scale: "Not even a Scotsman could live on that!" The legend began to take shape; yet it was not a legend. They said Field was shrewd; so he was. Honest; so he was. Cold; so he was. He was incorruptible. He was rectitude personified. He was the sharpest merchant in the United States, but the customer was always right. He never made a shady penny. If Marshall Field said no, Marshall Field meant no. Absolutely straight. No vices. A handsome man.

The ideology had found its *beau idéal.*

Chicago had changed greatly in a decade. With the Mississippi closed to commercial traffic during much of the war, lake and rail transport were the city's link with the world; with the South devastated and unproductive, imports rose sharply—from New England, from Europe, from the Caribbean by way of New York. Chicago had sufficient historical reason to resent the East,* to which was now added the suspicion that Eastern merchants and shippers were treating themselves to foreign wines and other pernicious ecstasies on profits they extorted from the Middle West. But Chicago usually managed to hold its own by passing some of the burden along to its own hinterland, and got as good as it gave by taking advantage of its function as hog butcher to the country (later, the world); by 1862 it was our leading meat packer, and in twenty years men like Swift and Armour were world-famous. After the war Chicago, like most of the country, was far too busy making money to give much time to sectional grudges. Even as they competed, Midwesterners worked ardently side by side with Eastern interests, to the point where good Illinois and Ohio names began popping up in the reports of splendid Wall Street scandals. It was a time of often stylish piracy. In New York Jay Gould used his Federal friends to depress the price of gold, and made—so they say— $11,000,000 in one day by selling his country short; and in Chicago men with sufficient resources could corner the market in hogs, wait for the consequent rise, and rake in fortunes ultimately composed of the two or three cents extra per pound contributed by housewives everywhere. Gould perpetrated another of the period's *grands coups,* when his Erie Railroad and Cornelius Vanderbilt's New York Central were competing ferociously for the Chicago-New York traffic in the 1860s and 1870s. The standard rate for shipping a carload of cattle east from Chicago was $125; Vanderbilt sprang a surprise, and cut his price to $100. Gould struck back at $75; Vanderbilt cut to $50. Gould slashed again, to $25; Vanderbilt trumped victoriously by dropping to $1, and for a time all cattle transport went to the Central. But Gould had meanwhile bought up every head west of Buffalo that he could lay hands on, and made a small fortune running them east on Vanderbilt's line.

Of such, too, were Ulysses Grant's myrmidons. Grant himself was an honest man, and died broke, but he was surrounded—even engulfed—by rich patriots whose unswerving devotion to the principles of liberty rarely made them poorer. "Money, and not morality, is the principle of commercial nations," Jefferson had written

---

* Of which much more in Chapter VII.

a friend in 1810; and sixty years later the United States achieved heights of commercialism to make a Phoenician blush. Among prominent politicians who, it was charged (and never quite denied), exerted influence in return for stock in Crédit Mobilier (a contracting subsidiary of Union Pacific, into which profits and subsidies were wantonly funneled) was Rep. James A. Garfield, R., Ohio; eight years later he became President of the United States.

But Marshall Field moves through these decades like a reactionary Galahad, not simply proper, but adamant—as outraged by a broken word as by labor unions, as indifferent to the whines of a ruined speculator as he was to the misery of the man's victims. Contradictions abound. Field was honest, but at his clubs and on his boards he sat with brigands—men of the highest class, but brigands. He was considerate of his employees, and occasionally even generous, but he hated—there is no better word—anarchists, union organizers, and strikers. He was rich, respectable, redoubtable— and now and then a Democrat. He walked to work, followed by his carriage in dubious weather, because he thought driving would be ostentatious; but he worked only from nine to four—among the hustling Chicagoans an unparalleled ostentation.

And he does not change. He ages, yes. Otherwise there he stands, reliable, calm, principled, quite cold; five feet nine, neither thin nor stout, his eye and tint clear, his dress distinguished, his hair and broad mustache graying; the uncrowned king, the reluctant *arbiter elegantiarum* of Chicago society; and probably the shrewdest merchant in the United States.

4

The first store, on Lake Street, handled both retail and wholesale dry goods. When Potter Palmer withdrew in 1867 he was forty, another archon, and he was retiring from one domain to storm another (real estate) and then a third (his splendiferous hotels). During the next year Marshall Field knew two triumphs. On April 21, 1868, Marshall Field II was born, a healthy boy who seemed to resemble his father. Field needed no heir to spur him along, but he liked children, and had suffered when his first son died shortly after birth. And by now he must have sensed hierarchy, permanence, generations; he was a builder, a dynast, and a crown prince was a confirmation of his work. The arrival of a son may have crystallized some of Field's hunches; at about that time he suggested to Leiter that the store was inadequate, and in October *le tout-Chicago* was invited to the grand opening of a new building on the northeast corner of Washington and State Streets, a voluptuous monument in Chicago Victorian, or Expensive Eclectic. Potter Palmer had built it, and richly. His fortune was in State Street land (already a $4,000,000 half mile; the "million-dollar miles" of our own time seem anticlimactic) and he and Field were undoubtedly agreed that State Street was to be the commercial heart of the city.

Three years later State Street went up in smoke. Mrs. O'Leary's cow kicked over a lamp; thirty-six hours later the blaze was extinguished, with the help of a timely rain. Half of Chicago was a smoking ruin. The first Palmer House, opened only thirteen days before, was gone (Palmer cleaned up the mess and talked the insurance companies into lending him enough for an even more splendid hostelry); so was Field, Leiter and Company. Field's first thoughts were characteristic. He posted a sign:

CASH BOYS AND GIRLS WILL BE PAID
WHAT IS DUE THEM MONDAY, 9.00 A.M.,
OCT. 16 AT 60 CALUMET AVENUE
FIELD, LEITER AND COMPANY

and immediately afterward bought the horse-car barns of the old South Side Railroad for $9,785; within two days clerks were once more bowing to their elegant customers.

Field's calm was more than characteristic; it was justified. He carried $2,200,000 worth of insurance, and he had not forgotten Cooley, Farwell: he did a cash business, and kept a large cash reserve on hand. Leiter wrote to a banker a month later that before receiving a penny of the insurance money the store had met its current obligations exclusively from accumulated daily receipts. Just after Christmas he wrote to Joseph Field, who had settled permanently in Manchester, England, to supervise the firm's European operations: "Our sales since the fire . . . will yield us a net profit of at least $125,000—making a surplus of $2,750,000. This does not include the personal property of either of the partners outside the business. Marshall, you know, has considerable."

Having considerable, he got the company out of the stables and into another store by April of the following year. The new store was ten minutes' walk west of State Street, but he never considered keeping the retail division in such a *banlieue*. Business was brisk on the corner of Madison and Market, but the agora was State Street. When the Singer Sewing Machine Company bought the old site from Palmer and defiled it with "five stories in the Italian style," Field moved back, but he left the wholesale division at Madison and Market. The move was, in effect, a serious expansion.

He also built himself a mansion, at 1905 Prairie Avenue, from the drawings of Richard Morris Hunt, "the most fashionable American architect of the late nineteenth century, and the first to return from the École des Beaux Arts," who was also to blame for several consummately hideous chateaux in New York. Field must have driven Hunt to agonies of self-restraint; the house "showed neither learning nor good manners. Its mansard roof was prim, its pressed brick walls were as mean as its sash windows, and its only concession to elegance was a Louis XVI drawing room in white and gold damask."

The mansion was put up in 1873; Field was thirty-nine. On August 28 a daughter, Ethel Newcomb, was born to the Fields; thirty days later the great banking house of Jay Cooke failed, and panic swept the country again. (Speculation and manipulation in the railroad business and wanton overexpansion in commerce, industry, and agriculture, plus a sharp diminution in agricultural exports to Europe in 1871 and 1872, had shaken the country's financial structure. That happened about every twenty years; sinners repented, and there was much loose talk about widows and orphans. The blame was usually thrown on an ill-defined group of men called "speculators." Ambrose Bierce wrote later, "The gambling known as business looks with austere disfavor on the business known as gambling.") Field was once again calm in the face of adversity; he had a son, a baby daughter, and cash on hand. The company distributed a circular:

We see no cause for general alarm, and advise merchants and others to keep on in the even tenor of their way. The partial failure of crops in Europe, creating such a large demand for our breadstuffs and provisions, warrants us in assuring you that no action of bankers can long retard their movements, and as the business of the West is almost wholly dependent upon the money realized for its products, it cannot suffer to any great extent.

As long as European crops failed, there was no cause for alarm; not even Eastern bankers could hurt Chicago.

Panics, rivals, natural disasters came and went; Field endured. He walked to work, occasionally joined by George Pullman, who lived a block up Prairie Avenue. He took his luncheon at the Chicago Club in the company of an opulent Sanhedrin. As a First Citizen he considered charities and sifted solicitations. He mulled suggestions from his brother Joseph, usually answering "Buy," and perhaps recalling wistfully the Democratic national platform in the year he reached Chicago: "The time has come for the people of the United States to declare themselves in favor of free seas and progressive free trade throughout the world, and, by solemn manifestations, to place their moral influence at the side of their successful example"; or perhaps smiling hopefully at the same party's platform in 1876: "We demand that all custom-house taxation shall be only for revenue"—and not for protection.

In 1877 he came through another crisis: Field, Leiter was razed by fire again, on the night of November 14th. The building was a total loss, and so was $750,000 worth of merchandise. Lightning had struck twice, but so had Field: he carried $959,000 in insurance, divided (considerately) among 152 companies. The Singer people, perhaps shying from a jinx, offered to sell him the lot with the picturesque ruins of the store, and he declined. It was possibly his only error of judgment in a fifty-year career. Singer immediately erected a "new palace" and Carson, Pirie and Company leased the premises. That hurt. If Field had a commercial motherland, it was that corner. Reversing himself with a minimum of outward agony, he paid out $750,000 for the building, free and clear. ($100,000 of that went to Carson, Pirie as a consolation.)

From then on the Four Horsemen left the store alone, and it must have been a relief. The company had occupied seven different buildings in ten years, but the gypsy life was over. Field could, and

did, concentrate on the store, on his investments, and on benefi-
cences.

On January 26, 1881, Levi Leiter withdrew, and the firm became
Marshall Field and Company. The decision was actually Field's,
and he broached it in an apparently sporting manner. He made
Leiter an offer: he would either buy out or sell out for the book
value. Leiter asked time to think. He might have spared himself
the effort. Field had reconnoitered and recruited; every competent
employee in the store had promised to stand by him, and none
would stay with Leiter. It was not a Machiavellian conspiracy;
Leiter was a hard man to live with, a social climber, something of
a blusterer, and a dogmatist. (The dogmas changed frequently, but
the dogmatism did not. He had once refused to sell to a man with
a bad credit rating; the buyer protested that he had the cash in his
pocket, but Leiter was adamant.) Field, on the other hand, was
consistent, if stern; he was also considerate. "How many boys came
down without overcoats and mittens?" he asked on a bitter winter
morning. "Outfit them all and say nothing about it."

So Leiter left, moving to Washington, D.C., with his accumulated
millions—roughly six—and there Mrs. Leiter played hostess, and
they lived happily ever after. Field was happy too. The store was
his, and in 1881 alone it netted $2,500,000, about 10 per cent of
the gross. He took on other "partners," but they were clearly sub-
ordinates, and though they did well for themselves, none retiring
with less than a million, they never presumed to consider themselves Field's equals. (Only Harry Selfridge did, years later; he was
sent packing; he went to London and founded his own great store.)

5

Field was a despot. He was benevolent, respectable, eminently just
and principled, possibly—by the articles of the national ideology—
the noblest merchant America has produced; but he was a despot.
He had every right to be. It was permitted, even encouraged, by the
rules of the game, and he had played, always, within the rules. But
resistance and rebellion were also allowed; they were even required
by any creed that valued individualism. It was only a century, after

all, since the Revolution; Jefferson and Adams were only fifty years
dead.

In the 1870s a serious reaction began. There had been sporadic
ripples of protest before, but never a ground swell; now, deep beneath the surface, a tide was stirring. Not against Field himself, but
against inequity and oppression—evils once imputed only to governments. With government and business thoroughly confounded
on the higher levels, political and economic resentments tended to
coalesce on the lower. Instead of faithful weavers scratching themselves and approaching the burgomaster with humble, ungrammat-
ical petitions for guild reform, the age bred strikers, anarchists, and
syndicalists, who challenged the ideology directly: God might exist
and then again he might not, and riches were not a sign of moral
superiority. The theorizing was limited. The philosopher of labor
did better in Europe, where societies were more ossified; from Saint-
Simon and Fourier through Marx and Kropotkin to a hundred modern exfoliations runs a grim and effective intellectual radicalism.
Its ideas were available in the United States, but its exegetes and
evangelists were few in the nineteenth century. The new world preferred action, and the reason for a strike was more likely to be
hungry children than the dignity of labor. Resistance was a new attitude; the illusion that anybody could be a millionaire had for a
time inhibited a man's inclination to identify himself as a laborer.
But in England Ruskin had sounded a pessimistic, weary, genteel
note of resignation (from his cozy study): "There is rough work
to be done, and rough men must do it; there is gentle work to be
done, and gentlemen must do it; and it is physically impossible that
one class should do, or divide, the work of the other. And it is of
no use to try and conceal this sorrowful fact by fine words, and to
talk to the workman about the honorableness of manual labor, and
the dignity of humanity." Here no one cared much about such well-
manicured sentiments, but in 1880 the Democratic platform glorified a large bloc of voters: "The Democratic party is the friend of
labor and the laboring man, and pledges itself to protect him alike
against the cormorant and the commune." Four years later Grover
Cleveland contributed his own clichés: "A truly American sentiment
recognizes the dignity of labor and the fact that honor lies in honest
toil."

It depended on where one stood. For a couple of centuries it had been preached that the reward of honest toil was wealth and God's grace; now it was being reduced to simple honor and defense against cormorants. The catch phrase had been "rugged individualism." Economically it required capitalism, and politically liberalism, but a liberalism in the old sense, which meant primarily freedom from government interference, and had nothing to do with responsibility to one's fellow man. But by the 1870s some revision seemed to be in order: a practical revision, if you were a workingman, or a doctrinal revision, if you were a capitalist. So, for example, gentle old Jeremy Bentham's services were no longer needed. At the end of the eighteenth century he had insisted that security was essential to the enjoyment of freedom—why should a man work hard and accumulate capital if he were not safe in his possession of it? This was agreeable, and considered wise, and during the early, acquisitive period it was understood that there was no freedom without security. But when sufficient fortunes had been made, and the threat to them was not from above but from below, it became apparent—at least among employers—that a workingman could not be both safe and free. If he wanted freedom to rise (and by a glib extension that encompassed all other freedoms—to change jobs, to migrate, to be buried in the cemetery of his own choice—except those which would win him security) he must not demand shorter hours and higher wages. Risk was noble, said the well-to-do; and security destroyed a man's moral fiber.

The middle and upper classes derived support for that argument from, of all people, Charles Darwin. The *Origin of Species* had been published in 1859 and was received hospitably in America, where the fear of hell-fire was relatively diffuse in the absence of an established clergy. Not Darwinism itself, but a variant called Social Darwinism, swept into the partial vacuum left as old-time Calvinism burned out. Its prophet was Herbert Spencer (who had actually anticipated Darwin, being originally inspired by Malthus); Spencer's American interpreter was William Graham Sumner, an admirably independent and stubborn professor at Yale (and coiner of the phrase "the Forgotten Man").

The tenets of Social Darwinism, complex if studied closely, seemed simple to men of business. If the "struggle for existence" and the "survival of the fittest" were the law in nature, then they must also be the law in society. If it was inevitable that the weakest fall and the strongest survive, then any artificial aid to the weak was contrary to nature; was a positive hindrance to the march of human evolution. Social Darwinism became "a kind of naturalistic Calvinism in which man's relation to nature [was] as hard and demanding as man's relation to God under the Calvinistic system."

Hard and demanding, yes; but it offered the hope of human perfection, as well as the grim truth of human struggle. It explained the realities of economics as a system in which virtue, thrift, industry, and self-sufficiency would ultimately prevail over laziness, improvidence, and ignorance. The doctrine supplied a perfect rationale for unbridled capitalism; Spencer's first book, *Social Statics,* published in 1850, had been "an attempt to strengthen laissez faire with the imperatives of biology." Spencer opposed poor laws, public education, public health, housing laws, tariffs, state banks, state postal systems. At Yale Sumner carried Social Darwinism to its logical philosophical end:

> Let it be understood that we cannot go outside of this alternative: liberty, inequality, survival of the fittest; not-liberty, equality, survival of the unfittest. The former carries society forward and favors all its best members; the latter carries society downwards and favors all its worst members.

"Sumner's synthesis," Richard Hofstadter wrote much later, "brought together three great traditions of western capitalist culture: the Protestant ethic, the doctrines of classical economics, and Darwinian natural selection." But those were not entirely compatible. Evolution itself horrified the religious, and the reduction of ethics to survival values disturbed the generous and idealistic. Darwin, who had gone considerably beyond Spencer ("Selfish and contentious people will not cohere, and without coherence nothing can be effected") and had discussed cooperation, generosity, and sacrifice as evidence of fitness and aids to survival, put a finger on one flaw; he wrote to Sir Charles Lyell, the great geologist, "I have received in a Manchester newspaper rather a good squib, showing that I have proved 'might is right,' and therefore that Napoleon is right, and every cheating tradesman is also right." But it would be some time before any significant number of people pursued that thought. It was only with the wider diffusion of power and the rise of the working classes that Social Darwinism lost its influence: as soon as the survival and improvement of the lower classes became probable, fitness ceased to be an ethical norm. What good was it as a standard if anyone could live up to it?

But that was later. Until the turn of the century the United States would remain a huge, clanking, greasy mechanical caricature of the struggle for existence, with the richer and more powerful justifying themselves, whatever their excesses of egotism and venality, as the fitter and therefore better.

Still, working people were beginning to see it differently. If freedom and security were mutually exclusive, how to account for the happy rich? * If security destroyed the moral fiber, why were capitalists not degenerate? † Perhaps they were; all the more reason to resist them. The Knights of Labor were organized in 1869; by 1886 they numbered 700,000, in a population of about 60,000,000, and had helped to win two major strikes. And then the working population became less Anglo-Saxon all the time; much of it was Roman Catholic, and to many Catholics the "best people" were, by the traditions of Europe, oppressors and not exemplars.

A practical result of all this was the economic rebellion of working people. Its implications for Marshall Field were rather sad, though if he thought of them at all he was probably more annoyed than depressed by them: as his accomplishments, wealth, and respectability increased, less and less of the public considered him the finest flower of Western civilization. (He was not vain, and would not have cared, for himself.) It was not his fault.†† He remained a superior individual by any measure he had ever been able to believe in. But the rules of the game were unfortunately not im-

---

* One answer, which achieved the force of truth though it was flagrantly false, was "The rich are really very unhappy people." Another, meaningless and often delivered with a doleful shake of the head, was "We are slaves to our money." No one noticed that these opinions, if true, were subversive of the whole ethic.

† Answer: because they were the best people.

†† "Superior want of conscience . . . is often the determining quality which makes a millionaire out of one who otherwise might have been a poor man," Henry George wrote in 1879. This was certainly not true of Field, whose conscience was highly developed. The difficulty was that his conscience never transcended its immediate context. Nurtured on a business morality, he made no effort to comprehend another. He was, in short, a man of his time: a respectable realist, dubious of what could not be named or numbered.

mutable. Ideologies are human in one sense: they begin to die the day they are born. Free-lance capitalism was past its prime, even if Social Darwinism could keep it healthy for another generation.

On May 10, 1869, a golden spike had bolted San Francisco to New York. On July 17, 1877, the men of the Baltimore and Ohio walked off the job at Martinsburg, West Virginia, in protest against the third wage cut in ten years—while the rich got richer—and the strike, disorganized, passionate, violent, blazed through railroad hubs: Baltimore, Pittsburgh, Buffalo, Chicago. State militias mobilized; pitched battles were fought; railroading came to a halt; and ultimately Federal troops entered the war, firing on pickets in five states. It was the most savage labor uprising this country had seen, and the swift counterattack was equally savage. When Chicago's railroad men called a general strike on July 24, the Field management armed the store's employees, and the next morning Field, Leiter delivery wagons were serving the police as squad cars. Marshall Field was in conference with the mayor. All that day rioters gathered, were dispersed, gathered again. The next morning ten thousand of them gathered in one spot, and repulsed a police charge; but they had no purpose, no program, no leaders. That afternoon Federal troops arrived, and the violence died quickly. The Chicago *Tribune,* which had identified the strike leaders as Bohemians and Polish Jews (this justified countervailing violence), rejoiced, announcing that the fight with the "Communists" was at an end.

It was; but only for a time. One of the hotheads was a young typesetter named Albert Parsons, neither Bohemian nor Jewish, "always courageous and almost never intelligent." He had managed to spend his life on the side of the underdog, aware of but not deterred by certain anomalies: he spent four years in the Confederate armies, and the next four fighting to win and consolidate Negroes' rights. Ejected from Texas, he had found work with the Chicago *Times,* and a forum in the *Tribune,* whose reporters enjoyed the sensational rantings of an unequivocal anarchist. His effect on Chicago's privy councils was seemingly disproportionate but actually justified; they recognized in him an effect and not a cause, a spokesman for far more power and unrest than Parsons himself dreamed. In 1877 the mayor advised him to leave town; he stayed, and was marked. In 1878 the Illinois National Guard became an object of solicitude on the part of thirty or forty rich citizens, Field among them; quietly, money was raised for modern arms and new uniforms, and training was stepped up. Some sort of battle was taking shape, and Field and Parsons are suitable symbols for the antagonists.*

When and how the fight would come, no one knew, and only extremists really wanted it, but in retrospect it seems as though there were only extremists involved. That was not true, of course; the measured tones of the middle classes and intellectuals could be heard if anyone cared to listen. When the furor of 1877 had waned, perfectly respectable voices were raised against the extravagantly immoral speculations of some Chicago tycoons, and it was even admitted publicly that an economy could not thrive where working-men lacked buying power. Periodically native labor rioted against cheap imported labor—poverty and xenophobia hand in hand—and journalists pointed out that employers must share the blame. In 1882 William Henry Vanderbilt, who had succeeded his famous father as head of the New York Central, delivered himself of one of those ringing, inspiring statements that become part of a nation's folklore: "The public be damned." The public's reaction was unsympathetic, and tension was not eased. Garfield was too tainted to raise any hopes in moderate hearts, and when Arthur succeeded to the Presidency he was thought too elegant and gentlemanly to care; yet he made a beginning. He established an equitable civil service, fulminated vigorously against government by pork barrel and fraud, and began to restore a tradition of independence and competence to his office.

Grover Cleveland, a Democrat, was elected to his first term in 1884, insisting that public office was a public trust and that he had done honorably by his mistress and his illegitimate daughter. He was so obviously superior to his opponent, James G. Blaine, that even Republicans respected him. (The election is the *locus classicus* of nip-and-tuck, but the Democrats were coming back. They had controlled the House since 1882.) Marshall Field was pleased. He

---

* But it was precisely the same despotic, principled Marshall Field who fifteen years later, during a financial panic, stopped a run on the Illinois Trust and Savings Bank by raising his voice in person to the angry mob: "If you will take your bankbook to my store," he announced, "your deposits will be honored. My name is Marshall Field."

was a free trader who appeared now and then before Senate committees to argue against tariffs, and Cleveland, for whom he had voted, was a low-tariff man who also stood for strict economy in government. (Even Thomas Nast, as pure a Republican as this country has produced, approved of Cleveland.)

The next four years were not, however, an easy time for anyone. Contradictions abounded still, and were reflected in politics. There was, for example, a surplus in the Federal treasury, which was theoretically healthy but actually served to withdraw large sums of money from general circulation at a time when population was growing. High tariffs added to that surplus, and raised prices; but then as always a reduction in tariffs was a threat to the American manufacturer. The debtor and the buyer tended to be Democrats; they wanted more money in circulation and lower prices. The creditor and the seller tended to be Republicans; they wanted prices maintained and tight money. To add to the troubles, farm prices began a decline in 1885 that continued for over a decade. Exports dropped, money was short, manufactured goods were expensive. Middlemen, industrialists, and moneylenders got richer; farmers and wage earners got poorer. Eventually they got William Jennings Bryan. More significant, they began to organize.

Field must have felt occasional dismay; so many of his fellow Democrats were Populists and union men. But he stuck to his guns: he wanted cheaper imported goods and more money in circulation, and in spite of all temptation to belong to another persuasion, he remained—for the time being—a Democrat.

He also remained an optimist, and decided in 1885 that the company needed a new wholesale store. His project was ambitious: he wanted a building that would occupy a large city block, bounded by Wells, Franklin, Quincy, and Adams Streets. Why he chose Henry Hobson Richardson to design it is a fascinating question; the answer is probably that Richardson had a splendid reputation and Field wanted the best. The choice was a stroke of luck for Chicago, and the building, whether Field knew it or not, was a consummately honest structure erected in a period of baroque trumpery. It mirrored the best in Field; it said what it did and did what it said. Richardson was born in Louisiana and educated at Harvard and the Beaux-Arts; perhaps because of his Harvard and Boston buildings, it is easy to think of him as a New England architect, who brought to Chicago the same sort of Yankee integrity that Field lived by. At any rate the building was a masterpiece.* It was also huge, and Field doubted that he could fill it; but in the 1880s Chicago's population doubled, and he needed all the space he had.

Meanwhile the United States Senate was investigating the causes of labor's unrest, and its questions were oddly impartial. The politicians were not at all skeptical about our destiny, but the phrase "robber baron" was in wide use, and agitation persisted—here and there, now and then, but always worse.

Riots, strikes, lockouts, assassinations, brutalities, exploitations, marked the economic life of this period: at no period in American history has the working class in America been more desperately enslaved. . . . But ideas were stirring; and if the dawn itself proved false, the hope it offered nevertheless was real.

Under Arthur the government had been jostled toward responsibility, and under Cleveland the lurch was accelerated. In 1884 the Republican platform, our most august transcription of revealed truth, had denounced "the importation of contract labor, whether from Europe or Asia, as an offense against the spirit of American institutions," and had flung itself recklessly into the Communist camp with this lunatic proposal: "We favor the establishment of a national bureau of labor; the enforcement of the eight-hour law." Admittedly platforms were for running on, and not for standing on, but this was heady stuff. The Chicago *Tribune*'s Joseph Medill, to whom even the Republicans were a namby-pamby pack of do-gooders, bleeding hearts, and friends of the unwashed, appeared before the Senate committee, and was categorical: the "wage classes" were in a fix because they were improvident and extravagant; they were therefore becoming revolutionaries; if hours were reduced the country would be flooded by immigrant labor; if wages were raised the employers would go broke. Alien doctrines of social welfare were pernicious; the solution lay in harder work, thrift, and less noise.

---

* It was torn down in 1930 by a society with even less taste than that of the 1880s. The building defied standard techniques of demolition; parts of the foundation simply could not be moved, and were left in place.

Medill's instructions were ignored. The eight-hour day was a national issue, and Chicago's radicals seized upon it. In the spring of 1885 there was a strike, with violence, at the McCormick reaper plant; the workers won minor concessions, but any concession at all was remarkable. Albert Parsons got back to work. When the Board of Trade tower was dedicated that same spring, Parsons led a parade of his followers to the scene, and when the well-equipped National Guard halted them short of their goal, Parsons made a speech, referring to the Guard as "Marshall Field's boys."

The climax of all this was the infamous Haymarket Riot of May 4, 1886. There had been strikes, and employers had been hiring scabs, and labor burst into savage protest. Parsons and his fellow anarchists, who had assumed the active emotional leadership of labor in Chicago, called a mass meeting for 7:30 in the evening, May 4, at Haymarket Square. Fifteen hundred men gathered. The speeches were incendiary, and there was truth in them; while Parsons orated even Mayor Carter H. Harrison was heard to murmur, "He is making a good political speech."

The police were already on the way. When they arrived, one hundred and eighty strong, there were some six hundred workers still in the square. The police ordered them to disperse immediately and peaceably; one of the anarchists, named Fielden, said, "We are peaceable," and climbed down off the platform. Calm was almost restored when someone threw a bomb at the police. One officer was killed, seventy were injured. The police counterattacked; later estimates were six anarchists dead, seventy-two wounded.

Good citizens have been arguing about the outcome ever since. Eight anarchists were tried, on the principle, enunciated on the spot by Judge Elbert Henry Gary, that "whoever advises murder is himself guilty of the murder that is committed pursuant to his advice." Seven, including Parsons, were sentenced to be hanged; two of them had not even been present in Haymarket Square. The eighth man, another absentee, was given fifteen years. The Illinois Supreme Court upheld the sentences.*

---

* The authorities were surely on thin ice when they indicted men who had not even been present, but they were forced to that by their own rationale. If Kropotkin had been available he too could have been tried, by the prevailing logic, but the young Clemenceau was just getting him out of jail in Paris. And Judge Gary was, to be delicate, not impartial.

Opinion, even among the best people, was sharply divided. Joseph Medill was gratified. George Bernard Shaw and William Morris were not, and spoke up for the anarchists at rallies in London. William Dean Howells led the protest of American writers and artists. Even Potter Palmer signed a petition for clemency. The agitation was almost successful. Governor Oglesby offered to commute the sentences of four of the men, including Parsons, if Chicago's civic leaders would agree. A meeting of fifty elders was called, and Lyman Gage, vice-president of the First National Bank, pleaded for the men's lives. When Gage had finished, Field rose to introduce the State's attorney, who would speak for him; the latter vehemently demanded the death penalty, and the assembled merchants, in no doubt of Field's sentiments, voted overwhelmingly and mercilessly to deny clemency.

Fortunately even that was not the end. When Oglesby received a petition for clemency bearing 41,000 signatures, many of them noble, he commuted two of the sentences to life imprisonment. Parsons and three others were hanged; another blew himself to bits in his cell. Three remained in jail, though the story was not over. No one ever knew who had thrown the bomb.

The net reaction was strongly against labor. Antilabor propaganda swelled. The eight-hour day was confounded, in dire warnings, with communism, free love, and hard liquor. The Knights of Labor lost influence and membership; the American Federation of Labor, founded in 1886, replaced the older organization, at first slowly and then, as it proved to be conservative and relatively untainted by foreign activist doctrines, more quickly. In general the shift was toward moderation and responsibility—and complacency. The Interstate Commerce Commission was created in 1887 because of public protest over railroad abuses; the Hatch Act * of the same year offered Federal subsidies to the states for the establishment of agricultural experiment stations. Cleveland vetoed an extravagant veterans' pension bill and came out all alone, without the approval of his advisers, for a radical reduction in tariffs. His timing was bad; the election of 1888 was fought over pensions and tariffs, and

---

* Not to be confused with the Hatch Act of 1939 regulating political activities by Federal employees.

although he won 100,000 votes more than Harrison, the latter beat
him handily in the Electoral College.

6

Marshall Field scarcely had time to be disappointed at Cleveland's
defeat. He was an extremely rich man with a complicated portfolio,
and he had a store to keep and a son coming of age. He also had
Chicago to take care of, already the Second City, still growing
wildly, still relying on its rich for responsibility and direction. In
his fifties Field had become Nestor, and while he never permitted
himself—never really desired—direct participation in politics, he
and his peers governed. Legends and anecdotes continued to pro-
liferate, and continued to attribute to Field supernatural business
talents and supernatural rectitude. In an age of banditti he became
famous for integrity.

Integrity was, to Field's mind, an absolute necessity; it was also
ingrained, and did not require constant reinforcement. Field was a
director or major officer of at least twenty-eight great corporations,
and was surely in no need of flexible ethics. Twelve of the corporations dealt in railroading or city transit; nine in banking. He seems
to have steered clear of oil and metals, except for a directorship of
the United States Steel Corporation; perhaps certain territorial
privileges were understood on higher levels, and perhaps he preferred to avoid empires significantly greater than his own. He was
once heard complaining, "It's useless to talk about getting rich when
John D. Rockefeller and a few others have all the money in the
world." Field continued to think of himself as simply a successful
merchant. Even his investment techniques were those of a careful
retailer. He allowed himself only two dubious flutters in half a century: the first was a small (some said $20,000) bet on silver mines
in Leadville, Colorado, which ultimately returned a million; the
second was $100,000 risked in a pool, the purpose being to buy up
small railroads and sell them all together to the Northwestern, and
once more the return was about a million. Much of Field's money
went into Chicago real estate, much of it into securities. Managing
his investments was heavy work, but he found it jejune, and was
never tempted into manipulation or buccaneering on the grand
scale.

He was not so quickly tempted into philanthropy, either. In America "good works" were still performed on the European pattern; charity was a function of the best people, and was offered in a spirit of oleaginous cliché. The poor would always be with us, and would inherit the earth (later), and then there was the needle's eye, and the old tradition that discomfort was good for the moral fiber, so that it was better to give than to receive. Private charity was a direct descendant of the first fruits, or the tithe: it was good in the eyes of the Lord, it was expected of certain people, and it propitiated the baleful demons of cosmic justice. It also made the rich feel good, like Scrooges hiding a furtive tear as Tiny Tim sank his carious choppers into a donated drumstick, and allowed them to distinguish between the deserving and undeserving poor, a distinction that has enriched our moral philosophy while impoverishing our affections. Withal, charity was necessary; the notion of social conscience was rudimentary, and private conscience had to stand in for it. The free Christmas turkey might taste of gall, but it was meat.

Philanthropy, however, was a different thing. Its purposes were broader, and it cost more. Its results were often abstract and unpredictable. Its recipients were often suspiciously unbusinesslike organizations that might require eternal deficit financing. And while an orphan home permitted large numbers of shivering pupae to enjoy the benefits of righteousness, an art museum might encourage revolutionaries like Cézanne. Nevertheless Field was a founding member of the Chicago Academy of Fine Arts, which established the Art Institute of Chicago; he joined the group in 1878, and the *vernissage* in 1884 gave him great personal satisfaction: one of its glories was Millet's "Harvest Moon," from the collection of Marshall Field. (He was not a connoisseur, and bought for respectability and price rather than out of esthetic conviction.) He was aware that the rich had a public responsibility, and once said, "Give us anything to elevate the tone of the people," which helps to account for the Millet. But he focused an excruciatingly canny eye on that process of elevation; when Nathaniel Kellogg Fairbank suggested, in the 1880s, that ten leading citizens put up $100,000 each for a combined public library and opera house, Field did his thinking aloud to a reporter: "Would I subscribe $100,000? Well, I am not prepared to say whether I would or would not today. Why should eight or ten gentlemen run the town as it might be with regard to a certain enterprise? Why should eight or ten gentlemen be called upon to subscribe $100,000? And will it take $1,000,000? Why is not the interest more divided? Answer me some of these things." In the end the project was abandoned.

Field was more amenable, but still canny, when the founders of the new University of Chicago came to him in 1889. The old University had gone bankrupt in 1886, leaving Chicago with little in the way of higher education. Three educators had prevailed upon John D. Rockefeller to do something about it. (They were Frederick T. Gates, corresponding secretary of the American Baptist Education Society; Dr. Thomas W. Goodspeed, financial secretary of the Baptist Theological Seminary supported by Rockefeller in Morgan Park, Illinois; and Dr. William Rainey Harper, a young and brilliant professor of Greek and Hebrew at Yale.) On May 15, 1889, Rockefeller agreed to put up $600,000 if another $400,000 could be raised within about a year; the founders did even better, coming up with $419,000. They also came up with a site: ten acres in the Midway Plaisance on the South Side. Owner: Marshall Field, who had paid $79,166 for it in 1879 and had watched it appreciate to about $125,000 in the decade since.

Field needed six weeks to make up his mind. They were taking inventory at the store, and there was a time and place for everything. Then he agreed to donate the land. Goodspeed was upset by his deliberation, but had no right to be; Field gave the land graciously, and was generous afterward. He donated more land, and sold other plots to the University on easy terms; he offered $100,000 once on condition that another $900,000 be raised in ninety days (it was); he gave $135,000 later on unconditionally. He contributed the land for an athletic field, and was probably as appalled as anyone when it was named "Marshall Field," an example of academic humor to vie with England's best. His donations totaled $361,000, one-thirtieth of Rockefeller's,* but, as Field had pointed

---

* John D. Archbold was another great benefactor, and when inaugural services were held at the University in 1892 the students sang this doxology:

> Praise John from whom oil blessings flow;
> Praise him, oil creatures here below;
> Praise him above, ye heavenly host;
> Praise Archbold too, but John the most.

out, Rockefeller was rich. (In a moment of irritation Field had also said, "It is exceedingly easy to give away other people's money," a sentiment echoed half a century later by Rockefeller's son, in a moment of equal irritation brought on by Field's grandson.)

Unquestionably Field was comfortable as a philanthropist, and gratified by his giving. His late start was a matter of caution and taste, and not of principle. He found satisfaction, once he had begun, and nothing in his attitude even hints that his contributions were conscience money. He subscribed $1,000 in 1891 toward the establishment of the Chicago Symphony, and two years later the Columbian Exposition offered him a unique opportunity to combine civic pride, profit, and philanthropy on the grand scale.

The World's Fair of 1893 marked Chicago's emergence as an international city. President Cleveland dedicated the "World's Columbian Exposition" on May 1, and by midnight 400,000 people had tramped the 600-acre fair grounds; in the next few months 28,000,000 admissions were registered. Royalty and nobility dropped in with often unpredictable results; the Infanta Eulalia of Spain appeared only reluctantly at a reception offered by Mrs. Potter Palmer, having stated, "I prefer not to meet this innkeeper's wife." Mrs. Palmer's revenge was deferred but decisive; asked to a reception for the same Infanta a few years later in Paris, she regretted: "I cannot meet this bibulous representative of a degenerate monarchy." But the social aspects of the fair were not Marshall Field's concern. He had bought the largest single block of Exposition stock, seeing the fair, correctly, as a spur to the city's trade and to its growth generally. He took no interest in Ward McAllister's analysis of the fair's effect on high society ("These Chicagoans should not pretend to rival the East or the Old World in matters of refinement"), if indeed he was aware of it. He was largely indifferent to the fair's architectural "splendor," as were most critics; with a couple of exceptions like Louis Sullivan's colorful Transportation Building, the structures ("Everywhere were white classic piles") were uniformly disappointing: imperial imitations of the Roman, substituting pretentiousness for style and pseudoantiquity for imagination. (Sullivan wrote later, "The damage wrought by the World's Fair will last for half a century . . . if not longer. It has penetrated deep into the constitution of the American mind, effecting there lesions significant of dementia," and thirty-five years later Mumford agreed with him, describing a period of "easy mechanical duplication of other modes of architecture, frigidly predicted by the Chicago Exposition of 1893.") But Field did not care. His interest was Chicago itself, and not a transient carnival, and his investment had been in growth and not in spectacle. Yet out of the fair came his largest single philanthropic gesture: the Chicago Natural History Museum, known for years as the Field Museum of Natural History.

Several people had felt that something ought to be permanently retained of the fair's exhibits. The man who acted was Edward E. Ayer, "a Chicago lumberman with a passion for American Indian relics." He was passionate enough to ignore Field's first refusal, and to ask again for funds to establish a museum. He appealed to Field's vanity—the perpetuation of a great merchant's name through altruism—and to his sense of stewardship. Field gave in cheerfully but conditionally, offering $1,000,000 provided another $500,000 were raised in the business community and $2,000,000 in World's Fair stock assigned to the Museum's trustees. In June of 1894 the Museum was opened, in Jackson Park; until 1921 it stood in what had been the Art Palace at the fair. By 1906 Field had donated another million, and the Museum was Chicago's pride. There was nothing parochial about it; it was, and remains, one of the world's great museums.

But 1893 was not just a year of fun and frolic. Grover Cleveland's solid conservatism had returned him to the Presidency; his firm defense of the gold standard had reassured the respectable, and free silverites and inflationists generally had stood by him because the alternative was the party of Rep. William McKinley's detested tariff bill of 1890. But international gold manipulations and extravagant pension grants under Harrison had depleted the country's treasury, and on May 5—five days after the fair opened—the market sagged sharply; late in June it crashed altogether, in the most severe panic the country had known.

As usual Field was secure. He was still doing a cash business, and neither the store nor his philanthropies suffered. He was comfortably above the battle. He kept an eye on "conditions," offered advice with his customary asperity, and criticized the abysmal morality of Chicago politics. He was the city's first citizen, and in 1893 he became more: a patriarch, if not a dynast.

7

Marshall Field II was a melancholy fellow. His father seemed a Jehovah, and he missed the consolations of a loving mother; in the late 1870s Nannie Scott Field had taken to spending much of the year abroad. The young man's life was a succession of proxies: the servants for parents, his father's achievements for his own, men's deference for their respect. He and his sister circulated among their peers, perfectly dressed, perfectly mannered. They were born to rank and money, and life offered little in the way of challenge and conquest. The high point of their childhood was their presentation to Chicago society, at a ball in their home on New Year's Night, 1886, when Marshall was seventeen and Ethel twelve. It was a "Mikado Ball"; sets from the first New York run of that operetta were shipped in and set up. There were about four hundred adolescent guests, many of whom had come all the way from New York, Boston, and Baltimore; an orchestra tucked into a pagoda sawed away while they waltzed. The favors offered to the young ladies had been designed in London by James McNeill Whistler.

Three years later, after the requisite private schools and tutoring, Marshall went off to Harvard, leaving Ethel behind to go on learning the graces. He showed little interest in the store; it was not of his creation, it did not need him, and the family fortune was already beyond danger—the Fields had so much money that it was impossible not to make more. Nor did he show any inclination to personal achievement in the arts or sciences.

He is almost always described as "sickly" or "unwell," but the debility is never specified. It seems to have been a general lassitude, a lack of purpose, a vagueness of identity, the kind of inanition that leads to snuffles and asthma and aches and pains of mysterious origin, sometimes to conscientious hypochondria. There is no record of these symptoms, but there is a strong impression of weariness. An Englishman in the same fix—not uncommon—would have been trained to manage the estates; failing that, to buy a seat in Parliament; failing that, to enter the armed services; if none of these sufficed, he might have gambled away his patrimony and headed for India. But Marshall showed no interest in a "useful" life, and very little in profligacy. He was not even a classic example of the *fils de riche;* he lacked the necessary egotistical nastiness. He was simply a young man of good mind and sound instincts for whom there seemed to be no place, no activity, that required his presence. His sickliness is best described by an old-fashioned word: he was neurasthenic.

Harvard failed to inspire him, but a young lady named Albertine Huck succeeded. She was beautiful, the daughter of a Chicago brewer, and—it was unimportant—a Roman Catholic. Marshall needed love, and with her he found it. He left Harvard in 1890, and they were married on October 10. He was twenty-two; she was eighteen. Three months later, on New Year's Day, 1891, sister Ethel married Arthur Magie Tree, son of a distinguished Chicago judge and diplomat; they went off to live in England, and shortly afterward Marshall and his bride joined them there.

From then on they spent most of their time in Europe, returning to the United States for a few months each year. In spring the elder Field usually joined his wife in Paris for three or four weeks, and there were family reunions. Chicago must have been puzzled; its first family had dispersed; only Field remained, the lonely patriarch. Young Marshall and his wife, from the reports that drifted back, lived an inexplicably passive life, alien to American ways: moneyed, empty, built around stylized social events, servants and horses and borrowed traditions, high tea on the terrace; spiced only by trips to the Continent and visits to galleries with Nannie Field. An aimless existence, redeemed only by a touch of connubial bliss.

Field missed his children. If they had never been close to him they had at least been present, and now he had no one. He was almost sixty, and loneliness at his time of life was an unforeseen and troublesome condition. The irony was surely not lost on him: having neglected his family to win an empire, he now ruled in solitary majesty—now, when he had need of company and affection, children and grandchildren at the hearth, flesh-and-blood reminders that the generations would go on.

He was elated when his first grandson was born, on October 28, 1892, and utterly disconsolate, as the whole family was, when the

boy died thirteen days later. Field himself had little time to brood.
Lifelong habits of activity bore him up, and there was good hope
for future grandchildren. A busy year was upon him. Chicago
claimed his attention constantly, a great city now, rich even in bad
times, swollen by armies of immigrant workmen, still attracting
businessmen, robber barons, and simple swindlers from all over the
world. A young Englishman named Samuel Insull arrived in 1892
to revivify the slumping Chicago Edison Company, and Field was
sufficiently impressed to lend him a quarter of a million dollars—
with which the young man bought Edison stock, and began an extraordinary career. In 1893 Field, aged fifty-nine, had the fair, and
his philanthropies, and the great panic; and in August of that year
he enjoyed a touch of family, when his brother Joseph's son Stanley
arrived from Manchester to begin a highly successful career in the
store.

Even the new Governor of Illinois provided excitement: a queer
duck named John Peter Altgeld, born in Germany and full of odd
humanitarian principles, he had been swept into office as a Democrat in the swing to Cleveland. Late in June, 1893, Altgeld pardoned the three surviving Haymarket agitators, and the business
community, led by the *Tribune,* burst into invective; the country
was falling into the hands of a new breed, and there was unease in
Zion.

But in the end it was a great year for Field. On September 28,
1893, back at 1919 Prairie Avenue, another son was born to Marshall II and Albertine. He was handsome and healthy, and he was
called Marshall Field III.

8

Field I did not decline slowly after sixty; he never declined at all
until the week of his death. In his last decade he lived almost another lifetime. Slow, but apparently irreversible, changes in American life posed a series of challenges to the public Field; the
nineteenth century was almost over (in all but the chronological
sense it ended with World War I and the Sixteenth Amendment),
and he resisted its passing stoutly. The personal Field, too, had his
hands full, and found himself coping with death, love, grandchil-

dren, and even—at seventy-one—marriage. He became less distant, less punctilious, and considerably more human.

On all levels government was becoming a less simple nuisance and a more necessary evil; the influence of the Social Darwinists seemed to be waning. The Federal government had to contend not only with Coxey's Army and free silver—symptoms of economic failure—but also with conservation, the annexation of Hawaii, a dispute between Venezuela and Great Britain, Cuba's rebellion against Spain. In Illinois Altgeld ceased to be a problem in 1896, when he was succeeded by the more amenable John R. Tanner, but not before the Pullman strike had shocked the country. In Chicago itself politics was slipping out of the hands of the imams into those of assorted fellahin (perhaps encouraged by Little Egypt's terp-sichore at the Fair); the Levee, followed by the New Levee, was in full flourish, being both a geographically bounded sink of iniquity and a human state of mind; an alderman's vote cost more than a state legislator's (Chicago boosters could take pride in that); and it was almost impossible for the righteous to participate in govern-ment without inhaling the prevalent corruption.

There were too many responsibilities for the few to fulfill. In a hundred years our population had leapt from 4,000,000 to 64,-000,000, and diffusion of power was inevitable. The frontier was almost stable; Manifest Destiny, or Vulgar Brawling, was much in vogue. There was simply too much national energy available. If the clamorous multitudes rejected peaceful service in favor of expan-sion and progress, even the confirmed Social Darwinists could not complain; if the latter insisted that life was a free-for-all, they had no moral right to pick the winner in advance. Social Darwinism had relied upon the ancient definitions of virtue and superiority, and the advance of technology was rendering those definitions obsolete. The technological revolution had introduced new mysteries, and Technological Man, the only one who could solve them, was no kin, and barely kith, to the Fields and Morgans, or even to the Pullmans and Rockefellers and Carnegies who had created him. In fifty years the technician would be king—in politics, in industry, even in "social relations," a term that could have been invented only by technicians; and if it was true that in the 1890s he was still just a workingman, it was also true that the capitalists were past their prime, and that an age of brilliant manipulators was upon us. Of these latter the two most successful—Insull and Kreuger—flourished in the 1920s, but they had a gold-plated archetype in Charles Tyson Yerkes, Jr., 1837–1905, approximately coeval with Field, and a perfect example of what the old gentleman was up against in his later years.

Yerkes, "the only Chicago capitalist with a prison record," was a buccaneer. He had started with nothing, worked his way into brokerage, and specialized in bonds. In 1871 he was convicted of misapplying municipal funds in Philadelphia. He was released betimes, largely at the urging of his fellow bankers, who appreciated the splendid job he had done selling municipal bonds. He seems to have felt from then on that because he could "get things done" for a big city, he was entitled to all the graft he could contrive. He entered Chicago's business world in 1881, with a stock and grain brokerage house, and was soon attracted by the almost limitless possibilities of municipal transport. He was not an intimate of Field, Pullman, or Palmer. When he "bragged of his special talent for corrupting aldermen, [Field] froze with disgust. Later . . . 'He shocked me,' the great merchant whispered. 'He is not safe.' " By 1896 Yerkes was building the elevated railway system. He subcontracted, padding bills extravagantly and pocketing huge profits; objectors were bribed. But piecemeal bribery was inefficient. In 1895, committed to his projects, he had rushed a series of "eternal monopoly" bills through the state Legislature. When Governor Altgeld vetoed them, Yerkes offered him $500,000 to change his stand; it was refused. "I admire that man!" Yerkes said, and, when Altgeld gave way to a new governor, promptly set about bribing the Legislature to pass the Allen Law, which gave the Chicago City Council authority to do what Altgeld had vetoed.

Field's public statements were unequivocal, but they were few, and they were whispered rather than thundered. He was not a party to Yerkes's machinations, but with his real estate and traction holdings he stood to make a great deal if Yerkes won. He was therefore restrained, by a kind of paradox that was a sickness of the times: for two centuries and more, moneymaking had been a sign of virtue; could it be virtuous when done by obviously vicious men? There were no more blacks and whites, and even Field came parlous nigh to iniquity. He was spared corruption by the courage of Carter

Harrison, Jr., the new mayor, and by the strident bellowing of Chicago's press, finally awake to injustice. (During the bloody Pullman strike of 1894 Harrison, publisher of the Chicago *Times,* had come out flatly—and alone—for the workers: "God knows the men involved . . . suffered grievously . . . no way humanly possible of righting the wrongs except through the strike." This put him shoulder to shoulder with Eugene Debs, but—and?—he was elected mayor anyway—therefore?) Harrison himself declined a generous proposition from Yerkes. After a series of votes in the Council, the issue stood or fell on one motion—to refer all traction ordinances to the Committee on City Hall, rather than to the Committee on Railways, which was packed with Yerkes men. The motion was passed by one vote, 32 to 31, but even here the war between virtue and vice was a free-for-all and not a confrontation: Harrison's hottest supporters were corrupt Democrats engaged in their own intraparty power struggle, and they voted with him because just this once, at least, power meant more than money. Three weeks later the Legislature killed the Allen Law. The *Tribune* estimated that Chicago's aldermen had saved their city $150,000,000; it was a good selling point for a ward heeler, and thirty-two councilmen had been aware of that. Incidentally Marshall Field had been spared a large and dirty profit. In the end he was pleased. It might have been the one great immorality that kills a man's faith in his own virtue.

The last years of his business life were relatively quiet. At the turn of the century he fought a hard battle with Charles Schwab over the expansion of U.S. Steel—Schwab favored the Monongahela Valley, Field the Chicago area. Field won, and the result was Gary, Indiana. He fought another, less noisy, battle to keep the United States out of war with Spain, and lost. He was by no means a pacifist in principle, but war was bad for business, and his fellow merchants supported his stand. Not so Medill and the *Tribune,* both belligerently American to start with, both confirmed in bellicosity by Field's opposition. When war broke out Field backed the cause, but wearily and warily: "This is the beginning, and what the end may be it is probable no man can foresee. War in general always seems to have been easier begun than ended. War unsettles, and while it lasts businessmen are compelled to be more cautious than in times of peace."

The war had one bizarre effect on his future. Teddy Roosevelt galloped into prominence, succeeded Garret A. Hobart as Mc-Kinley's vice-president in 1901, became President after McKinley's assassination, and naturally ran for re-election in 1904. In 1898 Field had been asked, discreetly, if he were interested in the embassy to the Court of St. James's, which John Hay had left to become Secretary of State; he had declined to discuss the matter, feeling no desire at all to become more of a public servant than he was. He had opined, however, that conservative Democrats ought to take such offices, to counteract Bryan's vulgar demagoguery. By 1904 Bryan was a two-time loser (he would try again in 1908, and be promoted to a three-time loser), and the party was ready for a steadier man. Rich and conservative Democrats spoke to Field; the South Bend *Times* editorialized strongly for him; but he declined. "I have a little reputation now," he said, "and might not have any left if I became a candidate." * The party shifted its ground, and urged him to take second place on the ticket, telling him that Morgan, for one, had approved the choice; but he declined again. When the convention met in St. Louis in July and his name was still being bandied about, he was forced to decline publicly, formally, and categorically.

He was a merchant, and he was getting on, and he wanted time for his family. Marshall II and Albertine had given him another grandson, Henry, on July 18, 1895, and Field became almost a commuter to England. His delight with a baby boy on each knee was obvious if uncharacteristic. What he felt when Nannie Scott Field died in Nice on February 23, 1896, no one knows; for twenty years they had spent little time together. Mrs. Field had enjoyed Paris in the spring, the south of France in winter, and England the rest of the year. Her life had been one of total luxury and little joy.

---

* He may have been reluctant—understandably—to go up against Roosevelt, who was a war hero and a trust buster. Field, who had opposed the war, was skeptical of Manifest Destiny, and represented the highest level of capitalism, would have suffered under the inevitable mudslinging. Bryan's supporters, the chewing-tobacco Democrats, might even have preferred Teddy to Field, who had been, and was still in many matters, a Republican in all but formal affiliation.

For ten years or so her marriage had sputtered along. She had become—probably with the exception of Mrs. Potter Palmer—Chicago's first lady, and then she had abdicated. Perhaps the bustle and
intrigue and backbiting of American society were not for her.
Surely Field was far from a loving husband—so far from it that
even the two children, even the money, even the eminence, could
not compensate for the barrenness of her life in Chicago. In her
last years she was weak, debilitated in spirit and easy prey to a succession of minor ailments. She may have found some relief in nar-
cotics; a legend grew later that she had been a drug addict, but she
remained a lady to the end, and her addiction, if any, was of the
genteel, medical kind. She returned to Chicago at last, and was
buried in the family plot at Graceland Cemetery.

The past and the future occupied Field more than usual during
his last few years. He did not neglect the store, and his responsibilities were undiminished, but intimations of mortality were upon him,
and his mind roved forward and back. His parents were buried in
Conway, in the Massachusetts he had left so long ago; and in 1900
the native returned. He brought with him money and an architect,
not to mention the simple power of his presence. On July 4, 1900,
was laid the cornerstone of the Field Memorial Library, large, free,
and badly needed. It was dedicated July 13, 1901; Field himself
supplied a community dinner, music, fireworks, and a speech, the
last being as brief as it was rare. From all accounts he remained
simple and reserved, with nothing about him of the local boy who
had made good.* He had a strong ego, but little personal vanity; he
had never been a complicated man, and as he aged he became even
more direct.

Back in Chicago, another trouble awaited him: Albertine gave
birth to a boy on August 29, who was named Reginald and died on
September 4. But Marshall III and Henry were thriving; and on
May 17 of the next year a healthy sister was born to them, and
Grandfather Field was happy again.

His social life was quiet: dinner with friends, luncheons at his

---

* He never even smoked cigars, and good Havanas were almost a necessity
among successful businessmen. In his last years he took an occasional cigarette in
company, to be sociable.

clubs, a good bit of golf. His private entertainments were limited to Sunday morning breakfasts—at nine o'clock—when a handful of male friends often joined him. He did spend time with Mr. and Mrs. Arthur J. Caton. He had known Mrs. Caton, the former Delia Spencer, for thirty years; she was a great beauty, and his admiration for her was common knowledge. It was not "gossiped about." Gossip, in any personal, malicious sense, would have been ignored or disbelieved.

Arthur Caton, lawyer and clubman, died in New York in November, 1904. Less than a year later, on September 5, 1905, his widow became Mrs. Marshall Field. Burne-Jones had called hers "the sweetest smile I have ever seen" and she was still beautiful. The ceremony took place at St. Margaret's Church in London, and Ambassador Whitelaw Reid was among the guests. Field looked grave, but became downright jolly during the lavish wedding breakfast that followed at Claridge's. He was obviously and thoroughly happy.

His happiness lasted about seven weeks. He and his bride were in New York on November 22, when they were notified that Marshall II had accidentally shot himself in the abdomen while cleaning a revolver.

9

A rich man's scandal is no more scandalous than a poor man's, but it is better publicized. When Field reached Chicago the next day, having hired a private train, reporters surrounded him, shouting and setting off flashpans; they pursued him to the steps of Mercy Hospital, where more of them were waiting. When he left the hospital they attacked again, and he turned on them fiercely, striking toward a photographer with his cane.

He had never cared for the press, and that day he hated all newspapermen. They were animals, and there were too many of them; they could not be tamed, could not be lectured, showed no slightest human decency; he moved through a forest of cameras; the shouts were maddening, unintelligible, a jungle gibberish. He was roused to one flash of helpless rage; trembling visibly, he roared, "Here, you, stop! Who are you? Why do you do these things? Aren't you ashamed?" They were not; they bayed him home. His house, too, was surrounded; he was barely given time for anguish. He locked his doors. Detectives were barred from the home and from the hospital room. For ten years Field had been mellowing, but this was the end; he was never again so much as genial in public. He had given away money, loved his grandchildren, married a woman he adored; but in one day of persecution the world lost his affection altogether.

Newspapers ignore grief; more, they punish contumacy. The family's brief statement—an accident—was not accepted. An expert reported that the revolver could not have fired accidentally. And Marshall II had bought the gun only a month before. The family had refused to allow the usual investigation. The doctors' statements sounded stilted. Field would say nothing of his visit to the hospital. Rumor ran high.

Meanwhile Marshall lay dying, only thirty-seven years old. The immediate abdominal surgery had been difficult and dangerous, but the patient rallied, and was conscious next day when he spoke to Field. He remained lucid for three days more, but on the 27th he failed, and that afternoon was given the last rites; he had become a Roman Catholic when he married. Shortly before five o'clock he died, with a crucifix in his hand. His eulogy was a bitter statement by his widow: "American wealth is too often a curse. I want it to be the means of the greatest blessing to my sons, the means of fulfillment of the highest patriotic ambitions. I should like to see them grow up into politicians, for they then would, it seems to me, employ their wealth to the greatest good for their countrymen."

For several days the newspapers were merciless, punishing Field's obdurate scorn. The speculation was obvious: Marshall II had committed suicide; in shame, the family had denied the deed. Field remained silent, and made no effort to refute the rumors. Even now, a full and formal statement might have ended matters, but it was never offered. The old gentleman had withdrawn, wrapped in sorrow and disdain. He had misjudged the press, antagonized it, withheld confidence, played the seigneur. Any man was free to think the worst, and some did: new rumors were whispered, denied, embellished. Field himself had made scandal inevitable, and the natural propensity of gossips to be "insiders" made it gaudy. Chicago de-

cided that Marshall II had been shot to death in the Levee, at one
sumptuous bagnio or another; preferably at the Everleigh Sisters',
which took pride in its tony clientele, which maintained a $15,000
gold piano and a rigidly correct standard of elegance and manners,
and which billed its regular membership monthly, sending each (to
his office address) an invoice under the name of a fictitious firm.
The whispers were only whispers for some time. About a year
after the event came the first circumstantial report, from a lady of
vague vocation in San Francisco who claimed to have been in practice in Chicago at the time, and an eyewitness. After that the race
was on, and there was fierce competition in details, adjectives, and
the niceties of rhetoric and oratory. Eventually the lie almost became truth.*

Marshall III, just twelve years old, had been in his nursery con-
valescing from the measles and playing with an assortment of musical instruments, birthday gifts from his grandfather. He heard the
shot, and remembered it clearly and sadly all his life. Later on he
felt sure that his father had committed suicide. Even that is open to
doubt, but it seems most likely. The abdomen is an unlikely target,
failure and long agony being possible; it may be that Marshall
II, like many suicides, wanted attention more than death, and unconsciously hoped to survive. One ingenious fabrication held that
Field had kept the newspapers from reporting the bordello story by
threatening to withdraw the store's advertising. It was blasted immediately by James Keeley, managing editor of the *Tribune* and
Field's old enemy, who answered, "If I could have run a story like
that I wouldn't have had to worry about advertising for the rest of
my life."

The tragedy was deeper than any of them knew at the time. A
nineteenth-century family had been shattered. In spite of the long
separations the Fields had a dynastic unity, with an awareness of
rank, with the hope of continuity, with self-respect and solidarity,

---

* Lloyd Wendt and Herman Kogan, whose research for *Lords of the Levee* was
exhaustive and punctilious, sat entranced one evening while an elderly lawyer of
high repute entertained them with a lurid and circumstantial account. They determined shortly afterward that almost everything the man had said about anything
at all was untrue. He was simply having another go at what had once been Chicago's favorite pastime.

all of this transcending individual unhappiness. There was even a strong sense of primogeniture: the first grandson, who lived less than two weeks, had been named Marshall, and the name had been used again. And now the family was reduced to an old man, closer to death than he knew; his daughter; his daughter-in-law; and the grandchildren.

But there was also the money. It was a far more unifying force than blood, and under its benevolent despotism the Fields survived as a family. With less of it the dispersion might have been permanent, and the fortune might have dribbled away at racetracks and casinos, yacht clubs and private galleries. But there was enough. Marshall Field I died just half a century after he came to Chicago, and the family survived; another half century and Marshall III was dead, but the Fields were still the Fields.

The old gentleman survived his son by less than two months. He had begun to recover from the tragedy, and he was happy with his second wife; but he had no smiles for the outside world. More than ever he withdrew into his work, into the circle of his close friends. He was not declining, simply withdrawing. His manner had always been austere, and a touch of added bleakness was not surprising. He was still the merchant prince. His taxes for 1905 were the highest in the country, but that may have been because he paid them a bit more honestly than most. (But only a bit. He was accused by the Illinois Tax Reform Association of paying only 10 per cent of his fair share. Still, in the 1890s the Chicago *Tribune,* netting over $250,000 annually, had paid taxes on an assessment of just $18,000; private citizens behaved no better, probably feeling that it was immoral to give the government money to do things that people should be doing for themselves.) The store was flourishing; volume grew every year. Field's largest investments were in real estate and blue-chip securities, and he tended them assiduously.

He also played golf assiduously. He played a round on New Year's Day, 1906, with his nephew Stanley (to whom was shifting more and more responsibility in the store), James Simpson (later the company's board chairman), and Robert Todd Lincoln, Abraham Lincoln's son and one of Field's oldest friends. They played on snow, using red golf balls, and Field was perky. He came down with a sniffle, but played two more rounds that week. In a conversation with Stanley Field he mentioned his Will; he wanted to leave the Museum $16,000,000 instead of $8,000,000, the additional money to go for a new building. He had board meetings in New York the following week; he would be back on Friday, and would see his lawyers then.

He was not back on Friday; he never went to the board meetings. On the Broadway Limited Monday evening he knew that he was very sick. His wife telegraphed ahead to Pittsburgh; a doctor met the train there, examined him, and prescribed. When Mr. and Mrs. Marshall Field checked into the Holland House next day, he was tottering.

Stanley Field was notified immediately; he made his own train reservations and then tracked down Dr. Frank Billings, the most respected physician in the Middle West. Dr. Billings was at the bedside of President William Rainey Harper of the University of Chicago, who was dying of cancer, and there is a desperate and macabre note in his answer to Field: he would rush to New York as soon as his patient died.

Stanley Field went on immediately. Billings arrived Thursday morning, examined the patient, conferred with the two doctors on the scene, and confirmed the diagnosis: pneumonia, and galloping. Field lingered for five days. Friends came to stand by and to offer Mrs. Field what comfort they could. Field's lawyer hovered decorously, available for eleventh-hour instructions. The dying man fought hard, weak, burning, in pain, but conscious; and at four o'clock on Tuesday afternoon, January 16, 1906, he died. Later in the day his widow said, "Mr. Field's last words were for me and not for the world."

The eulogies were flowery, almost fulsome; what evil there had been in Field's life was interred with his bones. *The New York Times* set the tone:

What a typically American career it is! The very rich man has died just at the psalmist's limit of life, leaving a huge estate, which ought not only to be unenvied but acclaimed, since the great merchant, whatever his motives, in order to accumulate it must have shared his profits and economies with his customers. And the opportunity to do what he did is still open to every beginner of native or foreign birth in this great and happy land. What is the use of talking about proletariats and classes in the face of such an object lesson that the hopes of American life are still as open as they ever were?

And even the Chicago *Tribune* melted, with praise of a man

about whose fortune [unlike many other great American fortunes] there has never been a suspicion of taint . . . whose faith in Chicago has been steadfast and true, and whose life will be a beacon light to guide future generations to honorable success.

Field's body was returned to Chicago on a private train. The store shut down until after the burial; nine hundred business houses in the city were closed all the day of the funeral. There was a family service at eleven at 1905 Prairie Avenue; a small service for friends at noon in the First Presbyterian Church; and a third at Graceland Cemetery at two. The minister took his text from II Samuel 3:38: "Know ye not that there is a prince and a great man fallen this day?"

To the citizens of Chicago, it was a good text. Field had been royalty for fifty years; he was a tough old reactionary, but he is remembered with the merchant princes and not with the robber barons. Chicago had been built on the dollar, and its builders were mainly freebooters whose chief concern was the dollar. Field too had a healthy appetite for profits, but he cared for his city. He detested labor unions, but he welcomed competition; he detested incompetents but bailed out bankrupts for the city's good. His philanthropies were deliberate and considered, and not expiations. His morality was distorted by the excesses of his century, but not disfigured by corruption. He was a stern, consistent, unaffectionate man with iron in his soul; a Yankee trader with a touch of Giovanni de' Medici. He knew little of human love because he never needed it until he was old, and then it was too late; he never learned to offer it, except awkwardly to his grandchildren; he distrusted compassion. He believed in "enlightened self-interest," the motto of his class, which reserved the privilege of defining it. If the right and wrong of his time were not the right and wrong of ours, at least he tried not to confuse the two. He knew only business, and he did it well, and he was faithful to his origins and beliefs.

Every epoch has its mystique and its truth, and following ages inherit a queer mixture of the two and do what they can with it. Periclean Athens exalted reason and lived on slave labor; we profit. Elizabethan England exalted the Nation and lived in treachery, intolerance, and bawdry; we profit. Martin Luther spoke directly to God, and crushed the peasants; we profit. The nineteenth century made its Deity a director in charge of public relations, justifying now child labor, now silicosis, now the murder of dissidents, now disproportionate wealth. The Industrial Revolution, like all revolutions, was careless of life; but what we are and what we have were determined by that revolution; what we value and what we abhor were made clearer by it, and if it produced no Sophocles and no Shakespeare, that may be because it produced so many more Anaxagorases and Bacons. When the survivors are gone new men will write its history, and the broken lives, the disease and oppression and personal tragedy, will become footnotes: everyone in the nineteenth century died this way or that, they will say, and the result was the twentieth century, in which likewise everyone died this way or that.

History moves, and few men move with it, and Marshall Field was no exception; but he lived by his lights and he told no lies.

He left something over $120,000,000, the bulk of which, appreciating steadily, went to Marshall Field III.

CHAPTER TWO

I call a complete and generous education that which fits a man to perform justly, skilfully, and magnanimously all the offices, both private and public, of peace and war.

—JOHN MILTON,
Tractate on Education, 1644

ALBERTINE FIELD'S DECISION to leave the United States was compound of Anglophilia and weariness. She and Marshall II had been happier in England, a more refined and languid setting for their unaggressive lives; feeling as she did that wealth in America was too often a curse, and brokenhearted at her husband's death, she must have longed for release from Chicago's commercial brutalities and waspishly competitive society. The move was not a difficult and daring expatriation; she was simply rejoining old friends, and in 1906 her friends composed the most rarefied stratum of the world's most self-sufficient society.

The Edwardian was a strange interlude, a postscript to Victoria, when the miseries of the nineteenth century seemed momentarily to have been assuaged, and the murderous glories of the twentieth had not yet made anxiety a way of life. Fifty years earlier Charles Kingsley had written, "Oh, England is a pleasant place for them that's rich and high/ But England is a cruel place for such poor folks as I," and it was still true, but the tone of life was gentler. The rich were still in charge, but the middle classes were taking over, and even the working classes were acquiring bits and pieces of power; persistent cranks like Keir Hardie in his cloth cap, and the Webbs, and Edward Carpenter, had nudged history. The Liberals were in office, and that stormy Welshman Lloyd George was, of all things, president of the Board of Trade; he detested the established church and the landed gentry, and had opposed the Boer War. Bernard Shaw had just written, "Englishmen never will be slaves; they are free to do whatever the government and public opinion allow them to do," but high society ignored the nasty Irishman. The swells were having a marvelous time. A few may have known that they were dancing in their own sunset, but Edward himself had set the tone, and crepes Suzette were the order of the day.

The Fields settled into a fashionable town house at 2 Carleton Terrace in London. A first concern was the children's education. Marshall and Henry had been exposed to some of the polite classicism of the Colter School on Chicago's Gold Coast, and to some tutoring at home; otherwise they had been almost completely sheltered. Marshall particularly had missed even the most genteel sort of rough-and-tumble. He was a victim of rheumatic fever—not a serious case requiring immobilization, but one bad enough to keep him from strenuous sports and games. Doctors had guessed that it might pass, or at least recede to unimportance, but Albertine Field worried; her older son was "delicate." Henry was robust, and Gwendolyn was a lovely little girl. Marshall was stockier than Henry, but softer, and it seemed probable even then that Henry would be the taller.

For a year or so the children led quiet lives at their mother's side. There were trips to the country, and there were private tutors. There were visits with Aunt Ethel, who was no longer married to Arthur Tree; they had been divorced, and she was now the wife of a handsome young British naval officer, Capt. David Beatty. She had two sons then, Arthur Ronald Tree, a few years younger than Marshall, and little David Beatty, who was only eighteen months old and not very good at games. Mrs. Field leased a country house in Hertfordshire, and entertained close friends. Among her guests was a Capt. Maldwin Drummond, who suggested that she send the boys to Eton. Drummond was of an old and aristocratic banking family, and his advice was always sound.

Entrance was not a problem. Marshall and Henry (Field major and Field minor) came well recommended. And getting into Eton used to be—it still is to some extent—an odd process.

These were the good, easy days before the Common Entrance examination, or indeed any entrance examination at all. . . . You were accepted for Eton in the week, if not on the day, of your birth, when your father sent a telegram to some Master likely to have a House in thirteen years' time. The examination was to decide, not your entrance, but your form. If it proved that you knew nothing at all, you were sent to throw ink-bottles at your peers in Third Form under Bunny Hare.*

Field was sent to the Third Form to throw ink-bottles at his peers; his tutor was Bunny Hare.

So it was, in a leisurely, gentlemanly fashion, that Field's formal education began, in the Michaelmas half of 1907. (There are three halves, or terms, at Eton: Michaelmas, Lent, and summer.) He was out in the world—a small, friendly world for the time being. Like all the boys, he had his own room, and was allowed a fire every other night in winter.

2

Back in Chicago the *sine qua non* was being published and proved. Marshall Field's Will and Testament consisted of some twenty thousand words of prose, divided into twenty-three clauses dated February 25, 1904; one codicil of two clauses dated June 14, 1904; and a second codicil of a single clause dated September 5, 1905— all before the death of Marshall II. It was an extraordinary document—in the size of the Estate it distributed, in the care with which it was drawn, in its opening note of affection and its mingling of family pride with business principle. It was contested later on three separate issues, and though it was bent to accommodate changing circumstances, it was never broken; two of the contests resulted in interpretations but not in revisions, and the third was unsuccessful.

The first clause was rather sad and sweet, and incidentally justified the twentieth:

---

* L. E. Jones, *A Victorian Boyhood,* Macmillan & Co., Ltd., London, 1955. This book and its sequels, *An Edwardian Youth* and *Georgian Afternoon,* compose an admirably written and remarkably charming autobiography. They are also wildly funny. Sir Lawrence is a man of little illusion and unlimited warmth, and although he was some ten years older than Field, his books offer a thoroughly winning explanation of Field's unwavering affection for England.

The health of my only son, Marshall Field, Junior, has long been a subject of deep solicitude to me. Never the possessor of a strong constitution he has suffered much from illness, and is at times compelled to make his own physical well-being almost his chief concern. With this in mind it is my aim to make provisions for his benefit in such form as shall lighten so far as practicable his burdens in the care of property.

The second left to Marshall, Jr., Field's house, with its contents and appurtenances, except for several paintings already given to Ethel. Should Marshall, Jr., predecease Field, those would go to the former's eldest surviving son.

The third through tenth clauses set the terms of generous trusts for Marshall, Jr., Ethel, Field's two surviving sisters, Nannie Scott Field's sister Nora, Albertine Huck Field, and little Gwendolyn. The eleventh left money for the "preparation and adornment," as well as the maintenance, of the family plot in Graceland Cemetery. The twelfth through eighteenth left cash or small trusts to various close or distant relatives, to friends, to employees, to the Chicago Orphan Asylum, the Old People's Home, St. Luke's Free Hospital, and the Presbyterian Hospital—and $5,000 to the selectmen of Conway, Massachusetts, for the care of Field's parents' graves. (The seventeenth was of special interest: Field left $8,000,000, including much Chicago real estate, to the Field Columbian Museum, of which $4,000,000 was to be considered a building fund.) By the nineteenth clause one of Field's sisters, and her family, were granted the right to use the Field plot at Graceland.

The twentieth clause was the heart of the Will: it directed the workings and destiny of the residuary estate. In essence the residuary estate was to be divided between Marshall III and Henry in the ratio of 3:2. When Marshall III reached fifty the Estate was to be divided finally and absolutely; until then the two boys were to divide part of the income, the rest of which was to be reinvested. Should either grandson die without issue, his share was to go to the other.

The last three clauses, and the codicils, took care of technicalities and included a few business suggestions.

More simply, Field left about $14,500,000 in various trusts, many of which were to revert to the residuary estate upon termination; * about $11,000,000 in outright bequests; and the rest to Marshall III and Henry. "The rest" was in the neighborhood of $75,000,000, but it was a rapidly expanding neighborhood; by 1917 the figure was around $100,000,000, and the accumulation was still accelerating. As a corporate entity for most practical purposes the Estate could buy, sell, invest, expand, retrench, increase or go broke. There were no Federal estate taxes at the time; the fortune went intact into the Estate. A few contemporary observers panicked: they saw the Estate swelling, absorbing, contributing nothing to the country and slowly acquiring more and more of the available wealth. It might last forever, an independent economic principality within our borders, compounding itself into the billions.

The Fields were already the stuff of legend; a middle-class country will believe anything of the very rich or the very poor. To the saga of the old gentleman and to the myth of his son's death was added a new legend (it still pops up from time to time): that in the face of this financial threat to the Union, Legislatures were hastily convened, and that in a flurry of lawmaking a new principle entered the books: henceforth trusts could run only for the lifetime of the youngest heir alive at the time of death, plus twenty-one years.

So great was the impact of the old gentleman's Testament that the principle is occasionally identified by laymen as "the Field Law"; but it is a principle as old as the English common law. For centuries English, and subsequently American, common law have limited trusts, and the wording of the Will indicates clearly that Field knew it. His maximum trusts are terminated when the youngest child of his last living heir reaches twenty-one, well within the traditional limit. The state of Illinois took alarm when the Will was published, and in 1907 passed a law limiting the period of trusts; while it was good to have the statute on the books, the law was superfluous. The rule on perpetuities—"life in being plus twenty-one years and nine months"—is considered not a guideline but a "peremptory command of law."

Still, the uneasiness was not irrational. The rich were too rich, and taxes were negligible. Suppose Henry and Gwendolyn died young and childless; suppose Marshall III lived to be forty-nine,

---

* $6,000,000 of this became, in effect, part of the residuary estate when Marshall, Jr., died.

and the Estate passed intact to his day-old son; suppose the son, at twenty-one, received the Estate and immediately established it, *in toto,* as another Estate, and lived to be forty-nine, and had a son— and so on, and on, and on. Six per cent per annum for a couple of centuries can alter $100,000,000 beyond recognition. And even within the limits of the original Will the Estate, running to its maximum life, might have reached half a billion dollars, to which could be added several millions disbursed along the way to the grandchildren.

But the very forces that generated alarm were working to change society. Field's estate would indeed be passed on intact (more: almost doubled)—but only once. Nine years from the day he signed his Will the Sixteenth Amendment went into effect, and a Federal income tax—"the art of so plucking the goose as to obtain the largest amount of feathers with the least possible amount of hissing" —initiated permanent changes in the American economy. Federal estate taxes were not far off. Field would not have approved.

The Will shows characteristics we often think of as English, though they are common to most societies. The boys, for example, are much favored, and the elder over the younger. Field's consideration for his son's health was also a relatively graceful pretext for passing him by; Marshall, Jr., would have received about $6,000,- 000, most of it in trust, and Field preferred to take a chance on his grandsons with the rest. The family, including nieces, nephews, and cousins to various removes, was taken care of; nothing was left to brothers unless no one else survived. The sisters were treated handsomely. Friends and employees were remembered. Trustees were selected with care and admonished with delicacy. Thousands of words were devoted to unlikely eventualities—some of which eventuated. The sentimental may miss the touching minor bequests ("My stuffed owl to my brother George"); the least of Field's gifts was $1,000 to a family servant who had been with him for less than five years. Field was not trying to be winsome, or to beguile opinion; he was the steward of a great estate, and could not be indifferent to its future. His respect for wealth was not casual. It was moral as much as practical, and he distributed the fruits of principle in a principled manner.

3

To the Fields in London the Will was, naturally, of surpassing importance. It left Albertine Field with half a million dollars free, half a million in trust, and whatever Marshall, Jr., had settled on her; it left the three children in the expectation of more money than they could ever measure in goods and services. That much money is abstract, and dangerous. It might have made thoroughly unpleasant men of Marshall and Henry. That it did not was due to no one event or condition, but to the accidents and choices of many years, and all his life Marshall acknowledged a great debt to the first of those accidents: Eton College. It was at Eton, the butt of so many American jokes with its silk hats and traditions and pride and playing fields, that Marshall discovered, by way of *noblesse oblige,* what social conscience was; and he never realized that until twenty years had passed.

The College is set in, and not isolated from, the town of Windsor, which lies on the Thames about 25 miles west of London. Eton was founded by poor old Henry VI in one of his lucid years, 1440. When Field arrived, aged fourteen, Etonians were not expected to go forth accomplished scholars; they were learning how to learn, and they were absorbing style; in a manner at once cumbersome and natural, inefficient and permanently effective, they were learning to be gentlemen. They were part of the Establishment, and what face England showed to the world in twenty, thirty, forty years would be to some extent of their making. Understatement and restraint were essential, as L. E. Jones makes clear:

. . . my brother and I soon found our paintings pinned upon one of the black pillars, with 'very good' scrawled across one corner. As the drawings were unsigned, we felt it to be only due to ourselves to inform the other boys, as they crowded around the pillar, of the identity of the artists. Any form of 'side' was taboo; and we had a swift lesson, by the scarifying and contemptuous comments of the crowd, on the wisdom of not blowing your own trumpet. We took it to heart and soon became as proficient as the rest in that endearing British false modesty which, skilfully used, can win so many games of tennis, so many rubbers of bridge.

Religious and moral probity was also essential:

The headmaster . . . addressed us. . . . He spoke of our responsibility as
Etonians; he was encouraging and kind. Then, out of the blue, came an
astonishing admonition. He told us to beware of 'filth', to avoid even talking 'filth'. I was completely baffled. I knew a great deal about filth. . . .
But here, at Eton? Could he be telling us to look where we trod, because
of the occasional dog-mess on the pavements? And who ever wanted to talk
about these horrors? . . . A year or two later, I should have understood
him; for it was a commonplace in those days, uncontested by Masters or
boys, and a particular obsession of visiting preachers, that sex, although
given to us by God, was a dirty little secret. The strongest of human impulses, the most delectable of human enjoyments, was equated, in our hierarchy of values, with ordure.

Responsibility and public service were exalted:

For even a new boy had his week of office as Praepostor, when it was his
business to mark in the Praepostor's Book the names of boys absent from
Division or from Chapel, and to collect an 'excuse' for them from their
Dame. The massive new houses had not then been built, and we lived, for
the most part, in intricate rabbit-warrens. When an epidemic of measles
or mumps broke out, a dozen boys might be absent at one time, and a small
Praepostor, wandering [about to collect excuses], had sometimes to skip his
breakfast. It was a bad system, now long abolished, but I loved my week
of office. It was the sort of thing that could be tolerated at Eton, and only
at Eton. And is there, perhaps, a taint of Original Jack-in-Office in all of
us? May only the French enjoy being functionaries? I suspect, from the
satisfaction I felt as I made my rounds with my long, narrow book, that I
had the makings, never yet given a chance to develop, of a successful small-
town Mayor.

And yet, and yet:

[I see most clearly] a picture, precise in the sunshine, of Jones minor
coming back up Keate's Lane from Lower Chapel on the morning of the
Fourth of June. He is wearing a button-hole; he has just been singing 'Now
thank we all our God' with immense and genuine fervour; he is walking in
a kind of intoxication. For everything that goes to the making of Eton,
the mellow red bricks, the elms, the river and the playing-fields, the traditions, the community, the high privilege of belonging to it, had suddenly
coalesced into a single flash of delight. It was a mystic moment for a Thomas
Traherne, not for him, to describe. But it left a mark; and I cannot help

thinking that a School which could visit with such a benediction a not very imaginative boy of thirteen must possess a singular grace.

Into that world stepped Marshall Field III. He was treated like everyone else. Eton had too much history to be impressed by money or rank ("That little fellow with the runny nose is the Maharajah of—what's that place again?"), or to feel superior about "fortunes made in trade," and Field was by no means the first American to be admitted. Like all Etonians, perhaps since 1440, Field fagged for an older boy for three halves, waiting upon him under threat of a flogging. The threat was not idle; when Field ma. served his fagmaster a bad egg and kept the good one for himself, he was found out and beaten. It never happened again.

He lived in Cotton Hall House, and his house tutor was a Mr. Booker. (Mr. Hare, mentioned previously, was his classical tutor.) The better rooms fell to the boys by seniority; when Field arrived he took what he found. It was a single bed-sitting room, with a desk and a chair; the bed folded away. The house had been built in about 1850; it was solid and dignified, but cold in winter. Not all Field's money could change the rules, and to a boy of fourteen learning moral fortitude in midwinter, with a fire only every other night, money must have been an irrelevancy.

On the whole Eton was conducive to anonymity. Its standards of social eminence were those of schoolboys and not those of the world. Diversity was considered exciting, and not dangerous: "At Eton you could think and love what you liked; only in external matters, in clothes, or in deportment, need you do as others did." In a Midwestern private school stocked with rich boys from one level of society, Field might have been set apart, deferred to as, at worst, first among equals; but at Eton were country boys, Londoners, Frenchmen, Indians, Jews, Australians, even, in the upper school, a couple of precocious Laborites. In the matter of glamour, an Indian princeling with a good snake collection had it all over an American millionaire. And Field ma. was not a striking young man: rather bland, healthy, fun-loving but not—because of the rheumatic fever —a great athlete. He was liked, but he was not special. Nor did he expect to be. At that age he was aware of his wealth, but his mother had taken pains to keep from him the thought that his money made him personally extraordinary. What *was* extraordinary was the outside world: the British Empire, if nothing else, a salmagundi of races propagating hundreds of political movements; a heterogeneous accumulation of real estate harboring incalculable riches and starving millions; a patchwork domain that demanded of any educated Englishman at least a surface cosmopolitanism—whatever his inner insularity—that Americans would not approach for decades.* This —plus Latin, plus Greek, plus history (which he always liked) and literature (in which his preferences were conservative) and science (to which he remained impervious)—he found at Eton. He ranked low in mathematics and classics; he was fair at French. But he was learning personal discipline too; being made aware that he knew very little; being shown the value of knowledge. The masters at Eton might be bound to the Establishment, but they were individualists, some of them even eccentrics, and simply to live among such men was an education.

His specific memories of that education were few. They were also self-deprecating (no "side"). The diffidence and understatement that later exasperated some of his associates began in Etonian modesty. "At Eton," he wrote later, "the only sop thrown to the modern world of technology was about an hour a week, officially called 'Science.' The situs was a rather ill-equipped laboratory, and the subject had acquired the label of 'Stinks.' Any pupil who evidenced undue interest in the subject was a 'Stinker,' of course, and the whole matter was scarcely tolerated and rarely referred to by either masters or boys. I got a vague idea at different times that water was represented by H_2O, that snakes shed their skins but were fun to fool with, and that caterpillars eventually became butterflies. But our chief occupation in 'Stinks' was mixing liquids, without any apparent idea or purpose except a general hope that a loathsome smell, or possibly even an explosion, might occur. History was taught with much understanding and imagination, as was the laborious translation of sundry 'classics' from the Greek and Latin.

---

* It is possible that for many of the boys one form of prejudice—loyalty to their social class and to Eton—precluded or diminished the more usual racial, cultural, and religious forms. Conceivably an old Etonian would have been more comfortable with a Nigerian classmate than with an English laborer. There is an ancient joke about cannibals and explorers the punch line of which is "One Balliol man *never* eats another Balliol man."

Mathematics was tolerated, but the teachers in that field had very little standing among their fellows."

And he once confessed in conversation, "I didn't really have a good time at Eton. You see, I couldn't do much in the way of athletics. I had rheumatic fever in those days." Here he was not being modest. The emphasis on sports and games in English public schools has raised hackles for decades; it has been charged with arresting the moral development of the Establishment at a schoolboy level and with creating generations of Colonel Blimps, or alternatively with hallowing hypocrisy, because in British foreign policy it has often been whether you win or lose, and not how you play the game. But until the Second World War Wellington's was the overriding judgment: "The battle of Waterloo was won on the playing fields of Eton." And Field was neither a wet-bob nor a dry-bob, but no bob a-tall. Which is to say that he was not a good oarsman and not a cricketer, and had to content himself with casual participation in minor sports of less prestige. "The main standard of achievement was, as in most schools, athletics," he wrote. "Proficiency at football, cricket, or rowing was the criterion of approbation. *Mens sana in corpore sano* was an Aristotelian precept which was followed more strictly as to its second rather than its first implication. Having been left temporarily with a weak heart . . . I did not, it may readily be conceived, find any great approbation."

But four years of compulsory games improved his health. He was growing out of the rheumatic fever, and when he was away from Eton he was on horseback much of the time; by 1911 he was an accomplished rider and a healthy man. He was still not a scholar, and never would be. He managed to squeak through all his examinations, but until 1918 Eton's examinations were rather loose affairs: to achieve excellence required hard work, but to get by was easy. Having got by, he was ready for the university. He was a normal, happy, exceedingly rich young man with all the makings of a nob; he took luxury for granted, though with a gentleman's restraint; he knew a good deal about horses, food, and wine, and not much about women; he had many friends, was handsome, and traveled in the best company.

But at Eton, and all unawares, he had been infected by—something. It could not have been called liberalism, nor yet conscience, but it was more than *noblesse oblige*—which may be, after all, nothing more positive than a Regency buck declining to thrash an old beggarwoman. Perhaps it was a notion of justice in human affairs, a rough, schoolboy's justice coupled with a contempt for unwarranted snobbery: "Eton, however, had a certain healthy contempt for the plutocracy which I found extremely salutary. The reason for the top hat and tail coat, which is held up to ridicule by those who do not understand it, is actually well founded. It is a uniform which obviates the invidious distinction of expensive clothes, without creating a feeling of militarism as so many uniforms are inclined to do." Perhaps he had simply learned, at eighteen, that there were different kinds of riches; no bob a-tall, he knew what it meant to be left out. And surely he had learned that someday a bill would be presented: that the price of privilege was responsibility.

He was not fully conscious of all this when he left for Trinity College, Cambridge. None of it showed. He was just an old Etonian.

4

In the fall of 1908 Albertine Field had become Mrs. Maldwin Drummond, and the boys were delighted. They liked Drummond; he liked them. They also liked Cadland, the Drummonds' estate (since the eighteenth century) near Southampton Waters; it was vast and Georgian, crowded with game—the pheasant shoots were particularly marvelous. (It may have been at about this period that some foreigner first said, "When the sun comes out in England, the Englishman says, 'What a beautiful day! Let's go out and kill something.'") From the house the view of the water was splendid, and there was a rich Englishness about the demesne: an island people, living in forests and meadows, yet masters of the sea. (There was, of course, another sort of Englishness in Birmingham and Manchester.) Marshall and Henry had their friends down for weekends; the sport was good—shooting, fishing, sailing, riding. Marshall loved the life, though he seemed inclined to an occasional mood, a passing moment of introspection; Henry was more dashing and gay. Maldwin's friends were of the best sort, and the surface of life was glassy. It was, as Field remarked years later, the last period in history when being rich was pure, careless fun. (Three centuries earlier

Sully had written of the English, *"Ils s'amusent tristement."* It was not true of Field's friends.) Weekend succeeded weekend, house party followed house party; the horseflesh was fine, the girls were pretty, the game was inexhaustible. Far over the horizon Germany was cementing alliances at a great rate; but Edward had confirmed the Entente Cordiale with France in 1904, and the Triple Entente with Russia in 1907. England was secure, and when Edward died in 1910, Englishmen knew that George V would do as well. The Labour party was growing, which seemed rather odd; but it was dominated by Fabians who addressed themselves to *conditions* (turning out volume upon volume of indisputable fact) and not to revolution. It was a good time.

Maldwin Drummond may have suggested Trinity College to Marshall; he surely approved. One of the boy's closest friends at Eton, Rudolph de Trafford, had chosen Trinity; his mother and Albertine Drummond were old friends, and Rudolph had been a guest at Cadland. The two young gentlemen matriculated at Michaelmas, 1912, leaving Henry at Eton. "I found Cambridge utterly delightful," Field wrote later; whatever his pleasure in Eton, it was as nothing beside the exhilaration old Cambridge offered. Trinity College itself was an amalgam of several ancient institutions, the most important being King's Hall (founded in 1317) and Michaelhouse (1324); the College flag is still the royal flag of Edward III. They had been joined together in one college by Henry VIII in 1546, a year before his death. Trinity boasted a unique distinction: its master was appointed directly by the Crown.* Its library was the work of Christopher Wren and was put up toward the end of the seventeenth century. Trinity was the largest college at either of the two great British universities, and was naturally full of history. Lord Byron, for example, lived in Merton Corner, an Elizabethan turret in one corner of the Great Court; he kept a tame bear because it was against the rules to keep a dog, and wrote to a lady:

I have got a new friend, the finest in the world, a tame bear. When I brought him here, they asked me what I meant to do with him, and my reply was 'he should sit for a fellowship'. This answer delighted them not.

Field, however, took private lodgings outside the college, in Mrs.

---

* The distinction is no longer unique; it is now shared by Churchill College.

Holden's house at 20 Portugal Street. He met his tutor, Mr. Harrison, and mapped out a program, largely in history. He proved to be conscientious enough, but not at all a hard worker. Much more is left to the individual in English universities than in American, and there was no nonsense about Field's being a freshman; a Trinity man was a Trinity man from his first moment, with all the rights, privileges, and obligations implied, and he could be brilliant in his first week or a damned fool for three years.

Field was neither. He was a well-turned-out young gentleman, more interested in recreation than in study, but aware that he was expected to become, somehow, moderately well educated. Perhaps not in the sciences; he found at Cambridge "every possibility of accumulating knowledge if one were so disposed; but, as might be imagined, my previous experience had not been conducive to enthusiasm about scientific subjects. I have since found it quite impossible to understand or manipulate anything like a radio, an electric device of any sort, or even an automobile or airplane. Perhaps this is just inherent dumbness, but I like to blame my education." The weakness was not significant; little science was expected of him.* In other areas there was no need to drudge, but to neglect his work would have been, at the very least, letting down the side. He had an active, if undirected, mind, and his mother had made it quite clear that he owed it to himself, to his fortune, and to the world to do something responsible with that mind. Not just yet but eventually. He could recall his father's death and be reminded of the dangers in an empty life, and some of his moodiness may be laid to that. But life at Trinity was the high noon of his youth, and the shadows were negligible.

There were some six hundred undergraduates at Trinity then, many of them from Eton, Harrow, and Winchester, a few of them peers of the realm, some later knighted or ennobled. Field liked

* Jones, in *An Edwardian Youth*, tells a story of A. L. Smith, the master of Balliol: "As a guest of honour at this same High Table [at Trinity College, Cambridge] he once sat at the Master's right hand, and so engaging was the Master's conversation that not until dinner was all but over did 'A. L.' remember that he had spoken no word to the Fellow of Trinity sitting on his other side. So he turned to him with some conventional, polite words, whereupon his neighbour turned scarlet, choked, dropped his fork, knocked over his wine-glass, and was thrown into a state of complete disorder. The Master of Trinity turned again to 'A. L.' 'I forgot to warn you,' he said, 'we never speak to the Mathematicians.' "

gaiety, and took pleasure in any company; he was most often bubbling and friendly, and kept his moods to himself. A classmate remarked years later that he had never heard Field say anything unpleasant about anybody, which is a considerable feat. He was not malicious, not egotistical, and not jealous of his friendships. If he was openhanded with all, it was the democracy of happiness and not of principle; his closest friends were all well off, and his clubs were of the most snobbish and exclusive. The Athenæum, for example (which is of course not to be confused with the Athenæum in London), had little to do with learning: its solemn and frequent conclaves were mainly given over to drinking. The Pitt Club was less bibulous but quite as aristocratic; membership was emblematic of a way of life, and Field was later described by a distinguished tutor who remembered him as a "cheery, horsy, Pitt-Club young man," which was, to Cantabrigians, sufficient definition. He belonged to two supper clubs, the True Blue and the Beefeaters. Admission to True Blue was solemnized by the quaffing of a pint of claret in one long draught. At their more elegant dinners the Beefeaters wore eighteenth-century costume, including wig, and smoked clay pipes.

Still, Field read his history and took his examinations. Somehow, among the hunts and house parties and trips to Deauville and Monte Carlo, he found time for books and lectures, not to mention the history and beauties of the university itself. Having been raised a Roman Catholic, he attended Mass, but Cambridge sheltered all sorts, and the indescribable splendor of King's College Chapel (another great debt to sad, pious Henry VI), transcending religion altogether, may have made him a latitudinarian on the spot. ("England," wrote an Italian in the eighteenth century, "has sixty different religions and only one sauce.") The study of history was doubtless tedious at times, but the Fitzwilliam Museum, housing "Egyptian, Greek and Roman antiquities, coins and medals, medieval manuscripts, paintings and drawings, prints, pottery and porcelain, textiles, arms and armour, medieval and renaissance objects of art . . . the music collection and literary autographs" could have fired the young man's imagination. We have no evidence that it did so; but it was there. George Herbert, Andrew Marvell, Macaulay, Tennyson, Elizabeth's Essex, Isaac Newton, Francis Bacon, all came out of Trinity; Field was likely more conscious that Edward VII had more recently trod its ancient footpaths, wandered through the Backs on sunny afternoons, lounged on the banks of the modest and lovely Cam. At nineteen Field was preoccupied with life, and not with immortals.

Being a horsy young man, he was made Master of the Drag at Trinity, which entitled him to special lodgings; being comfortably quartered, he declined the rooms, but enjoyed the honor. (The Drag is a version of the hunt much favored in underprivileged—i.e., foxless—neighborhoods; a bag full of assorted foxiness is dragged over the course to lay a trail for the hounds. Blowing the mort over a gunny sack is beautifully Edwardian.) And being a rich young man, he could pop off to the Continent when the humor was upon him. On one of his flutters at a race meet he won several hundred pounds, which he promptly bore to Monte Carlo; there he lost a few thousand, and was reduced to the last ignominy—he had to cable home for funds. (Apparently his affection for sports, ripening late, led to a less competitive notion of games; he said later that "all sports should be taken seriously and no games," and he was so busy riding and shooting that gambling never infected him permanently. He was a good bridge player, then and later, and would play for stakes; he also liked chess; but he preferred sports, and he preferred participating to watching.) He absorbed a few heavy losses in those years, but never gambled later on, beyond a gentleman's wager at the track. He and Oliver Lyttelton (a classmate, now Viscount Chandos) ran over to Deauville in Maldwin Drummond's yacht once and spent a wild night drinking and punting; Field woke late the next morning, and after the ritual snorts and ablutions found himself still foggy about the evening's transgressions. He ruminated, and then said in gingerly tones, "I have the feeling I did something very silly last night. Did I make advances to a woman?"

Lyttelton was drily unsympathetic. "No. You lost what would be four years of my income."

"Oh, that's it!" Field said, and brightened immediately. He might not have known that it was during this period that his mother went to the trustees of the Estate, in Chicago, with a request for more money for the boys' education. She was reminded that the old gentleman had been in favor of a sound and serious education for his

grandsons, though he had not referred to it in his Will. "They are
being raised as gentlemen" was her chilly answer. The trustees were
unimpressed, and equally chilly: "Yes, but as British gentlemen."
Their fears were not unreasonable. The family was happy in England, and it must have been obvious that Marshall loved England.
But even at twenty he knew that his was to be an American life—
not because he was unusually patriotic, or nostalgic, but because he
was sensible. The basis of his life was a huge fortune, and that fortune was rooted in America; it would need tending. At Trinity he
never thought of himself as English, or even as Anglicized; he was
American, and took deliberate care not to become sur-British. His
accent was gently British, and remained so all his life, but it was
closer to the refined accents of New York's old society families than
it was to the caricature Americans have come to think of as an
Oxford accent. He hunted the fox, but so had Americans, from
colonial times, and so they do still, in lonely outposts of empire like
Pennsylvania. It was not that Field was Anglophile, but that the
trustees, good Chicagoans of that period, were Anglophobes. America was never in the slightest danger of losing the young man.

Mrs. Field's request was granted, and life went on at Trinity.
Field was a wild horseman in those days—"later on he was more
buttoned-up about it"—and he had one bad fall, wrenching his back
severely. He was almost immobilized, and the Cottenham Steeplechase was three days off, and he had planned to ride. Friends repaired hastily to the hairdresser's, an establishment operated by Mr.
William Ewart Gladstone Beattie, who had resented his father's idol-
atry and become the most adamant of Tories. His barbershop was
an unofficial Jockey Club, the center of sporting gossip, full of toffs
and swells reminiscing about races older than they were. In an atmosphere of conspiracy and cologne Field's bad luck was brought
before the membership, and a man named Barker was recommended
—a quack osteopath much in favor that month. Barker was willin',
and went to work on the young American. The next day Field was
walking, and he rode in his steeplechase, out of the money.

There were ladies too, with floppy hats and parasols, at stylish
and stylized weekend gatherings. The times were old-fashioned but
no longer Victorian; the ladies laughed aloud and were witty, and

would stroll without chaperones, and *never* hid behind a fan. Some smoked. Some were suffragettes. Some actually attended universities. There were women in the world who could drive cars, and one or two who could pilot aircraft. If a mighty oath escaped a gentleman, there were ladies about who would neither blench nor swoon. Gentlemen tended to solve the problem of women by remaining gentlemen; that is, by ignoring it as far as possible. It was still a man's society. The ladies still retired after dinner, leaving the men to the inevitable port and cigars; women were attractive, and of course necessary in a way, and it was rather fun to watch them trying to break into a man's world; but in society the masculine attitude was more courtly than companionable. Women were just not good shots, and if you took them seriously they might turn out to be Emmeline Pankhurst or Beatrice Webb, and then where were you?

In the late spring of 1914 Field took his last examination at Trinity, formally designated as History Special II. He had passed History Special I in 1913. Nowadays a "special" connotes a certain *manque de sérieux*—someone muddling through for the sake of future conversation. But in 1914 it meant simply that Field was not a candidate for academic honors, or even a degree. He was studying for the sake of study, and he passed his examination. He planned to return for the Michaelmas term, but a trip to Chicago was necessary first: in September he would be twenty-one, and a trustee.

He had visited the United States two or three times on Estate matters, and had followed the news from home, but he was out of touch. He had missed another panic, in 1907; Taft's election and then Wilson's; the adoption of the Sixteenth Amendment, though this had been much discussed at home—out of every ten thousand dollars of income the Federal government proposed to confiscate *sixty dollars;* American concern with the Far East, mirrored in the "Gentlemen's Agreement" on Japanese immigration, in the Root-Takahira agreement on the territorial integrity and future of China, and in the completion of the Panama Canal; he had even missed an historical moment in American statecraft and jurisprudence, the passage of the Mann Act in 1910. The Armory Show had insulted New York, leaving scars so deep, painful, and permanent, outraging virtue and common sense so wantonly, that it would be perhaps thirty years before one of its paintings brought a quarter of a million dollars. Lincoln Steffens and Upton Sinclair had been baptized "muckrakers" by President Roosevelt himself; to keep journalism balanced, there was hardly a newspaper in the country that did not carry comic strips. Theodore Dreiser had begun an ambitious project: to write as many lumpy, gnarled, pedestrian sentences as possible in one lifetime and still project so much truth that he had to be taken seriously. And it is hard to see how Field acquired American culture at all, considering the best sellers he had missed: *The Shepherd of the Hills, A Girl of the Limberlost, The Winning of Barbara Worth, The Riders of the Purple Sage;* he was back in time for *Tarzan of the Apes,* but whether or not he read it is a matter of some doubt. Sigmund Freud and Carl Jung had lectured at Clark University in 1909, and Lee De Forest had invented something called the triode amplifier, which made possible ordinary microphone broadcasting. Automobiles were commonplace, and so were motion pictures. At about the time Field returned, a man named Robert H. Goddard patented a liquid-fuel rocket, of no conceivable value; two years later John T. Thompson invented a submachine gun, of considerable value during the subsequent Prohibition era. Bill Haywood and the Wobblies won a textile strike in Lawrence, Massachusetts, in 1912; New York State, following the Triangle Shirtwaist fire in 1911 when 146 needleworkers died, enacted a stringent building code and revised its labor laws; but in most of the United States child labor was still legal. Oklahoma, New Mexico, and Arizona had been admitted to the Union, rounding out the forty-eight states.

Before returning Field paid a brief visit to the Manchester branch of the family, and spent most of July at Cadland. His mother was quite sick, and the summer's social round was curtailed: Albertine Drummond had cancer. Guests dropped in quietly, even while she was hospitalized for an operation; there was naturally no fuss.

One of the house guests that summer was a lovely American named Evelyn Marshall, whose father had been a prominent New Yorker. Field had met her in London, and liked her, but they had never spent much time together. Now they did, in that last July; affection grew, and became love. But it was not a propitious season.

On August 4 England declared war on Germany, and the dancing on the green came to an end.

5

The end was not abrupt. Europe was baffled, but not surprised; one day there had been the regulation international quarrels, the next day policy had become war, and when all the alliances were honored almost everybody was in it. There were Englishmen who had warned for years that war was coming; no one had done much about it, and it was hard to see how it could have been stopped. It was also hard to see what the issues were, but no one hung back for that reason. A generation of Englishmen dropped its tennis rackets or trowels and became officers or other ranks; all over Europe the same thing happened. For a time it looked like a short war, another hot-tempered imbroglio followed by small territorial adjustments. The first extension of fighting was to the sea, and there were comic-opera incidents in various colonies, and few thought it would last.

Two years earlier, and Field might have tried to circumvent the early British rule against enlisting foreigners; but 1914 was his year of responsibility. He loved England; he was expected shortly in Chicago. He had begun to think of marriage, and to an American girl. His mother lay sick in England; his future awaited him in America. He surely thought about chucking everything and wangling a commission. His class at Trinity went in almost to a man. He could not join them, and he felt bad about it. His heart might have kept him out of it, but that was not the point: he owed much to England, and felt as though he were ducking out at a bad time. He envied Henry, who joined up in 1915, as soon as the British relaxed their regulations; perhaps that was some consolation to him.

Evelyn Marshall left England in August to visit her widowed mother, who insisted upon remaining in Paris to do hospital work. Miss Marshall booked passage shortly afterward on the *Lusitania,* and wrote to Field, who arranged to cross on the same ship. They were thoroughly in love; Field proposed marriage; and in the late fall of 1914 their engagement was announced.

Charles Marshall, Evelyn's father, was born in 1837—the year of Victoria's ascension—and had married late, taking a twenty-five-year-old bride when he was fifty. His own father, one of the founders of the pro-Lincoln Union League Club, was born in 1793 during the French Revolution; the three generations span a good deal of modern history. Charles Marshall was moneyed, and from his office in Nassau Street he supervised his own financial operations and performed good works, serving on civic committees and administering various charities. He was, among other things, a director of the Cunard Line—he had controlled the Black Ball packets to Liverpool—and had been on the *Carpathia* with his wife in 1912, en route to Paris, when that ship interrupted its voyage to rescue survivors of the *Titanic*. Starting again from New York, the Marshalls took the southern route; at Gibraltar Mrs. Marshall went ashore and caught pneumonia; she convalesced in Naples. Charles Marshall's heart was weak, and these events strained it; he died shortly afterward in Paris. For Evelyn Marshall it was a grim time, and she came through it not as a fluttering Edwardian miss, but with a strong and independent personality—perhaps like that of her maternal ancestors, the Lenoxes of New York, who had come down from Scottish fishing and farming families in colonial Nantucket.

Marshall turned twenty-one in September, and spent some weeks being initiated to the arcana of trusteeship. Chicago was a notable change for him. The other trustees were wary, possibly expecting waxed mustaches. Field's trips home had always been brief, but now that he was of age, and England was embroiled in a war of no interest to Americans, a more permanent interest was expected of him. He obliged in public, telling reporters, "I like English customs, but I want to get back to Chicago, where my grandfather lived." Privately he was not so sure. His sympathies, his personal ties, bound him more to New York and to England. The trustees liked him, however, and calmed down considerably as they came to know him better.

Field and Evelyn Marshall were married on February 8, 1915, at the Marshall home, 6 East 77th Street in New York, by a Roman Catholic bishop. Miss Marshall was not Catholic, but agreed verbally that the children could be raised in that faith; Field's religious sensibilities were not acute, and it is likely that he was as eager to please his mother as he was to guarantee his children's spiritual welfare. The wedding had been postponed from February 3; the influenza epidemic was at its height, and both bride and groom had been victims. The honeymoon restored them: a cruise along the Florida keys in a houseboat, warm, carelessly rapturous days, with the Estate and the war and family problems left behind. Later that spring they returned to Chicago, spending a few weeks in suburban Lake Forest. Here they heard that Albertine Field was quite sick, and in August they embarked for England. They were in mid-Atlantic on the 22d when the news reached them that Albertine was dead.

It was a mournful summer. For ten years Albertine had been the fount of wisdom and affection. The boys liked Drummond, but their mother ruled them; Gwendolyn, at thirteen, had been less attached to Drummond, and suffered more than the boys. Albertine had been not simply a mother, but a surrogate for the absent patriarch—Drummond was a good man, experienced in banking, in manners and mores, in grappling with the problems of a landowner, but he was not a Field. Nor was he American, and Albertine had known more clearly than the others that her sons' future was in the United States. The family had been almost more middle-European than English in some ways—an affectionate, preoccupied, easygoing father and a loving but rigorously conscientious mother. More than his coming of age, more than his assumption of trusteeship, more than his marriage, Albertine's death matured Marshall. He was *the* Field, with no buffer now between him and awesome responsibilities.

The three young Fields drifted apart, and were never again together for any appreciable time. Henry remained in London, in the armed forces. Gwendolyn went to stay with her Aunt Ethel, who was an unofficial quartermaster for the Royal Navy, commandeering warm clothes all through the war for the North Sea Fleet; her husband had been made an admiral in 1910 (the youngest in modern times), and commanded a squadron of cruisers.

Marshall went back to the United States, older and less cheerful, much sobered by the realization that over half his class at Trinity had been wiped out in the retreat from Mons and the first battle of Ypres. The bill for aristocratic pleasures had been presented, and was being paid very democratically.

The next year, 1916, was quiet and happy. Field was still entangled in the techniques of financial management, and spent months in Chicago under the tutelage of his fellow trustees. He did not, however, neglect the sportsman's life. He liked the Carolinas particularly: the climate was bland and there were polo clubs. The year was divided—part of it at 1200 Lake Shore Drive while he tended to business; part of it in South Carolina for pleasure; and part of it in New York, for both.

He was in New York at the beginning of June when news of the Battle of Jutland filtered through; his pride was intense. It was the only major engagement of the war between the British and German fleets, and if the British lost more ships and men, the Germans lost a far greater fraction of their Navy, and never again challenged British rule of the waves. Adm. David Beatty's First Battle Cruiser Squadron had distinguished itself particularly, drawing the heaviest German fire throughout the two-day battle. Beatty was a hero, and later in the year assumed command of the Grand Fleet. (For Gwendolyn, at home with Aunt Ethel and just fourteen, it must have been a triumphantly exciting week.)

Field was understandably moved, and was even more elated a few days later: on June 15 Marshall Field IV was born, at the Marshall home in New York. Field had paced the floor like any man; he shot off a cable to his old friend Rudolph de Trafford, by then a lieutenant: WANT YOU TO BE GODFATHER TO YOUNG MARSHALL. HE WILL DO YOU CREDIT.

But the war marred his happiness. He worried about his friends, about Henry, about England; he still felt, unreasonably, like a bit of a slacker. Late in 1916 he went to Plattsburg, a training center in upstate New York, and tried to talk himself into the Army. He was outwardly hale, indisputably intelligent, and prime stuff for a cavalry officer. But the old rheumatic fever was on his record, and he was turned down, though the authorities were appreciative. Six months more, however, and he would have his way.

6

On April 2, 1917, President Woodrow Wilson explained to the Congress that the world must be made safe for democracy and American shipping; on April 6 the Congress voted a declaration of war against the Central Powers. America responded wholeheartedly. As usual, there were crabby dissidents who scoffed, a potpourri of Anglophobes (who opposed our "pulling British chestnuts out of the fire"), Socialists (who saw the war, with some justice, as a struggle for markets, raw materials, and cheap labor, all to be purchased with the lives of unthinking young men), and subversive Teutons like H. L. Mencken, who considered Bach more musical than Stephen Foster, and Goethe a finer human being than Billy Sunday. But these were a minority. For most of America the war was an opportunity to prove once again that American men had hairier chests than anybody, and that American women could outshrill any other kind of patriot. The World War was an epochal, fateful war, an enormous complication of blind forces (some of them still at work) little understood at the time; its causes and consequences still plague the century. But too much has happened since, and the war is remembered now as a sort of carnival, in which certain men won medals and certain women gold stars, and slackers were handed white feathers by bloodthirsty viragoes of the highest social standing; or as a grim and bitter farce, in which Ernest Hemingway found cynicism and Scott Fitzgerald frustration and John Dos Passos disillusionment; or as a series of cruel battles, in which Château-Thierry and Belleau Wood joined Valley Forge as American shrines; or as an opportunity for great statesmanship, in which the Congress of the United States, straining every nerve and sinew to inspire Western civilization with the highest ideals of international morality, of democracy, and of religion, adopted and submitted to the states an amendment to the Constitution prohibiting the manufacture, sale, or transportation of alcoholic liquors.

But people were dying, and going back to Blighty without arms and legs, and to Marshall Field our declaration of war meant another chance to do what he could. He and Mrs. Field were in Aiken, South Carolina, on April 6; he was playing polo. They packed and returned to Chicago immediately. Sooner than argue with total strangers about his once-rheumatic heart, Field went directly to a family friend, Col. Milton J. Foreman, described later by Stanley Field, with fierce approbation, as "a Jew, a good man, and a fighter," who was commanding officer of the First Illinois Cavalry. The good Colonel was short on formality, and swore Field in on the spot.

Private Marshall Field had done the right thing. On April 15 the Chicago *Tribune* bestowed its laurel in an editorial:

America's richest young man has taken the direct step dictated by unadulterated patriotism. Many will rise to say that Field has done only what everybody should do. They will be careful to ignore the fact that everybody isn't doing it.

But Field required no one's compliments. His explanation to a reporter was well-bred and free of rodomontade: "I decided to enlist because I think there is a great chance for immediate active service and there is certainly no reason why I should not be willing to fight for my country, just as every other young man should do. From now on I am just plain Private Field, and I shall feel very uncomfortable if it is suggested that I be treated as anything but an ordinary private in Headquarters Troop. I am enlisting because it is my personal conviction regarding myself, and myself solely. I am not moralizing over what other people should do. I felt I ought to do my bit. My wife, after some reflection, agreed to my enlistment. Because I don't know enough about military matters to be an officer, I enlisted as a private. I chose the cavalry because I believed this organization was more likely than others to see service, and because I considered it the most distinguished of the Illinois organizations. The fact that I like horseback riding and have done a great deal of riding may have had something to do with my enlisting in the cavalry."

The statement is interesting. Its language is fairly simple; it contains perhaps the only patriotic utterance in the history of fustian consisting of eight words averaging two and a half letters each. Its tone is moderate, agreeable, and firm. Its style is not notable. It is considerate: of his wife, of Illinois, of the Army, of "other people." The proper attitude is expressed with proper deference. It is the statement of a young man who accepted the world as it was and his responsibilities when it came to preserving it. There are no quibbles, no homilies on the evils of war or the justice of the cause. Field was not exceptional; he belonged. He was twenty-three years old, and absolutely respectable.

For a cavalryman, he did little riding. A parade or two; but for the first couple of months, until the regiment was at full strength, army life was relatively informal. Field studied the red book—rules, regulations, tactics, leadership, the Articles of War; he learned discipline, the manual of arms, and the mysteries of artillery—big guns killed better than sabers, and the First Illinois Cavalry was shortly designated the Second Field Artillery, Illinois National Guard. The life was new and adventurous, but it was uncomplicated. Field enjoyed himself—until July 8, 1917, when he was notified that his brother Henry had died in New York, ten days short of his twenty-second birthday.

The blow was brutal. Marshall had loved Henry; they complemented each other perfectly. Henry was six feet two inches tall, handsome and mercurial, in an almost constant state of gaiety. He had got into the war as soon as the British would take him, and had been assigned first to armored cars and then to the balloon corps of the Naval Air Service, which kept huge, ugly inflated sausages hovering over London to confound the enemy's aircraft. His work was not arduous; he had weekends off. When Marshall was in England the two were constantly together. They had been together at a house party in 1915 when Henry met a lovely Virginian named Nancy Keene Perkins, a niece of the Nancy Langhorne who became Lady Astor. Miss Perkins, seated among a comely covey, had spotted the two men walking down a long green lawn. She took a sharp look, turned to her companions, and said, "I'll bet the tall handsome one is married, and the other one isn't." She was wrong both ways, and happy to be. She and Henry delighted each other from the start, and when Henry turned twenty-one, in 1916, they became serious. On February 7, 1917, they were married in New York City. Apparently they shared the kind of bliss we read about in ruinously escapist magazine stories. They had youth, beauty, and money; they were back in America, far from the war; the season was spring; even the rain must have been winy.

When the United States entered the war Henry's honeymoon was barely over. He set about enlisting in the American forces nonetheless, and decided to have his tonsils removed before joining up. The operation took place in Presbyterian Hospital, which was then at Park Avenue and 69th Street in New York. The procedure was routine; but a minor infection ensued, and it rapidly became major, spreading to an abscess behind Henry's heart. (The medical phrase is empyema of the pericardial cavity.) For almost two months the doctors held off, hoping it would drain of itself; it did not. They operated to insert a drain, and the operation was fatal.

Marshall was granted compassionate leave, and hurried to New York, and then Chicago. He discovered that Henry's affairs were in a snarl. Neither young man had yet received any sizable part of his inheritance. Marshall and Henry had previously agreed that if either died, the other would look after the survivors. (The agreement was made at Marshall's suggestion; it was he who had the history of heart trouble.) No one was quite sure at that moment just how the law would assign Henry's fortune, or his interest in the Estate; no one was quite sure what his widow's rights and privileges were. And there was no time now for friendly litigation; Marshall was a lieutenant and the country was at war. He could have requested a discharge, which would not have been impossible to arrange, but if the thought crossed his mind at all he discarded it immediately.

7

The regiment went into service on July 25, and on August 1 became the 122d Field Artillery, as part of the 33d Division. From Fort Sill, Oklahoma, where Field had made sergeant, leading the Fourth Section of Battery B, and then been commissioned a second lieutenant, he was sent to join the regiment at Camp Logan near Houston, where it was attached to the 58th Artillery Brigade. Houston was Field's home for six months.

It was not a bad home. Field took his job seriously and worked hard, but the regiment, known as "Foreman's Dog and Pony Show," was a good one, cheerful and efficient, and its men were proud of it. They were good gunners. Leaves were frequent, and if Houston was no Paris, it was not a bad town. The food at the Hotel Brazos was more than passable, and dinner there became a habit. In town the officers and enlisted men often ate together. Most of them were displaced civilians, and a volunteer army tends to be rough-and-ready about protocol. Field was firm on one point: no one else ever picked up a dinner check in his presence. He said once that he would think it "an abomination" for anyone else to pay, not because he couldn't stand favors but because it made no sense. And this in spite of the fact that Battery B was known as the "Millionaires' Battery"—half a dozen well-to-do Chicagoans were officers.

It was not always as easy to be generous. For the first time in his life Field was living among a great miscellaneous clutter of ordinary people, and among them were bound to be leeches. Here was no Cantabrigian code; a "gentleman" was any male over twenty-one (though the military tried to restrict the word to officers). Field was sensitive to tales of woe, though not at all embarrassed about being rich; he was constantly obliged to offer small loans. He could hardly accept the notion that a man who might be killed at his side within months should lack the five dollars that would make a leave successful, or even the fifty that would keep a mortgage running. But economic justice worked both ways, and to be victimized because of his money stung him. "He was no playboy and no miser," one of his buddies recalled. "He'd take a couple of drinks, and then he didn't want any more. If you needed money, he'd let you have it. Don't get the idea, though, that he was a sucker. He didn't throw his money away. He'd lend money to somebody that needed it, but he would expect it back. On the other hand, if it was somebody who needed it real bad, for his wife or folks or something like that, Field would just give him what he needed and never ask for it afterward."

It was a new experience just the same, and it left a confusion of scars. Field was not accustomed to doubting his fellows. He was not naïve; he knew there were scoundrels abroad, thieves, and outright swindlers; but he had never been exposed to them before. A new trait was born in him, and never quite died: he became wary. But not at all cynical: if Evelyn could join him in Houston, and take a suite at the Rice Hotel, it was not easy to be harsh in judging a man whose wife and children were a thousand miles away. At any rate his comrades were never made too sharply aware of his caution, and remember him as "a fine gentleman all the way through." Some recall incidents that may or may not have taken place: heavy loans to poor men, large term insurance policies for men with many children, the funding of accumulated small debts. He subdued his suspicions, and suffered quietly for the first time from a conflict that would be refought time and again in his life, between his belief that men were naturally good and his knowledge that some of them would take what they could get. Enough of them were good to justify the belief; enough were frauds to confirm the knowledge. From then on the repayment of a loan always gratified Field in much more than a fiscal sense.

He got along well. His men respected him. Those were the days when an officer never asked his men to do anything he could not do himself, and Field, with a thoroughly ingrained sense of honor, adhered rigorously to the principle. He was excellent with horses: he had a good seat and good hands and was considerate of the animal. As a gunnery officer he was sure and careful. He was less formal than many officers: he was accustomed to deference, was invariably polite in acknowledging it, and had no need to exact it. And he had already begun to understand that his wishes, whether commands or whims, might carry a disproportionate weight. Like it or not, he was more than a lieutenant: he was one of a mysteriously influential class of people. In the front lines it might not matter much; in training he was cautious. Such diffidence would have been unnecessary in the British Army; British officers were *ipso facto* gentlemen, and rich ones were of the Establishment, and class distinctions were the armature of society. No self-consciousness was necessary; no uneasy fretting about equality. But Field was still learning what Americans were like, and he trod lightly.

The 33d was several months in reaching the war. They were still at Camp Logan in 1918 when Mrs. Field returned to New York for her second confinement; Barbara Field was born on January 6, and her father distributed cigars. One of his fellow officers suggested that he apply for a dependency discharge, and Field roared, flattered by the razzing.

In May the welcome news was posted, and Field's unit was ordered to Camp Merritt, in New Jersey. They moved fast after that. On the 26th they boarded the tramp *Kashmir*. They were jammed together as soldiers always are on transports, but for most of them the departure from Hoboken was the start of an exotic cruise: they were Middle Westerners, and the sea was vast and new, and the ship was manned by Lascars. Exotic or not, it was a short cruise. On June 8 they docked at Liverpool. They were given a day's rest and ordered to Winchester; two days later to Southampton (Cadland was nearby, but Field had no time); two days later they were in Le Havre, and on the 16th they arrived at Ornans. The records are dry and the place names obscure: Valdahon, Pagny-sur-Meuse, Rambucourt, Montsec. On August 25 the 1st Battalion joined Group V of the Toul defensive sector; the Group flanked the St. Mihiel salient, nipped it off, and took 14,000 German prisoners by September 14. They marched northwest for five nights then, to Verdun and the Forêt de Herse. There were 700,000 American troops in the sector, and the Germans were rolled back steadily; the Americans were in the Argonne before the end of the month. Men in battle know little and care less about what happens outside their sector, but after the forced marches, constant barrages, and real if light casualties, the armies were happy enough to hear that Bulgaria had surrendered on September 29; it was as if crushing the salient had ended the war, and in a sense that was true. St. Mihiel was the last German thrust, and the next six weeks were a matter of triumphant mopping up for the Allies, revolution in Germany, and frustrated, last-ditch blundering by the Central Powers. The Ottoman Empire was collapsing of its own weight, and surrendered on October 30; the Austro-Hungarian on November 4. Mutinies swept Germany; the Kaiser abdicated; November 11 was the end. Four great empires had ceased to exist. Marshall Field was a captain.

Field and his battery had been in combat for a little over two months. He had done his work well; a no-nonsense correspondent named Bob Casey described him as "a hell of a good soldier." Like most soldiers, Field remembered the fighting with pride for a time, and then stopped thinking about it, and only much later asked himself why men did such things to one another. He remembered zeroing in on a farmhouse spotted as a German command post, and blowing it apart with the first salvo; it was what he had been trained to do, and he was proud of his gun, his battery, and his regiment. He was cited for gallantry by Generals Pershing and Bell, and while such citations were not unusual, there was generally good reason for them. He was proud of the citation too. And he was intensely proud when he heard that it was Adm. David Beatty who had accepted the surrender of the German fleet.

Years later, when he was an embattled humanist, friends wondered how he looked back upon his soldiering. He was still proud of it. He had fought as his classmates at Trinity had fought, as a volunteer; not for glory and not for gain. He may have been aware that the cause was at best ill-defined, the spirit of the times somewhat hysterical; he may have known that the fight was not for principle but for markets, raw materials, economic hegemony, and he may even have preferred it that way; it takes no great analytic talent to perceive that principle is the least tenable justification for killing. President Wilson knew it, in 1919 if not before; in St. Louis he asked, "Is there any man here or any woman—let me say, is there any child—who does not know that the seed of war in the modern world is industrial and commercial rivalry?" Suppose that was true; still, when the battle was joined, would anyone seriously have wanted the Central Powers to win? Would a perfect *kaiserlich-königlich* Europe have been better than an imperfect Manchester-Lille-Pittsburgh democracy? Shaw's comment on the Boer War is apposite: the British cause was unjust, but would anyone really have wanted a victory for Oom Paul and his Old Testament?

But ultimately none of this mattered. Field fought because with his background, his station, his friends, it was unthinkable to avoid the fight. He did what he had to do, did it well, and never regretted it. Years later, talking it over with his son, he said, "All right. We didn't save the world for democracy. But you've grown up thinking and saying what you like. We kept *something* alive that was worth saving."

Immediately after the war Field paid a quick visit to Rome, where he spent a few weeks with Ambassador and Mrs. Thomas Nelson Page. (Mrs. Page was the widow of the first Henry Field, the old gentleman's culturally inclined younger brother.) As a formality— Field was still in uniform—he was attached to the staff and given the privileges of the Embassy. The trip gave rise to a story that he had played some subtle part in the peace negotiations, which was not true. He was resting. Early in 1919 he returned to the United States, resumed his civilian life, and took a fresh look at himself and his country. Both had changed.

CHAPTER THREE

The social duties of a gentleman are of a high order. The class to which he belongs is the natural repository of the manners, tastes, tone, and, to a certain extent, of the principles of a country.

—JAMES FENIMORE COOPER,
The American Democrat, 1838

1919 WAS A BAD YEAR FOR HORSES AND BARTENDERS. City streets were yielded to the automobile; matched bays and spanking rigs faded into history. So did liquor, theoretically: the Eighteenth Amendment, of infamous memory, was ratified in January, and the Volstead Act in October. Mr. Wilson spent part of the year in Europe, chaired through various marketplaces by grateful millions; Clemenceau, Lloyd George, and Orlando were also grateful, but preoccupied with the practical business of revenge. Americans, preoccupied with the practical business of grinding valves and stockpiling red-eye, were insufficiently attentive to the President's pleas. Which is not to say that the League of Nations failed because of American apathy: in general Americans favored some sort of agreement that would end war forever. The Utopian spirit was abroad in the land. No more war, because we had won the war to end wars; no more crime, because we had abolished liquor; no more poverty, because industry was on the march; no more immorality, because women were getting the vote. Ways and means remained to be worked out, but American ingenuity was equal to any challenge.

Field came home sharing the general satisfaction and prepared to use himself constructively in this republic of noble savages. He was no longer a university blade; he was twenty-five years old, the father of two children, a tested warrior and a young chief. He had a place—possibly a high place—in the new world of hydrocarbons, sobriety, and respectability, and he intended to find and fill it.

He began in Chicago because there were problems with the Estate. He was in a responsible mood, and part of the responsibility was to himself. His affairs, with which he had barely become familiar before the war, needed to be set in order. Henry's death, for example, had raised questions: how, in the light of that tragedy, would the law construe Clause 20 of the Will? Did Henry's widow have dower rights? These were not matters of a few thousand dollars; they involved millions.

Field did three things immediately. He renewed his working relationship with the trustees; he set in motion three wholly amicable lawsuits against the Estate; and—fresh from the 33d Division, where some of his smooth edges had been rubbed rough—he became an associate director of an informal but effective veterans' bureau in Chicago, opening his own office in the Conway Building on West Washington Street, which had been built by the trustees in 1914. He was expansive as a veterans' adviser. It was his first step into altruism—he received no pay, of course; and it maintained the feeling of camaraderie, of belonging, that the war had strengthened in him. Primarily the work was simple rehabilitation—finding jobs for the returned men. Occasionally it was more complicated; there were real hardship cases, broken families, men who had no notion of their rights, men who had not applied, or had applied incorrectly, for pensions they had earned. Field worked hard, not a society chap doing his bit for the boys, but a biased and often indignant ex-captain still looking out for his men. When the American Legion was organized, he approved: the men had done their job, and were right to keep the country from forgetting.

The litigation that occupied him on and off for the next two years was magnificently complicated. Field appeared as both complainant and defendant, and then as cross complainant, in all three actions. The first had been initiated in April, 1918, and postponed during his absence. Its purpose was simply to secure from the Superior Court of Cook County opinions and instructions:

> Complainants . . . pray that the court may examine into all their acts and doings as . . . Trustees, and state their accounts as Trustees, and . . .

enter a decree herein, judicially approving all their acts and doings . . . and approving and settling their accounts . . . and finding the assets of said estate. . . .

And complainants further pray that the court may examine into and determine the correct method of computing the net income. . . .

To this action were now joined two others: a plea for dower rights for Nancy Perkins Field, and a plea for consideration of the possible rights of a natural son born to youthful Henry's mistress in 1915. Half a dozen eminent law firms ultimately joined battle, and the records of the proceedings, printed and typed, fill several thousand pages; legal fees alone finally approached a million dollars. There were forty-eight defendants—people or institutions who had a continuing interest in the disposition of the Estate—and twenty-six of them were minors, for whom the court had to appoint guardians *ad litem.*

Field's direct participation in all this was sporadic; his presence in court was rarely necessary. Lawyers jousted, and clients went on about their business. The records imply strongly that counsel enjoyed themselves, barring minor laryngeal complaints; the air was hazy with Latin, with Hereinbefores and Hereinafters; now and then the haze condensed to a rain of precedents, of which at least two hundred must have been cited. The hearings were a great corroboree of *stare decisis,* and the lawyers plunged in and out of Blackstonean thickets with the bright-eyed avidity of foxhounds.

Between April, 1918, and May, 1920, the case was entered and briefs were prepared and submitted. The hearings took place from May 11 to May 19, 1920, and on June 11 the court handed down its decisions: quick time, considering the tangle of forensic foliage. A major part of the decree consisted of reassurances: the briefs had been properly drawn, the witnesses properly notified; the trustees had done their work legally and well; the family relationships set forth in the various documents had been honestly and truly defined; the trustees were, indeed, entitled to a decree from the court judicially settling their accounts and instructing them; Marshall Field III had a perfect legal right to ask for judicial relief. The important decisions were these:

(1) that Marshall Field III was not entitled to receive at that time any of the principal of the residuary trust estate; that the trusts were to remain in being.

(2) that Henry's share in all trusts and interests was, for practical purposes, simply to be transferred to Marshall.

(3) that none of the provisions of the Will violated the rule on perpetuities.

(4) that Nancy Perkins Field was entitled to dower rights in Henry's share of the Estate.

(5) that Henry's son had "no right, title or interest of any kind in or to any of the property of said trust estate."

(6) that the trustees should alter their methods of accounting to conform with these decisions.

Disregarding the higher mathematics ("one-half of two-fifths," etc.), the decree meant that on his significant birthdays Marshall would receive the lump sums specified in the Will, plus the amounts specified for Henry; and that his interest payments would be increased by the interest that would have gone to Henry. Eventually, if he lived to be fifty, Marshall would receive the entire residuary estate. Marshall was free to work out an agreement with Nancy Perkins Field, which he did immediately. He was free of all legal responsibility to Henry's former mistress and her son, but he felt that his moral obligation persisted, and he provided formally for their support by means of a trust.

Marshall Field III never "broke the Will," though many claimed to remember the "hot legal battle" that "kept dozens of law firms alive for years." Another legend. The law firms were quite solvent without Field's complications, though they all relished the work and received good fees. The Will was not broken but construed in the light of contingencies. And the hot legal battle consisted of a couple of dozen pacific, well-barbered gentlemen arguing quietly in two languages. In the end there were no recriminations.

2

Meanwhile Field had a life to live, and he was living it in Chicago. Mrs. Field preferred New York; it was her home, and on the Fields' level of society it was more conservative and sedate than Chicago, quieter, governed by a more aristocratic taste. But Chicago was an exciting town in the early 1920s, full of bright young men, culture, sporting life, the buzz of big business. Eighteen legitimate theaters housed the full range of drama, from Hamlet to mellers with mustachioed villains; the restaurants served good food and scorned the exotic tidbittery, *flambé* and en brochette, that later displaced nutrition; outdoor operas were offered at Ravinia, and were well attended. Inevitably there was the classic contingent of ladies for whom culture was a pretext to display gowns and jewels, but the activity was constant, and for a few years Chicago looked down on even New York.*

Except for the war, Field's life up to then had been preparation for the future: the future was now upon him. At Cambridge Oliver Lyttelton had wondered what Field would do with himself, and had suggested politics; Field rejected the suggestion immediately, pointing out that American politics was "a dirty business." In 1919, when he took a vacation with his wife and children on Catalina Island, he invited Rudolph de Trafford to stay with them, and a couple of weeks later the two men found themselves in Santa Barbara drinking and talking until late at night with an economist from the University of Chicago and with Field's cousin Ronald Tree. It amounted to a one-night seminar in international finance, which Field had studied intensively, and of which he planned to make a career. Back in Chicago, he and de Trafford went deeper into the matter; Marshall saw several of his own friends, and Stanley Field introduced de Trafford to Lee, Higginson, who approved highly and passed him on to Higginson and Company in London.

Marshall too settled on Lee, Higginson. (It is hard to imagine that *they* chose *him*.) No question of credentials; equally, no question of undue deference: he started as a bond salesman. He did well; he had charm, knowledge, probity, and rich friends. Times were good, for the moment, in this country if nowhere else. For a few months Field lived in a world of bulls and bears, and polished his financial vocabulary. If he had not known before, he learned what bucket shops and boiler rooms were, and up-ticks and down-ticks,

---

* A decline began not during Prohibition, which made Chicago in many dubious respects the nation's first city, but in the 1930s, when the active leaders of the legitimate community—businessmen, philanthropists, landlords, directors of all sorts—moved to the suburbs year-round, instead of maintaining summer homes and living in the city. Their influence declined, and under Big Bill Thompson's successors there was a falling off of culture. You can run a town from the suburbs, but you can't make it think.

and selling against the box. He also rubbed elbows; he was becoming a popular Chicagoan.

Early in 1920 he left Lee, Higginson and gave his full time to the Estate. His schedule was somewhere between "What do rich men *do* all day?" and "We are the slaves of our money." He arrived at his office in the Merchants Loan and Trust Building around 9:30, and rarely stayed later than 4:30; but he was usually on the job five days a week plus Saturday morning. He took one long vacation that year, to Florida for the tarpon fishing, and his sister Gwendolyn joined him there. It was a happy reunion, all too short; when Field returned to Chicago, she went back to the home of the Beattys in England. The Estate Field was handling approximated the annual budget of a medium-sized city; it was about equal to the dollar value of all the heavy household appliances (refrigerators, electric heating, stoves) then in use in the whole country. It required diligent care. Field displayed assiduity and financial intelligence, but fell into minor pomposity now and then, as in this statement to a man from *The Literary Digest:*

What do you think made my grandfather a wealthy man? Courtesy— that's the first rule of every successful businessman, and without it you'll fail. My grandfather was a wonderful man, and it was his ability to make and hold friends that made him wealthy. Look at the big men the house of Field has given to the business world . . . you'll find upon close analysis that their entire business careers had for their foundation stone the stone of courtesy.

The lumpy style may be the reporter's, but the *naïveté* was Field's.

Soon enough he arrived at a natural limit of activity. Most of the Estate was in stable, relatively unadventurous assets, and barring sudden booms or busts would not require constant supervision. By the summer of 1920 Field was a bit restless. He took time out to participate informally in the Republican convention, which opened in Chicago on June 8. First he wangled a job (sergeant-at-arms) for one of his old enlisted men; then he plumped strenuously for Maj. Gen. Leonard Wood.

Field's enthusiasm for Wood—as against Hiram Johnson of California and Governor Frank Lowden of Illinois—was perfectly natural, and indicated a lack of political sophistication. Wood was a graduate of the Harvard Medical School; former commanding officer of the Rough Riders (T.R. had been only a lieutenant colonel) and of American forces in the Philippines; and former chief of staff of the Army. He had been governor general of Cuba from 1899 to 1902. He ran as a returned proconsul, confident that our colonial problems (if not all foreign problems) could be solved by the judicious use of force (justified because we were moral and others weren't), and not too clear about the nature of our domestic problems. His favorite issue was rampant Bolshevism, but A. Mitchell Palmer, Wilson's attorney general, had stolen his thunder with an orgy of unconstitutional raids and deportations, crowning Wilson's career as an idealist, and the public no longer responded to the usual apoplectic warnings.

Field was a good, solid, unreflective right-wing Republican, confident that if "gentlemen" were in charge the country was safe. (By then his grandfather would probably have joined him; neither party showed much desire to lower tariffs, and the Democrats had proved as hot for war as the Republicans.) When Gamaliel the Bloviator was nominated and duly elected, Field was puzzled, having had little experience of small-town sachems; but the man was patently safe. Of course Field voted for him. The opposition was not formidable. The Democrats had nominated James M. Cox, governor of Ohio, and Franklin D. Roosevelt, assistant secretary of the Navy; the Socialists had put up Eugene Debs, who was still in a Federal prison, serving a ten-year sentence for violation of the wartime Espionage Act, i.e., for believing the First Amendment; and there were the usual lost-cause parties: Socialist Labor, Farmer Labor, Single Tax, Prohibition.

The election is classically interpreted as a return to Normalcy and a gentle but firm repudiation of the League of Nations. It was also the first in which women voted. In 1916 a total of something like 18,500,000 votes had been cast; in 1920 the total was nearer 26,500,000. Cox lost by almost 2 to 1, but got more votes than Wilson had four years before. And the League was not so much defeated as equivocated to death; Harding's humility was exceeded only by his noncommittal rhetoric, and the League had been doomed since Wilson's rejection of Lodge's proposed amendments. Field was entirely in favor of the League, and regretted his party's attitude, as did much of the Middle West. When the senators from California and Massachusetts spoke against the League, it was often Hitchcock of Nebraska who defended it; young men like Wendell Willkie came back to Indiana and plumped hard for it. Middle Westerners in Congress favored the League generally, and were particularly attached to Article X, which pledged all to defend the independence and territorial integrity of member nations. Robert M. La Follette dissented, and opposed the League adamantly, which may be a key to the American attitude. The country was in agreement on the goal—to disembarrass itself of foreign complications—but divided on the means—settle them once for all by international agreement, or duck out of them altogether?

Field himself remembered the fate of his class at Cambridge, was naturally concerned about England, and echoed his grandfather's insistence that war was bad for business. Being a banker, he cared about prosperity, but he saw it as an international phenomenon, and not as a matter of daily buying and selling. Those were the golden days when the national debt was meaningful and there seemed a hope that taxes would remain a minor problem, and perhaps even diminish. Field's internationalism was strong, and tinged with a vague humanitarianism; what he really wanted was a quiet, thriving world and a close association between the United States and England. Events in Russia were disturbing, but surely if a just peace could be maintained Bolshevism would decline, or at least moderate itself into something a businessman could understand. Opportunities in the Far East seemed limitless, but only if stability could be imposed upon chaotic Asia. Field's opinions were up-to-date, but his attitudes were still fairly Edwardian, in the best sense: he wanted to diminish misery and confusion, and he thought the League would bring us into a healthier world.

He was "a damned nice fellow," brimming with charm, unfailingly considerate, a sportsman and a sound, conservative gentleman; no one was at all surprised when he decided to go into investment banking. The times—late 1920—were propitious. American production had been accelerated by the war, processes had been simplified, machine tools improved, management made more effi-

cient; the future looked good. Almost everybody owed the United
States money, and Harding was flatly against any abatement of the
debts, but bankers knew that one result would be large flotations
of foreign bonds. American exports might decline as the battered
warrior nations got back on their feet, but the decline would be
more than offset by domestic growth. The automotive industry alone
promised to carry the national economy; possibilities in electricity
seemed endless; and chemical industries, which had replaced the
country's former dependence on Germany, were already booming.

Older bankers had suggested that Field keep an eye on Charles
Glore, a bright and imaginative young Chicago banker. In 1920
Glore had joined forces with Pierce C. Ward (who was not related
to the mail-order house), Earle Reynolds, and Allen Withers, to
establish Glore, Ward and Company. Glore was thirty-two; he had
been vice-president of another banking house, and had accumulated
considerable capital of his own.

Field made his first suggestions in the fall of 1920, and Glore
was immediately receptive. The suggestions were ambitious: Field
had in mind a heavy participation in foreign bond issues, and perhaps the establishment of one or more investment trusts specializing
in Middle Western industrial opportunities. Glore, Ward liked the
ideas, and on January 1, 1921, the firm became Marshall Field,
Glore, Ward and Company. Field had hoped to hear it called simply
Marshall Field and Company; the hope was dashed at once by the
board of the department store. Stanley Field lectured his nephew,
pointing out testily that the young man had no right to the commercial use of his own name: in 1917 the store had bought its independence from the Estate, and had paid out $10,000,000 for the
name and good will alone. Marshall Field, Glore, Ward and Company would have to suffice—but not for long. Within weeks the
banking world was referring to it as Jesus Christ, Tom, Dick and
Harry—a witticism that first appeared in *The Bawl Street Journal,*
a parody newspaper of the financial community.

Field's Chicago friends were happy to see him setting up a business in the old home town—as were the trustees—but those close
to him knew that he had not retired from New York and Europe. In
that same year the firm opened a New York office, and brought in
new associates; and Field kept an eye on European opportunities.

Chicago was the center of the commodities market, but stocks and bonds belonged to New York.

So did Evelyn Field, who was far more comfortable in familiar surroundings, among her old friends. Chicago was the more brassy, aggressive city, and Ward McAllister, given half a chance, would surely have unburdened himself of the same old tired fatuities. New York's older families were still almost Jamesian: responsible stewards of old fortunes, at home in European culture if not in Europe, accustomed to an unofficial voice—or at least whisper—in government. In 1920 they might seem a bit played out by the side of the hustling Chicagoans; they were yielding reluctantly to hustling New Yorkers; they were barely capable of fathoming, much less serving, President Harding. Field was bound to them by Anglophilia, by his nineteenth-century background, by his courtliness; but he was also very much a doer—he liked big business and violent, all-out sporting life. He liked challenge, in other words, and that was a link to Chicago.

The tug of war between Chicago and New York was the first outward sign of an inner battle that he would be fighting for years. It was not a geographical problem, and it was complex. On the one hand was a secure, genteel, essentially unproductive existence, a life passed among "people of distinction," with philanthropy probably his most serious challenge. That life, and the proper political contributions, might lead to wider public service in the form of an ambassadorship, or an appointment to head up some temporary banking commission for the Federal government. On the other hand was a more direct plunge into the country's economic life, a deeper participation, a more genuine fulfillment of his mother's hopes. Field's notion of competition was, in 1921, the nineteenth-century idea of laisser-faire, with the usual unacknowledged and unexpressed overtones of Social Darwinism; and while he would have been the first to laugh at any suggestion that he was engaged in a struggle for survival, he unquestionably felt the need to prove himself as an individual—to assert his identity as a capable, competitive human being, worthy to be considered one of the "fit," and not just the keeper of a large inherited fortune. Jumping into the world of competition might expose him to, or even surround him with, disagreeable people, hard, lacking his own *courtoisie,* single-minded; it might throw him in with a good many bright young people, reckless, sporting, on the make; and he was aware that Evelyn Field would not be comfortable with either group.

Moving to New York was a compromise. A compromise between the Estate and Europe; between commercial cut and thrust and conservative stewardship; between his ties to Chicago and regard for his wife. He did not, however, make the move reluctantly. New York was the great cosmopolis, and if he wanted a businessman's battles, he would find them there. But the two years in Chicago had sharpened him, and from then on he was a citizen of two cities.

3

In 1921 the Fields settled into New York, with every sign that the move was permanent. For a few years they leased the home of Henry P. Davison, a Morgan partner; but only until their own town house was ready. The house was built on four lots, two adjacent on East 70th Street, across from the Frick mansion, and the antipodal two on East 69th Street. It was designed by David Adler and Robert Works, and was expensive. It was of course a town house in the grand manner, spacious and lavish within (though not at all light and airy), and discreetly Georgian without. There was no better neighborhood, there were no more respectable neighbors, anywhere in the city.

But a town house, rented or owned, could not be the center of Field's life; he was still too much the English gentleman for that. He needed a country home, and he saw it as a manor, and in 1921 he scoured Long Island for a suitable site. He took his time, realizing that he was about to make a major decision, and a major investment, in his and his family's future. Banking kept him busy, but the search for a home took up most of his spare time.

What he found, finally, now seems to have been ordained for him. It was an estate of 1,896 acres on Lloyd's Neck (also called Lloyd Neck), just above Huntington on the North Shore, and everything about it was right for Marshall Field. It was truly manorial; meadows and woodlands sloped to handsome beaches, and the views strongly suggested the Drummonds' estate at Cadland. Even the history of the manor was interestingly interwoven with English and Colonial history:

Three centuries ago Lloyd Neck . . . was known to the Indian inhabitants as "Caumsett." By adopting this name for the Marshall Field Estate, the owners strike a pleasant note that perpetuates the traditions of its locality. . . . From the earliest days of its occupation it has been a locality of absorbing interest. . . . Lloyd Neck was conveyed, in 1654, by the Indians to three white men living in Oyster Bay for 3 coats, 3 shirts, 2 cuttoes [large hunting knives], 3 hatchets, 3 hoes, 2 fathoms of wampum, 6 knives, 2 pairs of stockings, and 2 pairs of shoes. After this the property passed through various hands, and eventually came into the ownership of James Lloyd of Boston. His son, Henry Lloyd, made it his residence and in 1685 Lloyd Neck was erected into the only manorial domain in the country and was called Queen's Village.

In the turbulent time of the Revolutionary War, there were two forts on Lloyd Neck. . . . The splendid primeval forest that covered Lloyd Neck was stripped of its valuable growth of wood by the British and used to supply fuel and build cabins for the troops. . . . [In the Lloyd manor house] the Duke of Clarence (afterward William IV) was lodged on a visit. . . . Lloyd Harbor is claimed to have been a rendezvous for the British and Tories. The shores of Long Island have been favored by nature as a landing place for smugglers and pirates and even Captain Kidd has not escaped mention. Nathan Hale was captured on the shore of Huntington Bay. Tradition, legend and history give Lloyd Neck a romantic background. . . .

The property had been neglected for thirty years; it was "partly covered with woods, second growth timber, and overgrown with brush. A cottage of the Revolutionary period and several nondescript cottages and sheds existed on the harbor side." But the forests and foliage were exciting, and so were the vistas; and the peninsula afforded a natural geographic privacy. East of Oyster Bay and Sands Point, the estate was within comfortable distance—by boat—of the best North Shore society. The harbor was good, and commuting to New York by speedy yacht would be a matter of about an hour.

Field bought the land in 1921. He had ambitious plans for it, and memories of England must have crowded in upon him: the solid Georgian architecture he liked so much, and vast rolling lawns, and pheasant shoots, and stables; farmhouses and servants' quarters and gamekeepers' cottages; tack rooms and gun rooms, hay barns and garages, paddocks and bull pens and a dairy. He was not so much building a home as planning a town, a well-integrated rural town with a personality and an economy all its own. A whimsical map prepared for a magazine cover is labeled "The Property of the FIELDS, Gentry," which was perhaps an understatement, the gentry being the class immediately below the nobility. If the United States could claim a peerage, it was financial, and Field was of it, and Caumsett was to be his demesne.

The monumental work was entrusted to the office of architect John Russell Pope of New York, and in 1922 construction was begun almost from scratch. The paper work was voluminous. The first chart was a table of organization headed by the Business Office and divided between Designing and Engineering, with Architects' and Engineers' Field Offices, with Project Managers and Resident Superintendents and Contractors' Representatives, all joined by little synapses marked "Progress Meetings." The major divisions of work were Excavation and Grading; Landscaping; Building Construction; Electricity; Water; Drainage; Gardening and Fine-Grading; Roads and Drives—and these were only labels. The actual planning and construction busied hundreds for five years. The plot plan showed eighteen major structural units, and some of them, like the "farm group," comprised half a dozen separate buildings. Many of the roads were temporary, to be used only during construction; temporary telephone lines were strung; there were temporary supply dumps, temporary docks, temporary service buildings. Nothing was haphazard: from the composition of the main road to the hardware in the kennels, every material and every dimension was specified and approved. "In all cases where the original instructions were changed by later requests, the proposed changes were submitted to the client in writing, for approval or comment, before proceeding with the work. In the same manner, progress meetings and conferences were recorded and embodied in office reports, copies of which were sent to all parties affected."

It took more than money. It required a sense of position and family, a confidence, an appetite for life on the grand scale. It required a strong ego: building Caumsett was a massive investment in time, taste, and personality, and it takes a certain Alexandrian recklessness to build a manor every lintel and post of which will bear the mark of its owner. Field was accomplishing several things at once. He was expressing himself in a traditional way—constructing something vast yet personal. He was asserting a notion of fitness appropriate to his station and attitudes: not simply the estate, but the working part of it, the farm and herds and dairy and greenhouses. He was restoring to his life some of the grandeur of his English youth; not re-creating a corner of England—he was never prey to such affected strokes of sentimentality—but drawing from his memory and experience all the best that England could offer a man of his class, and adding to it the technology and amenities of a prosperous America. It was made possible by money, but not by money alone. For one thing, there had to be a climate in which Caumsett would be accepted and understood, and Field was lucky: the '20s basked in that climate, but in, say, 1932 Caumsett (though it "made work") would have been an affront not only to the depressed poor but also to the ruined rich.

So the bulldozers moved in.

4

Field's third child, Bettine, was born on February 18, 1923; young Marshall was almost seven, Barbara was five. The family was close-knit; Field was a good father. His love for the children was apparently boundless, and he refused to neglect his leisure. The family took a long vacation every year, and Field generally declined to bring work home from the office. He had an easy rapport with children, a real affection for them, a knack for the naïve complexities of their world, and they were never left with the empty feeling that their father was a big, important man with no time for play. He liked teasing and joking, most of all when the joke was on him, and was often found on all fours playing horsey. He had it easy in certain respects, as most fathers do: he could leave the discipline to Evelyn Field. He performed only one spanking all his life: young Marshall threw a domino at him in a moment of pique, and Field paddled him. Barbara believed later that he had allowed them too much leeway—they could talk back almost to the point of real impudence. But that independence had its advantages; the children

were included in sporting parties as soon as they could be trusted
with horses and weapons and conversation, with the result that they
were at home in an adult world very early on. Field himself taught
them to ride and shoot and fish; taught them bridge and chess;
taught his son to be a gentleman and his daughters to be ladies. His
gentleness of manner became, with the children, a vast, loving patience.

And Daddy was not just a good playmate. Shortly after the contests of the Will in Chicago he had established a large trust for
Evelyn Field, which he augmented from time to time; its purpose
was to give her and the children a security totally independent of
the Estate. He cared deeply about his children's future, and his
cheerful participation in their fun and games was also a kind of
tutoring. Field had lost both father and grandfather in the space of
two months, and knew what a parent should be. All through the
1920s he gave himself to his children, romping, teaching, deploring,
hinting, offering himself as companion and exemplar. Perhaps, with
Caumsett to remind him of Cadland, he remembered what Maldwin Drummond had meant to him. The children lived a luxurious
life at home, and were "spoiled" in that sense; but they were never
permitted to be brats. Their education was serious and disciplined.
Young Marshall was a brilliant student from the beginning, and led
the school academically at Fay;* it was impressed upon the girls
that this was a busy, wide world, full of more wonders than horses
and speedboats, and that while they were bound to be considered
ladies by others, it was important that they themselves share that
opinion. Their mother was a fine lady, and so was their Aunt Gwendolyn, of whom interesting news had gratified the family: on April
5, 1923, she had married Capt. Archibald Charles Edmondstone.
From Sandhurst, Edmondstone had been posted to the 9th Lancers
and sent abroad in 1914, before his eighteenth birthday; he served
with distinction, and after the war became aide-de-camp to Lord
Willingdon, Viceroy of India. By 1923 he had left the service and
settled down at Duntreath Castle in Stirlingshire, Scotland, to farm
seriously. Gwendolyn had been with the Beattys all this time; Admiral Beatty was by then First Sea Lord, Earl of Brooksby and of

---

* A private school in Southboro, Mass.

the North Sea. The Edmondstones' wedding reception was held at
Admiralty House in Trafalgar Square.

The winter cottage at Caumsett was finished in 1923, and became the family's fair-weather headquarters. The temporary dock
was ready, and Field commissioned a boat from Gar Wood, who
built a fifty-footer for him, the *Corisande,* capable of 30 knots. Field
hired a captain, John H. Stafford, who knew his way around motor
yachts and had skippered for other wealthy men. The *Corisande*
served chiefly as a vehicle for commuting. Occasionally when Field
took time off the family ran up to Massachusetts, but when they
were at Caumsett, Field appeared on the dock at 8 A.M. and commuted to the Wall Street slip; it was forbidden to tie up there, but
the boat could idle in, drop off or take on passengers, and scoot
right out. Commuting time was under an hour, and there were always hitchhikers to keep Field company—friends, neighbors, sometimes total strangers.

Field liked his work, and was bringing to it a sharp intelligence
and a shrewd financial sense. He knew capital, and he knew Europe,
and during the 1920s Marshall Field, Glore, Ward and Company
(which became Field, Glore and Company when Ward retired in
1928) was startlingly successful, in particular with foreign bond
issues. They floated issues of Italian Superpower to the extent of
$20,000,000; participated in issues of $10,000,000 each in Rhine
Ruhr, Est Road (French rails), "Montecatini" (Montecatini So-
cietà Generale per l'Industria Mineraria ed Agricola), Meridionale
Electric; $30,000,000 in the city of Milan; $4,000,000 in Hamburg
Electric. Their utility participations in Illinois Power and Light
alone aggregated $100,000,000. They handled a bond issue of
$17,500,000 for Marshall Field and Company, and—displaying
fine impartiality—$6,000,000 in preferred stock for Fair Stores, a
direct competitor.

Field was at home in the analyses and negotiations of international finance. In a way, the electrification of some remote Italian
valley was *why* he had chosen to be a banker, and with every successful flotation his pride in the firm's reputation grew; so did his
self-respect. He had nothing against making money, but he was
always happiest when some element of tangible industrial progress

was involved—the unstated assumption being that the condition of
society was being improved. A Victorian idealism, if you like—he
thought he was doing the world some good for a profit, which made
everyone happy. But it was also possible to make money without
doing anyone any good at all; he knew it, and was in a position to
do so, but was never even slightly tempted by empty and selfish
personal manipulations, however legal. He hated being defined by
money, even in a decade preoccupied with it. Always there were the
further definitions: his father's death, his mother's hopes, the war
he had seen, the restraints of an English education. There was a
lot of new money in the 1920s, and a new breed of condottieri, like
Kreuger and Insull. When the Big Boom swelled, corners could be
cut here and there, and restored later with paper profits; the average
financier, sniffing at the fresh trade winds, raised more sail instead
of making for shore and a storm cellar. The transaction itself was
all-important; it was hard to avoid making money if you only got
in there and did business. But Field was selective. He was not pre-
scient, and saw no objection to doing business with, for example,
Mussolini's Italy; but he preferred the business to have some bearing
on the future. As far as he knew, he would spend his life as a prosperous banker, and his attitudes and conduct as a banker would go
far to determine what he was as a human being. The closest he ever
came to immodesty was to call himself a good shot; but by his own
standards in the 1920s he was a good citizen and a good banker,
and a credit to his species, country, and class. He wanted to stay
that way.

His class, during a period of apparent industrial prosperity and
genuine hepatic frustration, amused itself mightily. The responsibilities of wealth were not ignored, but they were seemingly eased.
After a sharp recession in 1921, the economy bounced back vigorously. It survived such vagaries as Teapot Dome, on which the
public seemed temporarily to thrive: Sen. Thomas J. Walsh of
Montana, who had prosecuted the oil investigations strenuously,
was barely re-elected, while the somnolent Coolidge, who had
briefly given up his afternoon naps to thwart Walsh, piled up an
absolute majority over John W. Davis, Democrat, and Robert M.
La Follette, Progressive. There was a significant exception to the

rule of prosperity: the farmers, who were in bad trouble. But farmers were not much worried about on the Eastern Seaboard, and the fatback-and-sorghum states were at least momentarily diverted by the Scopes trial, in 1925. The East was developing a friendly interest in Europe. The government teeter-tottered from the Washington Arms Conference (ending war) in 1921–22, to the Dawes plan (reorganizing German finances and making a start on reparations) in 1924; to the Kellogg-Briand Pact (ending war) in 1927; to the Young plan (reorganizing German finances and making a start on reparations) in 1929; to the London Naval Conference (ending war) in 1930; to the Hoover moratorium (reorganizing German finances and suspending reparations) in 1931; to the Lausanne Conference (reorganizing German finances and making an end of reparations) in 1932. While governments discussed and commissions sat, private capital went on investing, and bond issues went on piling up public and private debts; but somehow the economy of the United States looked good. The Revenue Acts of 1926 and 1928 reduced income and estate taxes and abolished several excise taxes; money circulated; the market rose steadily. By 1928 Herbert Hoover could report that "The slogan of progress is changing from the full dinner pail to the full garage," a remark greeted with circumspection in South America, Africa, and Asia, not to mention inflation-racked Central Europe; but those were not his constituencies, and not an American responsibility, and the suggestion that they were would have been branded as imperialistic. For most Americans life was sweet, and for New Yorkers like Field whose garages were already full, it was a bedazzlement of pleasures: daily triumphs at the office; O'Neill and the Gershwins on Broadway; a thriving merchant fleet for the Caribbean and Canadian, or booze, trade, average displacement 1,000 cases ("A great social and economic experiment, noble in motive and far-reaching in purpose"); and, as happens in comfortable societies, a skepticism about personal morals. It was by no means a Sybaritic time, but it was at least Belasco-Byzantine.

Jay Gatsby lived on the North Shore of Long Island, and if he had existed he would have met Field at one party or another; they might have discussed English education, or the war, or, eventually, the Middle West. Gatsby's diary would have been fascinating:

"Marshall Field. Very handsome. Well-dressed. *Always* the

proper tie, accessories, etc. Always considerate, if anything over-polite. Shy, quiet voice, noticeable but not offensive British accent, natural result of life abroad. Drinks; partial to martinis and Scotch; never drunk. Sign of responsibility. Tipsy once; sat down and stopped drinking. Talked to the crew of his boat: they have never seen him drunk or really angry. (Possibly just being loyal; they like him; but I incline to believe them.) Generous; prefers to be host, but will accept invitations. Brings small gifts, always the best. Women very fond of him. Daisy says it's not his money but his calm, plus a remarkably attractive and hearty laugh. Some gossip about him now and then, but I suppose that's natural; they gossip about me, too. Newspapers call him a playboy, but I'm not sure he's happy. Moody now and then, in the middle of a party at that. Friends call him a good banker. Average polo player; has a practice field on his place, Caumsett; his children learning the game. Pheasant shoots almost imperial; he breeds them, and Charley told me that ten men, with twenty-five beaters, shot 1,500 in one day last fall. Awful, but then he raised them. What do they do with the meat? Refrigerate, maybe; or hospitals. Also raises Labradors. Likes to talk about his grandfather; terrific respect for the old man. Plays tennis (indoor and outdoor courts at Caumsett, with floodlights indoors) and golf; concentrated hard, and got down to the low 80s in his first year. Said he enjoyed chess. (I must learn. Buy necessary books.) Liked Surtees (first name?), now reads mostly nonfiction, voraciously, all subjects, but mostly history, biography, current events. Catholic, but not conscientious. (Religion doesn't seem to matter a lot here. All kinds of people. Must remember that. Occasional nasty remarks made privately; never by Field.) He lost $70 to M——— at golf the other day; sickening to hear M——— flatter him: 'Great drive on tenth; bad luck in that bunker on twelfth; classic swing,' etc. Field paid up with a laugh. Has a string of horses: Kentucky, and Newmarket in England. Brings Kentucky horses to Belmont for training. No big winners, but one of them took the Futurity at Pimlico last year. Paid 7-2. Look up name and jockey; drop it into conversation. Asked him about market; he said he didn't like to offer tips, but everything was on the rise. Reads Times and Herald Tribune, occasional afternoon papers. Very loyal—even adamant—about staff and old friends.

"Gentleman!! English shoes."

It was not Flaming Youth, but by any later standard it was an unreal life. As prosperity seemed the natural goal of work, so frivolous pleasures seemed the natural goal of leisure. At one party a lady arrived in a wheelchair and was consequently waited on hand and foot by a dozen attentive blades; after a few drinks she rose and waltzed, and they all laughed hysterically. Later a woozy gentleman fell asleep in the chair; two friends wheeled him to the garbage enclosure and left him; the next morning he was collected by the servants and wheeled to a shower. Field himself made some extra money one night when he was driving to New York; a tire went flat, and he was standing beside the car while his chauffeur rummaged for the jack. A black sedan screeched to a stop beside him, and an unidentifiable man pressed a fifty-dollar bill into his hand, and the sedan roared away. It was in the best tradition of Prohibition, and Field always believed that he had been mistaken for a down-at-heels socialite contact man, and had picked up an unearned bootlegger's commission.

Such was the aspect of his life—the anecdotal—that the newspapers cherished. It was a minor aspect. He took long vacations and played hard; he also worked hard, and now and then took a firm step beyond the borders of a financier-playboy's existence. He took Caumsett seriously, and if half his life there was pheasants and polo, the other half was estate management. He hoped that ultimately his herds of cattle would pay their own way, and considered crossing Guernseys with Ayrshires to breed a new strain incomparably rich in yield and butterfat, but he was told that the project would require several decades, and apparently he was not sufficiently confident that future generations of Fields would care that much; he abandoned the notion. He bought his first Guernseys in 1922, keeping them at a farm in New Jersey until Caumsett could accommodate them; officially, he became a professional dairy farmer on July 1, 1923, and sustained an average loss of $70,000 a year for the next five years. He lost money on his horses, too, but he was unquestionably improving the breed. He liked horses; winners were welcome but prize money was not Field's primary objective. He sold a yearling

named High Quest to Mrs. Dodge Sloan's Brookmead Stables, and
a couple of years later High Quest beat his famous stablemate Cav-
alcade to win the Preakness. Field himself had three Futurity winners—Stimulus, Tintagel, and High Strung. He was very proud to
own Nimba, one of the great racing mares of modern times; she was
a winner of the Lawrence Realization, among other races. In 1928
he became a director of the Saratoga Racing Association.

It was supposed later on that business bored him; that a man with
so much money could not really care about investment banking.
The supposition was perhaps wishful; at any rate, it was wrong. He
liked banking, and banished play from his office; he was at work
not to discuss ponies or Belgian shotguns, but to supervise international transactions. The office also became his strongest link to Chicago. He may have heard an echo of the voice that had told his
grandfather to grow with the Middle West; he may have felt responsible to the Estate and to the trustees; he may have felt that his life
in New York was half play, but in Chicago was all business. At any
rate when the Estate began, in 1926, to assemble a large plot of
ground (bounded by Sedgwick Street, Hudson Avenue, Sigel Street,
and Cleveland Avenue) in Chicago with an eye to the construction
of a large low-rent housing project, Field was enthusiastic. The
project was to consist of ten separate buildings set in greenery, and
was patterned roughly after an early New York development. Field
did not sit back; he shuttled between New York and Chicago, thoroughly absorbed in the planning, condemnation, relocation, and
construction—and kept a sharp eye on the financing. He was not
plunging into liberal, humanitarian activities. Coolidge was perfectly satisfactory, and the American system was healthy. (Only the
previous November the president of the National Association of
Manufacturers had expressed dismay that there should be criticism
of the status quo: "Listen to the strange philosophies of the living
wage: the check-off system, the minimum wage, government controlled children, the closed union shop, and the socialistic redis-
tribution of wealth.") The Marshall Field Garden Apartments were
a matter of business, an investment. They were not an experiment
in avant-garde social philosophy, or a concession to malcontents.
Field hoped to show that economical building techniques and slow
amortization could make low-rent housing profitable. Unfortunately,

he failed. Costs were—as usual—far above estimates. The Estate had hoped to acquire the land for $400,000; it cost them $1,200,-000. Local real estate taxes were high, and there was no basis, or precedent, for rebates. When construction was finished rents were set at $16 a room; not, in 1927, low-rent housing by a long way. Professional people moved in, and there was no difficulty in renting the apartments. But even at $16 a room the return hovered between 1 per cent and 2 per cent—perhaps enough to justify the participation of a very rich man, but nowhere near enough to prove a point, or to attract capital. Field drew interesting conclusions from the experience. Taxes were the problem. Costs—land, labor, materials —were, in a sense, a constant: if they went significantly up or down, then the economy itself was growing or shrinking, and "low-rent" would alter its meaning in proportion. Surprisingly, Field did not offer bitter comments on the tax structure; even more surprisingly, he told a friend that municipal participation might be the answer— an opinion not at all common in the business community.

He was not becoming less conservative; he was simply looking at the world without illusion, a good habit for investment bankers. He had no need to be embarrassed about any opinion. Field, Glore and Company, as it approached its tenth birthday, could compliment itself: it had been a principal in participations totaling over $2,500,000,000. It had also expanded—not only opening an office in Paris, but joining forces with bankers in Chicago in the creation of new houses, their precise category and function being moot. The Chicago Corporation, for example, established in 1929, was described as *not* a "so-called investment trust," but "a financial corporation designed to supplement the existing facilities of the Middle West." *Fortune* magazine commented:

This statement gratified the Board of Trade and the Chamber of Commerce; they were well aware, as were other local boosters, that before the inception of the Corporation, companies seeking capital were forced to go east to New York when Chicago banks, because of the nature of the loans, were unable to assist them. But the statement was of no such vital interest to potential investors, for they were not so much concerned with *where* (geographically) their money was to be loaned out as *who* was to do the lending. What impressed them, then, was the list of those Chicagoans on its directorate—an imposing list and worth setting down herewith: Sewell L.

Avery, president of the United States Gypsum Company; B. A. Eckhart, president of his own milling company; George B. Everitt, president of Montgomery Ward & Co., Incorporated; Marshall Field, Stanley Field (uncle); Charles Foster Glore (also the Corporation's president); Donald R. McLennan, president of Marsh & McLennan (insurance) and a financier of unquestioned ability; George A. Ranney, vice-president and treasurer of the International Harvester Company; James Simpson, then president, now board chairman, of Marshall Field & Co., Inc.; Silas Hardy Strawn, board chairman of Montgomery Ward, also a senior partner of Chicago's best-known law firm (Winston, Strawn & Shaw); Edward T. Swift, vice-president of Swift & Company; F. Edson White, president of Armour and Company; David A. Crawford, president of Pullman, Inc.; and Arthur W. Cutten. A more representative list of Chicagoans could not be compiled at any price.

Field, Glore was involved in other organizations, and the interlocking was spectacular. *Fortune* described two of them:

Another was . . . the Continental Chicago Corp., about as similar in operation as it is in name, with the noteworthy difference that Field, Glore in this later participation was second, not first, in the syndicate. Chief member of the syndicate is the Continental Illinois Co., and therein is seen the fourth spoke of a wheel of happy business alliances. First of all in these alliances there is the matter of the connection which Charles Glore and Donald R. McLennan had with the formation of the Continental Illinois Bank & Trust ("Largest bank under one roof"), parent of the Continental Illinois Co. Together they were largely responsible for the merger. Next there is the fact that both Mr. Glore and Mr. McLennan are directors of the Chicago Corporation, as above noted, and both are directors of the Continental Illinois. Moreover, the Chicago Corporation and the Continental Chicago Corp. have four other directors in common: White, Swift, Stanley Field, Eckhart. That is the circle—Field, Glore to Chicago Corporation; Chicago Corporation to Continental Illinois Trust; Continental Illinois Trust to Continental Chicago Corp. And back again.

The fourth spoke, Continental Chicago Corp., is presided over by Arthur Reynolds, which adds strength to the wheel, as he is the Brother Reynolds who is chairman of the board of Continental Illinois Bank & Trust Co. The Corporation has outstanding 1,750,000 shares of common, 1,000,000 of them owned by the Continental Illinois Co.

And that was not all:

Then there is still a . . . somewhat parallel Field, Glore enterprise— Chicago Investors' Corp.—which is frankly more of an out-and-out investment trust than either of the other two, and could not be so easily included in the wheel. It was formed some two years ago [1928] as a private business with about twenty or thirty Chicago financiers owning all its stock. It became public property on August 27 last year, when 150,000 shares of preferred stock were sold publicly.

Alarmists were delighted and terrified by this sort of thing, but most Americans took it in stride. In terms of Boom capitalism this was obviously sound stuff: honest men of the best class infusing new life into an already vivacious economy. Even Europe, until 1930, seemed to be coming to life. Secretary of the Treasury Mellon had visited Italy in 1926 (Will Rogers had cabled *The New York Times:* MELLON IS ESCAPING THROUGH FRANCE, TRYING TO REACH THE ITALIAN BORDER TO GO UNDER THE PROTECTION OF MUSSOLINI. YOURS W.R.), and while he took great pains to deny any discussion of politics or finance with Mussolini or Count Volpi, the Minister of Finance, Volpi announced that the visits were "personal courtesies to Premier Mussolini and myself . . . and he [Mellon] did not hide his keen satisfaction at the solidity of the political and financial situation." In that same month of August came another heartening report: "There is much speculation on the whereabouts of Hjalmar Schacht, president of the Reichsbank. What is certain is that where the Reichsbank president meets Mr. Benjamin Strong, governor of the Federal Reserve Bank, in Holland, on August 4, he certainly will confer with him and Andrew Mellon and J. P. Morgan before they return to America."

Heady news, and the kind of history that made good copy all through the 1920s. Seen from the left, it was all a concentrated effort to restrict power and money to the privileged few. Seen from the right, it was essential to the maintenance of prosperity; if the right people lost control, anarchy was inevitable. Seen from the center, it was all very mysterious—but it was the way of the world, so why worry?

5

The Crash of 1929 has been endlessly anatomized since. At the time it was a stupendously rude shock—so rude that it engendered a widespread unwillingness to take it seriously. *Fortune*'s article on

Field, Glore appeared in May, 1930, and contains the phrase "now that the general gloom has somewhat passed and Chicago once more takes a cheerful view of business activity." Apparently the shock had been absorbed in a mere six months; spirits, if not securities, were on the rise. The wistfulness ought not to be too severely condemned: the business community was in the position of an accident victim, plastered from head to foot, firmly insisting that modern science was invincible, and that he would be walking in a week. It was a combination of ignorance and blind optimism—a common enough human reaction to catastrophe. "One truth is clear —whatever is, is right," Alexander Pope had written long before; and when failure strikes, people are inclined to blame tactics and not strategy. Whatever the economic problems, for the first year after the Crash the psychological problem was confusion. Several centuries of belief and theory, much of it elevated to the status of divine law, had been called into question, and no one knew precisely why.

It would be fanciful to say that the country's malaise and Field's were directly related. He suffered in the Crash, but not terribly; much of his wealth was in real estate, in bonds, and while he felt the pinch, he was simply worth too much to be impoverished. His personal problems were rooted elsewhere. As early as 1927 friends had noticed minor signs of nervousness and dissatisfaction. His moodiness had intensified, and even his traveling—to and from Chicago, and Europe, and various Atlantic playgrounds—began to suggest restlessness and disaffection rather than pleasure. The captious might have suggested that his life, for all its glitter, was empty, but it was not. He was busy, he felt useful, he had never felt a need to question the world's organization; his own course in life needed no justification. He was aware of the critics of his way of life, of his class, but he was not overly sensitive to them. He suffered no *crise de conscience*.

But he was not happy. He had always had a streak of the dreamer, and his moods became vague yearnings and searchings, something like a young man's quest for lost ideals. He had not fulfilled his mother's hopes for him—which should not imply enigmatic Oedipal considerations; it was not so much that she had been his mother, but rather that she had been right. And while he was interested in

—at times fascinated by—larger economic and political problems, he was still a very conventional young man, and would have rejected any hint that his basic dissatisfaction was with his role in society. But somehow the thrill was absent, the *joie de vivre,* the pleasure in being what one was, the pride and excitement he had known at Cambridge, in the war, in his work and play up to perhaps 1925.

For Evelyn Field he became rather a strain to live with. He traveled a good deal, and socialized assiduously, and was developing a tendency to moon around the house. She felt that he was drifting, and even more important, becoming quite dissatisfied with the refined, bridge-party social life of sedate upper-class circles. He seemed to prefer a younger and more pleasure-hungry crowd—Long Island's polo players and crack shots, and racing men both here and in England.

What he missed—and this he barely sensed—was, in the most general sense, ecstasy. Somewhere it existed, that total commitment to passion, or to hatred, to any emotion, that drew a man out of himself and separated him from the world; and he sought it as though it were discrete, isolated, and attainable. He was tired of a vast accumulation of everyday responsibilities; he was also tired of "fun." Caught between two worlds, he seemed to have no direction, not even a marked inclination. He was a compartmented man: banker, husband, philanthropist, father, playboy, trustee, traveler, farmer, and each compartment held its own pleasures and pains; but not since the war—in which a man was a soldier and nothing more—had he lived in the heady delight of being whole, singular, himself. He was weary of being a sum of functions; he was weary of being Marshall Field.

He retreated more and more in the late 1920s; not sure which road to take, he chose the easy and obvious way, and became more than ever, for three or four years, a playboy. If his pleasures were not making him happy, perhaps it was because he was not trying hard enough. When he looked at himself he saw a ranking member of the leisure class, young, handsome, abundantly healthy, surrounded by entertaining men and beautiful women, by the best and most expensive of everything, basking in prestige and status: if he could not be happy in that careless environment, the fault must be his own.

He moved out of the town house into a flat of his own, in what amounted to a separation; he spent more time in England; and as the 1920s ended, so did the marriage of the Marshall Fields. It had been no marriage at all for some time; Field had created a life of his own outside the home, had made new friends and sought new diversions. Evelyn Field went to Reno. The grounds were incompatibility, and they were divorced on August 4, 1930. Evelyn Field kept a large trust established for the children, the income from which was to go to her in her lifetime; she also kept the town house; Caumsett, which had been in her name, became Field's.

Of course it was not that easy. The children took it hard. Marshall, Jr., was fourteen and intelligent beyond his years; he was told, as directly and simply as possible, and bore up well. Barbara was twelve, and less independent. She loved Caumsett, and was unhappy in the town house; it was gloomy, dark, and often lonely, and someone had killed her Cairn terrier by throwing him poisoned meat, and while she sensed friction between her father and mother, no one told her precisely what was happening. With the divorce her father simply "disappeared" from the house; she resented his absence, and his silence. Bettine was only seven, possibly more resilient but certainly more dependent, and she too was sad and subdued.

Whatever Field's superficial reaction, in his confusion and drift fifteen years of marriage and three fine children must have been some sort of anchor. He had been unhappy at home for three or four years, and the divorce was not a great wrench; but he was leaving the sum of his domestic life up to then. He and his first wife saw each other seldom afterward, and almost always in connection with the children. His consolation—possibly, for the time being, his salvation —lay in the world of youthful excitement, and for the next two or three years he concentrated on private happiness, on balm and heart's ease. He was thirty-seven.

Much more had ended than a marriage. The Boom was over, everyone knew that, but the crisis, they thought, was past. The Crash had been a matter of one or two hysterical, surrealistic months, almost a year before, and President Hoover was doing all he could; surely, they thought, we had touched bottom, and there was nowhere to go but up.

They were wrong. Out of the Crash came the Depression, and out of the Depression came a decade of wars and human misery. Life and liberty were becoming far more important than the pursuit of happiness.

CHAPTER FOUR

There is another man within me that's angry with me.

—THOMAS BROWNE,
Religio Medici, II, 1642

THE REACTION OF THE UPPER CLASSES TO THE GREAT DEPRES-SION is now one of the great comic episodes of American history, but in the early '30s it was tragic. For a year or two no one well off really believed that the Higher Capitalism itself was in question. A minor economic maladjustment could hardly shatter the ideological matrix of the Industrial Revolution, of American power, of—to some extent—the American government itself. But by 1932 a riddle had been posed. Either the elect, or the "fittest," and their philosophies had failed us, and we were in grave trouble, or our leadership was still right, still the pinnacle of history and evolution, and our difficulties were illusory. The American rich, with few exceptions, chose to believe the latter proposition.

In the first few months they seemed sincere and hopeful, and their ignorance and fatuity were not so immediately obvious. Henry Ford stepped into the breach as early as November 4, 1929: "Things are better today than they were yesterday." He was followed on December 10 by Charles Schwab, chairman of the board of Bethlehem Steel: "Never before has American business been so firmly entrenched for prosperity as it is today." The two statements were wishful, but the business community and its amenable economists had committed themselves to optimism; only a week before the Crash Irving Fisher had made his famous assertion that we had reached a "permanent plateau," and on October 26 Alfred P. Sloan had described the disaster as "healthy." (*The New York Times* of the 27th ran adjoining headlines: ALFRED P. SLOAN CALLS CRASH ON MARKET 'HEALTHY' and ENDS LIFE AS STOCKS FAIL.)

The pronunciamentos grew sillier as the crisis grew worse. By 1931 Schwab had been forced to admit that there was a problem; his solution was not complicated: "Just grin, keep on working, stop worrying about the future, and go ahead as best we can." Walter P. Gifford of American Telephone and Telegraph was more pious: "What we must have is faith, hope and charity, and perhaps someday we shall not need charity." Myron Taylor of U.S. Steel was less epigrammatic: "At no time have the majority of the people in this country been in distress. There has been a great deal of distress. Some of it has been very real, but some of it has been fancied. . . . It is our duty to deal generously with the minority who are in real distress, but it is equally our duty not to permit damage to the great system which has been created by patient effort and which in general gives great privileges and opportunities to those who are conscientious, willing, and faithful." The statement combines apparent objectivity with generosity and a moral defense of the American Way; it was a model for many others. Sewell Avery of Montgomery Ward, who was a friend of Marshall Field and remained all his life a tough and blunt man, was more honest: "To describe the causes of the situation is rather beyond my capacity. I am most unfortunate in having no friends that seem able to explain it clearly to me."

But most of those friends were very good at explaining it to each other. In January, 1932, Mr. Gifford, who was chairman of the President's Organization on Unemployment Relief, offered a Senate committee the benefit of his observations. The insufficiency of his facts was exceeded only by the self-sufficiency of his conclusions. He had no idea how many were unemployed; how many, if any, were getting help from the states; what standards the states were applying; what relief requirements were in different areas; how well local governments could raise relief money. He did not even know how much money had been raised by his own campaign of private charity. He did not believe that any of that information was important to the Organization of which he was chairman. But he *knew* that local communities could handle the problem. When the committee asked for the information on which that knowledge was based, he answered, "I have none, Senator." Asked further if he did not think citizens ought to worry if, for example, the people of Philadelphia were receiving inadequate aid, he answered with little humanity and less syntax: as human beings, yes, "but whether we should be concerned in the Federal government officially with it, unless it is so bad it is obviously scandalous, and even then we would not be obliged to be concerned. I think there is grave danger in taking the determination of these things into the Federal government."

The committee also questioned Albert H. Wiggin of the Chase Bank, who maintained, "You are always going to have, once in so many years, difficulties in business, times that are prosperous and times not prosperous. There is no commission or any brain in the world that can prevent it." Senator La Follette then asked if Wiggin thought the capacity for human suffering was unlimited. "I think so," Wiggin said. Gifford was not quite so despairing. Asked by Senator Costigan, "What evidence of human need in America would be required to convince you [that Federal help was needed]?" he replied, "If the state governments were absolutely broke and could not raise any more taxes, I think that would be satisfactory evidence." Most governors felt the same way—but not for long. At just about that time a young welfare worker named Aubrey Williams, who later became Marshall Field's friend, was being thrown out of the office of the Governor of North Dakota. Williams had been urging him to apply for Federal funds, of which President Hoover had made some millions available to state governments. Williams went back to the Governor: if the Governor would visit a few Dakota homes, and still felt as he did, Williams would stop bothering him. The Governor accepted; they saw eleven honest, God-fearing, hardworking North Dakota families in one day, and the Governor, horrified to the marrow, wired Washington that afternoon. "Part of the trouble," Williams said later, "was that nobody ever bothered to *look.*"

In June of 1932 Henry Ford rewrote Sir Thomas More: "Let every man and woman at this season of the year cultivate a plot of land and raise a sufficient supply for himself and others. Every city or village has vacant space whose use would be permitted. Groups of men could rent farms for small sums and operate them with several small families . . . or there are farmers who would be glad to give a decent indigent family a corner of a field on which to live and provide against next winter. Industrial concerns everywhere would gladly make it possible for their men, employed and unemployed, to find and work the land. Public-spirited citizens and institutions would most willingly assist at these efforts at self-help. I am urging Branch Managers of the Ford Motor Company and Ford dealers everywhere to study this suggestion, and find the best means of applying it to their communities."

Robert Wood of Sears Roebuck was less idealistic: "While it is probably true that we cannot allow everyone to starve (although I personally disagree with this philosophy and the philosophy of the city social worker), we should tighten up relief all along the line, and if relief is to be given, it should be on a bare subsistence allowance."

And all this was only a beginning. The rich had merely a Depression to contend with. Soon they would have Roosevelt.

For the first time the United States had to face an ancient question: "Am I my brother's keeper?" The answer was a qualified yes, and a change in the forms and attitudes of Western civilization. The rich were right about Roosevelt, and about the function of the Federal government: what remained of mercantile Calvinism, what remained of Social Darwinism, what remained of classical economics, lay under sentence of death. But all three were obsolete, inadequate, and unjust. They were deduced doctrines, and they were ultimately deduced from a cosmology that denied man's ability to define and shape his universe; it is probably accurate (though not immediately useful) to say that they were scotched as much by Isaac Newton as by the Depression. Since the seventeenth century science had become more and more inductive and empirical, and had produced wonders—most of which were put to the service of a civilization that rejected the application of a scientific morality anywhere outside the laboratories. Which is not to say that the New Deal was altogether scientific: it made mistakes, and labored under an emotional tendency to deduce from its own cosmology. But it was attempting to grapple with what *was,* and not with what an egotistical elite enjoyed supposing.

Most men of Marshall Field's class hated the New Deal, and in the process they revealed hatred of a good many other things. Robert Wood's disagreement "with this philosophy and the philosophy of the city social workers" is as revealing as it is spine-chilling: he felt that there was nothing intrinsically wrong with letting certain people starve; that urban altruists were suspect; and that social work—the plodding effort to help, to do *something*, to gather statistics, to formulate welfare programs, ultimately to legislate—was futile and dangerous. People like him thrived on technology but discarded science when it pinched; they were comfortable in their vague religion and talked much about faith, but they knew nothing of humility, brotherhood, or sacrifice. At the top of the heap economically, they assumed moral and spiritual superiority; but their morality was that of condottieri, and their spirituality was likely to be simple arrogance. When the law outraged their instincts, they ignored the law if possible: so in 1932 Col. Robert McCormick declared that his entire personal property, including securities, amounted to $25,250, on which the Chicago municipal property tax was $1,515. Silas Strawn (Field's colleague in the Chicago Corporation and a leading light of the United States Chamber of Commerce) was worth so little that his tax was only $120; S. J. T. Straus, chairman of the S. W. Straus investment banking house, paid only $18. Perhaps that was one of the "privileges and opportunities" available to those who were "conscientious, willing, and faithful." And if it were suggested that a country might take its economy in hand and learn to control it, rather than to suffer it, there was always Mr. Wiggin's view of economic catastrophe—"There is no commission or any brain in the world that can prevent it"—with its corollary, that the capacity for human suffering was unlimited.

But a great many Americans felt otherwise. They turned to Roosevelt in 1932 not because they liked his ideas, which were notably vague during the campaign and which, like those of most candidates, had to be quarried out of mountains of rhetoric, but because they wanted *somebody* to do *something*, even if it was only to bring back liquor. The rich, the conservative, and the Hoover administration had relied upon patience and inaction, or at best upon some slow, perfectly Darwinian accumulation of readjustments, and the Devil take the unfit. But the cosmos was stalled, and in 1932 the electorate took an intellectual decision—though few saw it as such—that had been centuries in the making. They decided to get out and push.

Marshall Field voted for Hoover.

2

Field had married again, on August 18, 1930. His second wife was an extremely beautiful Englishwoman, Audrey James Coats. She was the widow of Capt. Dudley Coats, of the British textile family, who had been badly gassed during the war and had died in 1925. Her own parents were thoroughly Edwardian. Her mother was Scottish and her father a prominent citizen of Liverpool. Miss James had been engaged to be married seven times during her first summer "out," and had remained, because of her elegant brunette beauty and her independent ways, one of the most popular young ladies in the British sporting set. She was a cousin of Gwendolyn's husband, Archibald Edmondstone, and Field had first met her in 1926. He was a member of the Fernie Hunt in Leicestershire, and on his visits to England during the '20s and early '30s he rode often. He liked to stop off in Ireland, where he owned good brood mares, and then go on to England to confer with Capt. Cecil Boyd-Rochfort, who was his trainer. In these hunting and racing circles he had met Mrs. Coats. Their friendship had persisted, and grown warmer; quite possibly she came to symbolize the carefree, glamorous life that attracted him more and more as his dissatisfactions grew. Her attitudes were of course those of her class and background, and Field, withdrawing as he was from indefinable but melancholy pressures, fell in love with her.

The honeymoon was almost a whimsical allegory of the times. Field bought a Curtiss-Wright amphibian and a lighter Moth, and they flew off to Kenya for big game. (Field had learned to fly in the 1920s, but of course hired a professional pilot for this trip. After about 1934 he never touched the controls.) The Moth was damaged in Khartoum, and the RAF warned them that the amphibian was unsuitable for the terrain. Ignoring the advice, they crash-landed three times, which was once too often. The last accident was near Entebbe, on Lake Victoria, and was followed by two days of hiking, after which a lorry picked them up and took them to the nearest airport. From there they flew to Nairobi, still in high spirits; but the business news from home was not good, and they proceeded as directly as possible back to New York.

Field had absorbed losses in the Crash, as had the Estate, but three factors limited the shrinkage: the portfolio was shrewdly diversified; the old gentleman's advice (real estate and blue chips) had been followed; and the principal was huge to begin with. Field had no need to panic. His capital required attention, and decisions had to be made—buy, dump, hold on, convert; but there were no desperate flurries of reorganization. Since the move to New York ten years earlier, Field's representative in Chicago had been George Richardson, who was a careful and industrious man. "I was living in Lake Forest in 1921," Richardson wrote later, "—an insignificant trainee in the Northern Trust Company—when Marshall called me one afternoon to ask if he could walk over to the station with me [a phrase perfectly expressive of Field's courteous diffidence]. On the way he told me that he was planning to move to New York and wondered if I would like to represent him in his absence as a Trustee of his grandfather's Estate. It seemed a God-given opportunity to me, and, when he suggested I might want to think it over, I told him I needed no time for decision. And so began, and lasted for more than thirty-five years, as satisfactory a relationship as ever existed between employer and employee, made so by such consideration on his part that I was always made to feel that we were associates, working together on the same level." Plucked out of nowhere, so to speak, Richardson was somewhat resented by the other trustees for a few years, and his efforts to plumb the mysteries of a great estate were resisted. He concentrated instead on familiarizing himself with the real estate, learning all he could about securities, and studying tax laws. He and Field were friends, but their primary association was in the office. Field's instinct about Richardson had been accurate: the latter was a man of calm, caution, and thorough moderation, all quite becoming in a trustee. And the trustees as a group had seen to it that none of Field's fortune found its way into dubious enterprises. There had been no wholesale shifts of capital into temporarily bullish areas, and Richardson's tone invariably became minatory when Field's expenses ceased to have "some relation to income." In April of 1929 Carl Weitzel joined Richardson's staff; as a C.P.A. he had been one of the Estate's auditors until then, and he became its comptroller. Field trusted Richardson absolutely. "I wrote Marshall an occasional letter," Richardson noted later, "but I seldom got an answer and finally came to recognize the fact that, having confidence in me, he didn't want to be troubled with matters he expected me to handle for him."

These two men, and the Continental Illinois National Bank and Trust Company, also a trustee, were something more than prudent arithmeticians. The year 1931 was hardly propitious for investment or construction, but in that year plans were completed for a major office building in Chicago, to be erected by the Estate; and after a series of slightly nervous conferences the trustees, including Field, decided to go ahead with the project. It was a big risk. Business failures were frequent, and there were vacancies in practically every office building in the city; portents for the future were not good. But costs were down and labor was cheaper; the construction would create jobs; if the economy recovered later the building would prove to have been an inspired investment. They took the chance.

The site was half a block in the Loop, bounded by LaSalle, Adams, and Clark Streets, north of Adams. The first section was begun in 1931, and as their leases expired the old buildings came down: demolition and construction proceeded simultaneously. Field was happy about the project, and buried himself in the details of design and construction. A public announcement was made that no tenants would be accepted from other office buildings—a strange, and at first glance dangerous, policy. It was public-spirited: there were too many empty offices in Chicago, and the trustees hoped to populate their new building with new firms, or with new branches of old firms. Construction would require three years, and the building was to be Chicago's most modern and comfortable; the first four floors (of forty-three) were air-conditioned from the beginning, rather a novelty in those days. The architects were Graham, Anderson, Probst & White, the designer was Alfred Scholl, and Field followed their work closely. He did not stint, and the gamble paid off. The work helped Chicago, and offered a psychological lift; first-class tenants moved in; the lower costs proved extraordinarily economical, particularly so as the dollar inflated slowly over the next twenty-five years; and the relative opulence of the building—its interiors were considered extravagantly modern in 1934—preserved it from obsolescence.* From any point of view, the Field Building was a good thing.

But it was probably the only enjoyable project Field undertook during those early depressed years. Field, Glore continued to breast the miasmal tide: Russell Forgan, a young and intelligent banker who had been Field's friend and golfing companion since 1922, joined the firm in 1931, undismayed by the moribund state of investment banking generally. Field's business satisfactions centered on the building in Chicago and the banking firm; he was jealously proud of the firm's reputation and adamant about keeping it in the first rank even during the bad years. Among his other concerns were the department store—he controlled over 60 per cent of the preferred stock and almost 10 per cent of the common, and the total holdings ran to over $15,000,000; the Continental Bank, of which the Fields were the largest stockholders; and Commonwealth Edison, which blew up in 1932 when Stanley Field had to fire Samuel Insull.

Business worries harassed Field, and accelerated his tendency to withdraw. He took long vacations, spent more time at Caumsett, played as though his life depended on distraction, and—as his friends began to notice—drank more than usual.

Caumsett was complete, and a wonderland. Swaths of forest had been leveled and replaced by deep grass. Most of the landscape had been left in its natural state, and where Field had cleared and planted, the new growth was cover for game, meadow for riding, or grasses for fodder. His landscaper was a Scottish horticulturalist, George Gillies, who had to contend with a twenty-year growth of dogwood, bayberry, and cedar, and who had a continuing responsibility for all the 1,896 acres, plus greenhouses. Field was lavish with the greenhouses, which sheltered a great variety of exotic flora; he was partial to calanthe orchids, and exhibited them at

---

* The whole building was later air-conditioned, and its maintenance was always conscientious: not a dingy corridor or a peeling wall anywhere. It remains a remarkably pleasant place in which to work.

flower shows. There was an addition to the estate during these years: a formal terraced garden, laced with balustrades and statuary. Its designer once confided to a member of the staff that there were only two such in the entire world, and added, "and I've already built twelve of them." Field himself was unimpressed; he remarked, "That's a lot of cement." He preferred organic decoration, and disliked irrelevant gingerbread. When Gillies was landscaping the main house Field admonished him, "Please, no little Christmas trees on each side of the door."

He had to cut his staff's salaries. (He cut their work week, but dismissed no one.) There was an obvious contradiction between that and his style of living—the expensive cement terraces, for example. His feeling must have been that if he made the contradiction a matter of conscience, and carried its resolution to any logical extreme, he would be obliged to ruin himself, a *reductio ad absurdum* for which he could not have generated much enthusiasm. His way of life was grand, and he wanted to keep it so; certainly during the up-and-down years of his second marriage he was in no mood to bring any rigorous order out of his own emotional chaos. He was beset by events, by economic problems, by himself; and while he was not too confused for decisive action in specific projects, he was reluctant to gather up the threads of a life that became more diffuse, more tenuously linked to any vital center, as time went by. The friends who came to visit at Caumsett were by and large less staid people than before, less responsible and more pleasure-seeking—a dizzier and younger crowd. (There were exceptions, and the exceptions were among his closest friends; it was almost as though he was trying to inhabit two worlds at once.) Their reaction to the general crisis was to ignore it resolutely, and up to a point Field let himself be carried along on their wave of indifferent frivolity. (One remark about Caumsett in this period, from a close and disillusioned observer, was "They turned that place into a roadhouse.")

Field tasted triumph once in 1933, and a sweet one it was, over the Bureau of Internal Revenue. The Bureau had questioned, reasonably, his tax losses and deductions as a cattle and horse breeder. (They had also questioned, less reasonably, a $1,000 contribution to the Insulin Fund.) Field was assessed over $300,000 in back taxes, and appealed the assessment to the Board of Tax Appeals. His careful bookkeeping proved of value; there had been an accountant-in-residence at Caumsett Farm, and the precision of Field's brief was impressive.

The government's questions had some basis. Caumsett-in-general had been in Evelyn Field's name, and Caumsett Farm, which raised stock, was leased from her by Field. Much of the fodder was bought by the stock farm from Caumsett-in-general. One of the commissioners took strong exception to this vest-pocket–pants-pocket commerce, and wanted to disallow all such intramural transactions. But the basic question was whether or not Field operated his stock farm as a business and for a profit, even potential; here the commissioners voted in his favor. Stock breeding takes years, and the returns begin to show only after a decade or so; one of Field's prime points was that if he had sold out in 1932, he would have shown a profit for the operation as a whole, and that therefore his losses for 1923, the year in question, were legitimate business losses. He had combined his American and British bookkeeping, which meant long lists of stock sales, races won and lost, stud bulls purchased; and the commissioners examined his operations thoroughly, including the fees paid out to his stables in Paris (Kentucky) and his trainers at Belmont Park in New York. They ruled that he had, indeed, been "improving the breed," for cattle as well as for horses, and cited the usual dozen precedents, including a decision in favor of George D. Widener.

The government appealed, and in December of 1933 the Second Circuit Court of Appeals delivered a final ruling upholding Field. (The illustrious Augustus N. Hand was one of the three judges.) They accepted Field's contention that while Caumsett-in-general was a country home, and a showplace, the Farm had been operated strictly as a business, for a profit, and should be considered separately. Field pointed out that no expense ever incurred elsewhere on the property had been charged to the Farm's accounts; that John S. Clark, whom he had hired in 1925 to take charge of the herds, was a professional stock-farm manager of the highest repute who, in his previous position, had increased the value of a herd from $50,000 to $700,000 in a few years; and that the Farm had sold bulls, the stables had won races and collected stud fees, and every penny of income had been declared on tax returns. The wording of the decision was firm, and Field—as well as certain members of Congress—would have occasion to recall it in 1944, when a different set of snipers launched a different kind of attack on him. The judges wrote:

> In the instant case, there is substantial evidence that the enterprises were conducted as a business for profit and with an expectation of ultimate profits. We cannot say that the expectation of profits is unreasonable or forecast continuous losses in the light of experience in cattle or horse breeding and racing. If the right to deduct losses under the statute required that profit appear to the court to be possible, that requirement would be quite general and would be applicable to any enterprise, whether it was farming, manufacturing, or promotion of any character. We may not, in this way, foredoom any business venture. Cattle breeding and horse racing projects are old. Some have been profitable; others have not. It is a matter of intention and good faith, and all the circumstances in the particular case must be our guide. In this case we think the respondent embarked in these enterprises with the expectation of making profits; at least he did so with an earnest and honest intention.

The case illuminates two aspects of Marshall Field. The court was right; he never engaged in any business venture without the hope of profit—a point his critics chose to ignore later on, when he engaged in ventures of which they disapproved. But the dissenting tax commissioner was also right, in a way: a man as rich as Field never starts anything on a shoestring, and there is a difference (though not a legal difference) between a man who borrows a thousand dollars to patch up a barn and buy a middling bull, and one who begins his career with an investment of several hundred thousand dollars. The commissioner must have felt that there was some injustice in Field's being able to afford so many deductible expenses— but that was not the point at issue. The commissioner was arguing with the law, or with the structure of society, and not with Marshall Field.

3

But sometime in 1932, shortly before Field cast his second vote for Hoover, the intermittent exhilaration of his private merry-go-round gave way to a queasy sensation. The happiness he had been seeking was still elusive. He confided to his cousin Stanley that "it got so one cocktail wasn't enough," which was surely understatement; the rule even among his happier friends was two or three. But Field's life had become fearfully compartmentalized, and its aspects were ceasing to relate closely one to another. From his Versailles he commuted to the River Club, shifting psychological gears as he approached his office to examine pessimistic reports from Europe or bank failures at home. Part of his mind wandered to the Field Building in Chicago; on his desk lay a balance sheet from the Garden Apartments, and a request for money from a former batterymate, and a memo about Samuel Insull. A note from Russell Forgan in Chicago required consideration; a telephone call from uptown confirmed a shooting party for Saturday. The reservations for Chicago on Monday were confirmed, and there were opera tickets for Tuesday night; Audrey Field wanted to wear her ruby-and-diamond necklace, Field's wedding gift. In another season the trip would be to Saratoga, for the races and the auctions and the flirtations; Field and his wife were both too attractive, and flirtation was an easy revenge upon either for the other's momentary infatuations. There were moments of humor, too: Audrey wanted to see old Charleston, in South Carolina, and Field arranged the trip. They woke up next morning, looked out the compartment window, and saw Charleston, West Virginia. But the Libbey-Owens-Ford Glass Company had offices there, and Field was one of its directors, so he visited his enterprise and they went on to White Sulphur Springs. They could go anywhere, do anything, invite anyone to Caumsett; if Field wanted a vacation there were sober and competent men to supervise his interests. The children came to Caumsett for a month in summer, and Field saw them frequently through the year; Marshall, Jr., was at St. Paul's and Barbara was at Brearley. Field had time to take visiting Irish horsemen to Kentucky, and then to play host to them in Chicago; he wired Stanley: ARRIVING TUESDAY. HOPE YOU HAVE PLENTY OF BOURBON. THERE'S NONE LEFT IN KENTUCKY. He had time for race meets in England. He had time for everything and anything, and he was not miserable, but it all left him strangely empty-handed, and it bothered him that he was drinking too much. The events, the activities, the days and weeks and months themselves, seemed unconnected; his life had no unity. A series of discrete pleasures did not add up to Pleasure; moments of exhilaration did not add up to Happiness.

A look at his friends brought him little enlightenment. Some were happy, some sad, some concerned, some indifferent, some divorced, some happily married. Many were neighbors, members of the Piping Rock Club, good people. Some were old friends from Chicago like Russell Forgan, or Charles Cushing, a gay, superlatively charming young banker who "always put more into a crowd than he took out of it," and was a first-rate businessman; Field was very fond of him. Some were more serious, more concerned about the state of the world; Forgan was, and James Warburg. These friends, perhaps more sensitive than the others, were distressed by Field's predicament, but gratuitous advice would have been bad form.

Somewhere, in some idle conversation, the notion of psychoanalysis occurred to Field. In the 1920s analysis—psychiatry in general—had been a rage, like mah-jongg or miniature golf, but its faddish excesses had subsided, and it was nothing out of the ordinary in urban America, though it was still the Devil's work in large swatches of the parsnip-wine country. Some of Field's acquaintances had been analyzed, with happy results. Field may have been momentarily startled at the idea; but he thought it over, and his interest grew, and finally he decided that it might help, and called a doctor who had been recommended by James Warburg's sister Bettina.

Gregory Zilboorg, M.D., played an important part in Field's life. His role was grossly exaggerated later by Field's critics; but it would be wrong to redress the balance by minimizing it out of existence. The story should begin with a flat warning: Zilboorg was never a Svengali, and Field was nobody's Trilby. The analysis was relatively brief, remarkably effective, and, as far as anyone knows, devoid of Freudian scandal. Field always looked back on it as the equivalent of a delicate and totally successful surgical operation, without sequelae, to the vast benefit of the patient.

Zilboorg was a Russian Jew of intellectual distinction. Educated in the feverish decade that preceded the Russian Revolution, he became, in his twenties, a minister in the hopeful but doomed Kerensky government. After the October Revolution and Lenin's accession to power, Zilboorg's services were no longer required; he made his way to the United States, continued his training, and became a psychoanalyst. He was a kind of man little known and less appreciated in this country: the rounded intellectual, idealistic and cynical at once, a professional man with a strong political sense, thoroughly cultured. He was closer to the upper-class eighteenth-century European, or to the Renaissance, than to the more specialized and pragmatic American. He took great pride in the fact that the successful English version of Andreyev's *He Who Gets Slapped* (still played) was his translation.

He was, in short, a brilliant, eclectic man, and the glitter was not superficial. He wrote, interpreting Freud to Americans and doing his best to counteract the absurdities and oversimplifications that emerged from Hollywood and the popular magazines; later in life, when he had become a Roman Catholic, he worked strenuously to reconcile psychoanalysis and the Church. Like many brilliant men, he had flaws by the standards of his society. He maintained a high theoretical disdain for money, but enjoyed a high income. He was not a "Park Avenue analyst," which sneering phrase, implying high pay for unnecessary or futile ministrations to the egotistical rich, refers to a probably nonexistent species. Zilboorg had far too much substance to be dismissed with any cliché. His patients were, however, often rich, and in his attitude toward their society was an undertone of testy impatience with financial problems. Perhaps it was the weary scorn of a man whose art, whose science, could not be measured precisely in dollars; of the kind of man that prefers not to handle money, not to be reminded of it, is irritated that it must exist at all, and resents the fact that men of lesser contribution have more of the world's goods and services. Perhaps that was true. There was more than a hint in his life that he was aware of the analyst's power and enjoyed exercising it, and was disrespectful of other forms of power—physical or economic, for example—that were derived from accidents of birth or commerce or politics, and not from the exercise of the intellect, or from a deep knowledge of man and his enduring works.

When the two met professionally, in 1933, curiosity predominated on both sides. For Field, as for so many, the early stages of analysis must have been an unsettling and mysterious experience; and Zilboorg's sharp mind must have focused on Field immediately as a perfect representative of the disillusioned rich. But Field's purposes were not mystical, and Zilboorg's function was not Voltaire's; shortly the two men found themselves dismissing preconceptions and getting down to the practical, and difficult, work of psychoanalysis.

Just what they talked about was nobody's business but their own. They met five days a week, vacations excepted, over a year and a half, and it is likely that few subjects or events of significance were omitted. Zilboorg must have seen in the first weeks that Field was becoming an undirected collection of aspects rather than a purposeful personality—the millionaire; the son of a suicide and of a strong woman with a sense of public service; the grandson of Marshall Field I; the husband twice; the father three times; the gay blade; the sportsman; the banker; the Chicagoan, New Yorker, Englishman; the conservative capitalist; the archgentleman; the ex-warrior; and, perhaps more important than one would think, the man who was about to celebrate his fortieth birthday and was not at all sure that his life added up to anything worthy of the world's or his own respect.

The analyst naturally came to know a rather different Marshall Field. Too much a gentleman ever to burden others with personal difficulties, Field found himself pleasantly obliged to air them. He "resisted," and at one point Zilboorg requested him to stop paying for a while; Field seems to have felt that as long as he made out the checks, he could think of Zilboorg as an employee—not the healthiest attitude for a patient. And while there was truth in the idea that payments ought to hurt the patient slightly, that was obviously an impossible condition. Zilboorg reversed the idea, and in the absence of a "salary" became what he had to be: the slightly dominant partner in the dialogue. What Field paid him, no one knows. Zilboorg was expensive. For Marshall Field, at any rate, he was worth it.

Field must have talked about money. He told his wife, years later, that he had once asked Zilboorg if his fear of being "taken" by hangers-on was a symptom of guilt over his wealth; Zilboorg had told him about a carpenter from the Bronx making $40 a week who had precisely the same fear. Field was disturbed about the uses of money, and felt that he was using his own badly; but the possession of it posed no moral problem. He was dismayed at some of the blather that issued from the rich during the Depression, but never believed that wealth was a flaw, or that he could improve society by ridding himself of it. Before, during, and after his analysis he lived richly.

But he must have realized that for all his money and position and presumed significance as a leader of society, he lacked emotional resources: strong ties to a few individuals, and an affectionate nature, were not sufficient. Socially he had a "great personality"; to a psychiatrist, it was not great at all, but purposeless bits and pieces which, if they were not integrated, might become debris. Zilboorg could not assign him a purpose; Field had to find his own. The best way to define Zilboorg's function is to say that he removed many formidable roadblocks from Field's path; he helped to give him a direction, and the confidence to take his first steps. That "direction" was not a straight line. Field was too various a man for a monastic solution, like the passionate study of lepidoptera, or a fanatical solution, like crusading for the chiropractic. Zilboorg rather opened up a segment of the universe in which he thought his patient would be happy. Roughly speaking, that segment was "service," but it was not a matter of kissing lepers, Christmas baskets, philanthropy, or weekly meetings over chicken à la king. It was a matter of involvement. To the world that had given him what he possessed—health and a good mind included—he could offer help, influence, perhaps leadership. How, he did not then know; but simply taking a hard look at that world was a good beginning. His commitment to his own class had left him empty and sad; a commitment to religion was impossible because he lacked real faith; commitment to a panacea, vegetarianism or socialism or whatever, was impossible for approximately the same reason. But he needed an involvement in something vastly larger than himself; and a commitment to the welfare of his own country—within the framework of its traditions and liberties—made more sense. (It made great sense, for example, to the British Whig in him. He was beyond simple *noblesse oblige* by then, but it was still a part of him.) When he came out of his analysis in 1935 he was treading softly, and looking at the world with new eyes; but—still within the moderately elastic limits of his position and background—he was concerned for that world, and a conscious part of it. He had a direction; he had faith in himself; he was not afraid of decisions. If he was not altogether *l'homme engagé*, he was at least *le gentilhomme engagé*.

At the time few knew, or cared, that Marshall Field had been analyzed. Field probably thought the subject would never come up again; it was not a matter for public discussion, and he was not, in any important sense, a public figure. But the time came when he was well-known, and by some detested, and the faith he had in human beings was sorely tried by the cheap and slanderous uses made of his analysis. The attacks were not beneath his contempt, but they were impossible to answer directly. He gave them the lie in his own way: stuck to his guns politically, remained Zilboorg's friend, and affirmed, when asked, that analysis had made him a better man.

4

Field's awakening was sensitively timed. Over the next few years his old friends came to think of him as somewhat starry-eyed, but the world was lumbering into an acceleration of event, of conflict, of scientific advance, of social change, of political development, of the amount and means of communication swifter by far than any in its history. Field was prepared morally and psychologically, if not academically, for that acceleration; many of his early friends and associates missed it altogether and never did catch up.

Those rumblings of history were hardly obvious; they seemed rather the ordinary flow of tragic incident. Japan, laughing at the Lytton Report, kept Manchuria and left the League of Nations. Mussolini was haranguing his Romans and preparing improved bombs for Ethiopian children. Hitler had become Chancellor of the Reich on January 30, 1933, but too few took him seriously, even when he was granted dictatorial powers in March of that year. Roosevelt had been elected, and had surrounded himself with a Brain Trust, and was almost assassinated even before his inauguration. The Hundred Days attacked the Depression with an unprecedented barrage of legislation (including the act that established the Tennessee Valley Authority); in June and July the London Economic Conference (to which Field's friend James Warburg was a delegate) grappled with European currencies and tariffs; in November the United States recognized Soviet Russia and established the Civil Works Administration, the beginning of a program of make-work projects; in December Prohibition was repealed. Through 1933 and 1934 Roosevelt worked out his Good Neighbor policy, which was not wholly disinterested, reaffirmed the Monroe Doctrine, and marked the first serious efforts at hemispheric cooperation in a century. The United States went off the gold standard, and the Federal government was granted power to regulate the value of the dollar and the disposition of gold reserves. Banking and commerce came under tight regulation. While both the Agricultural Adjustment Act and the National Industrial Recovery Act were later declared unconstitutional, many of their provisions were kept on the books by the passage of supplementary legislation. The mystery novel had become an American fad, and great days were still upon the theater: O'Neill, Elmer Rice, Kaufman and Hart, Maxwell Anderson, Sidney Kingsley, Robert Sherwood, Lillian Hellman, Clifford Odets led the way in possibly the only period in American history when a playwright could be honest, socially aware, popular, rich, and free of the need to compromise. Hollywood was still a haven for witlings, but Robert Flaherty and Pare Lorentz broke new ground, and an invasion of European talent (Dietrich, Garbo, Sternberg, Lubitsch, Clair, among others) gratified the intelligentsia. Artists, beginning to hobnob with refugee colleagues, were more aware of approaching disasters than politicians and businessmen were.

But even the richest businessmen had officially acknowledged the Depression; some of them insisted that it was, after all, not a bad thing. Henry Ford was asked what he thought about homeless boys riding the rails, looking for work, and answered, "Why, it's the best education in the world for those boys, that traveling around. They get more experience in a few months than they would in years at school." He was right: they experienced beatings, starvation, brawls, theft, rape, homosexuality, and other aspects of citizenship in the communal life of hobo jungles; most public schools lacked facilities for such an ambitious program. Myron Taylor of U.S. Steel was more ambiguous: "Out of the depression we have been going

through, we shall have learned something of great importance. . . .
It is too soon to say just what we are learning."

Quite a few industrialists and businessmen were learning one
thing: that Roosevelt was the Devil himself. Why that community
—with exceptions—preferred to deny the existence of a Depression,
or, admitting it, to insist that it had merits, remains a classic problem in rationalistic cruelty. An exemplary outline of their fears, and
a display of paranoia rarely paralleled in the morbid psychiatry,
was submitted in the form of the "Wirt charges," revealed to a subcommittee of the House Banking Committee at the end of March,
1934, by James H. Rand, Jr., of Remington Rand. The charges
were that unnamed members of the Brain Trust had told Dr. William A. Wirt of Gary, Indiana, that Roosevelt was to be the Kerensky of an economic revolution, and would be succeeded by a Stalin.
This exposé generated marked excitement among the committee
members, not to mention the American press. Dr. Wirt maintained
that the shadowy Brain Trusters had a fully developed plan to
overturn the "existing social order," and to control newspapers,
magazines, leaders of industry and labor, colleges, and schools.
According to Mr. Rand, Dr. Wirt was "an unusually well-informed
and internationally known leader in education, a student and financier."

The forces of reaction, who naturally called themselves "conservatives," and embarrassed a large body of genuine conservatives,
took their signal from these scandalous revelations. In August the
American Liberty League was founded, with an executive committee that included Al Smith and Irenée du Pont, and a membership
that included ten more du Ponts, Sewell Avery, Sloan and Knudsen
of General Motors, J. Howard Pew of Sun Oil, and scores more of
America's industrial elite. The Liberty League denied opposition
to the New Deal, or to Roosevelt, but announced that it would oppose all legislation it considered inimical to business. That was a
perfectly legitimate attitude, but other statements vibrated with
wishful overtones. Asked how the League could help the President,
its secretary answered, "If a tendency to extreme radicalism developed which the President wished checked, we might be most helpful
with an organization in which we expect to enlist two to three million people." The Wirt charges had indicated that there *was* a

tendency to extreme radicalism, and that it was personified by Roosevelt.

The Liberty League announced a more positive platform, however: To defend and uphold the Constitution of the United States, and to gather and disseminate information that would (1) teach the necessity of respect for the rights of persons and property as fundamental to every successful form of government, and (2) teach the duty of the government to encourage and protect individual and group initiative and enterprise, to foster the right to work, earn, save, and acquire property, and to preserve the ownership and lawful use of property when acquired. One of its executives added, "I look upon the American Liberty League as a nonpartisan organization which is determined to see that there is the proper respect for human rights as well as property rights." (The American Civil Liberties Union was skeptical, and wired: WITH THE EXCEPTION OF ALFRED E. SMITH, THERE APPEAR FEW NAMES AMONG YOUR MEMBERS OF MEN WHO HAVE BEEN CONSPICUOUS FOR FIGHTING FOR THE RIGHTS OF INDIVIDUALS, PARTICULARLY WORKERS. WILL YOU PROTECT THE RIGHT OF FREE SPEECH TO THE FULLEST EXTENT— HOWEVER DRASTIC AND RADICAL THAT OPINION MAY BE? WILL YOU PROTECT THE RIGHT OF ASSEMBLAGE FOR PEOPLE TO EXPRESS VIEWS OF WHICH YOU VIOLENTLY DISAPPROVE? COMMUNISTS, FOR EXAMPLE. WILL YOU INSIST ON THE RIGHT OF A FREE PRESS IN THE SAME SENSE?)

Through the mid-thirties the Liberty League grew. Its growth was not spectacular: many businessmen, particularly small businessmen, favored Roosevelt and had hopes for the New Deal, and some who might have sympathized with the League's goals distrusted its methods. In the beginning it was a fair example of selfish superpatriotism, but beneath the measured tones of the sorrowful Tory there came to be heard an occasional brassy note of gauleitery, more often as the elections of 1936 approached. Borrowings from European politics and techniques cropped up in the form of statements that were anti-Negro, anti-Semitic, anti-professor, of course anti-labor, and, in the corn-pone and night-rider belt, anti-Wall Street. In sum, Roosevelt and his New Deal were equated with foreigners, Jews, "undesirable alien elements," Marx, all forms of socialism, starry-eyed visionaries and "impractical" dreamers, and

intellectual meddlers who "never met a payroll." An adjunct of the
Liberty League called The Sentinels did much of the dirty work. In
March of 1936 a letter from its president to a follower read in part:

> I am doing what I can as an officer of the Sentinels. I think, as you say,
> that the Jewish threat is a real one. My hope is in the election next autumn,
> and I believe that our real opportunity lies in the defeat of Roosevelt.

And the reply included: "The Sentinels should really lead on the
outstanding issue. The old-line Americans of $1,200 a year want
a Hitler." Right-wing conservatives had a natural target in Roosevelt's labor-leader friends and associates, many of whom, like David
Dubinsky and Sidney Hillman, were Jewish. Hearst laid his anath-
ema on "the imported, autocratic, Asiatic socialist party of Karl
Marx and Franklin Delano Roosevelt." * The *Wall Street Journal,*
which maintained a bland manner, quoted Henry Ford on October
31: "Mr. Ford said he was not a party man. A real Democrat was
as fit to be trusted with the government as a real Republican. He
said, 'It happens this time that the members of both parties have
just one course to take—vote for the American candidate.' " †
  All this was distinctly unfair to Alfred M. Landon, the Republican candidate, who was incontestably a conservative but also a
man of probity and decency, a human being of quality who would,
in other times, have made a far better President than Harding or
Coolidge. What defeated the good Landon, however, was not public reaction to his less savory partisans, but the simple fact that
Americans making less than $5,000 a year—a great majority—
approved overwhelmingly of Roosevelt.
  There were also some very rich men who had supported the New
Deal from the beginning, and had been among its most reasoned
and effective, if friendly, critics: men like Averell Harriman, Edward Filene, and Gerard Swope, who as early as 1933 had supported the National Labor Board's procedures and purposes: "This

---

* An echo as late as November, 1961, is irresistible. Capt. Eddie Rickenbacker,
war hero and political theorist extraordinary, addressing a national convention
of real-estate dealers, denounced the "diabolical Mongolian philosophy called Communism" in a splendid salmagundi of religion, racism, and right thinking. But the
title of his address was "Conservatism Must Face Up to Liberalism."
  † Ford had nevertheless been one of the first big industrialists to recognize publicly the great importance of the little man's buying power.

is America, and that's the way we do things here." When Silas Strawn, Field's old associate and president of the United States Chamber of Commerce, voiced his desperation in 1935 ("Businessmen are tired of hearing promises to do constructive things, which turn out to be only attempts to sovietize America"), a few big business leaders demurred. The Business Advisory Council, which included Thomas J. Watson of International Business Machines, Henry I. Harriman of the U.S. Chamber of Commerce, Winthrop Aldrich of the Chase Bank, Averell Harriman of Union Pacific, Gerard Swope of General Electric, and Gifford, Wood, and Taylor, visited the White House en masse and publicly supported an extension of the NRA and other New Deal legislation. That Gifford and Wood were in this group did not make them New Dealers; it indicated that large segments of the Old Guard were willing to admit that we were in trouble, and that blind opposition to Roosevelt was no way out.

Field was doubtless gratified, though he had not yet discussed his new outlook publicly. He was not sure, for the moment, precisely what he thought of the New Deal. His awakened sympathies found a counterpart in the compassionate attitudes of the administration; but he was a capitalist too, and a banker, and was reserving judgment on Roosevelt's budgetary policies. He had too much reserve to become an uncritical "enthusiast," and too strong a sense of history to take the New Deal at face value. He knew that it was not a revolution, but he also knew that it was the most complex and delicate governmental overhaul in history. The Russian Revolution had been more violent, tragic, and difficult, but in one sense at least it was simpler: a body of doctrine was there, ready-made, and once the Bolsheviks had consolidated power they had no worries about the traditions of a restless electorate. They were, in their own metaphor, making an omelette, and if anything went wrong it was possible to break a few more eggs. The New Deal was not making an omelette but resuscitating a soufflé, and if anything went wrong there might be no dinner at all. Roosevelt had to work well within a framework of American values—his critics to the contrary notwithstanding—or forfeit support.

5

The Liberty League was a fascinating phenomenon, and its echoes still vibrate, but it was helpless against the New Deal. Field would never have joined it, but if he had not taken his life so firmly in hand he would never have bothered to oppose it either. He might have gone on, unchanged, considering himself complimented if anyone said, "Well, at least Marshall Field never joined the Liberty League." Two views of humanity, directly opposed, were in conflict, and the early Marshall Field would probably have remained above the battle. The dominant conservatives had been living in a world of helplessness and of assumed virtues: nothing could be done about the "natural" inequity of the universe, economic or other. Their sanctions remained pseudoreligious and neomercantile and quasi-Darwinian; they advocated Christian virtues, chief among them resignation and submission to an established order, and they maintained that legislating the economy was tampering with divine and universal law. They harked back to Adam Smith, insisting that self-interest was the mainspring of human activity; few of them had ever read Smith, much less noticed that he had inveighed constantly against the propertied and industrial classes for failing to distinguish between self-interest—a long-run interest that often required restraint and sacrifice—and selfishness. They emphasized the "early American virtues," like self-reliance, and chose to forget that the settlers had often banded together for survival, and were never averse on spiritual grounds to sending for the cavalry, and were in any case a far cry from the unskilled urban victim of assembly-line industrialists and tenement landlords. They feared planning, they feared people unlike themselves, they feared regulation; and on their fears they erected a political philosophy at once timorous and cruel that had nothing to do with the fate and desires of the average citizen.

The liberals also made mistakes. (This distinction between conservative and liberal is open to the usual semantic quibbling. Ambrose Bierce defined a conservative as "a statesman who is enamored of existing evils, as distinguished from the Liberal, who wishes to replace them with others.") In the surge of activity after 1932 there was necessarily a certain amount of experiment for its own sake;

panaceas had been pushed, which provided the conservatives with good ammunition. In the main liberals were men who believed, but did not always say, that no traditional dogma was necessarily sacred, and that if any sort of real democracy was to survive, its procedures and programs had to follow logically from its basic premise: that the people, or their freely elected representatives, were capable of controlling their environment, and were not the hapless victims of holy, immutable, inviolable social laws. The liberals liked planning; they paid little attention to differences of birth or background; and they preferred economic restriction of the powerful to the unlegislated oppression of the weak. When the conservatives defended "competition" the liberals answered that there was no possibility of competing for 95 per cent of the country, wholly dependent on the self-interest of the other 5 per cent; and that those who shouted the word loudest were, given half a chance, monopolists, protectionists, and price fixers, with no more love for true competition than other authoritarians. And without some economic and social justice there could never be any real competition of ideas; if the press, for example, felt responsible only to the upper echelons and to the deductions that tended to congeal the status quo, change and growth toward a healthier society would remain bitterly and painfully slow.

One later view of the New Deal, not unanimous, was that it had preserved the republic by saving it from revolution, right-wing or left, and by effecting necessary changes within the democratic framework. The truth of this was most obvious in 1933; after that first year, as the crisis eased, Americans forgot just how critical it had been. Gen. Hugh S. Johnson said later that no one would ever know "how close we were to collapse and revolution. We could have got a dictator a lot easier than Germany got Hitler"; Johnson was a fiery man but by no means an alarmist radical. Rexford G. Tugwell of the Brain Trust wrote, "I do not think it is too much to say that on March 4 we were confronted with a choice between an orderly revolution—a peaceful and rapid departure from past concepts—and a violent and disorderly overthrow of the whole capitalist structure." Walter Lippmann, not yet an elder statesman but certainly a sober observer, wrote, "At the end of February we were a congeries of panic-stricken mobs and factions. In the hundred

days from March to June we became again an organized nation
confident of our power to provide for our own security and to control our own destiny."

If revolution had come, it would have been bloody; the right was
extremely powerful and the left extremely bitter. Roosevelt was
hated by extremists on both wings (the right called him a communist, the left called him a "social fascist"), but the more powerful,
more vocal, and more dangerous reaction was from the right. It
would have been easier to warp the factitious "American tradition"
into a righteous fascism than into socialism. (It was in the early
'30s that Huey Long made a famous remark the gist of which was
that if fascism came to the United States it would call itself 100 per
cent Americanism.) So much of the New Deal is now firmly mortared into the economic structure of the country that the virulent
hatred of Roosevelt seems, in retrospect, surrealistic and even
psychotic. Probably some industrialists—and some "old-line Americans of $1,200 a year"—*were* so irrational as to believe that com-
munism was on the way,* that free enterprise was expressly
authorized by God, that regulation was Marxist, that the freedoms
of the Bill of Rights were tyranny; but most were simply using any
means at hand to hang on to what they had—money, power, prestige, a soul-satisfying sense of superiority. Marshall Field had
money, power, and prestige; but he had come to realize that they
had little to do with superiority, or even with simple goodness. His
statement that "mere possession of wealth is not in itself creative"
was hardly revolutionary, but the word "creative" is interesting; he
was no longer content with conserving, but sensed that there was
new ground to be broken.

He still traveled in conservative circles, and his friendships were
at first little affected by politics, but he felt more and more that
what his friends called problems were actually opportunities. He
became, first, impatient with their attitudes; but then, as the anti-
Semites and Roosevelt haters, the strikebreakers and quasi-fascists,
became more voluble, he experienced a new emotion: disgust. Too
many of his friends saw the world through their own problems.
They considered poverty natural and high taxes unnatural, Hitler

---

* Thirty years later a Texas oil millionaire said he thought Herbert Hoover was
too socialistic.

an interesting experiment offering hints in the suppression of unrest, labor unions the first step to perdition. Field was impressed by two facts. The first was that the men of his class (with exceptions as usual) were proving themselves by and large to be no gentlemen, no stewards, no willing bearers of responsibility; in a time of crisis they were querulous, egotistical, unfair, and not above flat prevarication. The second was that Roosevelt was making an effort; the President was himself of the upper classes, and was risking permanent obloquy, if not worse, for the sake of the country. Ten years later Field described his reactions:

So much about which we had felt so sure fell about our ears and jolted us to the very core of our beliefs. Was this cataclysm caused by a failure of democracy? Or had democracy ever really been given a fighting chance? These were questions with which our experiences were assailing us.

Like everybody else, I was forced to reconsider everything that I had taken for granted. Ideas that had before been matters of superficial inquiry demanded tougher analysis. Fixed points in my intellectual world had to be subjected to searching criticism in order to determine how far I was merely using them as anchors to avoid setting forth on journeys that promised to be strange and that might therefore prove uncomfortable or even dangerous. The process was not easy, as most of my fellow-citizens, who were under the same compulsion, can bear witness.

And he went on to discuss his conclusions in a few paragraphs that stand as a compact repudiation of the attitudes and behavior of most of his own class during the 1930s, and as a credo to which he was faithful all the rest of his life:

There is, of course, no such thing as an inherent right in private property. Theories to such an effect, like theories concerning the divine right of nobility, were invented by propagandists to justify otherwise untenable positions. What private property any of us enjoys represents the acquiescence of society in our private control of it. It is a privilege Western society has traditionally granted to its stronger or more fortunate members, and, like every privilege, it carries with it certain obligations as a kind of payment for the privilege. Those who neglect the obligations, I am convinced, speed the day when this privilege will be curtailed or perhaps denied. . . .

For the future of democracy to be secure, for freedom to be more than a word, those with financial and political power must regard the constant rejuvenation of freedom as their pressing duty. They must not hold their privileges lightly, and they must regard their obligations very seriously. One cannot help recalling a statement made in a different context by Abraham Lincoln when he told Congress in the dark days of the Civil War that "in giving freedom to the slave we assure freedom to the free—honorable alike in what we give and what we preserve."

He took his stand with Locke and Jefferson in an old stream of liberalism the chief concern of which was man and not ordinances. He wrote about it a decade after his decision; in the 1930s he refrained from rhetoric, saying only, "I got rather disgusted with the Republican Party and I got rather interested in Roosevelt and what he was trying to do." He voted for Roosevelt in 1936, and remained a liberal Democrat for the rest of his life.

6

This period of transformation, or conversion, was critical. On the surface a rich playboy had, through the impact of a Depression and a psychoanalysis on his natural human decency, amplified *noblesse oblige* until it became a budding social conscience. That the change was deeper and more complex is obvious; it included a re-evaluation of all the assumptions by which he had lived. His personal life too was seriously altered. On November 14, 1934, he and Audrey Field were divorced; their outlooks had diverged altogether. Glamour and the excitement of high life had lost their hold on Field; whether or not he was getting any closer to personal happiness, he no longer equated it with fun. As his disenchantment with the Republicans grew, he cared less for the repetitious concentricity of upper-class circles. His interest in racing, for example, ebbed, and his visits to England became rare. He began to read voraciously, concentrating on current public affairs. He attended, and offered, fewer gay parties. His conversation became more political and more frequently disputatious, though he never lost his mildness of manner and gentleness of tone.

In 1936 he was somewhat anomalous as a rich Democrat; that was a challenge, and if it was occasionally uncomfortable it was also exciting, and quite gratifying to a man of generous instincts. But he was becoming something else: a libertarian and a humanist. And among his old friends, that was carrying the thing too far; it was some time before he appreciated the bitterness his defection aroused among the well-to-do, and when he began to implement his ideas he was both astonished and amused at the ferocity of his critics.

All the major themes of the twentieth century had been sounded between 1934 and 1936, and were to resound forcefully in Field's personality: competition, planned economy, civil liberties, race relations, war and peace, authoritarianism and libertarianism, psychiatry, the welfare of children. In the next twenty years he took his stand on each issue as it came up, and suffered opposition that often took the form of hatred and slander. He discovered that it was not enough to be a good Democrat, or a consistent liberal; a talent for infighting was also needed, and the moral courage to reject his critics' more ignoble methods. He was about to undergo the rites of passage imposed upon every man in public life, and to accept without resentment the only reward that proves his value: he was about to make enemies.

When he announced for Roosevelt an old and dear friend, one of Philadelphia's best citizens, who was an enthusiastic sportsman and a staunch Republican, was incredulous. "Nonsense," he said. "No man who can hold a tired horse together like Marshall Field could possibly vote for Roosevelt."

CHAPTER FIVE

I knew that when I heard about Jimmy, a nine-year-old, kept in solitary
confinement for a week, with nothing in the room besides himself but a
board and a bucket, I could line up with him; I felt something of his
loneliness and hurt.

—MARSHALL FIELD,
Speech, May, 1952

I N LATE 1935, WHEN HE ACQUIRED A RENOIR, Field joked about
the changes in his life: "I'm changing my type. Just swapped some
sporting prints for a nude." His appetite for culture was greatly improved, and his mind for liberal arts, which had never been severely
taxed, worked overtime. He bought impressionists and postimpres-
sionists, caring less now for Romneys and Raeburns and Gains-
boroughs. (By 1939 he was able to make two gifts to the Metropolitan Museum of Art: the Douanier Rousseau's "Spring in the
Valley of the Bièvre" and a Gauguin "Tahitian Landscape," the
latter of which he gave anonymously.) His interest in music quick-
ened; he had been a member of the board of the New York Philharmonic-Symphony Society since 1923, and its president since
1934—happily active in both capacities—and now he found himself listening, as well as administering, with greater pleasure. He
enjoyed an occasional movie, caring more for relaxation than for
the art of the cinema. And he became a tireless reader. His background was good in the English classics, and he could refer easily
to Shakespeare, Thackeray, and Conrad (he neglected Jane Aus-
ten); he dipped often into lesser writers, like Kipling, Galsworthy,
Wilde, and now and then reread some of Maugham. He cared little

for poetry, except for an occasional narrative piece: Edward Arlington Robinson's *Tristan,* Stephen Vincent Benét's *John Brown's Body.* His tastes were obviously conservative. Philosophy attracted him for the first time; he preferred Santayana to all others, but he grappled with Bergson and went back to Plato, whom he remembered well from his university days; now he felt rather less sympathy for the rigidity of Platonic categories and hierarchies, and far more sympathy for the poor exiled poets. Political economy and current events were unavoidable; after a brief bout with Keynes he was likely to refresh himself with a biography of Liszt or Wagner or Van Gogh and then plunge back into the Beards' *Rise of American Civilization.* He had been a slow and thorough reader, who rarely reread; tempted to pick up an old favorite, he would usually be arrested by the knowledge that so much on Lincoln and Jefferson, whom he revered, lay untouched. Now he read faster, and for edification more than amusement. Books flowed in and out of the house; he was like a man who had just learned to read. His tastes in music, too, were catholic. He loved the opera, preferring Wagner but happy with whatever was on. At concerts he enjoyed Beethoven, and listened to Stravinsky with interest and occasionally pleased astonishment; Mozart, though, was his true love. In music particularly his delight was uncritical; with books and paintings he was more easily dissatisfied or displeased.

He still hunted, sailed, rode, and took long vacations. He was drinking very little and food tasted better. As his personal problems receded he turned his mind to a wide range of activities; observed politics closely; financed an investigation of suicide by Dr. Zilboorg —surely a kind of functional memorial to his own father—the results of which were read at a psychoanalytic congress in February of 1937; took more interest in the character of his own investments, and somewhat less in Field, Glore; became interested in public education, fiscal policy, the dissemination of culture; even his old interest in chess was revived.

Alone, he might have found all this simply distracting; but he was lucky. He had married again on January 15, 1936, and his third wife was the perfect companion for a trip into a new world.

Not that she was a liberal. Ruth Pruyn Phipps had been the wife of Ogden Phipps, living in highly conservative circles, and her own family background was Hudson Valley Dutch, well-to-do and traditional, aware of its responsibilities. Her great-grandfather, Robert Hewson Pruyn, had served Lincoln for four years at some personal sacrifice, leaving his comfortable bank-president's life to become Minister to Japan; his brother, John V. S. L. Pruyn, had established a citizens' committee in 1867 to investigate the care being offered the destitute and insane by New York State; Field's still unspecified desires to improve the world were supplemented by the Pruyns' consciousness of those obligations which Field later called the price of privilege. In her first marriage Ruth Field had been a good mother and a good hostess, quite popular—being a very pretty brunette with snapping blue eyes, an irresistibly charming low voice, and a mind of her own—on the frivolous levels of Long Island society. The Phippses and the Fields had met frequently in the early 1930s; Field had liked Mrs. Phipps, then been enchanted by her, then fallen in love with her.

Gossips said later that Ruth Field had been a flaming liberal all along, which was simply not true; she was a most conservative woman by birth and background, and politics had nothing to do with the marriage. But she had Field's respect, which added to the magic between them. It was apparently a permanent enchantment: fifteen years later a friend, watching them say goodbye before a three-day separation, turned away smiling; it was as though Field were off to the wars indefinitely. The marriage followed difficult years. Field understood the anguishes of divorce and Mrs. Phipps's fears about her two boys, Harry and Bobby; he was no less sensitive than she to the personal costs of broken marriages. Emotions were bruised, and there were delays. The wedding took place in the Pruyns' flat in River House, an elegant apartment building at the eastern end of 52d Street in New York City, before the bride's parents and a very few friends, Russell Forgan among them. It was a quiet wedding, and gave rise to only one anecdote, peripheral at that; Field liked to tell it as a joke on himself. His domestic staff had planned their annual party for the night of January 15, and when Field was invited to drop in by his old friend and major-domo Robert Hider, he was forced to decline. "I'm being married that day," he said. Hider was quite pleased: "Oh, well, of course, sir. Congratulations." Field continued regretful about the party: "I do hope it's a success." But Hider was still thinking of the wedding: "Yes, sir, indeed I do too. Other times have not been entirely fortunate."

This one was.

2

Field was making new friends. His life was full of Democrats, for one thing, and he was intrigued by the new breed of educated, imaginative, impassioned public servants that the New Deal nurtured. He was not blandly uncritical, and never just "followed along" with his new liberal friends. He had the example of James Warburg, whom he respected highly. Warburg had broken with Roosevelt in 1935, and had returned to the fold only when it became obvious, during the campaign of 1936, that the alternatives were impossible. Warburg's disagreement was with Roosevelt's monetary theory; he was violently opposed to manipulation of the price of gold (in an inflationary direction) as a solution to the problem of commodity prices. Field watched with a sympathetic but wary eye; he was learning to analyze and evaluate, and was alert. When the Securities and Exchange Commission was promulgating regulations in 1934 and 1935, he and Forgan had run down to Washington to talk to James M. Landis, its chairman, arguing energetically against rules that would reduce investment banking to a sort of super-bookkeeping; at one point Field remarked hotly, "I'm damned if I'll let them take my business away from me."

But in 1936 his interest in banking diminished, as his interest in public service (by the private citizen) grew. For one thing the social usefulness of banking was at best moot; for another, his participation was financially futile: whatever he made went out in taxes. What form public service might take was an open question, and he worried about it for a time. The beginnings of an answer were supplied not by Field's old friends, not by a British tradition, not by Dr. Zilboorg, not by Roosevelt or his administration, but by a lawyer from New York City with a genius for personal relationships, an apparently infinite understanding, and a deep commitment to humanism. His name was Louis S. Weiss, and for fifteen years afterward he was Marshall Field's close friend, personal attorney, and constant adviser.

Field had been introduced to Weiss in 1935 by Howard Cullman, with whom Field had served on the board of the Beekman-Downtown Hospital. He and Ruth Phipps had lunched with Weiss one day, when Mrs. Phipps had been separated from her husband, and was reluctant to proceed with a divorce so long as the future of her sons, Harry and Bobby, remained uncertain, a matter of dispute and possible heartbreak. Weiss offered intelligent advice that proved sound. Field had also had a tax problem—one of those chronic, nagging matters of interpretation—and his own attorneys had managed to pin it down, but not to resolve it. Weiss solved the problem, saving Field large amounts of money. More important, he impressed Field as a rare combination of compassion and integrity, intellect and insight, business sense and altruism. Weiss was a voluble, gregarious, brilliant lawyer; a zestful family man with a love of the festive; a born arbitrator with an uncanny knack for finding some small area of agreement and building on it. He could talk intelligently about almost anything, and the quality of his concentration was rare: whatever the subject, when he spoke to *you* he shut out the rest of the world. (When he died the occasional nurseryman at his country place wrote, "When I was with Mr. Weiss I felt the only thing he cared about was his trees.") Field was also impressed by a resolve Weiss had made as a young man, and kept: once he was making a decent living for his family, half his time and energy would go to philanthropy.

Weiss's background, too, was interesting. For one thing, he was the only man Field ever knew who was born on a farm in Manhattan. (An approach to the George Washington Bridge now covers the site.) His father, from a small town in Pennsylvania, had been poor, and had worked his way through Yale Law School; he had been a man of no special social concerns, and had practiced law in a dry, almost weary manner, but he was a man of great dignity and rectitude, and his sere approach to the statutes masked a passion for justice. He was also passionate about learning, and that passion too he passed along to his two sons and two daughters.* Louis was

---

* One of Weiss's sisters, Carol Weiss King, also became a lawyer. She was famous for defending left-wingers whose civil liberties had been jeopardized, and was

the younger son, and grew up with a greed for ideas. (He had read Freud, for example, before the First World War, and was challenged and stimulated by him.) Compassion and intellect, mingling, became a commitment to social justice that transcended politics. Weiss was by no means a metaphysician; his interest was not the principle of philanthropy, or the function of charity in this or that society. It was rather the immediate predicament of the hungry man, the homeless child, the marginal citizen. But he was too much at home in history, in political thought, in psychology, in economics, to neglect those causes of injustice that arose from the structure of society itself, from its built-in myths and immanent tensions. Weiss had a sharp intelligence, and no reluctance at all to cutting through old patterns and prejudices. He was also intense and persuasive, with much of the teacher in him; indeed, he had first planned to be a teacher.

The meeting of these two men was lucky for both. Field, with his desire to act, to participate, was moving in Weiss's direction; Weiss, with his ideas and strong feelings, welcomed a congenial and thoughtful ally. They became friends quickly, meeting in New York often, traveling together to Chicago. Their relationship centered on work, and was never diffused to a bridge-and-barbecue partnership; the Weisses and the Fields dined together formally perhaps half a dozen times in ten years. Field enjoyed Weiss's erudition; the lawyer, a year younger than Field, had loved poetry in his earlier days, and was as likely to quote Byron as Bentham. Once more Field was being impressed with the essential unity of men's lives, with the impossibility of divorcing the mind from the belly, morals from society, government from culture; but he was also acquiring a fuller notion of the infinite variety of needs and desires within that unity.

Neither man was interested in reorganizing the United States, or in stunning the world with some original political theory. If nineteenth-century capitalism had fallen upon evil days, the United

---

consequently often maligned. It was she who interested Wendell Willkie in the Schneidermann case, which he successfully argued before the Supreme Court in 1942. Without any personal introduction to him, she had sent him the brief and the court's writ of certiorari. Willkie saw the justice of her case, and bravely argued the cause of an admitted Communist. Field and Weiss were sometimes "linked" to her by antiliberals; but regardless of her own political beliefs, which critics never bothered to determine, she and her brother were not close.

States remained a magnificent experiment in human freedom, committed from its birth to more liberty, more tolerance, a freer pluralism than any country in the world; it was the only nation in history that had charged itself (in writing!) with the pursuit of happiness as a national goal—and to the sentimental but perfectly clear-eyed Weiss this apparently gratuitous stroke of hedonism was an acknowledgment of a deep psychological truth. What concerned the two men was not so much the preservation of freedom as its extension, and the New Deal offered them hope, and a favorable climate. Their quarrel was not with those who claimed that only unrestricted capitalism could bring men freedom and happiness; that claim had been exploded by a century of boom-and-bust and by the growing rebellion of its presumed beneficiaries. Their argument was primarily with those who denied that freedom and happiness were important, or who believed that fidelity to ancient doctrine was more important. They saw not only a third of a nation ill fed, ill clad, ill housed, but nine-tenths of a nation confused, in the grip of conflicting mythologies, frightened by the possibility that self-improvement might be sacrilegious, taking shelter in old prejudices. Field believed that without education, democracy had no chance; he also believed that without food, shelter, and clothing education became a luxury. He had already pondered mass education, though he deferred action. He had also thought again about low-rent housing, though with some hesitation: he owned a great deal of real estate, and would be open to charges of self-interest; he had been through one bad experience, with the Garden Apartments in Chicago; and the government itself was entering the field.

His discussions with Weiss were sporadic, though intense, and lasted for several months. In late 1936 the two boarded the Twentieth Century for Chicago, and sat up late, deep in conversation. A contrasting pair: Field stocky (he had been putting on weight), debonair, beautifully dressed, puffing occasionally at a pipe, the picture of patrician distinction; Weiss intense, bespectacled, gesturing and quoting as he argued, rumpled, waving a cigarette, the picture of dedicated brilliance. On that trip Field made his first decision, and it may have been a surprise even to him: the place to start was in child welfare.

3

Over the previous couple of years other decisions had been made. Mussolini had decided to bring culture to Ethiopia. The United States had passed, and then extended, a Neutrality Act, carefully amended by the House Foreign Relations Committee so that while the President might declare an embargo on arms shipments to belligerents, nothing would hinder sales of oil or steel. Japan had formally abrogated the Washington Naval Treaty. Senator Nye's investigations of the profiteering munitions industry had confirmed Americans in their fairly general (and fairly sound) belief that wars were a matter of profit to the few and death to the many; American isolationism was much strengthened. The Wagner Act gave labor the right to organize and to engage in collective bargaining; the Social Security Act completed the disintegration of American moral fiber by dragging the Federal government into unemployment compensation and offering the great mass of the aged (of whom there were more every year) an alternative to misery by attrition. Hitler had entered the Rhineland in direct violation of the Treaty of Versailles; resistance to the reoccupation was weakened by a vague awareness that the Treaty of Versailles had been unjust, and a more specific awareness in Europe's privy councils that the Nazis, while their relations with Russia were equivocal, were at least a firm bulwark against excessive liberalism. General Franco had revolted against the Spanish Republic.

The Depression was not over; it seems true in retrospect that it was the war, and not the New Deal, that ended it. Its attendant miseries had, however, been much alleviated. Unemployment was still high, buying power low; critics were more bitterly vociferous, partisans more defiantly hopeful, than ever. Roosevelt was re-elected with a majority that was almost dangerous: better than 3 to 2, with an electoral vote of 523 to Landon's 8. The minority parties were interesting. There was a Prohibitionist, as usual, who won some 37,000 dry and cracked voices; the Socialist Labor candidate trailed badly with only 13,000; the Communists, that ever-present, Gargantuan threat to American institutions, managed to muster 80,000 votes against the "Social Fascist" Roosevelt; and Norman Thomas's quadrennial calm, plausible effort in behalf of socialism was approved by about 190,000. The real third party in 1936 was the Union Party, headed by Republican Rep. William Lemke of North Dakota; it drew support from the rabid fringes of the Liberty League and from outspoken American adherents to the newer forms of European *Realpolitik,* chief among whom were a man of the cloth, the Rev. Charles Coughlin, and a political metaphysician of the feudal persuasion, Gerald L. K. Smith. This party amassed 890,000 votes, approximately what Norman Thomas had received in 1932. Obviously the New Deal, by assimilating the less radical goals of socialism, had decimated the American left; the third force in American politics was, and would remain for many years, the "old-line Americans of $1,200 a year" who were the objects of so much right-wing solicitude. Poor Huey Long had been assassinated, and missed this small vindication.

Field meanwhile had a private life to enjoy. He was not by any means a figure in the New Deal *; he approved of Roosevelt but was not interested in personal participation. And if he was groping toward active liberalism, he remained a rich man. In the spring of 1936 he leased a six-bedroom flat at 740 Park Avenue; a year later he bought Chelsea, a 13,000-acre plantation near Ridgeland, South Carolina, saturated with quail. He had thought—not for the first time—of retiring from business altogether, and had decided that he would need a more comfortable boat. He found a good one in the yards at Port Washington. Over the next few years *Corisande II* was a happy vehicle for the Fields: Marshall and Ruth, Bettine, and the Phipps boys. (Marshall, Jr., and Barbara, no longer children, had begun to lead their own lives.) The family's summer headquarters in Maine was Dark Harbor; *Corisande II* took them there; and on extended vacations Field and the children raced sailboats against the families of Winthrop Aldrich and Douglas Dillon (races Tuesday, Wednesday, Thursday, Saturday; a cup awarded at the end of each season), who were the closest of friends ashore but cutthroat enemies in a race.

Field was happy. His friends were not sure what to make of all

---

* He is not even mentioned in Schlesinger's *Age of Roosevelt,* and his name does not come into Harold Ickes's voluminous diary until 1940.

this: he held forth as a liberal, and his wife was coming to agree with him; yet he bought Chelsea. He had not yet come to the attention of middle-class or administration liberals, who might have wondered just how serious he was; on the other hand he was not yet being called a "traitor to his class." He rode, hunted, swam, played tennis and golf. (He gave up polo at about this time.) Outwardly there seemed to be little more than a conversational change in the man.

His friends were all the more surprised, then, when he left Field, Glore and Company. He did not break with the firm; he simply bowed out late in 1936. His interests lay elsewhere. It was a good firm; he was proud of his part in it; he considered investment banking a useful and constructive profession. But he did not depend on the firm—taxes took his profits anyway—and he needed his time. He may have considered his departure the first in a series of withdrawals the end of which would be his retirement in philanthropic works; if so, he was wrong, but there was no indication in 1936 that he was considering further gainful employment. His investment in Field, Glore was substantial, and his manner of leaving financially courteous: he left his equity in the firm as a non-interest-bearing loan, without recourse (a polite phrase meaning that if the firm went broke he would have no claim on it). In 1937 the firm became Glore, Forgan and Company. Many of Field's friends were mildly astonished. They did not know that he had been allowing many of his affiliations to lapse since 1932. Between that year and 1937 he gave up directorships in twenty-three corporations,* positions on the finance committee or executive committee of five,† and two trusteeships (of The Brookings Institution and the Bank for Savings of the City of New York). He had resigned some of these offices because new SEC regulations limited interlocking directo-

---

* American & Continental, American Light & Traction, Bank of Manhattan, Manhattan Co., Continental Chicago, Chicago & Northwestern R.R., Chicago, St. Paul, Minneapolis & Omaha R.R., Columbia Gas & Electric, Continental Illinois National Bank and Trust, European Electric Ltd., Field, Glore, General Rayon, Guaranty Trust, Italian Superpower, Libbey-Owens-Ford Glass, Owens-Illinois Glass, Staten Island Edison, Toledo Glass, Ulen Engineering, Ulen & Co., United Light & Power, Willys-Overland, and Bank of the Manhattan Co., which last was not the same as the third or fourth companies above.

† American Light & Traction, Bank of the Manhattan Co., Chicago & Northwestern R.R., Continental Insurance Co., United Light & Power.

rates, but on the whole he was pleased at the chance to free his time and energies for new interests.

One of those interests being current events, he took an immediate look at the Spanish Civil War, which broke out in July of 1936 and was an education to him on several counts. He disapproved of Franco from the start, and seemed genuinely amazed, and worried, that the revolt showed such strength. To him it was akin to the war in Ethiopia and the reoccupation of the Rhineland; he was quicker than before to judge events as "progressive" or "reactionary," and to rejoice or lament accordingly. The position taken by England, France, and the United States troubled him; he thought it not only a matter of international law, but also one of good politics, to support the Spanish Republic, and was dismayed at the transparency of the democracies' weakness; their righteous embargoes were clearly a form of aid to Franco, in view of the German and Italian supplies (and troops) coming in on the rebels' side.* But he knew little about Spain. He was shocked to learn that there were not enough educated people outside the Church to provide teachers for any appreciable part of the younger generation, and that only the rudiments of a school system existed; and that consequently communication, the simple dissemination of history and news, played a small part in the national life. Spain was a desperately poor country, and civil war was not making it richer. There was insufficient food, there were not enough hospitals, housing was often primitive.

The American attitude was, generally speaking, casual during the first year of the war. Many liberals in the administration fretted and chafed, but kept silent; some private citizens—usually those who had already been worrying about the Axis—were alarmed and an-

---

* A quarter-century later United States congressmen were felicitating one another on the 25th anniversary of the "Spanish people's uprising against Communism," which is unusually nonsensical even for the elected members of that august body. There were no Communists in the Spanish government in 1936, and only 15 Communist members in a parliament of 470. Franco had Italian aid from the beginning; the first Russian aid reached the government a year after the war broke out. Franco's coup was an antirepublican military revolt and not a crusade for freedom; it was also (in retrospect, anyway) an unmistakable prelude to Hitler's inhuman adventures. But the Spanish War has since become a prop for opportunists: liberals who ignored it can now prove their good faith by nostalgia for the Loyalists, and pious congressmen, or impious congressmen with pious constituencies, can praise Franco and prove that they are right-thinking.

gered; Roman Catholics tended to favor Franco, who would presumably restore the Church to its former influence; but the mass of good Americans just didn't care. We had been legislating to keep ourselves out of Europe's backyard quarrels, and to most of us Spain was no place to begin making exceptions: an almost moribund country, comatose since the seventeenth century, connoting only bullfights and guitars. Roosevelt sympathized with the Republic but was helpless: he was committed to firm neutrality, and the electorate was hypersensitive about it, and he had a campaign coming up. After the elections it was too late: inertia had become policy.

Field's efforts were humanitarian: he set about raising $250,000 for the purchase of wheat to be sent to the Spanish government. He thought it would be easy. But the experience was grim, and a sharp note of disenchantment—almost bitterness—was superimposed on his growing disillusionment. Of all his moneyed friends only one— Gerard Swope—was enthusiastic. Some "didn't want to get mixed up" in the political issues; some thought it would be a disservice to the Spaniards, because Franco would end the war more quickly against a weak Republic; some favored Franco outright, and refused to help the government; some simply had no interest in so degenerate and medieval a corner of Europe.

Field was learning.

4

Considering his first burst of approval, and the tendency of a convert to become *plus royaliste que le roi même,* Field observed the New Deal with great caution. "They" did not approach him, of course; in 1932 he had been a socialite firmly for Hoover, and if he was displaying unusual interest in social and economic developments, he was doing so quietly and privately. He had no desire to participate in government. He remained a conservative in many respects, and reserved the right to criticize. There had been some justice in Warburg's warnings about inflation—during 1937, in fact, Field bought real estate as a hedge against the possibility; he had been obliged to argue energetically with the SEC in its early days; he had a banker's distaste for deficit spending without a healthy tax base—though he preferred public works programs to relief; and in foreign policy the administration was, temporarily at least, hog-tied. The ebb and flow of power within the government made prediction difficult.

In 1937 Field's circumspection was justified spectacularly, when the President announced his proposal to pack the Supreme Court. The ensuing battle was the toughest in Roosevelt's career, and resulted in his most crushing defeat, though it apparently frightened the Court into a reluctant acknowledgment that there had been changes since the second Grant administration. Field opposed the President's plan sharply. He was clear about one reason: it was necessary, and often desirable, to experiment with methods, but sharp changes in the structure of our institutions were dangerous. His second reason was not altogether clear in his own mind, but was close to an idea that lay at the heart of his thinking later on: that any enterprise, any institution, any innovation could live only in an organic relationship to the society in which it arose. Filling a real need, deriving support from the people, it would survive; failing that, it deserved to perish. He did not see the court-packing scheme so clearly and simply, but his conservative instincts resisted attempts to bypass the legislative process—even if the ultimate goal was congenial to him. He was aware—as who was not—that the Court was fogyish, much given to obsolete dogma and to the citation of conservative rather than liberal precedents (both are always available); but it was the Supreme Court. It had been, and would be again, ahead of its times; the price of that was its right to hang back. More important, and to Field, with his British background and ingrained *noblesse oblige,* perhaps most important, was a principle of political morality: if, as he had come to believe, the welfare of the people was one of the responsibilities of a just government, then that government must proceed in an unalterably just manner: no democratic end could be achieved by arbitrary means, and a government that had accepted votes for a promise of justice was obliged to stay honest or forfeit support. By July Roosevelt had lost, amid great public clamor, and Field was relieved. He had been equally relieved when, in March, April, and May, the Supreme Court, with a nervous glance over its shoulder, upheld the constitutionality of several New Deal measures, chief among them the Wagner Act of 1935.

That Act, which guaranteed to labor the right to select its own representatives and to bargain collectively, accelerated labor's drive toward independent power. Management resisted, and the labor war was intensified. Field did not know that in 1933 Secretary of Labor Frances Perkins, forbidden by the mayor of a company town to use town property for a question-and-answer session, had ingeniously moved her meeting into the United States Post Office building; but he was acutely aware of the strikes, shootings, riots, and beatings that characterized labor relations in the mid-thirties. Some of the violence was approved, or even authorized, by men he knew well, men with whom he had served on various boards; some of it was labor's rebellion. Field favored the unions, but realized again that he had a good deal to learn about labor. He set about learning it.

But nothing, he had discovered, could be studied in isolation. What he learned about child welfare, Spain, deficit spending, taught him something about labor. Or race relations: Negroes as a group were beginning to agitate for their rights, and took heart from the New Deal; Eleanor Roosevelt's flat egalitarianism was new and exhilarating from a First Lady. Or public works. Social Security— Bismarck, of all people, had introduced it to Germany in the 1880s. AAA and TVA and CCC and NRA. People were talking, quoting, arguing, doing. Democrats and Republicans stood more distinctly apart than they had since the Civil War, but both parties were split and fringed. Extreme right-wingers warned that Roosevelt would spend the country to death, and then offered their own give-away programs. Progressives and radicals were no less isolationist than protofascists. Southern Democrats campaigned as Roosevelt's friends and then voted with Republicans in Congress. There were progressives who were extreme nationalists, and conservative bankers who believed that monetary problems were ineluctably international. The Secretary of Agriculture, Henry Wallace, who shared Roosevelt's faith in the people, and who coupled a background of great accomplishment in scientific agriculture with a streak of mystical idealism, opposed American recognition of Soviet Russia as adamantly as any rock-ribbed Republican. William Randolph Hearst maintained that anyone accused of being a fascist was most likely a real, 100 per cent American; certain farmer-laborites maintained that all real Americans were radicals.

Being for the moment outside the battle, Field had time to sift the confusions and complexities. Occasionally his reactions were quite personal. It was appalling to note that child labor in the textile industry—the phrase itself must have recalled those horrifying vignettes of nineteenth-century Manchester—had been finally outlawed only in 1933, by the NRA. His dismay was compounded by the fact that Marshall Field and Company owned mills in North Carolina, and he was relieved to find that its labor policies, while not ideally advanced, had always been more liberal than those of its often Neanderthal competitors. And within a few miles of Caumsett he had firsthand experience of the rationale of child labor: men were jobless and hungry, and in other times their children might have been out earning pennies. Field's first step in political economy was local and paternalistic, but welcome. With the help of the American Luggage Association he created Suffolk Craftsmen, Inc., in the early '30s, rented a two-story building in Huntington, Long Island, and put thirty-five people to work manufacturing "different kinds of good luggage which was sold wholesale in New England, New York and Chicago and in parts of the South," as John Clark later wrote. "After the local labor situation became better Mr. Field sold his interest to [Sam] Balterman [who had been the plant manager; Clark was president and represented Field], who continued on his own for several more years. . . . Thank the good Lord I don't have to pick out the colored linings for women's suitcases ever again." Field's was not the smug satisfaction of the benevolent capitalist: he knew many of the employees, and their despair was not abstract. The firm cost far less than relief would have; profit and loss aside, Field knew how degrading charity could be, and preferred a business arrangement. ("Incontrovertible, unfortunately, is the inference that the power to distribute philanthropy is likely to give the one who dispenses it a feeling of superiority over the person or group who may be the recipient," he wrote later; he knew.)

But his primary interest remained child welfare. Louis Weiss had pointed out that a healthy society could not be created by fiat; that one generation carved out law which the next polished to habit and custom; and that unhealthy, ill-educated children were not likely to become the kind of adults who could shape their own destinies. Whatever the New Deal did now, or did not do, the children of the '30s would make the world of the '50s, and stopgap soup kitchens were not the answer to their problems. Nor were unctuous benefactors; for every Oliver Twist there were a thousand underfed, undereducated potential Bill Sykeses.

The intellectual justice of Weiss's case was obvious; more, Field's affections were engaged immediately. He loved his own children extravagantly, and knew how lucky they were, never having lacked. He had lost father and grandfather at twelve; losing his father, as Freud says somewhere, is one of the two or three crucial events of a man's life, and Field had been still a boy. And Field, still relatively apolitical, was a good man for welfare: entrenched politicians, doughtily defending the taxpayer, consistently resisted efforts at reform from within, using political threats and red tape, but as a well-known outsider of impressive social standing Field did not immediately menace the existing power structure.

Weiss introduced him to a remarkable woman, his first guide through the labyrinth of child welfare. Justine Wise Polier * was not only an authority on welfare and compensation but also a veteran of strikes, relief battles, fights with Frank Hague's henchmen, the war against municipal corruption; she was a lawyer and the stormy petrel of the New York City administration; and she was a lady who had no use for sentimentality. She was the daughter of Rabbi Stephen Wise, a liberal so outspoken that Mencken had tried to make fun of him; and Roosevelt had been her friend since she was a baby. She was not long out of Bryn Mawr, Radcliffe, Barnard, and the Yale Law School, but from her the Fields took an intensive seminar in big-city politics, with animadversions on the labor movement and state and Federal government.

Her various reports on abuses in compensation, on antilabor bias in relief administration, on unemployment, and on medical costs and insurance practices had been of immediate working value to Mayor La Guardia, burdened with the remnants of James J. Walker's corrupt coterie and with a press that steadfastly refused to

---

* She became Mrs. Shad Polier in 1937. When the Fields met her she was the widow of Lee Tutin, who had been a brilliant young professor of law.

see relief as anything but a grab bag or a source of sensational "exposés." In 1936 La Guardia offered her a judgeship on the Court of Domestic Relations, but she was more interested in social problems than in individual cases; she preferred Magistrates Court, where strike cases and civil liberties cases would demand decisions that might, by a slow accumulation of precedent, work a permanent change in the judicial attitude toward labor. But La Guardia asked her to look into the Children's Court; its inadequacies worried him, and brought out all his strong sentimental anxieties. She looked; she was appalled; she accepted a temporary appointment— for thirty days, renewable ad infinitum—and tried to make a start on cleaning it up. It had resembled the magistrates' courts of eighteenth-century England. Representation was bumbling, inadequate, and indifferent; language barriers were ignored; families were separated with small reason or kept together with less; and there were simply no facilities for the kind of compassionate counseling that tempers justice with mercy.

The judge accepted a second thirty-day appointment, during which time she became embroiled in a violent quarrel with the mayor and Gen. Hugh Johnson of the WPA (the latter had vilified New Yorkers as slackers and spongers). She made it up with the mayor quickly. There was real and strong affection between the two (it was probably impossible to know La Guardia at all well and not be fond of him) and they had hated the dispute. La Guardia called, sent his car, had a long talk with her in his office, embraced her, and offered her a ten-year term as judge of the Children's Court. She accepted.

What happened next caught Field's imagination and sympathies, when she told him about it, more than all the rest. In 1936 Children's Court was an unconscionable mess. It was always full, for one thing; aside from the more common trespasses of slum children, many of them now lived so close to starvation that they habitually stole to eat. And the tensions, with a couple of million sullen, marginal citizens squeezed into filthy, decayed tenements, were terrific; in those conditions misdemeanors can become a way of life through sheer hopeless frustration. The easy way out for the officer of the court was to label the children "delinquent." If they were over twelve, and the delinquency was felonious, they could be sent to the State Training School. But for the others, many thousands, under twelve or minor transgressors, the answer was private organizations: homes or special schools.

These were run mainly by religious groups, each of which took care of its own. The Roman Catholics and the Jews accepted their charges without question; but Protestant facilities were limited to whites, and most Negroes are Protestant. Peopled by the oppressed and rejected, Harlems were bad enough in normal times; even if there were jobs, Negroes lived in a world of difference, of closed doors, of forced solidarity and justified bitterness, unable to be individuals, obliged by a hostile (the polite word is "unthinking," which is a lie; it was hostile) white society to consider themselves always Negroes, always special, never just people; obliged to suffer the condescension and clichés of the stupid, damned if they lost to despair and anarchy, patronized if they won out. In 1937 it was far worse. There were no jobs, and the few that opened up—even on the menial level to which Negroes were condemned—went to whites. Negro children were in a desperate spot: they were pushed, pulled, and battered toward the "antisocial" by every possible influence, and when they got into trouble there was no hope for them. There was nowhere to go.

The judge's reaction was characteristically unjudicial: she got good and mad. Poor La Guardia, who in the name of New York City would take on any opposition up to and including the President, could not fight the city itself, and when Mrs. Polier set before him a report on twenty-five instances (out of thousands) of flagrant injustice, all evidence of the rankest segregation, the mayor too simmered and percolated. For the moment there was not much to be done about it. La Guardia threw his weight behind expanded municipal services. If private organizations were so fastidious in suffering little children to come unto them, then the city would do the job; and he encouraged Mrs. Polier to keep hunting for private help.

By then Mrs. Polier had met Marshall Field, and the first lesson he learned from her was a good one: that there can be no effective child welfare without good race relations. (Again, he was to generalize that later: there could be no effective *anything* in society without good race relations, preferably so good that people forgot to think about them. But that condition was, and is, a long way off.) To start him off Mrs. Polier introduced him to a very wise woman, and an expert in child welfare, Agnes King Inglis. Miss Inglis, knowing how complex and sensitive an area child welfare was, educated him thoroughly. She talked, she gave him books (not by any means easy books), she discussed conflicting theories. So did another friend, Sophie van Senden Theis; and these two ladies urged him to go out into the field and see for himself.

He did. He sat in Children's Court and listened. He made a tour of existing facilities, and what he found was humiliating to him—an American version of Manchester charity, consisting largely of S.P.C.C. shelters built in the 1870s, when even Marshall Field I would probably have thought them insufficient. These were temporary homes for the orphaned and "wayward," and were presided over by genteel descendants of the original nice ladies who cleansed their souls one afternoon a week by bringing light to the less fortunate. Field had many friends on the board of the S.P.C.C., and had put off his visits on the reasonable grounds that the shelters were run by responsible people and could not be so bad; he was wrong. In Boston, Buffalo, Chicago, he saw the vile bodies. They had food and a place to sleep—which was, in 1938, something—but that was about all. Spiritual guidance was available, if any of the children felt the need of humility and forbearance, but there was no education, no psychiatry, no recreation, and in sum no hope. Fifty years earlier those homes had been all that society offered, and without them there was nothing. But in half a century they had not changed. They were an apology by the generous rich to the God who had made them rich enough to be generous, and while they might have been restful luxuries to a ten-year-old mill hand, they offered no hope of rehabilitation, of citizenship, of productive (much less happy) life to their tenants. Field returned from his tour determined not to reform them, but to have them abolished. The days of needle-point-and-New-Testament charity were numbered; social work was a profession now and not a hobby; psychiatry was a science and not a dirty joke; society was not Society.

Field was especially interested in establishing diagnostic services for serious emotional problems. If treatment were made available, more children could remain with their parents. But there were many parents who refused such treatment, and that posed knotty problems. The delinquent could be housed and cared for; but what about the predelinquent, the younger child, the disturbed child? A partial answer was clinics for social and psychiatric work within the Children's Court itself. Parents who declined to place their children in the hands of diabolical, meddling doctors and social workers were likely to change their minds once the children were in the toils of the law. Social work was still suspect, and so was psychiatry; the suggestion that their children needed help often angered parents, who apparently preferred to think of their offspring as vicious rather than sick. (Social workers themselves were divided on several issues, though united on the need for action. Roughly speaking, those with a sociological orientation, which included those of the political left, liked to deal with the child in the total context of his family and society. Those with a psychiatric orientation put more stress on specific individual problems. Of course the approaches overlapped. The quarrels were occasionally bitter, but were kept within bounds by the presence of the children, whose needs were immediate and indisputable, and of the enemy—the many who would have been delighted to see social workers annihilate one another.) The public shared, to a great extent, Gen. Robert Wood's contempt for "the city social workers," which was itself only a special case of Herbert Spencer's Social Darwinism. Field's attitude was by now free of that particular cant, and was reminiscent of Robert Owen's, back in 1813, in *A New View of Society*. Modern ideas about juvenile delinquency were not much different from Owen's: he believed that it was an inevitable result of the stresses and strains of economic hardship and emotional disturbance, and that the only way to save children from it was to get hold of them early and improve their living conditions.*

Field worked hard. He addressed himself to four different goals. First, abolition of the S.P.C.C. shelters. Second, an experimental program to find foster homes for Negro children. Third, the establishment (or expansion) of diagnostic services within the Children's

---

* The comparison ends right there. Field was no Utopian; even more important, he never felt, as Owen always did, that he had a monopoly on truth and that if people would only do what he said the world would be perfect.

Court. Fourth, direct support for an institution in Esopus, New York, recently inherited by the Protestant Episcopal Missionary Society and projected as a home for troubled youngsters and the destitute aged. It was called Wiltwyck, and in September of 1938 Field and Mrs. Polier toured the grounds and discussed cash with the home's administrators. Their ideas were good, their resources low. Field offered sufficient capital for renovation of the existing facilities and the addition of separate facilities for old women; money for case work and psychiatric services; and a guarantee of the annual budget for three years, after which the Society would be on its own. He saw the need to go beyond conventional charities; his deeper concern was for attitudes, for climates. Refurbishing the S.P.C.C. shelters would perpetuate archaic modes; Wiltwyck, firmly in the twentieth century, offered real hope. From 1938 on the fight would be for nonsectarian, integrated welfare, with local, state, and Federal participation.

Of course Field was called a "do-gooder," particularly after 1940, when he was more in the public eye. The word was used as a cheap sneer, and directed at those who believed that poverty was a social, and not a personal, sin. It was a favorite of people who insisted that the unemployed and destitute were not victims of a social order but good-for-nothing villains, and it was much brayed by those numerous and noisy critics—including a large part of the press—whose only objection to relief was that it went to the needy. Many of those critics were themselves willing contributors to established charities; now and then on the more exalted levels they went so far as to subject themselves to the ennuis and discomforts of a charity ball. But they invariably objected to serious efforts to remove the need for charity—efforts to reduce economic injustice, to effect some organic alleviation of poverty. They could not have liked poverty, knowing nothing of it; it was fair to assume that they saw a formless, disquieting threat in a healthy society. Perhaps it was simply that they cherished their own *obligeance*, believing it lent them *noblesse*. Perhaps it was simply that they feared altruism, having so little personal experience of it.

5

Meanwhile there was the private life of Marshall Field. He was more than ever *the* Field; his aunt Ethel, Lady Beatty, had died in 1932, and Delia Spencer Caton Field, the old gentleman's widow, died in July, 1937. Field's third marriage was extraordinarily happy. A daughter, Phyllis, was born on November 3, 1936; a second daughter, Fiona, on Christmas Day of 1938. Field was starting all over again as a father; of his first three children only Bettine was still at home. Barbara had married Anthony A. Bliss on December 21, 1937. Marshall, Jr., had been married on June 20, 1938, to Joanne Bass, daughter of a former governor of New Hampshire.

Field loved his son, bearing for him some of that special affection inspired by an only son, and some of that special solicitude which accompanies a sense of primogeniture. That they were good companions in the sporting life was no more than Field might have expected; his greater pride was in his son's scholarship and initiative, the more to be respected as its absence would not have been criticized. Young Marshall led the school at Fay, was awarded a gold medal for scholarship at St. Paul's, and entered Harvard with the class of 1938. (Barbara, incidentally, had been president of her graduating class at Brearley.) Students were notoriously political in the late 1930s, mainly pacifist and isolationist, though as the war approached, large groups of them swung toward intervention, or at least more support for the Allies. But young Marshall was not political, and took no part in the rallies and parades and manifestoes. In his personal life he was conservative: he dressed well, lived well, worked hard, enjoyed his clubs. He was also curious about the world: in the summer of his freshman year he took a job on the floor at the Republic Steel mill in Buffalo—he called himself "Mike Farley" and that was all the others knew about him—and did heavy labor for two months, shoveling slag into the open hearth. (If he had waited a couple of years he might have been shot at; one of the great bitter strikes of 1937 was at Republic.) He went back to Harvard; he was graduated in June of 1938 *magna cum laude* in English literature (his thesis was on A. E. Housman). His marriage to Miss Bass was naturally a social event, and it was also a happy occasion for his father. By now Field was not a dynast, being more interested in ideas and people than in empire, but as his energies and impulses were released his affections ran deeper, and he took pleasure in the thought of another Field family, a new focus of domesticity; in brief, he looked forward to grandchildren. Meanwhile the Fields, Jr., settled in Charlottesville, Virginia, where Marshall entered the University of Virginia Law School. (Field and Marshall, Jr., were oddly contemporary. When Marshall V was born Fiona was only two and a half. Field began a new life in 1936; his son married in 1938. Thinking of them as near contemporaries throws a strong light on their relations after 1945.)

And in New York Field, Sr., was once more a paterfamilias. Harry and Bobby Phipps were seven and five and Phyllis was two when Fiona was born. Field had never tried to replace Ogden Phipps as the boys' father, but he offered them—and received—unlimited affection and kindness. They called him "Marshie"; as the girls grew up they called him by a variety of nicknames. He had not lost his ability to shed the years, and when he played horsey or Indians with his daughters and the boys dignity vanished. He was forty-five in 1938, but his family life was that of a man fifteen years younger: full of love, excursions, games. For the next few years he was likely to come home from a day of intense professional strife and find himself in another battle: a din-din fight, wherein he was the poor pioneer and the four girls and boys were Indians in ambush. He always lost.

Field's affection for children was often translated into a kind of personal rejuvenation: not the pleasure of an adult who feels that he has done right by the young ones, but the warm excitement of a grown man who enjoys becoming a child temporarily. In 1940 two young nephews of Maldwin Drummond came to America to stay with the Fields; R. E. A. Drummond, known to family and friends as "Bendor," and his brother Maldwin. With Harry and Bobby Phipps they composed a quartet whose ages ranged from eight to ten, and years later Bendor Drummond recalled mischief at Caumsett:

Somehow we [the four boys] found out that dry ice when screwed down in a jar would eventually blow it up. We tried to get some from Horace [Field's butler] but he wisely refused to supply it, making things more fascinating by saying that dry ice would burn. We were all about to go down to the pool when Bobby told Marshall about this marvelous stuff and said that

Horace had some. Horace was sent for lumps of ice and jars which after being filled by Marshall duly blew up as predicted. What struck me then was that Marshall was as gleeful at the idea and its execution as we were and went on making explosions until either the ice or the jars ran out. . . .

One of us found a broken bow and some very tatty arrows in the play-room. We were trying to rig up the bow on the front lawn when Marshall came out and seeing the situation was hopeless summoned Risebrow [his chauffeur] who returned in about half an hour with four bows, masses of arrows and a colored target. It seemed like magic that the old bow was so quickly replaced, and Marshall playing with us that afternoon made the whole thing feel like a special occasion, almost as if one could have gone up to him and said, "Let's have Christmas Day today."

Sitting in the front seat of Marshall's car, a place hotly contested, coming up the Bath House hill and thinking about switching off the engine, I sud-denly did so; the surprise was almost as great to me as it certainly was to him. There was a certain amount of difficulty in getting under way again, and Marshall was addressing the people in the back seat with "He switched it off, he switched it off" over and over again with occasional looks of amazement at me but never a reproach. I sat very quiet.

Not a good driver, Field had been startled; but his reaction was one of real wonderment and not anger, as though he were asking quite seriously, "Now why did he do that?" and might even like to do it himself some time. He played not out of a sense of duty, or with a consciousness of "unbending," but because he identified en-tirely with children, and loved to play.

In those days, of course, little Bendor paid scant attention to even smaller Phyllis Field. In 1958 they were married in London.

Field's happiness served him twice: it gave him youth and energy and high spirits, and it made him more acutely sensitive to the un-happiness of others. The world was spiraling downward, and war and misery seemed to be the order of the century. Field was in no position to do much about the Japanese rape of China, or *Anschluss,* or Munich, or Franco's victory in Spain, or the American recession of 1938. Individual human beings seemed helpless; they were being sucked unwillingly into tragic history. Democratic governments blathered and hesitated, backed and filled; totalitarian governments counted on the moral and physical sloth of their enemies. Superfi-cially the United States seemed divided between isolationists and interventionists; actually most of the country bumbled along without strong opinions either way. A man might be forgiven for thinking that a world of decency and hope would have to be postponed for at least a generation. Field never yielded to that sort of despair, but in the years between Ethiopia and the Fall of France his preoccupation was children. That implied faith in the future, and a desire to shape the future.

But when war broke out in September of 1939 the future receded even further. And when it shortly became obvious that in an age of bombers there could be no noncombatants, Field's first concern was for the children of Europe.

6

The troubles of children in war were nothing new, but organizing their relief, or outright rescue, had begun only in World War I. Civilians had never been immune, but for some centuries war had not been total, either. Wars had been fought not for annihilation, not even for subjugation, but for bits and pieces of land, or trade routes, or sources of money; populations could be spared, and even used afterward. (In 1757 Lord Chesterfield wrote to his son, "Even war is pusillanimously carried on in this degenerate age; quarter is given; towns are taken, and the people spared; even in a storm, a woman can hardly hope for the benefit of a rape.") But technology brought the wheel full circle, and the bombings of World War I brought civilians back into the fight—if only as victims. World War II promised to be infinitely worse. Its causes, back in the mists of final analysis, were economic-psychotic, but the conflict was so permeated with ideology, racial mysticism, and mass psychology, on both sides, that it might almost have been pre-Malthusian, even pre-Reformation, even pre-feudal; once combat began, it might have been a tribal war fought in a thunderstorm on a darkling plain by naked animists snarling gutturals. Gods, idols, rituals, whole societies were at stake for the first time since ancient Rome. Outside of Poland the land war was quiet for the first few months, but Poland served as a warning: it was flattened and partitioned as quickly, as ruthlessly, as a small town in a border dispute between the Han Chinese and the nomad barbarians. At sea ships full of civilians were torpedoed; by air, bombs killed indiscriminately. The threat of mysterious gases lay heavy. Annihilation was in the air.

The first, most obvious, victims had been Jews, and as far back as 1934 Jewish groups in America had sent out lifelines. There were Jews in Germany who were willing to stay, either to resist or because they thought the terror would blow over, but wanted their children out of the country. Many were killed, and dead Jewish adults left live Jewish orphans. One of the first American organizations was the German-Jewish Children's Aid, which became, as *Kultur* spread, the European-Jewish Children's Aid. By 1940 they had brought 443 children to the United States; "only" 443, but there could be no "only" with even a single child. The U.S. State Department had cooperated, and had set a pattern of "corporate affidavits," by means of which an organization could accept financial responsibility for its charges—for their transportation, orientation, placement, and, to a point, future.

But the quota restrictions of American immigration law made large-scale rescue operations impossible. Great Britain had accepted 20,000 refugee children, and in 1939 the National Non-Sectarian Committee led efforts to persuade Congress that America could do the same, but Congress was not interested. When the war broke out borders were sealed even tighter, and Central Europe was cut off.

There remained the children of Britain, France, and the Lowlands; but for the first few months—the Phony War, the *Sitzkrieg*—there was an atmosphere of stalemate, a lack of urgency. There were interventionists, many and vociferous, but they were also called alarmists, which was a good indication of the hopeful caution that slowed Allied responses. Most Americans were lulled by a seemingly ineradicable human predisposition to ignore the remote bad until it became the immediate worst.

But the conquest of the Lowlands and France took about one month, and that month jolted Americans harder than any other of the war, barring December, 1941. When France fell, and Mussolini kicked her as she toppled, America woke up. The interventionists gained ground; the isolationists grew more adamant. There might have been a violent emotional split, with paralyzing strife between the Hitler haters and the Roosevelt haters—there were still Americans who had a higher opinion of Hitler than of the President; but the middle-of-the-roaders, the indifferents, were stirring, and the trend was toward a tough defensive unity.

Sympathy for France, alarm over England, and a stiffening of our own backbone marked those days. Possibly the best symbol of the new awareness was the astonishing nomination of Wendell Willkie by the Republican convention of July, 1940—which opened two days after the Pétain armistice. Willkie was a decent, honorable, intelligent capitalist and ex-Democrat, by no means a New Dealer, but at the same time in favor of Selective Service—a hot issue—and the swap of aged American destroyers for British bases. He was in a bad fix politically, unable to oppose Roosevelt's international attitudes with any conviction; that, and the genuine desire of a majority to hang on to a leader they knew and trusted, made a Willkie victory improbable from the beginning. (The Fall of France, which helped to launch him, also took the wind out of his sails.) But he put up a good fight. Roosevelt, even in that year of crisis, won fewer votes than in 1936, while Willkie did almost 6,000,000 better than Landon, and the right-wing opposition vanished altogether. The usual Prohibitionist martyr drew about 58,000, and poor Earl Browder had to settle for 48,579. Norman Thomas dropped off to 100,000, and the Socialist Labor candidate just missed 15,000. The total minor-party vote was the smallest since the middle 1800s, when the electorate numbered only a few million altogether: in 1880, when less than 10,000,000 votes were cast, the Greenbacker had done better than all four of the 1940 outriders put together. Unity was indeed upon us.

Against the new background—Europe gone, Britain endangered —and the growing sense of urgency

action swiftly followed words. Friends sent for the children of English friends, or of friends of friends. Families offered to open their homes to the offspring of British business acquaintances they hardly knew. Clubs and organizations announced projects to find homes for British children. Industrial firms with subsidiaries in the British Isles formed plans to bring the children of their overseas employees to employees in this country. University faculties extended hospitality to the children of English dons. A great city newspaper asked its readers to open their homes to British children. Immigration offices were swamped with inquiries about entry requirements.

. . . In a few weeks the [British Children's Overseas Reception] Board had registered 200,000 children whose parents were anxious to send them to . . . safety. . . .

In May 1940 a group of socially concerned men and women met in New York. Though sympathetic with the American surge of hospitality, they had become apprehensive over what might happen to large numbers of imported children admitted without safeguards and placed in a hit or miss fashion with families who might not understand them. . . . They saw two needs: to extend the opportunity of refuge to British youngsters with no American connections; and to provide protection for those who would come. . . .

. . . Their efforts bore fruit in early June when Mrs. Franklin D. Roosevelt invited a large number of people to meet with her in New York to consider organizing into a Committee which would carry a concern for all European children and would set up an immediate program to channel the swell of pro-British sentiment into a supervised child care program with good placement practices. A few weeks later the group became incorporated as the United States Committee for the Care of European Children, under the chairmanship of Marshall Field.

The Committee was by no means a hobby for socialites. It received wide, heartfelt, and nonpartisan support from the beginning. Even the Chicago *Tribune* approved, and its one reservation was intelligent: transportation had to be paid for, and there was a danger that the children of the well-to-do would be favored. The Committee knew that, and was also aware of dangers that the public hardly considered. At the first four organization meetings, held between June 19 and July 3, these were some of the problems discussed:

Would the assurances of the proposed Committee be considered sufficient guarantee by the United States government?

How much responsibility should the Committee accept once the children were placed in foster homes?

How could existing placement agencies best be used?

Should a religious balance be maintained?

Would the inevitable preponderance of British children cause a bad public reaction?

Should participating private organizations have a vote in the Committee?

What kind of liaison was necessary with the State Department, the Red Cross, the Immigration and Naturalization Service, the Children's Bureau?

Who was to be responsible for medical examinations and care?
Would the Committee sign a corporate affidavit for children too
poor to pay their way?

What was the best way to cooperate with Canadian authorities?
Should the Committee as such lobby in Congress?

And these were chiefly administrative questions; the more detailed and specific problems of child care and case workers would
have to wait.

The problems were solved, which was to be expected, but they
were solved quickly, which was not usual among new organizations.
The temporary administrative committee appointed by Mrs. Roosevelt at the first meeting wasted no time. Field was on it, with Winthrop Aldrich, Mrs. Dorothy Bellanca, Dr. William Haber, Agnes
King Inglis, Dr. Frank Kingdon, Shepard A. Morgan, Clarence E.
Pickett, Bishop Bernard J. Sheil, George L. Warren, and Louis
Weiss. At the third meeting it was suggested that the committee be
enlarged. Archbishop Joseph Rummel, Alfred Bergman, Mrs.
Frederic R. Coudert, Sr., and Dr. Henry L. Stevenson were pro-
posed for membership, and were later asked to serve as directors,
together with the original committee and these newcomers: Mrs.
John Allen, Mrs. August Belmont, Eric Biddle, Dr. Samuel McCrae
Cavert, Dr. John Lovejoy Elliott, Mrs. Douglas Gibbons, Dr.
Marion Kenworthy, Bishop Charles H. LeBlond, Mrs. David Levy,
Lady Lindsay, Bishop Henry St. George Tucker, Alfred F. Whit-
man, and Rabbi Stephen S. Wise. Mrs. Roosevelt remained the
Committee's honorary president, and Field its president, throughout
its fourteen years.

The Committee and its directors were oddly assorted, which was
a good thing. Some were high society, some religious dignitaries,
some experts in child welfare. Some were very rich, others were not.
What they shared was a working concern for children, and they
were not relying on their own little group for funds: they went to
the public, to the foster parents, to various national organizations
like the National War Fund, and ultimately to religious organizations active in saving refugees.

Within a very few weeks the government had recognized the
Committee's value. Members of the Committee

were meeting almost daily with officials . . . in an effort to find an opening for groups of children in immigration laws written to prevent the exploitation of foreign child labor. They found it in mid-July when the Attorney General's office issued a ruling that preserved the individual character of immigration but made it possible for the Committee to import numbers of unaccompanied children, including those unknown to anyone in this country as well as those specifically requested. The magic tool was a device called the "corporate affidavit" which allowed a non-profit organization to guarantee the support of a specific number of children and within forty-eight hours to receive as many "blank visas." These it could send abroad to be filled in with the names of children awaiting exit.

And soon the Committee became a quasi-official organization; it stood on, two official rocks: the United States Children's Bureau, to which it looked for standards of child placement; and the U.S. Immigration and Naturalization Service, which chose to keep the importation of children centered in the Committee. Only once in the eight ensuing years did the State Department grant a corporate affidavit to another organization for a group of children. . . . With the corporate affidavit the Committee stood responsible for every child it helped to bring into this country, thereby gaining power of supervision over the child's care.

So the Committee became the leading agency for wartime (and, later, postwar) children's immigration. Private and religious organizations that wanted to help found that cooperating with the Committee was more efficient than establishing independent programs. The Catholic Committee for Refugees, the National Lutheran Council, Church World Service, European-Jewish Children's Aid, and the American Hellenic Educational Progressive Organization joined the work on a national scale; and close to three hundred local or state organizations—most of them religious, all of them voluntary rather than governmental—accepted responsibility for the Committee's children. The work of coordination was not easy, and Marshall Field did much of it: for the first year of the Committee's life he gave more time and energy to the children than to any of his own enterprises. The work might have been *made* easy, if the Committee had chosen to leave it in the hands of the Omaha *World-Herald*, which had its own ideas about child welfare and expressed them in this editorial:

There was an item in the paper the other day that needs some clarification for the uninitiated. It said:

"President Roosevelt asked congress today to make available immediately 125 thousand dollars to be used by the children's bureau in establishing and maintaining standards for the care of European refugee children."

Now, what can this mean?

It probably means that a group of social workers has been appalled by the very idea that Americans, moved by a powerful sympathy for the victims of war, should simply and straightforwardly open their homes to refugee children. No, this must not be! Charity must not be left in the hands of individuals. Aid to the distressed must not remain a simple matter of heart responding to heart—it must be formalized, institutionalized, filtered through all the elaborate apparatus of organized social work.

So no doubt those social workers have gone to the president, and he has agreed with them, and congress is asked to appropriate funds for the "establishment of standards."

Which means that before an American can open his home to a refugee child he will have to be visited by a case worker. And the worker will write, in the best technical jargon, a report on that home. And a supervisor will "review" the report. And there will be reports on the reports; memoranda establishing "standards of placement;" perhaps second "visitations;" probably memoranda to clarify the memoranda; and no doubt, before long, a full-fledged graduate course in the schools of social work dealing with problems of placement as regards refugee children.

And maybe, in the end, the generous Americans will finally receive refugee children into their homes. And maybe the war will be over by that time, too.

Not really; within a month of that editorial over two hundred children had arrived and were being placed. And the editorialist had failed to indicate a preferable course: perhaps he would have favored placing Catholic children in Protestant homes, giving parties with snappers for neurotically depressed orphans, dispersing children to maudlin alcoholics making sentimental offers, dispensing with medical checkups in favor of epidemics, or simply gathering the children in a public square and letting bighearted American families draw lots for them. The appropriation was not to be used to screen the children, or to screen the foster parents, but simply to draw up standards (e.g., the foster father should be gainfully employed), and the editorial—fortunately the only one of its know-nothing kind—was a perfect reflection of that envious distrust of intelligence so ably enunciated a few years before by Gen. Robert Wood.

There were problems that not even the *World-Herald* could foresee. A well-born matron in New Orleans asked if she might have a handsome little peer for the duration; should that sort of request have been honored? There were a handful of Spanish children from anti-Franco families who managed to get out in 1942, and whose parents had felt bitter antagonism to the Catholic Church:

> Church representatives here, however, reminded the Committee of the American tradition of placing children in homes according to their religion. Consequently the parents were appealed to through the relief agencies abroad and the placements made according to their individual wishes. By the time these became known, however, some of the children were already settled in Protestant foster homes, and a few had to be changed.

And the bitter, tragic personal problems:

> There was, for instance, Henry, whose father had been killed in Germany and whose mother was last heard from at the infamous Camp de Gurs. Henry received his first shock here when he learned that his uncle's willingness to take him home only involved temporary hospitality; and his second, when his newly married brother failed to include him in his family circle. He reacted to a foster home placement with outrageous behavior, but settled down placidly enough to institutional living. All through the years of growing up Henry tried desperately to become a part of his brother's family and resisted any effort on the part of "outsiders" to come close to him. However, when a distant cousin he had never before heard of turned up one day to say "hello" he was overwhelmed with emotion.
>
> . . . Jean, a brilliant French teen-ager, given to temper tantrums, teasing younger children, and alternate aloofness and extravagant demands for affection from his foster parents, would not talk except in polite yeses and noes, in a year of acquaintance with an agency's social worker. One day, he broke into a flood of recollection about the days when France was falling— the bombings, the hordes of frightened refugees, his responsibility as a twelve year old Boy Scout to take care of the babies in a railroad nursery. "I grew up overnight," he said, "but here I am expected to be a little boy—so I act like a little boy."

These problems, and many like them, could not have been solved without standards and supervision. There had to be not only good will, but deep understanding and responsibility. Neither the Committee nor its social workers claimed infallibility, but at least they were aware of the range and subtlety of the difficulties.

The country approved. From Hartford, Baltimore, Butte, Chicago, Philadelphia, Richmond, Washington, Kansas City came editorials of encouragement, and when the children began to arrive —in August, September, and October of 1940—their rescue was matter for a thousand feature stories. Most were from England, but others were from anywhere in Europe: Germany, France, Romania, even Turkey. They came over on the *Samaria,* the *Antonia,* the *Scythia,* the *Empress of Australia*—on whatever ship had room for them. There were about as many boys as girls. They were of all religions, predominantly Protestant in the early days. A great majority were between nine and fifteen years old. One ship brought only three children; another, 138. When the children disembarked in New York, and the reporters and photographers had finished with them, they were taken to reception centers. Most went to the Gould Foundation in the Bronx or the Seamen's Church Institute in Manhattan; others went to the New York Children's Aid Society or the Vacation Camp in Rye, New York, about twenty miles outside the city. At these centers a paid staff—director and house mothers— made the children welcome and saw to their living arrangements, while volunteers helped provide medical care, nursing service, supervision and recreation, entertainment, transportation, allotments of clothing and toys, and the routine secretarial work. The medical care and examinations were extraordinarily thorough, and included psychiatric service when necessary.

The care included everything from haircuts, shoe repair, and dry cleaning to the actual placement of a child in a foster home. Many children arrived hungry, owning one shirt, one pair of pants, one pair of shoes, wearing an oversize patched sweater that had been donated in England. Some spoke no English. Most were nervous, exhilarated to be in the Promised Land, still terrified by memories of war, lonely and cut off from the only life they knew. The Committee tried to get them into foster homes as soon as possible, and worked so efficiently that most of the children spent less than a week in the reception center. When they left, scrubbed and dressed and somewhat fatter but still nervous and confused, they were sent on to regional centers, and thence to foster homes. There was one exception: fifty-four children from the British Actors' Orphanage had been sent over with the understanding that they were to be placed in comfortable Hollywood homes. Apparently the promises made by Hollywood had been misunderstood, or believed; at any rate it was found that no homes were available. The children, who had lived together as a unit for years and been through night after night of bomb-shelter existence, stayed on at the Gould Foundation and were eventually placed there permanently, an arrangement they enjoyed. Of the others, over half were placed in homes in New York and Massachusetts, and another quarter in Connecticut and Ohio. In the first year Committee children went to twenty-one states, Canada, Hawaii, and the District of Columbia.* A good many children had specific destinations, but as a group and not as individuals. The Hoover Company in Canton, Ohio, for example, took 84 children of employees of the Hoover Company in Perivale, England; Kodak in Rochester took 156 children of employees of Kodak in Harrow; 47 from Warner Brothers, London, went to Warner Brothers employees in New York and California; 110 children of Oxford and Cambridge professors were sheltered by families at Yale.

There was trouble, of course. The Committee stood firm on a policy of placement by designated agencies, experienced and fairly objective, who could do more than just "size up" the child and the foster family, and were "equipped by training and experience to sense whether a couple's offer of hospitality emerged spontaneously from a genuine love of children or from a more or less conscious need for prestige and admiration; whether the couple's own children would regard the little foreigner as an intruder or a playmate; whether the young visitor could take the competition of other children in the family or would be repelled or attracted by an abundance of affection; whether the couple would be apt to be driven by emotional needs to try to wean the child away from his parents in England." This was the sort of thing some Americans resented; one group sponsor flared up, "We know our employees better than any-

---

* But not to Nebraska. The "powerful sympathy," "heart responding to heart," that had brought tears to the eyes of the Omaha *World-Herald* was apparently an out-of-state phenomenon.

one else, so why shouldn't we know best where to put the children?" His impatience was understandable, but the Committee was
firm. As a result, only 68 of the first 850 children had to be replaced. Of 46 cases, these were the reasons:

Illness of foster parent	7
Foster parents moving	2
Transfer to relatives	1
Foster parents inadequate	3
Boarding school placement	6
Shift from temporary home	4
Child unable to adjust	23

One family, disappointed that their charge displayed all the usual
quirks of childhood and was not a model of Old World perfection,
actually wrote to the girl's parents in England asking them to take
her back. The Committee found another, less purist, family for her.

Not everyone approved of the Committee's purposes. Louis Weiss
was its legal workhorse and a founding member, but his own wife
had serious and intelligent reservations which were, in time, echoed
by many. Was it really better for a British child to leave home and
country in a time of trouble? Wouldn't a boy or girl grow up a bit
tougher and a bit prouder, and a good deal less dislocated psychologically, by staying home and sharing the lot of his countrymen?
Children from the Continent were a different matter: they faced
horrors, and they faced them, often, alone. But the British children,
who were happy to come to America, were sometimes not as happy
to stay. Some—particularly the older ones—withdrew and seemed
to feel almost guilty at being behind the lines. "Almost all expressed
the desire to reach the age of 17, when they would be allowed to
go back home and do their bit." Some of the little ones became furi-
ously American: one ten-year-old was heard to say that she was
"glad we had won the Revolution because they are all too stuck-up
over there." Others were both delighted and depressed by American
ways: the older schoolchildren "tended to worry about subjects
needed for further study back home, but found the self-discipline
required in an atmosphere where 'nobody makes you study' difficult
to maintain." And occasionally a charming atavism came to the

surface: "One little girl who had struck her foster parents as 're-markably free from the bonds of old home ties' flared up in anger when her foster mother did not put on an evening dress to greet the English visitor at luncheon."

As time passed, and the original batch of British children grew older, more and more people felt that they might have been just as well off at home with their parents. But that was later. In the first year or two public approval was practically unanimous.

Practically. One loud opposing voice must have reminded Marshall Field that nothing in this world was nonpolitical. On August 9, 1940, the Indianapolis *News* carried the story:

CHAILLAUX HITS CHILD REFUGEES
Legion Director Asserts Many Are From Communist Families of Spain

Proposals to admit refugee children "from Communist-Loyalist Spain" into the United States under the guise of "providing asylum for refugee children from England" were attacked by Homer Chaillaux, national Americanism director of the American Legion, in an address to the national convention of the Military Order of the Purple Heart Thursday night in the Claypool hotel.

"A lot of us have fallen for that tommyrot—the poor little kiddies of Europe," Chaillaux told the delegates. "But only a few hundred of these children are from English families. The rest are refugee children of the Loyalist group in Spain who were driven from that country because their parents were Communists."

"These," Chaillaux added, "are what the English want us to take. Let's be sensible for once."

"Furthermore," the Legion director said, "we have 2,000,000 boys and girls of our own who are juvenile delinquents for economic and social reasons. Let's solve that problem first."

The gentleman's sources of information were not specified, which was just as well for his purposes. Aside from assuming that all Spanish Loyalists were Communists, he seemed to be assuming that uncounted thousands of children were on the way, of whom "only a few hundred" would be British. As it turned out, only 1,315 children had arrived by the war's end, of whom 860 were English, 209 German, and only 42 Spanish. These last were indeed of Loyalist families: they crossed the Pyrenees * and embarked for America at Marseille. It is hard to believe that they represented a clear threat to American institutions. The sole remark they occasioned from their guardians here was this: "Only the Spanish children [of the Continental group] seemed to have preserved something of the normal lightheartedness of childhood. Forty of them spent the reception period at the Gould Foundation where they made a great hit with the staff, the British actors' children and the people of the surrounding community, because of their infectious gaiety and their proclivity to song and dance." These subversive minstrels were not, of course, the real objects of Mr. Chaillaux's remarks. He was keeping righteousness alive, and was being traditionally cautious in dispensing the benefits of God's country, though his God seems to have been one who punished the child for the sins of the father.

His 2,000,000 American delinquents did rather well in World War II. Afterward many of them joined the American Legion.

Field was very much at the center of all this; his presidency was far from honorary. He traveled, raised funds, posed for pictures, visited reception centers, supervised the red tape that threatened occasionally to become a tangle. He also worried. He was not objective about children. A bad report on a depressed child could make him wince; the news that a ship had cleared a European port with a full load of children brought him immediate exhilaration. (He had hazel eyes, and several friends noticed that they seemed to grow darker and warmer when there was good news about the children.)

He never cared much about personal popularity, but the work he did with the Committee brought him a good deal of favorable notice. Even those who thought he was only a conscientious socialite approved of the Committee's work. Those who knew him better saw clearly the fulfillment he found in it. Ultimately—by 1952— the Committee had brought 4,122 children to this country, refugees,

---

* It should be said, and gratefully, that General Franco was not harsh to refugees from other countries. While the Vichy French ultimately rounded up and deported many thousands—mostly Jews—to certain death, Franco's officials tended to wink at refugee border-jumpers headed for Lisbon, and—provided the recipients were recommended by someone, Spanish or not, known to the Spanish government —granted transit visas with a minimum of red tape.

displaced persons, orphans; had worked with the United States government, with UNRRA, with the International Refugee Organization; had done *something,* had acted specifically and unselfishly, to reduce human misery. Those children went on to become teachers, nurses, clergymen, doctors, tradesmen, skilled workers; some of them died in Korea. Some of them simply survived, and remembered that America had cared. Many of them never even heard of Marshall Field, or had thought of him as a department store.

In the Committee's final report was one item that made him smile, one category for which he may have felt a special, unquenchable affection. It read:

> Stowaways accepted for care: 13.

7

The Field Foundation, Inc., was established in October, 1940. It was not an extension of the Committee, or even of the attitudes that had led Field to preside over the Committee. It was a natural and inevitable issue of his political-social-philanthropic education. Foundations were nothing new in American life, but before the First World War most had been either expiatory gestures or echo chambers for special interests. There were only about 30 tax-exempt foundations in 1915, 179 by 1926, 243 by 1939. As the technological world became more complex and perilous, and taxes rose, the number and range of foundations increased; there were more problems worth attention, and extra money was as easily disbursed to nonprofit organizations as to the government, with noticeably more renown to the donor. By 1946 there were 505 foundations. Practically all of these were educational or philanthropic and tended, with a very few exceptions to the left or right, to reflect the Establishment. They did good, and they maintained their occasionally precarious tax exemption by working well within the limits of acceptable American thought.* They consequently radiated an often bland amiability. Field knew that; he also felt, and said a few years

---

* Many, including the Field Foundation, have become more adventurous in the last fifteen years, and their exemptions have become correspondingly more precarious. Dunderhead congressmen delighted in baiting them; in 1962 they were accused of having caused a recession for their own selfish ends.

later, that there ought to be at least a few of them prepared to do what the more respectable would not: work directly in areas of tension and controversy.

The Foundation's first formal report was not issued until 1949. It opened with an introduction by Field:

> From time to time, I am asked about the origin of the Foundation. There are several reasons why I decided in October 1940 that I should establish the Field Foundation, Inc. For one thing I found that a busy schedule of civic and business responsibilities did not allow time to exercise thought and discrimination in deciding upon the merits of the hundreds of appeals for donations addressed to me personally. Moreover, I am opposed to giving of money on a paternalistic or emotional basis. Such gifts, made impulsively and without appropriate study, are frequently resented by the recipients and in any event are extremely unlikely to achieve constructive results.
>
> With these considerations in mind and convinced that the inheritance of large sums, which public opinion is more and more likely to limit in the future, imposes on the recipient of such funds something in the nature of a public trust, I decided to organize the Foundation. I found that there are many devoted men and women—experts in their fields—who are willing to give of their time and experience in order to assist in the constructive distribution of funds available for philanthropy. The members of the Foundation are residents of Chicago, New York, Philadelphia, Washington and New Haven. They are highly qualified in their respective fields and sensitive to the social needs of the community. I am glad that I have been able to vest control of the Foundation's policies and funds in these members, and I am very grateful to them for the time and thought that they are giving to the Foundation from day to day. It is the hope of the members that by experimentation a few ideas and social techniques may be helped to germinate which will eventually prove to be of enough value to be adopted by the community.

Note that he thought "public opinion," and not some repressive, arbitrary government, would cut down on large inheritances; and note too his early accent on the germinal, plus his feeling that the only worthwhile projects were those that the community itself would ultimately adopt. He never abandoned those attitudes.

> Among the first decisions a foundation faces is whether to operate research and experimental projects directly, [or] to focus its efforts on making grants to other organizations, [or] to do both. Our Board decided that for

the present the Field Foundation, Inc., would be primarily a grant-making foundation.

The Charter and By-Laws give the Board of Directors wide discretionary powers. In accordance with the provisions of its Charter, the Foundation limits itself exclusively to "charitable, scientific and educational" purposes and operations. The Foundation cannot and does not seek to influence legislation or to engage in propaganda. No grants are made except to organizations having similar purposes which have been granted Federal tax exemption. The Foundation is not limited to assistance to organizations and institutions within the United States. Both principal and income may be expended. Thus, the Foundation is assured freedom of action to meet changing conditions. . . .

In the beginning, the Foundation's grants were distributed over a relatively wide range of recipients. More recently—as appears from the report —the Board of Directors has decided that the principal areas of interest of the Foundation will be the problems of children and those arising in the field of interracial and intercultural relations. A small percentage of income is allotted to germinal projects outside the fields of major interest.

It was a quiet sort of foundation, with no extensive fellowship program, no spectacular news releases, no multimillion-dollar grants, no museums, no showcases. With about a million dollars a year to offer, the accent remained on the germinal. That word clarified Field's ambitions as both philanthropist and, later, publisher: he wanted to create climates, and not to propound dogmas. The Foundation did not seek to "prove" anything; it sought to learn and to make the fruits of learning available to the widest possible public.

By 1949 its assets totaled around $11,000,000; its yearly gross income was something over $1,500,000. But far less was available for grants; some of its assets were subject to mortgages and depreciation. All in all it was not a huge foundation, though it was larger than the average. Andrew Carnegie, whose concept of stewardship was broad enough to include the notion that it was a disgrace to die rich, had distributed some $330,000,000 to over a dozen foundations and endowments, six of them in the United States. By 1960 three generations of Rockefellers would have contributed over a billion dollars to various family-founded institutes. In that same year the Ford Foundation, established in 1936 with assets of $25,000, would represent about one-fourth of all the foundation money in America; its assets would have grown to something over $3,300,000,000.

But only about 10 per cent of all American foundations controlled over a million dollars. Even in an age when charitable contributions might cost a rich man only nine cents in the dollar, more than 11,000 of the approximately 12,000 foundations were modest in assets and limited in function. The Field Foundation probably ranked about 100th in size. More important was its function. It was established in the tradition of the Rosenwald Fund (which served "the well-being of mankind" by aiding Southern rural education, ameliorating race relations, and contributing to the health and education of Negroes; and of which Field became a trustee in 1941) and the Twentieth Century Fund, chartered in 1919 by Edward A. Filene to improve economic, industrial, civic, and educational conditions through research and publication.

The Field Foundation's board was not, however, composed of financial experts. (Carl Weitzel, comptroller of the Estate in Chicago and Field's business confidant and adviser, was not on the board but served as treasurer.) The board consisted of people whose interest was the grants, and not the income. There were always Fields on the board, but at Louis Weiss's suggestion, and Marshall Field's insistence, they were always a clear minority. The Foundation might be a family affair; its functions were not. Before the decision to give priority to child welfare and race relations, the board had offered grants in civic betterment, general education, health, protective and correctional services, social work education, all of which required the advice and approval of experts. (Even so, it turned out that child welfare and race relations had absorbed over half the value of all grants in the first eight years.) There were certain areas in which the Foundation had no ambitions. A paragraph in the report headed "Limitations" reads:

Among the categories of assistance which the Foundation views as outside its scope are: contributions to building funds, to endowment, to ordinary budgets and accumulated deficits; support for propaganda and efforts to influence legislation; scholarships and fellowships; and medical research and programs for the prevention and treatment of disease which is primarily physical or somatic.

There were five Fields on the board in 1949: Marshall, Ruth, Marshall, Jr., Barbara and Bettine. With them were James Brown IV, a Chicagoan with ten years of social service work at the University of Chicago, which he advised on legal aspects of child welfare; Homer Folks, of the State Charities Aid in New York, who also served as vice-president of the Foundation; Agnes Inglis O'Neil, one of Field's close friends and early tutors in child welfare; Clarence Pickett of the American Friends Service Committee; Justine Wise Polier; Helen Ross of the American Psychoanalytic Association; Dr. Milton J. E. Senn, director of the Child Study Center at Yale; Hermon Dunlap Smith, a Chicago businessman; Dr. Channing Tobias of the NAACP; and Louis Weiss, who was also the Foundation's secretary. The Foundation's executive vice-president—i.e., the administrator in charge of the heavy day-to-day work—was Maxwell Hahn, who had once been a newspaperman in Canandaigua, New York, had raised funds for colleges and hospitals with the John Price Jones Corporation, and had directed publicity and education for the United Hospital Fund in 1935. He had later directed national publicity for the Associated Hospital Service, and still later raised funds for the U.S. Committee. With the Foundation he did little fund-raising; its finances were sound and its original goals modest; its staff was small and its administrative expenses low. The work at hand was not accumulation, but grants. Hahn was perfect for the job. His knowledge was great, his probity and dedication were absolute, and he was there to get things done: he never suffered the occasional occupational diseases of foundation executives like the itch for prestige or the compulsion to power.

Most of the grants were a source of pride and satisfaction to Field. Some of them resulted in an immediate improvement in living, working or educational conditions for various socially handicapped groups. Others resulted in published reports of the factual kind that authorities ignore until there are enough of them, at which time it becomes apparent that important realities have been neglected. The names and projects of only a few of the beneficiaries, in welfare, give some idea of the Foundation's range: the American Academy of Pediatrics, Washington and Philadelphia (health services for children); the American Public Welfare Association, Chicago (foster home requirements); the Bank Street School in New

York (teacher education in child behavior); the Ryther Child Center in Seattle (psychiatric social work with children); the State Charities Aid Association of New York (improvement of the Children's Division of the Department of Welfare); and the Wiltwyck School in New York State.

Field took a personal interest in that last organization. As a Foundation report noted, it cared for "boys for whom the community takes little or no responsibility; a large percentage of these boys are Negroes. They all have presented serious . . . problems to their families, schools, communities. While still young, many have become potential dangers to society and many have come to Wiltwyck called 'hopeless.' Eighty boys live at the school, twenty in each of four homes, with counsellors who bring to the homes intelligence, kindness and understanding. A boy's average stay is two years. There are no locks, no gates at Wiltwyck. Corporal punishment is forbidden and all punitive and custodial methods have been left behind." (Field had seen at first hand what a timely break could do for a reputedly "hopeless" boy; he did not believe in that kind of hopelessness. In Judge Polier's Children's Court he had met one boy, half Cuban half Jewish, whose father had deserted the family; he liked the boy's manner and appearance, and arranged to get him into a private school. The boy shortly won a scholarship, later served with distinction in the Air Force, and went on to finish college. What the slums would ultimately have done to him could only be guessed. Field knew that the scale of help had to be large, ideally including the whole society, but occasionally he made a very personal gesture. In the fall of 1937 a Negro boy of perhaps eight was brought into court; his family had disintegrated and he was sleeping in parked cars. "I'll get along," he assured Field, who liked his self-confidence and rushed through breakfast the next morning to stop off at Bloomingdale's and buy him a windbreaker.)

In race relations the awards were equally effective and their impact equally slow, unobtrusive, and steady. Grants were made to—among many others—the American Council on Race Relations, Chicago (equal rights and opportunities), Provident Medical Associates, Chicago (helping Negro physicians to acquire specialized training), and the Research Center for Human Relations, New York (integration in housing).

Occasional grants were directed at less immediate but equally important improvements. One of these established the National Opinion Research Center in Denver (to discover, test, and perfect new methods, techniques and devices for measuring public opinion). Another went to Sheldon and Eleanor Glueck of the Harvard University Law School, and helped them to produce their classic investigations into the causes and nature of juvenile delinquency.

There were also grants to colleges and universities, to educational institutions of many kinds: to the University of Illinois Medical College; Roosevelt College in Chicago, with which Field himself had a long and close relationship; the New School for Social Research in New York City ("While it is not the Foundation's practice to contribute to regular operating expenses of established organizations, special wartime conditions that threatened to cripple the New School made the grants appropriate"); the Reading Institute of N.Y.U.; the Child Study Center at Yale; Fisk University in Nashville; Howard University in Washington, D.C.; Black Mountain College in North Carolina; Princeton University. Awards went to New York, Illinois, Washington, Pennsylvania, Indiana, Michigan, Tennessee, Utah, Connecticut, Minnesota, Ohio, Massachusetts, New Jersey, Georgia, Missouri, Virginia, Colorado, Kansas; to London and Liberia; to the Highlander Folk School and the Massachusetts Institute of Technology; and to points and organizations between. Do-gooders, every one, and tax-exempt, and seedbeds, if not hotbeds, of new ideas. They had one idea in common: they were trying to understand what was in order to improve what would be.

Up to October of 1940 Field was still a fairly obscure millionaire, vaguely associated with a store in Chicago and with Roosevelt; a philanthropist; one of those very rich men who might be assumed to have some influence on the upper levels of society, and perhaps in Wall Street and Washington, but none really with the public. Still the perfect gentleman; the whispers of liberalism were an acceptable eccentricity.

A year later his class was calling him traitor.

CHAPTER SIX

We hear about Constitutional rights, free speech and the free press. Every time I hear those words I say to myself, "That man is a Red, that man is a Communist." You never heard a real American talk in that manner.

—Mayor Frank Hague of Jersey City,
Speech, January, 1938

A WIDER PUBLIC BEGAN TO NOTICE FIELD IN LATE 1940. Not too wide; his name was not associated with a product, or a political movement, or show business, or crime, and those were the four keys to national fame. He was best known among the worriers, the concerned, the committed, and even they were not sure how to take him. Most thought him knowing but naïve, too rich to know reality; and because he was so much the gentleman, refusing direct rebuttal, murmuring his diffident contributions to difficult debates, it was often some time before they realized that the quiet manner might be his modest way of concealing the fact that he was a jump or two ahead of the conversation. It *was*, now and then, hard to take him seriously: here was a handsome, refined, rich Jeffersonian, presumably a sheltered idealist, a gentleman of the most gentle kind, distinguished in appearance, impeccably accoutered, nonviolent almost to the point of passivity, making an occasional point in a beautifully modulated semi-English voice. But the point he made sometimes lingered in the mind, and proved to be subtle. He went to dinner at the White House in the fall of 1940, and had occasion to make a few such remarks. His hostess was Mrs. Roosevelt (the President, whom he had known casually since the 1920s but whose close friend he never became, was not present). The guests were assorted:

Sidney Hillman, Ben Cohen, Will Alexander, Paul McNutt, Aubrey Williams, three or four others. The topic—the reason for the dinner—was the problem of employment of Negro youth. The more conservative guests were rather pleased when Hillman, of all people, suggested that "things" would work themselves out, and that the government should keep its distance from the problem. There was general agreement that ultimately economic considerations would move employers to disregard prejudice. "Do you mean because they can pay Negroes less?" Field asked innocently. Answered by silence, he went on. "This kind of thing has to rest on moral, and not economic, inclination," he said, glancing briefly at Hillman. "Most employers have a sense of fair play; all other things being equal, they'd be willing to hire Negroes. But all other things aren't equal—I suppose they never are; and there are a lot of people who *aren't* employers who have to share the blame. I think if they knew some of the facts that have come out tonight, things might change. We need some way to get the facts to them."

On the surface that was a naïve, idealistic proposition, giving the employers far too much credit for social awareness, and placing too much confidence in "facts" as a remedy. But everyone at the table understood what Field had been saying. That the hard core of resistance to Negroes in the labor force came from the unions; that there were employers willing, some even eager, to hire Negroes, but unwilling to fight the unions, many of which were rigidly segregated; and that when Hillman proposed to let "things" work themselves out, he was simply ducking the real issue: whatever the economic inclinations of employers, the immorality of segregation was the real shackle on the Negro workingman.

That sort of elliptical comment made it easy to misunderstand Field. When he delivered a speech on September 18, 1941, to the American Public Welfare Association, at the Park Lane Hotel in New York, he made natural but misleading headlines: MARSHALL FIELD SCOFFS AT WEALTH: 'Don't Give a Damn' What Happens to His Fortune in Crisis, He Declares; WORTH SEEN IN SERVICE. The story went on:

. . . Mr. Field, grandson of the Chicago merchant who created the great Field fortune and one of the world's wealthiest men today, emphasized the importance of individual service. . . .

"I don't know what is going to happen to me. I happen to have been left a great deal of money. I don't know what is going to happen to it, and I don't give a damn.

"If I cannot make myself worthy of three square meals a day, I don't deserve them."

That sounded awful, so earnestly condescending, and the newspaper treatment was no help. John D. Rockefeller, Jr., delivered one of his rare witticisms: "I don't care what happens to Marshall Field's money either, but I do care what happens to mine." It was only two years later that Field protested the misinterpretation, in an interview by *The New Yorker*. The remark had of course been taken out of context; he had been in the process of saying that he would never encourage or even tolerate fascism in the hope of keeping his fortune. "I'd rather not have my money than have my social feeling warped," he summed it up; a sentiment either very naïve or very confident.

These were simply verbal misunderstandings or obliquities, but it was not always easy to get behind them, to discover precisely what Field's meaning was. Those who tried were put off by a baffle of clichés: fair play, give and take, decency, justice—all of which bore plain, unmistakable meaning to an early British Whig but were less simple to pragmatic Americans—and occasionally that mysteriously ambiguous word, "competition," which seemed to have a special significance for Field. His old friends wondered; if he had to be a Democrat, all right, and if he had to be an FDR Democrat instead of a manageable Jack Garner Democrat it was just as well that he confine himself to platitudes; but where was the man headed?

They had a fair indication in the fall of 1940, when Marshall Field, in defense of free enterprise and a free press, became the sole owner and proprietor of the noisiest and most colorful newspaper in America, which was almost immediately labeled Communist.

2

When Harold Ross gave Ralph McAllister Ingersoll a job on the infant *New Yorker*, in 1925, he groaned, "Hell, I hire *anybody!*" His recruit was, in the patois of that stratum, scion of an old New

York and New Haven society family; his mother's uncle was that
same Ward McAllister whose edifying comments on Chicago's
barbarism graced nineteenth-century drawing rooms. Ingersoll
lacked his great-uncle's instinct for classification and condemnation;
at Yale he abjured sherry and genealogy, taking instead whiskey
and a B.S. in mining engineering. He had then adventured briefly
in Paris and Rome, done some mining in the Southwest, seen Mexico and written a book about it, and returned to New York, where
he took a job reporting for Hearst's morning *American.* Shortly
thereafter he threw a roundhouse right to his city editor's nose—
with absolute justification—and left the Hearst empire, landing on
his feet in Ross's office.

Ingersoll had talent; he also had a flair. He lost his small capital
in the Crash, but not his natural sense of independence and im-
punity; he often rushed in where fools feared to tread. He became,
for example, the managing editor of *Fortune* magazine; and then a
vice-president and general manager of Time Inc. He was a first-rate
magazine editor, and liked challenge. New York's entrenched newspapers were a challenge. Except for the *News* and the *Mirror,* they
were stodgy and unimaginative; the *News* and the *Mirror* were sensational and unimaginative. By and large the metropolitan dailies
offered little courage and less edification. They carried features,
columns, and canned news. The *Times* wore piping on its weskit;
the *News* toted a lunchbox; the *Mirror* had Hialeah, and the *Journal*
had a line cut of William Randolph Hearst; the *Tribune* had Lippmann, grave and authoritative; the *Telegram* had Pegler, savagely
illiberal and often brilliant; the *Sun* had "Silent Sam," "Reg'lar Fel-
lers," and "Pop." Particularly noticeable in a melting pot like New
York, there was only one newspaper, the *Post,* that could be called
at all liberal. And there had not been a new newspaper since 1924,
when the *Mirror* and the short-lived *Graphic* debuted.

Ingersoll did what for him was the natural thing: he gave Henry
Luce a year's notice, and in 1938 formed Publications Research,
Inc. He took offices in the old Time-Life Building and, with Ed
Stanley as his one assistant, set about preparing a prospectus, a
dummy, and a budget.

In the first expansive months of independence he and Stanley
worked out an estimate of his capital needs; it came to $6,000,000.

A nice round figure, of no practical use whatever. They trimmed it to $3,000,000. Less round, but of no more use. They began again—Stanley did the major part of all this—and worked it down to $1,500,000. That looked more realistic to the man who had to raise the money. It was wildly low, considering the job: to found a newspaper, hire and house its staff, buy into wire services, promote the paper, and get it printed and distributed—all in the city of New York, where wages and prices were high and where eight major dailies (plus the *Telegraph,* for the morning line) had already parceled out the market. But that wasn't enough: Ingersoll's real recklessness lay in the nature of his proposed newspaper. It would carry no advertising, and would pay its own way by newsstand sales and subscriptions. The fact that no such newspaper had ever succeeded added spice to the effort.

The conception was not new, but the attempt to bring it to life on such a large scale was radical. In its economics, and not in its later politics, lay the revolutionary nature of the newspaper. Ingersoll knew that there was sufficient talent in New York—not to mention the rest of the country—to create an exciting, literate, witty, uncompromising daily. There was no real need to be stuffy and pretentious; there was no real need to run sex murders on Page Two and chorus girls on Page Three. The news in the '30s and '40s was far more exciting than any possible "entertainment." There were strikes, riots, wars; economic scandals and profiteering; municipal inefficiency and graft even under La Guardia; above all, there were millions of ordinary people being dragged by the scruff of the neck into a new world—a world of Hitler and air travel and Social Security, of literacy and technology, of ideology and psychiatry, of dangerous national quarrels and spurious international agreements; of, as it turned out, everything from global war to the illegal sale of sick chickens. If, given that material, a classy staff could not turn out a newspaper that people would scream for, the fault would not be Ingersoll's.

In early 1939 the form and function of the newspaper were clear in Ingersoll's mind. He had completed a dummy, Volume O, Number O, with the help of an all-star cast of enthusiastic friends. For this one dummy Heywood Broun wrote sports; Dorothy Parker a drama review; Louis Fischer and Leland Stowe foreign news;

Dashiell Hammett a book review; Erskine Caldwell national news; Oscar Levant music; and playwright Lillian Hellman a movie review. Two hundred copies of this thirty-two-page sample were printed up. Ingersoll had also completed a long document entitled "A Proposition to Create a Newspaper," plus a condensed version of the proposition; with those and the dummy he began scouting among his friends for advice and money. Advice was plentiful. One of his friends recommended that he talk to John Wharton, a ranking New York attorney whose clients included not just the usual run of magnates but many professional people, some of whom were in or near the world of arts and communications. Ingersoll did so; he and Wharton dined together, and Wharton liked his ideas. Nothing spectacular came of their talk for the moment, but on Wharton's advice Ingersoll took a trip to Washington. SEC regulations would certainly bear on any large-scale limited partnership; and certain Wall Streeters had discouraged Ingersoll, declining involvement on the grounds that the New Deal "wouldn't let him start a new business." They were wrong, of course. The SEC saw no obstacles, but offered three warnings: Ingersoll would do well to set $100,000 as a minimum investment, dealing only with men who could afford the loss; he should accept no commissions from anyone for anything; and he should guarantee to his backers that they were committed only if *all* the money was eventually pledged. Cheered by his interview, Ingersoll decided that January 11, 1940, was his target date. He set it arbitrarily; *some* deadline was necessary. Then he began to beat the bushes. Meanwhile Wharton set about drawing up a "stockholder's agreement" which was a concise and uncompromising document. One of its major stipulations was that no backer would exercise any editorial control—the direction of the newspaper was to be Ingersoll's alone.

John Wharton was a partner in Louis Weiss's law firm, but Wharton was not a scout for Ingersoll, and in any case Marshall Field was Weiss's client and not the common property of the firm. Wharton never proposed to approach Field, but one day in early spring Weiss got a look at the dummy on Wharton's desk; he shoveled it into his briefcase and scanned it that night. He read through the prospectus, and called Ingersoll immediately. "This is Louis Weiss," he said. "I've just read your prospectus, and I want to see you right away."

"Fine," Ingersoll said. "Shall I drop around tomorrow morning?"

"I said right away," Weiss told him. "I'll be over in fifteen minutes."

At Ingersoll's apartment on East 80th Street the two men talked. This was perfect, Weiss announced, for Marshall Field. Furthermore, if Field came in Weiss would want to take over the legal aspects of the project. "I can't do that," Ingersoll objected. "John Wharton's helped me from the beginning, and you can't just—"

"John and I'll settle that ourselves," Weiss interrupted. "Marshall Field is my client, and he'll be interested in this as more than an investment. He likes ideas."

Ingersoll said he'd be glad to send Field a copy of the prospectus. "Wait," Weiss said. "At the right time."

That phrase, as Ingersoll was learning, meant that Weiss required time to investigate a bit more thoroughly. From the very rich—those among whom Ingersoll was pushing his idea—a commitment is only the prelude to a symphony of experts: lawyers, accountants, close friends, unnamed advisers. That was the real work of raising money: cutting through questions, objections, hesitations, "impartial hostility," simple lack of enthusiasm, and often plain suspicion. At any rate Weiss and Ingersoll parted, and Ingersoll heard no more for a couple of months.

On a balmy afternoon in June Weiss telephoned. Would Ingersoll be kind enough to meet him and Field at Field's apartment, at five o'clock? Ingersoll would. He arrived five minutes before the hour and went straight up. Weiss introduced him to Field, who impressed him as shy, very gentle, and almost absent in his manner—preoccupied, barely attentive. The two shook hands, and Ingersoll launched his spiel. Field nodded now and then, and even yawned politely a couple of times. Ingersoll was sure Field was bored; he raised his voice a bit, spoke faster, compressed his arguments. Field looked at his watch—he carried it in his trousers pocket; it was the kind that snaps in and out of a flat rectangular leather case—and Ingersoll went on almost by reflex, the enthusiasm draining slowly from his voice. Field stood up; so did Ingersoll, still talking. The two men drifted toward the elevator, Weiss behind them; Field pushed the button. The elevator arrived. Field shook Ingersoll's hand, said very amiably, "I couldn't take more than two units. Good night, and thank you," stepped aboard the lift, and quietly vanished into the nether regions.

Ingersoll, in a state of mild shock, turned to the smiling Weiss. "What did that mean?"

Weiss was matter-of-fact: "It means you have another two hundred thousand dollars."

Ingersoll sat down and took a long, slow, weary breath. Field later signed the necessary investor's agreement, and Ingersoll did not see him again until January of 1940.

Ingersoll's impression of Field's lack of interest—a first impression shared by others—was doubtless reinforced by an odd habit that puzzled, and occasionally even offended, Field's acquaintances. He yawned a lot. When he felt like yawning, he yawned. He might be having a marvelous time, but when his system called for oxygen, he supplied it. Whether this was simply a slight nervousness or a bizarre sequel to the early rheumatic fever, it was dismaying to casual friends, who were often alert to his slightest reaction, and disconcerting to closer friends. The habit persisted until about 1946, when the James P. Warburgs and the Archibald MacLeishes were visiting the Fields at Chelsea. MacLeish was holding forth rather brilliantly after dinner, and Field was yawning his way through a delightful evening. The next morning MacLeish asked Warburg, "Jim, was I really such a terrible bore last night?" A militant delegation marched on the host in protest; Field answered feebly that yawning was, after all, a natural function; and the habit disappeared for good when Mrs. Warburg reminded him with fond asperity that there were other natural functions which he was kind enough to spare his guests.

Ingersoll was not sure why Field had come in, but many of Field's reasons later became obvious. Above all he liked the independence of the proposed editorial policy. Field's liberalism reached full flower in 1940 and 1941. He retained a gentleman's respect for those he considered honest conservatives, but he was more than ever alert to unconscious motivations, to the built-in bias that even intelligent conservatives might be unaware of. His dislike of the

Chicago *Tribune* had become disgust, and though *PM*—the name finally chosen for the new newspaper—was not direct competition for the *Tribune,* it was a beginning. He was intrigued by the decision to do without advertising—far too intrigued, and unrealistically so, as he himself pointed out later. The sponsors of the new paper seemed to be responsible people, and the other backers, up to that point, were eminently sound. Liberalism needed a bracer in a dangerous time. The newspaper promised excitement; it would provoke and air ideas; Field gave it his support. Never, then or later, did he consider running it himself.

That, in essence, is the story of Marshall Field's introduction to *PM*. Ingersoll was presented to him in his own apartment by Louis Weiss; he was the seventh (in order of commitment) of eighteen backers; and he wanted Ingersoll's project to have a fair chance in a bruisingly competitive field. A later mythological account, all compound of Franz Kafka and the Protocols of the Elders of Zion, took hardy root shortly afterward, when Field had become a "traitor to his class." It was infinitely more exciting, and melodrama pays, and the press—free—loved it. It was not true, but man does not live by bread alone. It angered Field, who believed in facts, and toughened his contempt for kept journalists. But that was later.

3

In early fall Ingersoll telephoned William Benton, a good man to call for three reasons. He had been a brilliant advertising man as half the firm of Benton & Bowles; he had sold his interest in that firm when he became vice-president of the University of Chicago; and he had been a classmate of Ingersoll's at Yale. The two were not close friends; they had played bridge now and then at college, and had lunched together a couple of times a year in the 1920s. But Benton had a quick mind, and knew all kinds of people, and threw off ideas by the dozen. Ingersoll asked him to cocktails. They were joined by Laura Hobson, then a ranking promotion writer for *Time* and not yet a famous novelist; in 1923 she and Benton had been copywriters, at $50 a week, for George Batten, who later joined the other B., and D., and O. Ingersoll wasted no time; they ordered drinks and Miss Hobson said, "Ralph wants to start a new newspaper in New York."

They talked. Benton suggested that they would need a succinct memorandum stressing two points: why the paper was needed, and why it would be profitable. They gave him the long prospectus. He read it on the train, on his way home to Connecticut, and sat down that night to type an eight-page letter. Ingersoll read it and called him back. Cocktails again, the three of them; and Ingersoll asked Benton to boil down the prospectus for them. Benton sat down at 8:30 that night and finished at 5:30 the following morning. He had written the "Blue Book."

It was twenty-eight pages long, which made it only relatively succinct, and it was called the Blue Book because Ingersoll put it between light-blue paper covers. It was a propaganda piece, a good condensation of Ingersoll's ideas, using many of his more memorable phrases, and it created a fair amount of excitement in the newspaper world. It also impressed a few potential investors: its title was "A Financial Proposal," which sounded a practical note immediately. The first purpose of the new paper was "to make money for its owners." It would accomplish this by fulfilling its second purpose: "keeping its readers more *intelligently, entertainingly,* and *truthfully* informed, each day, on what has happened in the world in the previous twenty-four hours." These purposes were not strikingly original, but the editorial and production techniques proposed were at least different. The paper would crusade: a lost, or at any rate enfeebled, art for these many decades. And a new paper would have one advantage over its established competition: existing newspapers had a huge capital investment in techniques and machinery that were slowly becoming obsolete. The new paper could, for example, plan to use color lavishly and set up its presses accordingly. It could work in easily readable nine-point type without having to junk its fonts of seven-point. It could start right out with half its space given to photographs. It could use better paper and better inks. Its layouts could be original and imaginative without annoying a readership accustomed to a tradition.

Other techniques were possible: the stories would run continuously, and not (continued on p. 8). Good writers could be hired and paid well (of all the innovations, the most revolutionary). The paper would be slightly smaller than existing tabloids, and bound like a magazine with wire staples. Above all: no advertising.

Five pages of the Blue Book were given over to proof of the proposition that a newspaper so conceived and so dedicated could sell for a nickel and long endure. (Newspapers were two and three cents in those days.) Ten reasons were offered why readers would spend that much ungrudgingly. A table of profit estimates, on the basis of different circulations, was drawn up. Capital requirements and investment procedures were outlined. One point was again made unmistakably clear: Ingersoll would have complete control. The purchasers of the $1,500,000 in preferred stock would receive half the common; the other half would be reserved for management, Ingersoll and his chief assistants, with perhaps a broader distribution as time passed. The preferred was to be retired by an annual sinking fund of one-third of net earnings; no dividends were to be paid to management until capital had been fully reimbursed, after which capital and management would share alike in the profits.

Ingersoll was the key to the whole proposal, and the last half of the Blue Book was devoted to the man and his ideas. Included were two quotes from Henry Luce, who had written Ingersoll on August 31, 1939, "What you have in mind . . . may prove to be of great importance in the history of American journalism and in the life of the nation. . . . In so far as its success depends on the leader of the enterprise, all the omens are favorable, for you have obviously demonstrated unusual talents in the journalistic field," and whose announcement, when Ingersoll was made general manager of Time Inc., in 1935, had read in part, "He took over the management of *Fortune* when it was in the red and when its circulation was 30,000. Today its circulation is 130,000 and its profit this year is over $500,000." Ingersoll's qualifications were unimpeachable, and his ideas ranged wide: a complete and interpretative guide for radio listeners; news of the American press ("The American press does not report news about itself. Its proprietors are 'members of a gentlemen's club' in which it is bad taste to discuss the affairs of fellow members. We do not propose to join this club"); news about labor, with emphasis on the unions; news of the unemployed, of whom there were about 10,000,000; news about living: a food page with daily price fluctuations, news about health and education, about both fashions and bargains.

The last two pages of the Blue Book set forth the proposed newspaper's editorial policy, quoting freely from the original "Proposal." Some of this later made its way into dictionaries of quotations. Here was the core of it:

We believe that any newspaper should crusade in the interests of truth. This is particularly important for a new newspaper. Its success may depend upon it.

Most great newspapers became great by their crusades. We propose to follow this tradition. But we shall crusade in a modern way.

We are without political affiliations because we believe political affiliations circumscribe crusades for the truth.

However, we who are working on this new newspaper, as human beings, love and hate certain things. We shall not be unbiased journalists. We do not believe that unbiased journalism exists. Claims to emotional disinterest are, consciously or unconsciously, usually fraudulent.

We are against people who push other people around, in this country or abroad. We are against fraud and deceit and greed and cruelty and we shall expose their practitioners. We respect intelligence, honesty, sound accomplishment, religious tolerance. We propose to crusade for those who seek constructively to improve the way men live together.

Since we wish not only to change the approach to newspaper publishing, but also actively to crusade for what we believe to be right, many will call us "radical." We look upon ourselves as radical in the same sense that Joseph Pulitzer, Senator La Follette the elder, Theodore Roosevelt, and even Woodrow Wilson were once regarded as radical. This is not only in line with our personal convictions. It is good publishing and good business policy.

The Blue Book ended optimistically:

We are prepared to publish ninety days after the completion of our financing.

Ingersoll met his deadline. On January 11, 1940, he was ready to go. Eighteen separate backers had committed themselves, in this order:

Mrs. Marion Rosenwald Stern (later Mrs. Max Ascoli), the basis of whose fortune was Sears Roebuck, and whose background was one of liberalism and philanthropy.

Howard Bonbright, of the investment banking firm of Ladenburg, Thalmann, a most conservative businessman.

John Loeb, of the investment banking firm of Loeb, Rhoades.

Deering Howe, of the Deering tractor family, a friend of John Wharton.

Garrett Winston, a distinguished lawyer of the firm of Sherman & Sterling, also a very conservative man.

Elinor S. Gimbel, of the department-store family.

Marshall Field.

Huntington Hartford, of A & P.

Harry Scherman, head of the Book-of-the-Month Club.

Dwight Deere Wiman, theatrical producer, who was the great-grandson of John Deere and the grandson of Charles Deere, both of whom made a fortune in agricultural machinery.

Chester Bowles, then a successful advertising executive.

Ira Williams, Jr., of Philadelphia.

Dorothy Thompson, writer and commentator.

William and Lessing Rosenwald, Mrs. Stern's brothers.

Philip Wrigley, of the chewing-gum Wrigleys.

George L. de Peyster.

John Hay Whitney (later Ambassador to England and owner of the New York *Herald Tribune*).

To these was added, on January 25, the name of M. Lincoln Schuster, of the publishing firm of Simon and Schuster.

The list was impressive. It was notably lacking in "radicals"; *PM* cannot by any stretch of the imagination be said to have sprung from the left. If a political average could be struck it would lie distinctly to the right of center. But these people had seen the documents, and knew they were not backing another journalistic stuffed shirt. For some it was purely an investment; for some an opportunity to share in the excitement of newspaper publishing; for a few, an effort to balance the sharply skewed scales of American journalism. And of most, this was true: each felt, with a beautiful, confident optimism, that a truly independent newspaper would naturally reflect his own views.

In a celebratory mood, Ingersoll called Field, and invited him to lunch. The two had not met since their first interview. "I'd be delighted," Field said. "Can you come by my office?" Ingersoll walked in shortly before one; the two did not enter a limousine and dash off to the Chambord, but went downstairs and around the corner to a "Schrafft's or the equivalent." They ordered a drink and were silent briefly; then Ingersoll said something like "I wanted to have lunch with you because you're the one stockholder I don't know anything about. I'm curious." Normally Field shied from that sort of conversation, but he smiled; without the brashness Ingersoll would never have conceived *PM*. "I think you'd be surprised to know how much like other people I am," he said, and the chat proceeded from there. Field talked about Chicago and England and the New Deal, while Ingersoll listened; then he asked about Ingersoll's progress, and received a full report. The waitress took their order for dessert. Field had ordered a businessman's luncheon, one of those ironclad contracts for ironclad stomachs, from the left-hand page of the menu; he asked if he could substitute pie for ice cream. The waitress was sorry; no changes were permitted. Field submitted with good grace, but looked grumpy when she had left. He ate his compulsory ice cream, drank his coffee; the two men ambled out onto the sidewalk and shook hands. Field wished Ingersoll luck and went back to his office.

Ingersoll liked him: the first impression of abstraction and preoccupation had given way to a budding admiration for his calm and his quick grasp. But Ingersoll still had no clear idea of Field's motivations. It was obvious—and it became more obvious as publication day approached—that Field had no interest in editorial control. Nor could he count on profits for a long time. (Longer, as it turned out, than either of them dreamed.) One of Ingersoll's three largest stockholders had simply presented him with capital, asked enough intelligent questions to be sure that the investment was not being misused, and patted him on the back.*

For some months after that luncheon the two met rarely, most

* Ingersoll felt later that he might have done better to be less naïvely honorable and more aggressively businesslike at this point. He could easily have doubled his capitalization. The list of backers was a formidable advertisement, and when it was announced that Ingersoll was over the top quite a few potential investors—cautious men who had been waiting for the dust to settle—asked to buy in. But Ingersoll had promised his original backers that each $100,000 invested would represent one-fifteenth of the newspaper, and he thought it would be ignoble to suggest a revision of terms to them. The extra capitalization might have made a big difference; or *PM* might have flopped anyway.

often at board meetings. Field remained unobtrusive. Some curiosity, some pestering, would have been justified: New York was full of rumors. One insisted that Henry Luce was behind the whole project; but Luce, while an interested observer, had declined to enter daily journalism. The news got out quickly that *PM* was to be liberal, but Ingersoll's office refused to comment further, even denying for some time that it would be called *PM*. An art contest was announced: Ingersoll planned to go back to the Civil War tradition of artist-reporter, and had asked John Sloan, William Gropper, and Wallace Morgan to judge the entries. (There were 1,926 submitted; the twenty-five winners included Reginald Marsh and Don Freeman; but only Freeman joined the staff. Nothing much came of the idea. Photography was simpler and more popular. Later on Dr. Seuss—Theodor Geisel—drew for *PM* with great success.) Other newspapers reported Ingersoll's progress, generally in muted or slanted stories. Magazine writers speculated. Ten days before the first issue Richard Rovere delivered the first accurate descriptions, in an article of welcome in *The Nation*. *PM* would be a tabloid, but of slightly different size from the others; its local news would concentrate on people, and its stories would be more like naturalistic vignettes than dry reports; its photographs and stories-in-depth would reflect Ingersoll's magazine career; it was true that no advertising would be carried, but a consumer's guide would be printed as a legitimate part of the day's news. Precisely what the editorial attitude would be, no one knew for sure, but it was reasonable to think that the newspaper would support Roosevelt strongly.

Roosevelt himself thought so. On May 21 he wrote to Ingersoll:

Dear Ralph,

This is to welcome PM to the New York and to the American scene. Your interesting prospectus leads me to believe that you are about to add a notable chapter to the history of our free press.

It is more important than ever in these fast-moving times that the people be fully, reliably and quickly informed about the march and counter-march of significant events. They should get all the available facts and get them straight.

As you know, I have been critical at times of a part of the daily press. Too often the news of this part of the press has been colored because of front office prejudice or "business" reasons.

Your proposal to sustain your enterprise simply by merchandising information, with the public as your only customer, appeals to me as a new and
promising formula for freedom of the press.

Such encouragement from high quarters was welcome, because
by May Ingersoll had noticed that his competition, when not edi-
torializing about a free press, showed signs of combining against
him. Mild ridicule was the first weapon; then doleful regrets that
New York City could not support another daily; then overt suspicion of the quality, background, and politics of *PM*'s staff. Ingersoll, knowing that any publicity was good publicity, fought back
with frequent statements to the press, continued his preparations,
and kept a wary eye open for unforeseen complications.

They popped up just before publication. A meeting of New York
distributors was called, and was presided over by a surrogate for
Capt. Joseph Patterson, publisher of the New York *Daily News*.
Patterson was a narrow-minded but shrewd editor. He had once,
in his flaming youth, been a bitter (and very temporary) socialist;
the socialism had been transformed into an unreliable liberalism by
1932, when the *Daily News* supported Roosevelt. Field liked Patterson (years later he said, "There's something about Joe I've always liked"), and noted approvingly that the *Daily News* stayed
with Roosevelt in 1936, and again in 1940; what fascinating arguments took place between the Captain and his cousin, Col. Robert
R. McCormick, can only be guessed at. After 1940 Patterson suffered a sharp revulsion at the drift toward war; and once he broke
with Roosevelt he went all the way, becoming a fierce reactionary.
Field rarely disliked a man personally because of political differences, but his affection for Patterson may be said to have cooled.
Even in 1940 the *Daily News* was moderately schizophrenic: it supported Roosevelt, but came out flatly for appeasement of Hitler,
disliked unions and Jews, and thought highly (when it thought at
all) of the lowbrow. (The *News* never attacked the Catholic
Church; there was an unwritten rule in the right-wing newspaper
business that Catholics could be attacked in the Middle West, but
not in the East.) At any rate Patterson's spokesman had a few
pungent words for the distributors, which, stripped of their poetry,
were a flat warning: anyone who carried *PM* would not carry the

Daily News, and on the *Daily News,* which sold 2,000,000 copies a day, depended the living of many distributors. (In one version of this story the orator twirled a pistol as he spoke. The detail is probably apocryphal but the story itself is true.) Not being merely an idealist, he had practical suggestions. The size of newsstand surface was fixed by city ordinance, the stands being legally "sidewalk obstructions." The ordinance was passed in the 1920s, when there were five evening papers; there were only four in 1940, because the *Graphic* was long gone, so there was room for *PM,* but Captain Patterson's flunkey had solved the problem: they could lay out the four papers the long way instead of the narrow way, making less room on the stand and an excuse to decline novelties like *PM.* The distributors were helpless; one of them actually wept with rage when he told Harry Feldman, *PM*'s circulation manager, that their agreement was annulled; but they relayed their instructions to the individual stands.

This happened a week before publication, and put *PM* in a desperate spot. Ingersoll had been congratulating himself on the success of his distribution program; and now this. His lawyers assured him that he had a perfect antitrust suit, which he would win in three or four years at a cost of perhaps a quarter of a million dollars.

Ingersoll waited until eleven that night, for dramatic effect, and hied himself to the mayor's modest apartment on upper Fifth Avenue. La Guardia greeted him, not too cheerfully, in pajamas and bathrobe. The colloquy has been variously reported, always too formally. It ran, roughly, this way:

La Guardia: "Ingersoll! For God's sake what do you want at this time of night?"

Ingersoll (hopping mad): "I thought you were running this town."

La Guardia (matching his mood): "I sure am. Who says I'm not?"

Ingersoll: "Then why can't I get a newspaper on your newsstands?"

La Guardia: "Who says you can't?"

Ingersoll explained; La Guardia fretted and fumed. He had small affection for Patterson, and less for the kind of "freedom of the press" that amounted to despotism.

La Guardia (majestically): "Those stands are licensed by *the City of New York*. Nobody can do that to you!"

Ingersoll: "They're doing it."

La Guardia: "I'll tell you what. You get some auxiliary racks and set them up outside the stands."

Ingersoll: "That's a violation of the ordinance."

La Guardia: "It won't be. Just do it."

Ingersoll did. Within the week he had ordered and received 6,000 makeshift racks. They would do for a start.

Next was Patterson. Ingersoll went to the Captain's office. Patterson welcomed him, swinging a toy baseball bat a boys' club had just honored him with.

Ingersoll was cooler; two days had passed. "Captain Patterson," he said, "I came around because I think it's pretty rough of your boys to keep my paper off the stands. We're an evening paper and you're a morning paper. We don't even compete for your advertising. You're big, we're little. Why go out of your way to get us? And why let yourself in for a lawsuit?"

Patterson took a couple of swings with the little bat. "You know," he said, "when we started the *Daily News* in 1919, the wise money said we'd never last. They're saying the same thing about your paper, and I can't take the chance."

Ingersoll tried again: "Your paper's always talking about how the New Deal kills enterprise, how Washington makes it tough for a new business to get started. But I'm not having any trouble with the New Deal. I'm getting all my trouble from the *Daily News*. How do you square that with your ideas?"

Patterson chuckled. "Put it this way. Sure, I'm making things tough for you. But if you're tough enough you'll stick, and then you'll be a member of the club. It's kind of like hazing a new boy."

Samuel Johnson defined a club as "an assembly of good fellows, meeting under certain conditions." Patterson's conditions were those of an adolescent bully. Perhaps he had taken seriously an anonymous editorial in the *Wall Street Journal* in January, 1925: "A newspaper is a private enterprise, owing nothing to the public, which grants it no franchise. It is therefore affected with no public interest. It is emphatically the property of its owner, who is selling a manufactured product at his own risk."

Ingersoll walked out.

Volume I, Number 1, of *PM* appeared on Tuesday, June 18, 1940, in a run of half a million copies, not enough by far for the curious city; by sunset copies had changed hands for fifty cents. The newspaper was different, all right; immediately obvious was the new typography. The headline, in upper and lower case, read DICTATORS AGREE ON ARMISTICE; the subhead was "Terms to Be Demanded of France Are Decided But Not Announced"; beneath that was a photograph of Hitler and Mussolini reviewing German troops. The masthead ran halfway down the left-hand quarter of the page ("PM 5 cents New York Daily," then a weather report, and then the index, "Today's Sections," which were Foreign, National, New York, Labor, Business, Opinion, The Press, Theater, Movies, Radio, Living, Food, Adv Digest, and Sports), the lower half of which was a schedule of news programs on the various metropolitan radio stations. Page One was, then and for some time afterward, bordered in color, most often a rather *fané* Burgundy; the motif was repeated inside to mark off sections or articles of special interest. Body type was nine-point. *PM* ran proportionately more photographs than the other tabloids. News stories, done with emotional slant and insider's detail, tended to carry built-in analysis. Serious stories were far more informative than the usual tabloid headline-plus-footnote, less thorough than *The New York Times*'s Dreiseriana, and infinitely more *engagés* than either. The appearance and emotional drive of the stories, the lack (at first) of advertising and comics, the photographs and the decorative layout (for which *PM* was to win more than one major award) accented the newspaper's kinship to magazines, though the absence of ads smacked of the serious quarterlies rather than the big slicks.

No single element of *PM* was altogether original. Green sheets and blue-streak editions had used color; tabloids were nothing new; neither were photos; a liberal slant had centuries of broadside-and-coffeehouse tradition; European penny sheets, American newsletters, and the *Reader's Digest* had forgone advertising. Even combining all those elements was not revolutionary: there were small country weeklies, subsisting on a minimum of advertising and a maximum of personal, critical, local reporting, that bore an odd resemblance—though they were most often conservative—to *PM*.

But *PM* had bustled noisily into the world's busiest city, elbow-ing its way through shades of Brisbane and Greeley, chattering in-cessantly and waving its hands and making rude remarks about things that mattered. It was, to change the figure, something like an undernourished, brilliant sixteen-year-old in plaid knickers, an orange shirt, Persian shoes, a purple satin cape, and an alchemist's pointed hat, interrupting the Congress of Vienna to announce that democracy was on the way. (Laughter; derisive applause; tumult on the floor.) For the newspaper's staff, the first weeks must have been tense but exhilarating. Deadlines were still deadlines, and by-lines often became merely initials, but *PM* was the premier topic of conversation in New York, and there was plenty of important news, starting with the Fall of France and the Republican conven-tion.

All was not rosy, however. During the first two weeks a bad, disappointing howler was perpetrated, no one quite knew how, that may have been more important to the history of *PM* than anyone could realize at the time. Harry Scherman had supervised a promo-tion by mail consisting of a sharp, strong distillation of the major points in all the previous proposals and prospectuses. A response of 5 per cent was considered fair for such mailings; *PM*'s response exceeded 30 per cent, which was almost miraculous. With *Time* and *Fortune* Ingersoll had learned that the wall of public apathy was best breached by a phalanx of charter subscribers; and *PM* had acquired 60,000 of them, carefully entered on business-machine cards. But in the second week of publication Ingersoll—who had been busy enough putting out the paper and fighting Patterson—discovered that none of those subscriptions had been serviced. No one even knew where the cards were.

It was the sort of thing that makes strong men sniffle, and that leads observers to speculate that enthusiasm may have outstripped professionalism. Ingersoll was furious, but the damage was done. It was small comfort when the cards were found a couple of months later, heaped up in bushel baskets behind and beneath an assort-ment of boxes and crates in a back hallway. How they had disap-peared, no one ever knew.

And even the rehearsal issues had pointed up flaws: for all the flair, for all the excitement, for all the real talent at work, there was a streak of the amateurish in the finished product. A touch of the coy, the self-conscious, the cute. The first issues were described as "an adult *Current Events*." The newspaper's emotional bias was obvious, though it took no fierce editorial stands until midsummer; but its principles were festooned with verbal mistletoe. The very intensity of the writing was a danger, because it became stridency; and that was a problem that *PM* never did—perhaps never could—resolve.

To do what it wanted to do *PM had* to be strident; so it lacked that grave, moderate tone which often passes for truth. (The value of moderation has always been assumed, but is still moot. "A great soul prefers moderation to excess" was Seneca's ethically loaded emendation of the Greek idea, and great souls must have agreed; but—to be immoderate for a moment—what about the slaves who made Greek philosophy possible, or who served Seneca's guests a jug of the best Falernian? Was the American Revolution moderate? Moderation is a conservative quality, and a good one in a stable, just society; but progress toward a stable and just society seems to require a continuing series of small, nasty excesses.) *PM* was in a fix. Moderate, it could never have pulled an audience away from its moderate competition, and it would not have been the newspaper Ingersoll had conceived; strident, it repelled a large part of that audience. It was even laughed at. And the Blue Book had offered one perfectly prophetic sentence: "Since we wish not only to change the approach to newspaper publishing, but also actively to crusade for what we believe to be right, many will call us 'radical.' " Many had, even before publication, and some of the backers and executives felt regret almost immediately.

William Benton had grave reservations. He had been a midwife, and the baby, he thought, sure was funny-looking. Much of it corresponded to one point or another in the Blue Book, but the early issues were far from what he had expected, and in the first two weeks Benton experienced the queasy distress of a man who realizes too late that someone has put butter instead of chicken fat on his corned beef sandwich. He had done much of the promotion, and had put his $7,500 fee into common stock, but he had worried: during the two or three months before publication Ingersoll had not consulted with his backers, the most remarkable group ever associated with one newspaper, all of whom had wanted to help. Ingersoll's reasons were good: he wanted to avoid a bad precedent, feeling that if the backers grew accustomed to being consulted, they would meddle unduly forever after. But when the early issues proved disappointing, Ingersoll's independence took on an aspect of stubbornness.

Benton bailed out. Two weeks after publication he told Ingersoll he wanted to leave and sell his stock. Ingersoll asked him to stay on a bit longer; Benton did so, but he turned in his stock just the same, and shortly received a check for $7,850, which made him the only man who ever took a profit out of *PM*. (He never found out why the extra $350, but he discovered a few months later that it was Field who had bought the stock.)

By mid-August circulation was down to 31,000—abysmal. Though the figure rose slowly thereafter, it was obvious by October that *PM* was close to utter failure. Circulation was then nudging 100,000, but more than twice that was needed to break even. The backers were incensed. *PM* was, if not a dirty word, at least a snigger on the lips of the public. Commentators persisted in calling it radical, or even Communist—though *PM* was, and had been from its first day, interventionist, lined up with Britain and France against both America First and the signatories of the Nazi-Soviet Pact. Max Schuster, a backer who remained enthusiastic, asked his associate Leon Shimkin to do a survey of *PM*'s prospects; Shimkin, a perceptive and intelligent businessman, did so, and concluded that the backers should cut their losses. For the major backers, all of whom were in high tax brackets, the loss would not be crippling; and the others could hardly afford to throw good money after bad. Even with singleness of purpose and perfect coordination the prospects would be gloomy; with the existing dissidence and creeping disillusionment, they were black.

Field and Weiss talked it over. The paper was a mess, but something of permanent value was being slighted. Each backer had warped the image of *PM* into a personal view of what it should be; none had been quite sincere in agreeing to let Ingersoll run the paper his way. The paper had been oversold in early promotion: no publication could have been that good. All that remained was a few faithful readers and a good idea. That the idea *was* good, Field believed firmly. If its execution had been sloppy, that might be rem-

edied. It seemed to him grossly unfair that a new concept in journalism, brought to life under difficult conditions, should be allowed
to die for lack of a year's support.

In August and September a series of meetings was held: a couple
of board meetings and one full-dress stockholders' meeting. At an
informal board meeting in the Brooklyn offices of *PM* the matter
came to a boil. Some of the backers were angry because they were
losing money; some because *PM*'s politics annoyed them. There
were cries of liquidation, and of litigation. When the tumultuary
protest had diminished, Field rose and made his offer: he would
buy out the other backers at twenty cents on the dollar—but only
if he could buy them *all* out, and only if they decided quickly.
There was silence, and then there were objections, and then there
was deep thought. One backer suggested to Field that they support
PM together for a few weeks and try to work out a more palatable
editorial policy; Field said, "I'm sorry. I'm not supporting a newspaper, I'm supporting an idea. It wouldn't be fair." When Huntington Hartford and John Hay Whitney accepted the offer, resistance
died. A couple of backers remained disgruntled, and later threatened a large lawsuit, but nothing came of it.

As the others continued to debate the event, Field and Ingersoll
retired to the latter's office to discuss the future. After fifteen minutes or so John Loeb stepped over to Ruth Field and said, "I want
you to know that I consider Mr. Field's offer very gentlemanly and
more than fair. I've got to run now, but I wish you'd tell him that
for me." It was an acknowledgment that Field always treasured.

At a full meeting of the stockholders shortly afterward Louis
Weiss (representing Field; Ingersoll had, for this meeting and to
relieve Weiss of any conflict of interest, retained another attorney,
Henry Root Stern) presented Field's offer to an audience some of
whom were rather shocked to hear of *PM*'s desperate condition.
Others had been kept *au courant*, and the explosive hubbub of the
previous meeting had faded to a murmuring. There was discussion;
the questions were rather superficial; sadness and resignation prevailed. When the meeting ended, Field's offer had been accepted.*

---

* Ingersoll here did something very considerate: he arranged to have the corporation repay Dorothy Thompson the balance of her $50,000 investment. Of the
original backers she alone was not rich and would have been badly hurt by the loss.

The general feeling was that Field had behaved honorably and generously. A few of the various stockholders' advisers said later that they would have been happy to get out for ten cents on the dollar. Certainly if *PM* had simply folded after three months its backers would have seemed a sorry group of feckless financiers. William Benton, who played no part in these final proceedings, said later, "I think we were all lucky to get through the whole mess without more embarrassment than we had, and we owed that entirely to Marshall Field. He was the generous and kindly gentleman who bailed us all out. We should build him a memorial."

But Field had not done it to spare his friends anguish.

4

No good history of *PM* has been written. Field's own account, written in 1945, was of his relationship to the newspaper and of his basic attitudes toward American journalism.

The theory of *PM* has been, since its beginning, that it should be a kind of newspaperman's ideal. This was to be true in three respects—its social outlook, its internal structure, and its makeup and method. The idea was that men who worked as independently as they wished would say the things that most needed to be said. . . .

Can a newspaper so conceived—a crusading, anti-authoritarian, staff-dominated paper, run without advertising, and challenging many of the sacred cows of the status quo and of journalism—make its way toward a balanced budget and an effective impact on public opinion? That is the question *PM* has sought to answer. It is a question many a newspaperman had asked for years as he and his fellows vented their frustration at publisher domination in bull sessions over glasses of beer.*

. . . Ingersoll told the readers of the first issue that "the news is too big, too terrible to seem for a second like a break for a newspaper coming into being. Instead, it dwarfs us. And it pitches us without preparation into the midst of horror. It means that we, who wanted time in which to grow up, shall have no youth—shall be gray-haired from birth—and that with no experience we must rise instantly to a sense of enormous responsibilities."

---

* Not really. Field was melodramatic here. Bull sessions are for college boys; a lot of newspapermen drink whiskey, now that they have Guild salaries; and while there are occasional complaints about publisher domination, a weary resignation is more common. You take the King's shilling, you fight the King's war.

But this was only one of the difficulties *PM* met. A big obstacle which *PM* . . . had to surmount was that of obtaining access to the news dealers and newsstands—the existing distribution system. This was probably the last thing a newcomer to journalism like myself expected, but it was a difficult problem. In any city the existing papers have traditional rights on the newsstands, have well-developed distribution facilities, and have created a degree of dependency among dealers. They have also ways of making their control of these distribution systems even more effective by alliances with police, politicians, and even underworld elements.

But *PM*'s greatest obstacle was the resistance it met from those whom it hurt. Because it had set out seriously to fight the "people who push other people around," and had met the concerted opposition of the reactionary press and the other reactionary forces in American life, it was smeared as "communistic" and ridiculed as "half-baked" and "do-good." Something like that effort to smear has continued almost from the start of the paper down to the present time.

. . . I therefore took over responsibility for the venture and promised to underwrite its probable deficits for a long enough period so that the experiment might be given an adequate trial. In taking this step, I made no change in the structure of control within *PM*. I wanted the paper to continue as a publication operated and controlled by working newspapermen. Occasionally I sit in on editorial conferences, but I do so strictly as an observer. . . .

With respect to myself, some people seem to consider it strange that I should have paid out money to meet a paper's deficit without throwing my weight around in an effort to manipulate the paper's editorial policies and news content. I do not, however, find it so in the least. Even though I have no editorial control, I respect the basic conception with which *PM* was started and with which it has continued, and I am convinced that it is paying dividends to me and to all other Americans who care about the promise of American life and the early traditions of freedom in American newspapers.

Like all honest newspapermen, the members of *PM*'s staff are aware of what still remains for them to do to achieve their ideals. Yet *PM* has had and is having a healthy and important impact on American life, not only in New York but throughout the country.

. . . *PM* is geared to the day's news. But it does not consider its job done when it has retailed press-service dispatches, when it has taken the "facts" as they come in and dished them out at random. What is known as "news" today is often an implement in the struggle of groups competing for power, and its indirect bearings on that struggle must often be scrutinized before the newspaperman can tell whether or not he is being used to grind someone's ax. What is known as "news" today is usually only a fleeting fragment of a larger whole. It is usually a surface projection of a cluster of difficult issues whose substance and reality are, like an iceberg, nine-tenths hidden below the surface.

Thus *PM* comes to its conception of news with the conviction that the world of economics, politics, and international affairs has become at once so dangerous and so complex that the ordinary man cannot find his way around in it without warnings and aids. Hence *PM*'s emphasis on "debunking" current "news stories"—"debunking" being journalese for the scalpel dissection of the interested motives which certain power groups may have in propagandizing a given version of the news. Hence also *PM*'s emphasis on the research which will present the background and framework within which the isolated "news" items take on intelligibility. . . .

Take, as an instance, the question of the war economy and its adequacy for the task that lay ahead of it in 1940. Among the most typical and most important of the *PM* campaigns to date was the series (in November, 1940) on the monopoly held by the Aluminum Corporation of America, which told of the throttling of American production of aviation metals and materials. At the time both the business interests involved and the government officials charged with the neglect of these critical defense materials denied the charges and the reasoning in the *PM* stories. Yet the subsequent production figures, and the Truman Committee reports on critical materials shortages, bore out the *PM* articles.

Or take another area in which *PM* has every reason to be proud of its work. The TNEC (Temporary National Economic Committee) had been holding hearings on the structure of American industries in Washington for several years before *PM* was started. In February, 1941, *PM* ran a full report of the current TNEC hearings on the insurance industry. The reports on these hearings were careful, objective records of testimony on monopoly tendencies within the industry, internal price controls, the relation of premiums to risks, irresponsibilities in the writing of industrial insurance, and the need for some form of federal control. It did not require any "scoop" or extra research on *PM*'s part to uncover this story. It was available to every newspaper that had a staff or a correspondent in Washington. What happened was that *PM* saw the importance of what other newspapers may have considered too technical, and, above all, *PM* had the courage to present material that other newspapers probably also thought too "hot," because of the powerful interest concerned. It was partly as a result of the publicity given to these TNEC insurance hearings that the effort of the powerful insurance lobby in 1944 to put through Congress an act exempting insurance companies from the antitrust laws was properly met and frustrated under the leadership of Senator O'Mahoney of Wyoming, chairman of TNEC.

I have mentioned several *PM* campaigns which might go unnoticed by the side of *PM*'s persistent crusade against isolationism, international appeasement, and internal Fascist forces in America. This crusade has become almost synonymous with *PM* in the minds of millions of Americans, whether they be sympathetic or not with *PM*'s purposes. The articles which form part of this have included Ralph Ingersoll's eyewitness reports of London under the blitz, the steady and persistent exposure of the nature of Franco's regime and the dangers of appeasing it, the reports on racial injustices and discriminations against Negroes in southern and northern cities alike, and the exposure of the anti-Jewish cancer in the American body politic. . . .

Through this type of democratic newspaper crusading, which might be called "spearhead journalism," the American public learned that *PM* is the place where people can get a hearing if they have a just cause. This is true whether they represent racial or religious minorities, pro-labor groups, independent businessmen fighting the monopolists, consumers, or individuals deprived of civil liberties in one way or another.* *PM* became and remains the focus of whatever cries out for courage against injustice; and so completely has it come to epitomize efforts to remedy injustice that newspapermen working for other papers often seek out *PM* reporters and give them material they know their own editors would not accept.

Field met one common criticism squarely:

One might say that *PM* has not fought with equal militancy for the rights and interests of the big corporations and the conservative groups in America. I suspect that that would be an accurate statement, at least in a superficial sense, even though *PM* has promoted a more healthy American society, and all legitimate organizations benefit from a more healthy society. More directly, the answer is that *PM* has not considered its function to be that of viewing with equal impartiality both sides of the struggles between the strong and the weak, the big and the small, the monopolists and the independents, the intrenched and those who still have their way to make. The *PM* writers have seen their function as best expressed by Justice Holmes when he spoke about "the equality of position between the parties in which liberty . . . begins." To do as much as possible to help create that "equality

---

* He might have added that when Negro groups in the South were in bad trouble they often put in long-distance calls to *PM;* now and then a family or an individual would scrape up the money and do the same.

of position," to aid in establishing conditions "in which liberty begins," has been the aim of *PM* staff members.*

There are some who will raise the question of the lack of our traditional gentlemanliness in this sort of crusading journalism, which is willing to attack individuals it regards as the representatives or the symbols of evils it fights. But . . . a certain lack of gentlemanliness is a requisite of democracy. Gentlemen are comfortable associates, but they are seldom as constructive socially as those who treasure social welfare above social formalities.

Ungentlemanliness is nothing new in crusading journalism. It is, of course, essential to it. In fact, any invective culled from *PM*'s pages would seem mild in comparison with what was flung about in the days of the Bennetts and the Greeleys, the Wattersons and the Danas. Restraint is not always a virtue when crying injustice needs to be met head-on. Ingersoll early imbued his staff with the importance of getting mad, and staying mad, at the right things. . . . It would have been impossible and immoral for any thinking and feeling writer and editor to have remained placid and constantly good-mannered in the face of the facts being brought to his attention.†

PM's attitude on crusading tactics is based on two premises, both of which are crucial if we are to have a great daily journalism in our time.

The first of these premises is that anonymity may become a mask for injustice and that, where it does, names must be named to strip the mask away. Most people think in terms of personalities and not of abstractions. That is why so many politicians will be willing to defend or attack an abstraction: it draws no blood and leaves no mark. If a newspaper attacks a generalization, and those who are meant by it are left unnamed, the attacked can rest secure in their intrenchments. Thus it becomes apparent how important depersonalized journalism may be in protecting the present distribution of justice and injustice, privilege and underprivilege, power and impotence, wealth and poverty, freedom and slavery. And while the exposure of the role of particular persons should never be an end in itself, there are

---

* It was also the aim of Marshall Field's public life after 1935. The conditions in which liberty began were approximately those in which true competition began. Special privilege—unmerited, assumed, rationalized—was the villain, but it usually took the form of special oppression; that is, it was not that Southern whites established a special system of justice for themselves, but that Negroes never got an even break in the courts; not that gentiles made better doctors than Jews, but that Jews couldn't get into medical schools. Efforts to destroy special privilege by removing special oppression were called left-wing tyranny.

† Attacks on special privilege and injustice were always called radical and vulgar. Contrast with that the snickering approval given Westbrook Pegler, within the industry, for his vicious attacks on a lady of Eleanor Roosevelt's quality and humanity.

times and situations when only the naming of names can blast away apathy and lay the truth open to all people.

The second premise is that the evils of our time have real social causes and do not come into existence by the mere fact that the evils are named and attacked. There is a curious current superstition that if a newspaper attacks discrimination against Negroes and Jews, it thereby fosters that discrimination and creates racial and religious strife. That seems to me superficial to the extent of being fatuous. It seems to me related to the taboos in primitive tribes which forbid one's speaking of disease or drought lest one should bring on such a calamity by the naming of it. I believe that social evils like racism and religious hatred have real sources and real causes. These sources and causes cannot be traced and treated adequately except through public exposure and through the co-operation that comes from public knowledge and understanding.

PM has become a leader in public exposure and, I am convinced, performs public service by bringing to the people knowledge and understanding of many matters about which they would otherwise be uninformed.

5

Field neglected to mention many things, because he was not writing about gossip and workaday details. He left out the charges that Communists were doing *PM*'s hiring and firing—not true (the first managing editor, and ultimate authority, under Ingersoll, on hiring and firing, was a solid ex-Scripps Howard man); that there were Communists on the staff—perfectly true, and probably true of every newspaper in New York City; that *PM* followed the Communist line —often enough true during the war (when, for example, *PM* opposed dealing with reactionaries in liberated territory; or conscientiously reported Gen. Douglas MacArthur's message to Stalin on the anniversary of the Red Army in 1942: "The world situation at the present time indicates that the hopes of civilization rest on the worthy banners of the courageous Red Army. . . . The scale and grandeur of [the Russian] effort marks it as the greatest military achievement in all history"; or agitated for permanent peace, for punishment of war criminals, for industrial democracy, for civil liberties—all of which, at one time or another, the Communists also hurrahed for). Field left out some of the grim humor, often not funny at the time: *PM,* violently attacked by business, by other newspapers, by Roman Catholics, by America First, was attacked with equal violence by the *Daily Worker* and by the Newspaper Guild (which in New York at that time—1941—was supposedly under left-wing control) when Ingersoll tried to discharge men he thought incompetent who happened to be Soviet sympathizers. *PM* was the only New York newspaper to support Mike Quill in a transit strike; Quill won, and shortly afterward damned *PM* as an interventionist rag. A Texan refused to support Ingersoll on original grounds: "I've only got one thing against you, Ingersoll, but it's enough: you've never had a failure"; three years later the cruel joke about Ingersoll in New York was "Never has failure gone to a man's head so quickly." *PM* was sued with monotonous regularity, but only two cases reached the courts. In one, a man who had been called a "pre-Pearl Harbor fascist" brought an action, and settled out of court; in the other a New York lawyer representing one defendant in the lackadaisical sedition prosecutions of 1943 made a speech to the jury that *PM* called "Jew-baiting," and when he sued for libel, *PM* won. The newspaper was Mayor La Guardia's best friend, but attacked even him now and then; during one such period of hostilities Field and the Mayor appeared together at the opening of the new open-air lion habitat at the Bronx Zoo, and La Guardia, introducing Field from the speakers' platform, referred to him as "my good friend in the A.M., anyway." (Ingersoll's original prospectus had quoted Charles Darwin: "I shall steadily endeavor to keep my mind free so that I may give up any hypothesis, however much beloved, once facts are shown to be opposed to it," and even the hypothetically magnificent Fiorello stumbled on a fact now and then.)

But all this had little to do with Marshall Field, who was the newspaper's financier and nothing more—though he said later that he had agreed with 90 per cent of what *PM* printed. He rejected control; he did not want power over *PM*. Twice Ingersoll pleaded with him to "come to work on *PM*"; Field declined. ("Ralph *thinks* he'd like me there," he confided to Mrs. Field, "but after a week or two he'd resent sharing authority.") In the eight years of *PM*'s existence Field wrote precisely one letter to the editor—correcting certain facts in an article critical of Westinghouse, of which Field was a director. He knew that Ingersoll went to the White House now and then for luncheon with the President, who might give him an idea for a trial balloon or ask his direct support for one measure or another (as in the exchange of American destroyers for British bases), but he never intruded upon that relationship.

Once he intervened in a journalistic crisis, but he did so privately. Ingersoll was drafted in 1942. He was forty-one, married, supporting another dependent; other editors had been deferred almost automatically. (Six months later the rules were changed, and he would have been exempt.) Ingersoll felt that the draft board had been biased. Employees of *PM* went to Washington with a petition, and Ingersoll made a bad tactical error: he made the story big news in *PM*. But after talking it over with Field and with other friends, he came to the conclusion that he had to go. When the day came he went to the rallying point, a large drafty hall in Manhattan, and stood in line with his fellow conscripts, chaffing with the reporters and photographers who were there to cover his adieux. After an hour and a half he was informed that he had been declared exempt.

Field had wired Gen. Lewis Hershey on his behalf the night before, and had received an exemption for Ingersoll on the grounds that he was an indispensable employee, and had filed the exemption with Ingersoll's draft board. Ingersoll had known nothing about it —a fact that was greeted with cynical disbelief, but a fact nonetheless.

In a matter of hours there were two picket lines outside *PM*'s offices, one bearing scurrilous posters from the right (including, sadly, Roman Catholic organizations), the other bearing hortatory posters from the left (including the Newspaper Guild and other unions) suggesting that he be exempted permanently. There was no violence, but there was a good deal of name-calling. Field felt rather strongly that Ingersoll had been put upon, and was willing to back him all the way. But *PM* was hurt by the week of brouhaha that followed; and at the end of the week Ingersoll took the subway to Whitehall Street and enlisted. The news traveled fast: he had not yet completed his applications when a radio twenty feet from him announced his enlistment. The story might have ended in a magnificent irony, because the doctors found a small spot on one lung and were about to reject him. His life insurance company, hastily consulted, certified that he had had that same spot for twenty years;

and Ingersoll went off to war. The day before he left, Field threw a big dinner party for the staff, announced that John P. Lewis would carry on as editor, and gave Ingersoll his World War I field glasses. Ingersoll carried them all through the war, and returned them afterward.

Nor did Field discuss the quality of the writing, often high, and the interesting *bizarrerie* of some of the features. Crockett Johnson's "Barnaby," a superior comic strip, drew raves everywhere, and Coulton Waugh's "Hank," which ran briefly in 1945, was another departure: its hero was a veteran who had lost a leg and had a social conscience. The photography was the best in the business. Even the sports pages were excellent, though *PM*'s readership was less athletically preoccupied than most. Its drama criticism, written by Louis Kronenberger, was the most perceptive in the country. Its foreign coverage, which made use of the Chicago Sun Syndicate after Pearl Harbor, was far above average (Frederick Kuh was a leading light) and its Washington Bureau was fiery and pertinacious. With the acquisition of Max Lerner the newspaper could even boast a budding American Tocqueville. But its coverage was limited. The Associated Press, a "cooperative monopoly," denied *PM* membership; and the AP was far and away the best wire and photo service available. What it missed in breadth, *PM* tried to make up in depth.

But—and this may have been *PM*'s real flaw—there was little in the newspaper to capture the unmilitant. It was read by people who didn't need it, who were supporting it rather than drawing on it. Field once asked Russell Forgan, "Isn't there anything about my newspaper that you like?" and Forgan's answer was "Yes. It's got the best radio columns in the country." Which was not enough. As Field learned with the Chicago *Sun,* a newspaper must not only affirm, it must attract. *PM* was like a skyrocket going off in the front yard every afternoon: you couldn't help noticing it, and if you liked fireworks you were grateful, but otherwise there was no need to go and investigate. You knew what it was, you could count on it, and you could therefore take it or leave it. Too many left it.

Still, by 1944 it was breaking even, and it broke even for a year, until rising costs after the war dropped it into the red again. Like that of an early ascetic saint, its following was faithful but without increase.

Field was obviously not trying to write a true and complete history of *PM:* the precise political orientation of its reporters and editors, the internecine rivalries, the cliques and feuds, the political makeup of its readership, its effect on other newspapers in New York, its participation in national politics, its place in the historic stream of American journalism, its accomplishments, errors, triumphs, stupidities, brilliancies. He was not interested in all of that. He wanted only to see if an independent, frankly archliberal newspaper, erratic, ebullient, friend to any underdog, could make its way in a free society. James Wechsler, once of *PM*'s Washington Bureau and later editor of the New York *Post,* wrote in 1953, "Field was a gracious, sensitive, modest man and the . . . pain he suffered was not all financial. Undoubtedly *PM* offended his tolerant instincts and his sense of propriety, but he never gave public vent to his discomfort. He . . . believed that there was an idea beneath the clamor, and his faith endured unimaginable reversals." And when in 1946 Wechsler and three others resigned with a blast at *PM*'s rosy view of Russian foreign policy, they included in their statement regrets for "any embarrassment our action may cause to Marshall Field, an honest and courageous American." *PM* was a minor part of Field's existence, but the idea behind it was a test of his democratic faith. He stood by *PM* until he was convinced of two points: that *PM* without his support would not survive; and that one-man support was a greater danger to any newspaper than pressure from advertisers.

John P. Lewis, who had met Field in the early days of *PM* and who later replaced Ralph Ingersoll as editor, wrote about Field long afterward:

When I think it over, it seems to me that this [Field's combination of modesty and impressiveness] was one of many seeming contradictions in the man—which weren't contradictions at all. He wanted to do things, but he was diffident about saying how they should be done. He had firm opinions, but he did not like to argue or contend—and yet he wrote a book of his opinions. He was not a man of controversy, yet he backed the most controversial newspaper enterprise of his time, and stood up under a good many personal calumnies as a result. I think Marshall had courage and patience and a stronger sense of historical perspective than most—and these were the things, not the seeming contradictions, which really were reflected in his personality. In many things he had an air of hesitance, but in the years I knew him I believe he was more firmly headed in the direction he wanted to go than most.

. . . Marshall was willing to stand behind his editors, but he wished a way could be found to make the point without riling the others concerned. . . . Looking backward, I think if we'd had more of his feelings for getting along with people—been less contentious on little points while standing firm on big ones—our wearing qualities would have been better.

The one thing that stood out in Marshall's relationships with us at *PM* was his willingness—something more than willingness—to give a group of working newsmen, freed of the traditional restraints of journalism, a chance to find a better way to meet the obligations of a free press. That we didn't find it was not his fault, but ours. In the process, though, I think we did— that Marshall did—make some real contribution toward strengthening and broadening human rights in the political and social fabric of the country. There never was a paper more intently read among the law and policy makers of our country than *PM* during its day, and the weight of that influence was on the human side of the ledger.

The demise of *PM* belongs to another period of Field's life. In the early 1940s *PM* was very much alive, and was the only spokesman in the country for a liberal-radical attitude far more widely held and appreciated than *PM*'s circulation indicated. It was a strange and exciting newspaper in a strange and exciting time, and what was later remembered as its "left-wing excess" was not, in the context of these years, excessive at all. The national mood had altered. The American right wing had been insisting for so long that any efforts toward humanity, decency, and compassion were equivalent to communism that segments of the public had begun to wonder if perhaps communism was compatible with precisely those qualities; at any rate Russia was putting up a good fight against Hitler, and we began to hear that 'way down deep they were a lot like Texans. It was easy enough to make fun of *PM*, but harder to refute what *PM* stood for.

A strange and exciting time, surely, when one issue of one American publication could offer all this (and much more):

A full-page portrait of Lenin, with a legend beginning "Perhaps the greatest man of modern times was Vladimir Ilyich Ulyanov."

A photograph of the Supreme Soviet in session, with a legend beginning RED LEADERS . . . THEY ARE TOUGH, LOYAL, CAPABLE ADMINISTRATORS.

A story on the industrial growth of Magnitogorsk, headed MAGNITOGORSK IS AN EPIC.

A two-page color reproduction of Surikov's romantic-heroic painting, "The Storming of the Winter Palace."

A long and friendly discussion of future relations with Russia by former United States Ambassador Joseph E. Davies.

Articles on Russian painting, theater, ballet, history, literacy, and sports.

Laudatory accounts of Russian agriculture and industry.

An editorial measured in tone, including: "But the Soviet Union has extended modernity to the people. For instance, Russian electric power plants are among the most modern in the world. The new Soviet architecture is very advanced. The Russians are great aviators. And they have come to have a feeling for modern machinery almost as intense as their feeling of patriotism," and: "Clearly it is up to both the U.S.S.R. and the U.S. to seek a broader and more enlightened base for a future relationship."

A horrifying photograph of heaped-up corpses, with the legend: SINCE 1941 VIOLENT DEATH HAS COME TO 10,000,000 OF RUSSIA'S PEOPLE.

PM?

No. *Life* magazine, March 29, 1943, with a benign and noble cover portrait of Stalin.

6

Right-thinking Americans, as represented by the largely Republican press and the mass-circulation magazines, had not honored Field with much attention. They had foreign wars to keep out of, and a New Deal to destroy or mitigate. Field's work in child welfare was good for an occasional item, though not nearly as interesting as his former sporting activities. About the man himself, there had not been much to say. A good fellow, mixed up with some odd people;

still one of the country's best-bred gentlemen. Seen too often with long-haired men and short-haired women, i.e., Democrats, and he had spoken up for Roosevelt, but he seemed harmless. Even his direct association with Eleanor Roosevelt was in a good cause, barring Mr. Chaillaux's reservations.

Then he became *PM*'s financier, and the microscopes were hastily refocused. Maybe he was serious about civil liberties, and even about civil rights. He had attacked monopolies, which everybody did—but he behaved as though he believed they might really exist, which was not playing the game. He was making a name for himself among the benighted; the underprivileged and the disenfranchised were turning to him for help. He would bear watching. An exposé might be necessary, or at least a touch of deft ridicule. Perhaps if his associations and motives were questioned, in a gentlemanly way, he would be more circumspect. *Verbum sap.,* after all.

Meanwhile he went on doing good, apparently not caring who thought that nefarious.

For a short while there was only occasional speculation in various newspapers,* until the first note of sober warning was sounded in a piece called "Muddled Millions," in *The Saturday Evening Post* of February 15, 1941. It was an expertly confused article wherein Communists, liberals, and millionaires were indiscriminately stirred into the boiling pot, so that a casual reader might have assumed that Mrs. Roosevelt, William Z. Foster, Edward A. Filene, Joseph Stalin, and T. S. Eliot were loosely associated in a Communist conspiracy. A careful reading would make it clear that the *Partisan Review* was not to be burned, because it welcomed the most varied opinions; and it was explicitly stated that neither Field nor John Hay Whitney, the "two largest stockholders" in *PM*, nor any of the other wealthy stockholders, "could possibly be called a Communist or a fellow-traveler." The effect of the statement was a strong implication that *PM* was a Communist newspaper backed by dupes; and the gist of the article was that most liberal publications were, when you got right down to it, Communist-dominated or -manipulated. In discussing Ingersoll the author reached heights of indignation: "While he was publisher of Time that magazine followed the

---

* The fulminations of Col. Robert Rutherford McCormick, after the establishment of the Chicago *Sun*, were of a different order and are discussed further along.

party line, cleverly and subtly, but none the less clearly, in its labor and book-review departments. The record is in Time's back numbers, for anyone to read." As if anyone would go to the trouble. Those who did would find a conscientiously pro-business bias, coupled with a reasonable insistence that business accept its social responsibilities and admit a diversity of economic opinion. But Field himself was treated kindly: "It was only some six weeks after Marshall Field took over the control of the paper that Mr. Ingersoll at last came out with an unequivocal anti-Communist editorial. . . . Marshall Field has made PM a strong pro-Roosevelt, pro-Ally paper. The majority of 'the most brilliant newspaper staff' in America were fired. Today, PM is another New York tabloid, competing with the New York Post as a New Deal organ." The implication was clear: Field had assumed direction of the newspaper, weeded out Communists, and taken a stand against communism and for the Allies. That was not true. Field never did assume active control of the newspaper, or even an editorial voice. The staff had included Communists,* and probably still did, but the paper had been interventionist from its first issue, during the year that preceded Hitler's invasion of Russia—a year when the Communists (some of them reluctantly, but discipline was discipline) condemned the fight against Nazism as an "imperialist war."

The most interesting point of the *Post* article was overlooked later: in the opinion of a bastion of righteous conservatism, *PM*— whatever its earlier orientation—had become clearly noncommunist within eight months of its first issue.

The *Post* returned to Field a few months later, in honor of the appearance of the Chicago *Sun*. The issue was dated December 6,

---

* Ingersoll later estimated that there had been half a dozen confirmed party members and two or three dozen close sympathizers. Of course to those who saw no difference between liberals and Communists the whole staff of *PM* was Bolshevik. Ingersoll was quite open and not at all apologetic about one of the party members: he had felt that somewhere in a free newspaper there must be room for a clearly identified expression of the Communist view, and that the immediate demise of democracy as a result was unlikely, so he had asked Earl Browder to send him a journalist. "Let him fight for his point of view," Ingersoll said, "and we'll fight back," displaying considerably more faith in the strength of democracy than the book and witch burners ever did. The man did not last long on *PM;* Ingersoll decided later that he had been wrong to assume that a party journalist would thrive in a competitive situation.

1941, and the next day many journalistic attitudes were rendered obsolete. The article on Field was called "Do-Gooder." It was by Jack Alexander, and its tone was fairly friendly, though hints of the exotic, of mysterious background and influences, flitted through its pages. *PM* was examined without overt hostility, though the language was often loaded:

PM started off with a rush in June, 1940, on capital which had been contributed [not invested?] by an impressive array of fat cats, including Field, most of whom were of an unsuspecting nature. [Some of them, then, must have been of a suspecting nature. Why did they invest?] Two months before the November election, the till was bare and most of the fat cats, alarmed at a reddish glow which they thought they saw in PM's editorial complexion, were in confusion. In the uproar Field quietly moved in with a new handful of his own money and with a reorganization plan which squeezed out his fellow cats and gave him full control. [That is, he wanted the idea to have another chance, and made a gentlemanly offer to take the others off the hook.]

His coup preserved for President Roosevelt something which the New Dealers then thought he needed [did they later change their minds?]—the only daily in New York with all-out applause for the Administration. Since the November victory, PM has continued on its strange way. [Applause for the administration is rarely considered strange in Republican years.]

And so on; which was, however, the normal tone of political journalism. Ingersoll was given several paragraphs; *Time* magazine's communist propensities were not mentioned.

But a new villain was introduced: Gregory Zilboorg. "The extent to which Doctor Zilboorg has influenced PM's editorial policy, if at all, is a popular topic of argument in New York newspaper circles." Hardly. The popular topics of conversation in New York newspaper circles have always been, on the upper levels, circulation and advertising; on the reportorial and pressroom level, salaries, women, sports, crime, and politics, in any order. *PM*'s policies were Ingersoll's and everybody knew it. But Zilboorg was too colorful a character to ignore, and the coincidence of his having analyzed, or permanently hypnotized, both Field and Ingersoll was heaven-sent. He was described as a "minor darling of Manhattan's intellectual cocktail set," and it was pointed out that he was "often seen in the paper's editorial offices, particularly during the early days." But the sinister implication was clarified further along: Zilboorg had become a stockholder, like Huntington Hartford, and he was also a contributor. "Once, after the Fall of France he contributed a nostalgic article on Paris as he had known it before the war, and he wrote a few others on European subjects. All were carried under a pen name. . . . Thus does the face of the psychoanalyst go through cycles of appearing and then fading into thin air [leaving only the sinister smile?]. Both Field and Ingersoll have remained on friendly social terms with Doctor Zilboorg since meeting him on a professional level."

Oddly—for a piece with the title of this one—only one paragraph was devoted to Field's philanthropies and public service. *PM* and the Chicago *Sun* were becoming symbols of his desire to do good, which was an interesting comment on the state of American journalism. The surprise in "Do-Gooder" was its equable, almost approving tone; hostilities were not suspended, but they were hardly waged *à outrance*. A friend was quoted: Field was "a nice fellow with a messianic urge and a hell of a lot of money," but nothing in the article even hinted at messianism, much less identified the friend. Field was said to discuss "his own psychoanalytic adventure as casually as a tonsillectomy"; but he considered it serious work rather than an adventure, and while he referred to the fact of his analysis casually, he kept the details to himself. He and Ingersoll were referred to as "brother alumni of the Zilboorg office," but the author had the grace and honesty to point out that neither had known this until after the birth of *PM*.

Field was irritated by the article; the bland tone masked certain misrepresentations and distortions. A blasting attack might have been easier to answer. But he had no time for a reply, and no real inclination to bother. If he had known that the worst was yet to come, he might have been better able to ignore this rather unimportant pousse-café of history and gossip.

He made *Time* magazine on July 6, 1942, with a brief letter to the editor, here reproduced as it appeared:

Sirs:

. . . "One of the speakers at the convention was Marshall Field, backer of Chicago's *Sun* and New York's *PM*. He urged the Negro press to go easy on the race issue. The advice was interesting, since he is also the backer of a Negro paper, a four-month-old Harlem tabloid called *The People's Voice* (to which last week he extended 'another $25,000 of credit')" [TIME, June 15].

I am deeply sympathetic with the efforts of the Negro press to improve the lot of the Negro. Nothing so impairs the moral position of America in the present war as our treatment of the Negro population, and every sincere effort that seeks to ameliorate the present status of the Negroes should be encouraged. The conclusions here stated are, I take it, axiomatic to all loyal and understanding Americans.

This brings me to the excerpt quoted above. I have no connection whatsoever with *The People's Voice*. I did not extend during the "last week" before your issue of June 15 "another $25,000 of credit" or any other amount. *The People's Voice* is printed on the presses which print *PM*, but under a contract which requires that such printing be paid for in the usual way. Bills are due and payable 15 days after charges have been incurred and there is no arrangement for any other credit to *The People's Voice*. . . .

MARSHALL FIELD

New York City

—To Marshall Field, apologies for an evident error. TIME's statement was based on information that apparently came from the horse's mouth: Publisher Adam Powell told TIME's correspondent covering the Negro publishers' convention that Mr. Field was indeed his backer and had at luncheon only the day before extended him "another $25,000 credit."—ED.

In all Field's dealings with the press, it was taken for granted that he himself told the truth: whatever embroidery a magazine or newspaper indulged in, a note from Field had the force of gospel. But he was not inclined to personal disputation, and not the type to keep a scrapbook; as public comment increased he tended more and more to ignore it. He was a busy man; more, he was learning that the record could never be set straight once for all. Most magazines required, particularly of their Lord-High-Executioner writers, "merely corroborative detail, intended to give artistic verisimilitude to an otherwise bald and unconvincing narrative." Beyond that, their function was to create an agreeable gallery of recognizable, uncomplicated types, immediately understandable to their readers —i.e., totally and satisfyingly comprehensible within a reading time of perhaps fifteen minutes. These were called popular magazines.

Those that reported in depth, or that confined themselves to reality, were unpopular magazines.

The most complete *trompe-l'oeil* portrait of Marshall Field III, painted in the prose equivalent of bilious green, was unveiled in *Life* magazine on October 18, 1943. The legend had been exfoliating like a skunk cabbage because *PM* remained noisy and irritating, the Chicago *Sun* was flatly pro-Roosevelt and prolabor, and Field himself had been making speeches on politics and education and child welfare. Those who had been merely curious about him were now turning surly; the very word "welfare" had, for conservatives, assumed new and dangerous ideological overtones.

One unalterable fact was annoying: Field was of the upper classes, qualified by birth, training, associations, and—more recently—accomplishments to be a respectable leader of men. His kind of maverick was always a problem. Either he was dead wrong, in which case it had to be proved that he had been traduced from the straight-and-narrow; or he was right, in which case decades of oracular wisdom needed modification. (Usually, of course, a rich liberal did some things right and some things wrong, and Field was no exception; but in the heat of judgment it was the attitudes rather than the actions that were called into question, and they were seen as black and white.) By 1943 a kind of "insider's" science fiction had been adduced to explain Field's "defection"; a splendid yarn, threaded with mystery and dark derring-do. If it had been offered to Hollywood, the synopsis would have run something like this:

> Out of the steppes of Asia slouched a brooding mystic, Comrade G. Zilboorg, dangerously steeped in culture, mustachioed, in a wide-brimmed black hat and a long black cloak; bearing a round black bomb with a sputtering fuse, he settled in New York, muttering Marx in Yiddish and showing dirty movies in the cellar. Under his spell came two dupes named Field and Ingersoll. He hypnotized them. Then he persuaded them that they were neurotic, but that their neuroses were complementary, and could be cured if they would join forces to publish a revolutionary newspaper. Glassy-eyed, they did so, and took over the leadership of the American left as unwitting agents for the sinister doctor.

It would have been a shame, and a betrayal of the highest standards of bread-and-circus journalism, to let facts kill a good story. The

effective alternative was to weave the yarn—or those delicate, tenuous, colorful threads—around an armature of known fact, exercising implication, indirection, and omission, the trinity of tendentious
journalism. In the process it was essential to stress Field's putative
weaknesses: the guilty conscience of the rich do-gooder, and his
extreme susceptibility to the disquieting, vaguely obscene influence
of psychoanalysis.

The prevailing American contempt of the do-gooder has been
mentioned; the national view of psychoanalysis was more complex.
By 1943 no one of any intelligence disputed the legitimacy and
value of psychiatry. But the intellectual hinterland (not always
identical with the geographical) remained suspicious, and with good
reason: the particular branch of psychiatry called psychoanalysis
reeked of immorality and heresy. To a man whose ingrained morality told him that righteousness would make him successful on earth
and blissful in heaven, analysis was genuinely dangerous: if he took
its tenets seriously he might lose the balance that had kept his family's feet on the ground for generations. Analysis was not even dignified by statistics and formulae; it was a qualitative science, in
some senses an art. And yet it was a product of "materialism," without the spiritual sanction of traditional philosophies; it was an
animalistic and un-American science, introduced mainly by Jews
and other foreigners, and on the surface it was totally disrespectful
of ancient concepts of right and wrong. Its emphasis on sex and the
brute unconscious horrified many, and a large part of the theoretical
work in this country was devoted to establishing some other basis
for human psychology—an effort that failed intellectually but succeeded on the higher levels of popular culture, which seized with
great relief upon Jung and the various religio-psychiatric schools
that happily de-emphasized sexuality. Distrust of Freud, and of
"materialistic" psychoanalysis, remained strong, though—paradoxically—Americans were considered a materialistic and sex-ridden
people. It was more true to say that they adored the romantic and
feared the erotic. The word "morality" itself reflected that fear: it
was almost always applied to sexual behavior, a private matter normally, and rarely—unless something absolutely scandalous occurred—to society's public transactions, where morals were of

supreme importance: business, entertainment, government, the press, the manipulation of myth and symbol.

So in 1943 psychoanalysis was still a slightly dirty word to the general public. It was either a tool for handling the insane or a toy for the delectation of the depraved rich. The prevalent attitude was still that of good, solid, middle-class America in the 1920s, when psychoanalysis was anti-Christ, unpatriotic, eminently disrespectful of mother, Bolshevistic, and a plot of the wets. That attitude was changing, but slowly. Many Americans approved of psychiatric care for the armed forces but were unable to repress a snigger in other contexts; psychiatry was respectable in the medical columns of newspapers, but not in the social notes. Hollywood and the popular novel were using it in a corrupt and drastically oversimplified manner, but even so they were influencing the public toward greater tolerance and receptivity by making the jargon and techniques a commonplace of popular culture.

The article in *Life,* written by Francis Sill Wickware, was consciously set against a background of do-good and psychoanalysis. It was a superior example of snide journalism, and it affronted Field greatly. It also hurt him deeply. The misstatements of fact were perhaps to be expected, but the invention of conversations that had never taken place, or the casual quoting of previously invented conversations, was simply shoddy reporting. The subtitle alone roiled him on several counts: HE TRIES TO ATONE FOR HIS MANY MILLIONS BY GOOD WORKS AND PROFITLESS JOURNALISM. First, he was not atoning, and had never felt a need to atone; second, he considered his works not "good" but necessary; third, the journalism was not profitless by his choice: he wanted his newspapers to pay their own way. But the tone of the piece was set, and the text was even worse. A figure in the first paragraph was wrong by a couple of million dollars; a conversation made much of in the third paragraph never took place; the famous statement about not giving a damn what happened to his money was wrenched entirely out of context (as it had always been). His money and early extravagances were emphasized, and his professional accomplishments denigrated: "He also is known as a 'financier,' mainly because he once set up an investment banking house—Marshall Field, Glore, Ward and Company —from which he withdrew when he 'retired from business' at the age of 42." (That sentence may have irritated him most; the rest of the article was fairly obvious buncombe, but that cavalier dismissal of fifteen years of successful professional life cut deep.) Minor errors abounded: the name of the Chicago Natural History Museum was given incorrectly, and the Court of St. James's kept appearing as the Court of St. James—but everybody did that, and minor cavils were unimportant. What was wrong, to Field, morally and professionally wrong, was the slow, polite accumulation of bias in the classic manner of hatchet journalism, so that ultimately the article was one massive misrepresentation. Even the layout was used with finesse: far down in the text, available only to the conscientious reader (and few readers were conscientious about picture magazines) was this passage:

Many people drew the obvious conclusion that Dr. Zilboorg had decided to kil! two birds with one stone when . . . Field turned up as the chief backer of *PM*. This deduction was seized upon and wildly embroidered by the press. Field has denied explicitly that Zilboorg had anything to do with his taking an interest in publishing. He says, "I met Ralph Ingersoll, who was then seeking support for *PM,* through an entirely different source and decided to participate in the enterprise because, and. solely because, of my great interest in liberal and honest journalism."

But the legend under a fair-sized photograph of Zilboorg, much more salient than any of the text, read this way:

Dr. Gregory Zilboorg is the psychiatrist consulted by Field. It is thought Zilboorg brought Field and Ralph Ingersoll (p. 108) together, out of which meeting grew *PM.*

"It is thought" presumably kept the sentence from being a lie; and the reference to p. 108 was not—as it might so easily have been— to the explanatory paragraph in the text, but to a photo of Field and Ingersoll together. The treatment of that one point was emblematic of the whole profile. Truths were glossed over or omitted; half-truths were prominent; and instead of libelous lies there were nonactionable suggestions, all tending to support, though not to repeat directly, the political science-fiction of that Hollywood synopsis. Having "established" Field's money guilt, atonement, subservience to Zilboorg, and helpless *naïveté,* the article ended with an amiable paragraph, almost a concession to good taste—in which, nevertheless, were two Parthian shots:

The needle's eye may not have widened appreciably for Field since his conversion to good works, but he is leading a useful life and—perhaps for the first time—a thoroughly happy one. The *Sun* is work which absorbs him; his third marriage is a model, with Mrs. Field enthusiastically interested in both the *Sun* and *PM*, and the inner man seems to be content. At least, Field says he no longer requires the services of Dr. Gregory Zilboorg [Field had been out of analysis for seven years!]. Perhaps in another ten years or so Field may even lose his guilty sense about his money. If this happens, it will be the end of a magnificent Horatio Alger story in reverse.

Much of Field's anger at all this was the contained, glacial resentment of a gentleman who has been near-slandered; some of it was the helpless resentment of any honest man derided by cocky and inaccurate journalism; but some of it was the moral dismay of an idealist devoting more and more of his life to responsible publishing. As an honest publisher he must have felt lonely, betrayed, apprehensive: if a major magazine could do no better in something as unimportant (his modesty would have insisted) as a profile of Marshall Field, where could people turn for any sort of reliable interpretation of the people and events that were changing the world? Part of the answer—and this he had known before—was that the press as a whole had no interest in changing the world. Its weapons, from editorial polemics to gossip columns by way of slanted news, were at the service of a comfortable *status quo* (if not *ante quo*), and anything that happened anywhere was interpreted in the light of the assumption that traditional American prejudices were the highest possible flights of man's spirit. It was discouraging, to say the least, but it confirmed him in a resolve so simple and naïve as to be almost embarrassing: he would keep his own life, and his own publications, honest. Maybe it was all that a man could do; maybe it was the least that a man could do; at any rate, he would do it.

7

Field's new critics were understandably confused. The man was taking heavy financial losses on *PM* (in Chicago, on the *Sun*), and there seemed no logical, straightforward, selfish explanation. If he had been dropping two or three million a year on an oceangoing yacht, champagne and mistresses, and the tables at Monte Carlo, no one would have cared; those were red-blooded millionaires' pursuits. His willingness to dissipate money on *PM,* an unsuccessful and boisterous left-wing sheet, was inexplicable by the vocabulary of free enterprise and the profit motive. The obvious conclusion— and in some quarters anything not obvious was intellectually inaccessible—was inescapable: a sinister, subversive machination of some sort.

The security of the United States had always been in good hands, and of all the agencies concerned with it none had exceeded Congress in selfless, ceaseless, silent vigilance. Composed by definition of individuals of the highest intelligence and rectitude—it was necessary to mention only Huey Long, Theodore Bilbo, and Martin Dies—Congress was considered America's most sensitive body of public servants: sensitive not only to the general welfare and the perfection of our Union, but also to its constituencies, to publicity, and to the contaminations of un-American thought and utterance, e.g., "I have sworn upon the altar of God eternal hostility against every form of tyranny over the mind of man," or, "It is error alone which needs the support of government. Truth can stand by itself," or, "The sword of the law should never fall but on those whose guilt is so apparent as to be pronounced by their friends as well as foes." As one result a Congressional committee recommended, during the war, the dismissal of 3,800 government employees considered unreliable; the Department of Justice, investigating, determined that precisely thirty-six of these were, indeed, suspicious characters. That the committee's efficiency was something under 1 per cent did not dismay Congress as a whole; heaven only knew how many heterodox schoolteachers, nonconforming journalists, prolabor scoutmasters, or sexually deviant longshoremen menaced the American way.

None of this was new. But governmental fear of the dissident became, during the Depression and the war, Congressional policy. Whether it was a preoccupation or an obsession only the medically qualified could say, but it was chronic and severe. At first glance it was logical: we were in a great struggle with Germany and Japan, and sedition, treason, espionage were to be expected. At second glance an observer would have realized that he was one war behind: Congress took little interest in right-wing corruption. The legislators seemed consistently opposed to deviation toward liberty, equality, or fraternity, and consistently hospitable to narrow-minded *echt*-American men on muleback. A decade before, that had not been so. The first House Committee on Un-American Activities had investigated impartially Silver Shirts; Nazis; Gen. Smedley Butler's charge that American fascists, tied to Wall Street, were actively plotting a rise to power; and Communists. The investigations were conducted fairly and rationally. But now the atmosphere was more that of a circus, a gladiatorial afternoon, and in spite of—perhaps because of—our alliance with Russia the emphasis was on the noisy exposure of radicals. Ten years before, that work had been left to William Randolph Hearst, who had expressed admiration for Hitler while his newspapers exposed "reds" in American universities—almost as good for circulation as a puzzle contest. Raymond Gram Swing had pointed out that a good Communist scare was a necessary precondition for the rise of fascism, and Arthur M. Schlesinger, Jr., writing about it years later, said of Hearst, "His primary object was evidently less to uncover genuine Communists than to frighten liberals out of expressing opinions on public affairs."

But now, in the 1940s, Congress—and, increasingly, other agencies of government—had taken charge. To say that Congress was hospitable to fascism would be a silly lie: a few of its members were fascists, authoritarian, despising liberty; more were nineteenth-century reactionaries, authoritarian, mistrusting liberty; many were simply opportunists desiring re-election; very many who disapproved of thought control found it difficult to oppose it publicly; a few stood up and fought hard against the dangerous trend toward monolithic complacency. But if it was dubious to speak of fascism, it was essential to speak of privilege. A major goal of Congressional archconservatives and superpatriots had always been the maintenance of special institutionalized superiorities: of white over black, of the rural vote over the urban, of the farmer over the factory worker, of the gentile over the Jew and the Protestant over the Catholic, of the godly over the agnostic, of the Anglo-Saxon over the Middle European (Orientals and Southern Europeans hardly counted except in big cities at election time)—and of course of the rich over the poor.

No one man, or even group, embodied all these prejudices. But taken together and made permanent, those congealed superiorities would have formed an adequate skeleton for fascism, *or for any authoritarian political system.* Liberals distrusted them singly and as a whole, and fought them all—except when liberals, too, fell into expediency. Marshall Field considered them vicious moonshine, and said so at every opportunity, and in 1944 Congress honored him with its direct attention.

Low comedy followed. A reasonable and necessary piece of legislation was almost lost because it was offered in a spirit of vendetta; the proceedings provided extraordinary fustian and splendid confusion; and at least one senator seized the occasion to demonstrate that he was unfit for public office.

The brouhaha centered on an amendment to a tax bill; but certain senators were clearly aware that only three months before, the Chicago *Sun* had won a decision against the Associated Press in a United States District Court, which decision, when enforced, would render both the *Sun* and *PM* considerably more effective as liberal organs.* The result was obvious: Field was here to stay as a publisher. He was an aggressive force in American liberalism, and a few politicians became prickly. To its credit, Congress had never up to then entertained proposals to suppress newspapers directly; but Field was a patrician-turned-democrat who had been criticizing freely, and conservatives decided that there was more than one way to skin a Catiline.

The amendment was called the Danaher amendment, or the hobby amendment, or—to the wide-eyed, innocent astonishment of Danaher himself—the Marshall Field amendment. It was introduced to the Senate on January 15, 1944, having been reported out by a majority of the Committee on Finance. (The District Court had delivered its summary judgment, enforcing the decision in favor of the Chicago *Sun,* only two days before.) The amendment's author was Sen. John A. Danaher, R., Conn. Its meaning eluded the

---

* The AP case is discussed in the next chapter.

Senator's colleagues for several thousand words of the *Congressional Record,* but essentially it was this:

If a taxpayer claimed more than $20,000 annually as deductible losses from a secondary business, for six consecutive years, the excess over $20,000 would be disallowed as a deduction, and his taxes for the first five years would be refigured in that light. To avoid the problems of ex post facto legislation, all years previous to 1944 would be exempt from the refiguring, but would count as years of loss. For every consecutive year of loss after the first five, the maximum allowable deduction would be $20,000.

The amendment had the backing of the Treasury Department, which had requested only that a certain flexibility be provided to allow for unusual cases. The measure was obviously aimed at people who had large incomes and expensive pseudobusinesses as hobbies. The Senator saw no reason why the public should support those hobbies, and there was sufficient justice in his view to set off a lively debate. Senator Danaher and Sen. Millard Tydings of Maryland first discussed the real meaning of the amendment. Tydings had several questions; Danaher reviewed the purpose and probable effect of the amendment, citing figures and referring to published opinions by the Commissioner of the Board of Tax Appeals. Perhaps wistfully, he quoted this sentence: "Every good citizen values the privilege of contributing to the public income in proportion to his ability to pay." There was no laughter. Then Sen. Alben Barkley of Kentucky rose to state the case against the amendment.

Mr. BARKLEY. Mr. President, this matter is not quite so simple as the Senator who has explained it would have us believe. He has selected an outstanding breeder of thoroughbred horses, Mr. Joseph E. Widener, who has for many years been engaged in the breeding of fine horses and in racing them. The Senator has picked that out as a typical case which would be affected by the amendment. It is not at all a typical case. There have been in this country very few Joseph E. Wideners . . . and there is nothing that I know of, morally or socially, against the development of thoroughbred horses, any more than there is against the development of thoroughbred cattle, or thoroughbred hogs, or thoroughbred men and women, for that matter. We are all seeking excellence in the breeding of all sorts of live things, even including chickens and turkeys, and everything else alive.

There are many individuals in this country who are engaged in that sort of enterprise for profit, not as a side line, but as a business. All the individual in the so-called typical instance referred to by the Senator from Connecticut has to do in order to avoid the effect of the amendment is to incorporate, and some have already incorporated. It applies only to individuals.

Mr. [Joel Bennett] CLARK of Missouri. Will the Senator yield?

Mr. BARKLEY. In just a moment. It applies only to individuals, so that every farmer who desires to develop a line of thoroughbred livestock, as the Senator from Maryland indicated a while ago in his question, may be compelled to take losses for 5 years in developing that thoroughbred line of cattle, or hogs, or horses, and in order to avoid the evil effects of this proposed amendment he would have to incorporate his farm and his land, and thereby he would escape the effect of it. . . .

I now yield to the Senator from Missouri.

Mr. CLARK of Missouri. Mr. President, this is generally known as the "Marshall Field amendment," as I understand it. The idea has been that Mr. Field was engaged in the activity of starting newspapers and other publications around over the country for the purpose of influencing and, as some of us think, corrupting, the public mind, simply as a device to reduce his income taxes.

I may say that I voted for the amendment in the committee, under the impression that it would have some effect on Mr. Field's activities. It was on that basis that the amendment was carried in the committee. I should like to ask the Senator from Kentucky whether it is true or not that the amendment as at present drawn would apply to such a case as Mr. Field's.

Mr. BARKLEY. It is my understanding that Mr. Marshall Field has incorporated his newspaper enterprises, and therefore, it would not apply to him.

Mr. CLARK of Missouri. It would not apply to him?

Mr. BARKLEY. No.

Mr. CLARK of Missouri. Then, of course, I would be against the amendment.

"It was on that basis that the amendment was carried in the committee"! Senator Clark had just said, in effect, that in committee he (and presumably others) had voted for an amendment of which he disapproved, *for the sole purpose of striking at Marshall Field.* Field apart, he was against the amendment, either in principle or because it would work hardships on his constituency; but none of that mattered; possible damage to the country was of no consequence provided Field were injured. None of his colleagues commented on

this aspect of the matter: a United States senator disregarding conscience and constituency, using a Senate committee for private
satisfactions in utter disregard for—or, by his own feeling, in opposition to—the general welfare. ("The law," Aristotle wrote, "is
reason free from passion.")

Senator Clark went on, possibly in a tremulous voice:

I should simply like to point out an illustration along the line of that suggested by the Senator from Maryland, a case with which I was very familiar.
It was the case of my own father-in-law, the late Wilbur W. Marsh, of
Waterloo, Iowa, who was probably the most prominent and most eminent
breeder of Guernsey cattle who ever lived in the United States. [There followed a few hundred words of eulogy and statistics, directed *against* the
amendment, which culminated in this flat reversal:] It does seem to me that
any amendment which would be calculated to stop such activities as that is
an unfair amendment.

In committee the Senator had gone so far as to vote against his
late father-in-law's better interest, possibly the most heinous aspect
of his action; what domestic tortures had he risked? And with what
relief he must have found himself able to change his stand!

There followed more technical discussion, and then this:

Mr. DANAHER. . . . Let me say further to the Senator from Kentucky that
he has said that this amendment in its inception was the "Marshall Field
amendment," so-called.

Mr. BARKLEY. That is what it was called.

Mr. DANAHER. I do not know anything about the vulgar nomenclature to
which the Senator refers, but it is not mine, and I will tell the Senator that,
so far as I am concerned, this problem first rose back in the district of Connecticut, when it came to my notice [in a Connecticut tax case]. . . . It has
nothing to do with Marshall Field, and, so far as I am concerned, he is a
department store.

Mr. BARKLEY. It was known, as the Senator from Missouri [Mr. Clark]
has indicated, when it was first brought in, as the "Marshall Field amendment."

Mr. CLARK of Missouri. I voted for it under that misapprehension.

Mr. BARKLEY. It is now known as the hobby amendment. It is designed
to reach persons who have a hobby, but it reaches hundreds of thousands of
persons in this country whose hobby is to try to make an honest living out
of some business into which they have placed their money and in which
they have exercised an initiative, in connection with which they recognized

before they got into it that they might have losses over a period of years before the profit stage was reached.

Mr. DANAHER. I have no knowledge whatever of Mr. Field's losses in the newspaper field. For all I know he is making money. But I have the record of the case in which the Commissioner of Internal Revenue had to act in reference to Marshall Field in 1932. From 1924 to 1928, inclusive, the losses on Marshall Field's racing stables were as follows: On his American racing stables, in 1925 the loss was $130,000; in 1926 it was $134,000; in 1927 it was $72,000, and in 1928 it was $50,000. On his English racing stables, his loss in 1924 was $37,000; in 1925, $36,000; in 1926, $36,000; in 1927, $22,000, and in 1928, $51,000. I supply only round figures. I want to insist to the Senate that every single dime of that, to the extent of the taxability of the income as of those dates, was coming out of the American taxpayers, without his sharing in the losses which he thus absorbed in the interest of horse racing.

Mr. BARKLEY. Mr. President, it has been easy and would be easy for any Senator to pick out a few individuals of great wealth who interest themselves in some activity in which they may sustain losses. It is not in their behalf that I am speaking, although I do not think there is any rule of society or law or philosophy that ought to prevent a man from having a hobby if he wants one.

Mr. DANAHER. I want them to have hobbies.

Mr. BARKLEY. I have a hobby. I do not make any money out of it.

Mr. DANAHER. But I do not want the taxpayers to be called upon to pay 92 per cent of the loss.

Mr. BARKLEY. Some man may think his hobby is a legitimate business.

Mr. DANAHER. In that case, if the gross income of the individual is derivable from that business, he may charge off the loss.

Mr. BARKLEY. This amendment was adopted rather nonchalantly by the Senate at the last session.

Mr. DANAHER. But not in the Senate Finance Committee in this session.

Mr. BARKLEY. I think it was. No one was heard on it. No one was invited before the committee to testify as to the effect of the amendment. The Senator offered it during the last days of the consideration of the bill, and it was adopted. In connection with the last tax bill, it was adopted by the Senate without much debate, and went out in conference, because the House of Representatives felt—I think properly so—that the Senate ought not to devote itself to these little chicken-feed things in order to clutter up a bill with apparently innocent amendments which affected hundreds of thousands of people in the United States.

There followed three or four pages of pro-and-con; hypothetical hardships were dwelt upon. When the story was told of a man who had paid $38,000 for a first-class bull, a senator essayed humor:

Mr. ROBERTSON. I am interested in the telegram which the Senator read, stating that one man purchased a bull for $38,000.

Mr. THOMAS of Oklahoma. That is correct.

Mr. ROBERTSON. Turner bulls are known all over the cattle-raising country, particularly among Hereford herds. Anyone who has a top Turner bull is assured of the sale of his livestock at the highest price; and when he pays $38,000 for a bull he gets about $8,000 worth of bull and about $30,000 worth of advertising. In his income-tax return he should deduct $30,000 for advertising.

The debate ran on for half an hour more. Senator Barkley suggested the absence of a quorum, and the roll was called: sixty-nine senators were present, a good turnout. After a discussion of the amendment's potential effect on a manufacturer of shoe fittings in Maine, the vote approached; this was delayed for a moment while Senator Clark posed a parliamentary inquiry, wanting to know first if the amendment under discussion was indeed the Danaher amendment, and second if members in favor of it should vote "yea" and those opposed "nay." Confirmed in his suppositions, he yielded to the vote.

The amendment was passed.

In the House of Representatives the allowable deduction was raised to $50,000 annually, and the questions and answers were considerably more businesslike. One representative spoke against the amendment:

Mr. COCHRAN. Mr. Speaker, there is one provision of this conference report that does not appeal to me and I think the House conferees made a grave mistake in accepting the Senate amendment, although the amount was raised from $20,000 to $50,000. I am referring to the so-called hobby amendment. At the outset it was always referred to as the Marshall Field amendment. It seems that some wanted to tax properties of Mr. Field, especially his newspaper enterprises. When the matter was debated in the Senate it was shown beyond doubt by the Senator from Kentucky . . . that the amendment would not affect Mr. Field's newspapers. I might say that this was confirmed by one of the outstanding authorities on income tax law in the Treasury Department. So far as I can find no hearings were held by either the House or Senate on this subject.

This amendment, in my opinion, places a penalty on progress as well as science. . . .

Great benefits accrue from hobbies. . . .

Representative Cochran went on very sensibly to discuss Adolphus Busch's investment in a hobby that produced a workable Diesel engine, and Henry Ford's losses in soybean experiments. No representative was courageous enough to sacrifice conscience, honor, and the public interest in order to rebuke the tyrant Field.

The amendment was not capricious, and its passage, with the limitation raised to $50,000, was not evil. Two points were noisome: that the personal element should have been so strong, and that the legislative process should have been so obviously at the service of antiliberals. Colonel McCormick in Chicago had been blattering away about Field's deductions, and much of the archconservative wing of the press had joined him; but these were not men famed for their public service or—particularly—for their conscientious obedience to tax laws. They objected to Field because he was a liberal and a competitor. They should, in view of their own patriotic oratory, have welcomed competition; it was, according to them, the lifeblood of the body economic. But they did not; they suppressed their own competition whenever, and almost however, possible. One of their more violent objections to Field was that he called them out for it, publicly; *they were up against a man who honestly believed in competition, and they fought him as hard as they could.* Not as a lobby; the press had no need of a lobby. It made its wishes known, and as often as not an alert, sensitive Congress took note. The Marshall Field amendment had a basis in justice, but it was timed as a blow against Roosevelt and rich liberals who supported Roosevelt. It was a futile blow. Its effect on Field was salubrious, to the bafflement of its proponents. Before the matter even came to a vote Field was reorganizing his holdings. He was immune to the legislation. Its only effect on him was that he was forced to create a solid, profitable, enduring financial establishment: Field Enterprises, Incorporated. He had to seek out profitable businesses, and make them more profitable, to balance the losses he remained willing to absorb in the name of good journalism. Congress had forced him to lay the foundations of what would be, twenty years later, one of the two or three richest and most stable privately owned enterprises in the United States.

He accomplished that with determination, with consummate ability as a businessman (and in the face of the myth that he was a bad businessman); and he did it well without betraying his liberal principles. He displayed all the awareness, all the insight, all the energy and purpose of his grandfather. And he was shrewd enough to keep his enterprises intact for generations in just the way that his grandfather had: much of the fortune ultimately went to his grandsons in trust. They may someday give thanks that a relatively undistinguished senator impelled Marshall Field to the full exercise of his financial talents.

It must have been frustrating for Field's critics. The only way to get rid of democrats seemed to be to get rid of democracy, and they really didn't want to go that far.

Illustration
Section

Marshall Field I about 1900

Mrs. Marshall Field II with Marshall III

Mrs. Marshàll Field II with Marshall III [LEFT] and Henry

[ABOVE]

Private Field,
1st Illinois Cavalry,
1917

Field in his
early twenties

Pirie MacDonald

Field
as a pilot,
aged about thirty

Marshall and
Ruth Field
at Belmont Park,
1937

Field with children brought here by the U. S. Committee, 1940

Field and Thomas E. Dewey fact-finding for the USO at Fort Knox, Kentucky, 1941

[ABOVE] Marshall Field and Silliman Evans with the first-rehearsal edition of the Chicago *Sun*. Behind Field and to his right, full-face, is his good friend Charles Cushing. [BELOW] Field, John Golden, Mrs. Eleanor Roosevelt and Mayor Fiorello La Guardia, 1942

Marshall and Ruth Field: the *Sun*'s first birthday

The Publisher, 1943

[ABOVE] Marshall and Ruth Field with executives of *PM,* 1944

[OPPOSITE TOP] Field in Miami with the Churchills and Colonel Frank Clarke, their host

[OPPOSITE] With Vice President Alben Barkley, 1950

Associated Press wirephoto

Chicago *Sun-Times*

Chicago *Sun-Times*

Receiving the Rosenberger Medal from Chancellor Lawrence Kimpton of the University of Chicago

CHAPTER SEVEN

The most serious danger that menaces the freedom of the American press is the obvious anxiety of rich publishers about the freedom of the press.

—WILLIAM ALLEN WHITE,
Chicago *Times,* 1939

C HICAGO WAS ONCE IN WISCONSIN.

Which proves nothing; but any attempt to account for the Chicago *Tribune* should begin with at least an oddity. George Rogers Clark was not responsible for the geopolitical disposition of the Northwest Territory, but he won the area for the United States in 1778 and 1779 with two surprisingly easy victories, at Kaskaskia and Vincennes, after a remarkably difficult march through the wilderness. The British yielded the territory, to the hearty gratification of its few settlers, but maintained their fur stations on the Great Lakes in flagrant violation of the terms of cession. That was the first of a series of British nastinesses much resented by the Middle West and was—barring the American Revolution itself—the remote inspiration for Mayor of Chicago William Hale Thompson's reported promise, in the 1920s, to biff King George V on the snoot.

By the Ordinance of 1787 (the Revolution was over, but Washington was not yet President) the territorial authorities ceded sovereignty to the Federal government (the territory had originally been claimed for Virginia) but reserved the right to determine the boundaries of states to be formed from the region. Ultimately three to five states were envisioned, and in them slavery was to be prohibited.

The prospective states were duly mapped out: and the original

Illinois lacked the fourteen northern counties (the "northern tier") of the present state. Its northern line ran westward from the southern tip of Lake Michigan, roughly what is now Hammond, Indiana, to roughly what is now Davenport, Iowa. And in 1817 this small Illinois, its population over the requisite 60,000, applied for admission to the Union.

There was a snag. Sectional rivalry was already strong in Congress, and slavery had begun to be an issue. Most of Illinois's early immigration had been from Virginia, Kentucky, and Tennessee, and its political personality was Southern. New York and Massachusetts, leaders of the Northeastern Congressional bloc, were hostile to the idea of a new "Southern" state so far north; they were also fearful that ultimately the antislavery clause of the Ordinance would be abrogated or ignored. They therefore opposed the admission of Illinois, unless a large slice of lakefront real estate—north fifty miles along the lake, and westward to the territorial line—were added, to make immigration from New England and New York by water (the Erie Canal, on which construction had begun, and the Lakes) easier than the overland trek. The territorial authorities complied, and the fourteen counties were subtracted from Wisconsin. The expanded Illinois was admitted to the Union in 1818.

The expected migration occurred, and the state's political personality was consequently a bit schizoid—though both halves were conservative. Downstate, now popularly considered safely Republican, was Southern Democratic, and large pockets of it remain so. But northern Illinois passed through Federalism to the Republican party—with the obvious exception of Chicago. That city's Copperheads, during the Civil War, reflected the Southern origins of much of the state. They also reflected a disillusionment with the East that was statewide. Ex-Easterners often had good reason for moving west, and cut their ties to the coast quickly; Southerners in Illinois had little use for the increasingly industrial and abolitionist East. And as a debtor state Illinois was understandably hostile to its creditors. The result was a natural conservatism coupled with a fierce provincial pride.

The state's creditors were resented for a hundred years. The first out-of-state money invested in Illinois was British, offered to the state for internal development in the 1830s. A normal (for the

time) series of panics bankrupted many major enterprises, and
Illinois, created and settled by tough, independent men, found itself
obliged to grovel before British bankers. Railroads failed, toll roads
failed, canals failed. Gubernatorial campaigns were fought over the
single issue of repudiating the debts. By 1840 Illinois was so broke
that the fourteen northern counties held a convention in Rockford
and asked Wisconsin to take them back.*

There was one way out: New York banking houses were by then
rich, and seeking investment, and Illinois asked for sufficient credit
to disembarrass itself of the Britannic incubus. New York obliged.
Illinois's debts, and resentments, were transferred to New York.

By 1847 the state was struggling to its feet. In June of that year
the Chicago *Tribune* commenced publication. Eight years later a
man named Joseph Medill became its half owner. He was a violent
partisan of the new Republican party. He was also a violent xeno-
phobe, of impeccably Scotch-Irish Protestant background himself.
He had been editor of the Cleveland *Leader,* a Whig paper, and was
one of the first to use and promote the word Republican ("National
Republican" at the very beginning) as a name for the new coalition
of Whigs and Free-Soilers. Medill was not hospitable to the more
generous Free-Soil ideas. He was an abolitionist of sorts, but hated
Negroes; and he did not approve of throwing new land open to
unrestricted immigration. He believed that the United States belonged to a free white race—by which he meant clean-living Protestant Anglo-Saxons who were not New York bankers or railroad
owners. One of the *Tribune*'s first crusades was against abuse of the
public by the railroad industry, and it reflected Chicago's bitter
dependence on transport monopolies based in the East.† But the
newspaper did not rest there. It struck out at foreigners, Eastern-
ers, and slaveholders with equal fervor. When Medill was finally
granted a wish—war against the South—he failed completely to
understand that war, considering it at once an abolitionist crusade,
a war of liberation for the Northwest Territory, and a cleansing of

---

* Wisconsin declined. The matter was brought up again in jest a hundred and
twenty years later; Wisconsin stood firm.

† It was an honorable crusade, if the product of mixed motives. Twenty years
later its major demands were in the Republican national platform.

the nation that would leave it in the best high-tariff mercantile Protestant hands.*

He was not alone in those views, and must not—precisely as his most famous successor must not—be taken for a simple psychopath. He reflected much Middle Western opinion. Middle Westerners were only a generation or two removed from pioneers (Lincoln himself had fought Indians); they were hard, lean, religious sons of the soil with all the virtues and all the narrowness of such men everywhere—but they were free men and proud of it, and they were wise to fight the bondage of industry. They scorned dependence, on slaves or on monopoly railroads. Often they seemed to be fighting the third side of a triangular war; their concern with Vicksburg and an open Mississippi was not that the South be deprived of a waterway, but that the Northwest come out of the fighting with a free outlet for its grain. Theirs was an agricultural economy, and they felt an odd sympathy for the Southern farmer, even as they despised him as a slaver. They were proud of the Wisconsin cavalry, and proud of Sherman's magnificent army; and when that army finally reached Washington, via Georgia and the Carolinas, many of its men asked, with bitter humor, if they could keep fighting until they had licked the Army of the Potomac—with which they resented marching in the victory parades. They, and their families, were unaware that Medill had lost hope in 1863 and come out privately for abandoning the war and acknowledging secession; when the men got home they bought his newspaper. They read it because it was tough, patriotic, populist, and well distributed: as a reward for his support of Lincoln, Medill had sought and been granted several postmasterships, invaluable to his circulation department.

But the original immigrants from New England and New York and Virginia who, with their descendants, had composed a suitable audience for the *Tribune,* were now joined by others, less reputable: Central and Southern Europeans. Medill was annoyed and depressed by them; he vented his anger in his newspaper. But he left the *Tribune* in 1866; it passed temporarily into more moderate

---

* He agitated passionately for the war, and then tried to give the President, whom he had helped to elect, the benefit of his wisdom. Lincoln was rumored to have said something on the order of "You got your war; now go home and let us win it."

hands. Elected mayor in 1871, he went out of his way to enforce an ordinance banning the sale of drinks on Sunday—and discovered suddenly just how radically the population of his city had altered. A sixth of it was German, and the loss of Sunday afternoon's beer was a catastrophe. Americans of all descents protested, and Medill, disgusted that immigrant voters could challenge a real American, resigned his office and went off to Europe (!) to recover. When he returned he wanted the *Tribune* back, but to buy up control he needed a large amount of money.

He borrowed it from Marshall Field I, some said at 10 per cent per annum. He bought back his newspaper, cleaning out the noxious free-trade-and-tolerance elements; he suffered, but never acted upon, occasional advice from his new creditor until the loan was repaid; and he thenceforth concentrated on what was to become the World's Greatest Newspaper. No un-American elements escaped his notice, and his remedy was monotonously drastic: kill them. He suggested that radicals (he called them Communists, but he meant anarchists and syndicalists and socialists too, and probably single taxers and maybe free traders) be lynched publicly en masse, and that beggars be mercifully dispatched by a touch of arsenic in the handout. There was simply no room in his cosmos for failure, for dissidence, for foreigners, for charity, for compassion. Granted the power, he would happily have transformed Illinois into one vast Sabbatarian presbytery.

The point of all this historical filigree is, however, that the Chicago *Tribune* was never, even when run by men of precarious mental health, simply a crackpot sheet. Gibbon, writing about Zoroastrian institutions, said, "But in that motley composition, dictated by reason and passion, by enthusiasm and by selfish motives, some useful and sublime truths were disgraced by a mixture of the most abject and dangerous superstition." Roughly that might be said of the *Tribune*'s outlook. Local pride, independence, and a love of freedom were so far perverted by the Byzantine neuroses of a publishing dynasty that only those upon whom the violence had been worked gradually were able to continue taking the newspaper seriously. In the twentieth century the common reaction to the *Tribune* outside "Chicagoland" was one of clinical amazement or fierce detestation; yet the newspaper had grown in its own soil, and if it rarely reflected truth, it usually refracted some sort of reality.

In 1909 Medill's grandson, Robert Rutherford McCormick, became treasurer of the Tribune Company; his cousin, Joseph Medill Patterson, became its secretary. McCormick had not been corrupted by his sojourn in the East, at Groton and Yale; nor by his career in Chicago politics—he had been elected first alderman and then head of the Sanitary District, his earliest experience in regulating the flow of sewage. In 1911 he became president of the Tribune Company, and the newspaper became, officially and with no embarrassment, the World's Greatest Newspaper. It also became a participant in the most savage circulation war this country has known—men were crippled and killed; but in the next seven years circulation rose to over 400,000, and the *Tribune* stood first in Chicago.

Both McCormick and Patterson served during the World War. Patterson saw action in four heavy battles and came out, like Field, a captain. McCormick, who had toured the Russian front as a civilian in 1914 and had written, "I have tasted the wine of death and its flavor will be forever in my throat," did his sipping as a soldier behind the lines, where his executive abilities and Larger View were more valuable; he became a colonel and won the Distinguished Service Medal. When the two returned, the Tribune Company backed Patterson's *Illustrated News,* which quickly became the New York *Daily News;* and the Chicago-New York axis was born.

McCormick was much like Medill, and pined for the same sort of Golden Age. But if Medill was behind his times in 1870, McCormick was in another universe altogether half a century later. He was a fourteenth-century duke—of a great family, splendidly groomed, an impressive six feet two, elegantly mustached, educated, a power in politics, and a Gothic paranoid: secret panels in his office, armed guards outside it, a wolfhound at his heels, the world populated entirely by peasants, traitors, and latitudinarian troubadours.

His writings and speeches—which should have been gathered together for the entertainment of an incredulous posterity—ranged from Heliogabalan purple to Apocalyptic black, and the infelicity of his style (Victorian Vulgate) was matched only by the extravagance of his ideas (Caligulan). Aside from the œnological nobilities of war, he discoursed on the dangers of friendship with England; on the perfidy of intellectuals; on the unreliability of the foreign-born; and on the dangers of communism, which he defined generally as that doctrine advocated by anyone who disagreed with him, and specifically as whatever Roosevelt was trying to do at the moment. To his credit, he was impartial enough to point out that we had been brought "to the brink of destruction" even before Roosevelt, by the extravagant fiscal policies of wastrels like Comrades Coolidge, Hoover, Mellon, etc. Throughout McCormick's life the United States *lived* on the brink of destruction; it was a matter of seconds, or at most a day or two. To maintain his charges he distorted, omitted, implied; when necessary he lied outright. Charged with knowledge of, if not complicity in, the murders incidental to the great circulation war, he replied, "It is well known to all newspapermen in Chicago . . . that in 1911 I was not editor, publisher, or business manager of the *Tribune*. . . . I had not been brought up in the newspaper. It was not contemplated by anyone that I would enter the newspaper. The events which led to my entering it three years later were not in sight." He had been elected president of the Tribune Company on March 1, 1911.

Through the 1930s he opposed the New Deal viciously; opened his editorial columns to officials of the Nazi government, one of whom wrote a two-part panegyric for successive Sunday editions; calumniated the British at every opportunity; accused Roosevelt of heading a "war party" composed of Communists; and praised the clean (their baths were coeducational, but they did bathe) and industrious (Nanking was sacked efficiently and without remission) Japanese. ("What vital interests of the United States can Japan threaten? She cannot attack us. That is a military impossibility. Even our base at Hawaii is beyond the striking power of her fleet." These dicta, the fruits of meditation by the Greatest Military Mind of our era, were offered on October 27, 1941.) And these were not occasional sallies into editorial omniscience: they were the steady diet of *Tribune* readers.* McCormick is not open to the charge of

---

* There are *Tribune* readers even now—primarily among the well-to-do—who claim to have the only accurate, unbiased, insider's view of the 1930s and 1940s, everyone else having been misled by Communists in high place. They find it hard to admit that two or three decades of *any* single newspaper will warp a reader's vision.

inconsistency on all counts: he was consistently irrational, and consistently wrong. He was of sound mind; he knew who he was and where he was and what year it was (within seven or eight centuries); but it is impossible to exaggerate his irresponsibility. Perhaps his crowning service to the people of the United States was a great newsbeat, a journalistic coup, on December 4, 1941, headlined F.D.R.'S WAR PLANS! It was a deliberate release of top-secret information—"the construction of a strategic and tactical plan for the fighting of a global war in case it should eventuate," in Henry Stimson's official prose—in an effort to prove that Roosevelt (who would have been an incompetent commander-in-chief indeed if he had not ordered the plans drawn up) * was a warmonger bent on the destruction and betrayal of the United States. McCormick was rebuked immediately and fiercely by Republican Secretary of War Stimson:

What do you think of the patriotism of a man or a newspaper that would take these confidential studies and make them public to the enemies of this country? . . . While their publication doubtless will be a source of gratification to our potential enemies, and a possible source of impairment and embarrassment to our national defense, the chief evil of their publication is the revelation that there should be among us any group of persons so lacking in appreciation of the danger that confronts the country, and so wanting in loyalty and patriotism to their government that they would be willing to take and publish such reports.

McCormick's answer appeared on December 7, 1941:

We regard the achievement as among the greatest contributions to the welfare of our country which this or any other newspaper has ever made.

The Japanese attacked Pearl Harbor that afternoon. The next day McCormick reversed himself without blinking:

America faces war through no volition of any American. Recriminations are useless and we doubt they will be indulged in. Certainly not by us.

Certainly not.

A "gentleman," member of the best clubs, active in charities, a powerful publisher, a liar and an egomaniac, McCormick was not

---

* The public may have been naïve enough to be shocked, but McCormick was after all a military expert, and must have known that there have always existed war plans for even the remotest contingencies—invasion of Canada, for example—in even the most peaceful of times.

often called a fascist. In his day a man could be called a Communist if he came out for public housing or Negro rights; but no one was ever called a fascist until he put on a colored shirt and an armband. Americans were very polite about that. But the great tragedy of McCormick's life was that he, with a few select lieutenants, could not control the economy, morals, and foreign affairs of this country. He knew better than even to consider a grab for power, but if a right-wing coup had ever been remotely possible he would surely have supported it (he discussed the possibility with obvious approval in early 1941), and would probably have accepted any after-the-fact offer to lead. He would have relished a corporate state and a place on its board. Everywhere he looked he saw the enemy: anarchists, Communists, foreigners, "hyphenates," effeminates, libertines, waiting only for the chance to sell us out for Russian gold. If facts failed to support his allegations he created his own facts, a technique seized upon and refined ten years later. His hatred of Roosevelt was psychotic,* and to the stock arguments that the New Deal would destroy American character, cripple American business, and make peons of us all, he added his own Napoleonic taste for the totalitarian. He used the pronoun "I" as God might have. "The Germans are not so tough," he told a Senate committee early in 1941. "I have been up against them and there is no use being scared of them." Asked what he would feel if Hitler conquered England and occupied her bases in the Western Hemisphere, he answered in majestic simplicity, "I would not let him do it."

It was difficult to find one redeeming feature in the man, one quality that fitted him, however slightly, for his position as publisher and pundit. He had a sense of humor, but it never showed in public; † and if he was affable, polite, and articulate at his club,

---

* Denis Brogan wrote in 1951 (in *The Price of Revolution*), "I have known men who had been in German, Spanish, Russian concentration camps who could yet speak of Hitler, Franco, Stalin with far more self-control and objectivity than many rich Americans spoke or still speak of Roosevelt."

† Meeting with his high-powered editorial staff one day, he ran down the first four editorials, all anti-Roosevelt, and approved. His editor then informed him that Lloyd Wendt, the youngest of the editorial writers, was going to do a short piece on a bad tree blight that had been depleting local forests, including McCormick's own woodlands. "Really," McCormick said gruffly. "And what do you propose to write about it?"

"I thought I'd blame it on Mr. Roosevelt," Wendt drawled drily, and a couple of hundred thousand dollars' worth of editorial personnel froze in mid-breath.

that qualified him for club membership and not for publishing. Many of his readers took him seriously; most did not. A prevailing reaction to the *Tribune* was gratitude for its features and its city and suburban coverage, coupled with casual derision of its national and international editorial policies. (Chicago was, after all, full of loyal Democrats, who bought the *Tribune* for its local news and features.) Still, there were believers, and for a time they were a force in American politics. Movements ranging from America First, which had the support of some intelligent and honest people, to various fascist organizations found strong support in McCormick's domains. Some of the Middle West was a northerly Bible Belt, and it was easy enough to equate grass-roots virtue and provincial pride with McCormick's authoritarian flag-waving. Starting from the natural resistance of pioneer farmers to capitalists and bureaucrats, the *Tribune* had progressed to the most vicious kind of man-on-horseback hatreds. It survived and grew by telling Yahoos what they wanted to hear: that they were better than others, that only they were loyal, that everybody else was weak and evil, that they were *right* in their fears and dislikes and therefore had no need to be tolerant or even reasonable—in short, that ingrained prejudices were absolute, revealed truth. The burden of the *Tribune*'s message, repeated often, sandwiched between appeals for charity and brotherhood, was that anyone who shared its political views—*anyone*, not only the Anglo-Saxon even if he was a useless drunk and wife beater, but also the Negro if he was properly segregationist and the Jew if he was well assimilated and right-thinking—was superior to alien-oriented Eastern Seaboard democrats like Albert Einstein or Franklin Roosevelt or, in good time and *toutes proportions gardées,* Marshall Field.

That was the Chicago *Tribune* up to 1941. To a significant area of the country, including a truly great city, it was the daily interpreter—in the morning, the only interpreter—of a world far beyond its own comprehension. Field despised it. He did not hate easily, and he never hated Colonel McCormick; an old-fashioned Whig-and-Tory tolerance made real hate impossible. In a loose, upper-

---

Wendt gazed innocently at the Colonel; no one else even dared look up. After a long five seconds, McCormick's eyes twinkled and he roared "Ho! Ho! Ho!" like a benevolent walrus.

class-citizen way, the two were associated. They belonged to some of the same clubs; they had many friends in common; they both owned tracts of Chicago real estate. If McCormick called Field a traitor to his class, and if Field scorned McCormick's Neronian megalomania, the two nevertheless nodded and spoke briefly at charity luncheons. When Field left on one of his trips to Chicago in the summer of 1941 he remarked whimsically to Mrs. Field, "I suppose I'll have to drop in and say hello to Bertie."

The *Tribune* and its monopoly were his enemy, and not the Colonel. Whiggishly he refused to pursue politics over the threshold of his club or drawing room. It must have been a strain at times, but it was civilized behavior in the best paleo-Victorian manner, and McCormick, perhaps surprisingly, maintained an equally patrician affability in personal confrontations. There were not many of those after 1941, when Marshall Field announced the imminent establishment of a morning newspaper in direct competition with the Chicago *Tribune*.

2

The real danger, to Field, lay in the lack of competition; at stake was access to facts. New York had four morning papers, Chicago one. There could be no real debate. And it was galling to think that the *Tribune* was considered by the rest of the world a spokesman for Chicago. Having outlived its identification with gangsters, Chicago was cursed with another undeserved trademark. McCormick had rivals at a distance: the St. Louis *Post-Dispatch* to the south and the Milwaukee *Journal* to the north; but within the *Tribune*'s range no one was making a fight of it.

Field had other reasons, too, for coming back. He was still a part of Chicago, and would be pitting one great Middle Western name against another. And New York was not the city for a Field-run newspaper. *PM* was Ingersoll's; Field had no wish to take it over or to interfere with Ingersoll's execution of his own concepts, techniques, and editorial program; still less did he want to set himself up as a competitor, of which *PM* had a sufficiency. In Chicago the return of the native would add drama; in Chicago the liberals needed more help than they were getting, and the rumor of Field's return was a tonic. (At one gathering of liberals and academicians, including Saul Alinsky, a neighborhood planner and Field's friend since 1939, it was suggested that a one-man newspaper was dangerous; that it ought to be backed by a group. Alinsky asked, with asperity, "Who the hell else *is* there?")

But primarily isolationism was Field's reason: a doctrine strong in the Middle West, remote from the seacoasts and foreign traffic, historically suspicious of the European entanglements of Eastern banking houses, historically true-blue and virtuous in its defense of the American Way—which had been a very satisfactory way for several decades.* Field was of course spoiled for all that: he was half a New Yorker, and his British sympathies were pronounced, permanent, and public; even before 1939 he had believed that we must go to England's aid before it was too late. McCormick was a natural focus of Field's campaign. Generally, because he represented what Field had come to detest. Less generally, because Roosevelt needed an ally in Chicago. Specifically and personally, because Field was worried about the state of the American press; because McCormick stood at the head of the opposition to what Field and many of his friends were trying to do in political and social areas; and perhaps even because Field remembered so clearly a noisy, frightened committee of the Illinois State Legislature.

That committee (which was later called the Broyles Committee) had been established to keep the state safe from un-American thought, word, and deed. In 1935 its attention was drawn to the plight of Mr. Charles R. Walgreen, the eminent pharmacist, who had withdrawn his niece from the University of Chicago, charging that she was being instructed in communism.† The *Communist Manifesto,* for example, was on her reading list. The University, under its brilliant young president Robert M. Hutchins, had already drawn fire for its bizarre insistence on education, if necessary to the detriment of football, fraternities, and bibulous *bel canto.* The Walgreen charges were timely (because timeless), and the Committee

---

* Field, who understood tradition, never underestimated its strength or legitimacy. He felt that traditions were a cumulative fulfillment of deep and important needs; but he knew too that they became obsolete as the needs did.

† Twenty-five years later such instruction was mandatory *in high school* in many states; the University of Chicago had been a quarter of a century ahead of its times. But in 1935 ignorance was bliss.

investigated. It had the support of all Chicago's newspapers except the *Times*.* Frank Knox's *News* was restrained, but the Hearst paper, and of course the *Tribune,* let themselves go.† Hutchins defended himself ably, but it was a time when friends counted, and Marshall Field proved to be a friend; at the height of the melee he sent Hutchins a brief note on academic freedom, folded around a check for $10,000.

Hutchins did so well, in fact, that the Committee cleared the University of all charges. William Benton then mediated conversations between Hutchins and Walgreen, in the course of which the latter displayed more understanding and generosity than the former had expected; by early 1937 Walgreen had given the University $550,-000 toward the establishment of the Charles R. Walgreen Foundation for the Study of American Institutions, designed to "forward the development of good citizenship and the improvement of public service."

But the stigma remained, and for a time it was almost as chic to make jokes about the University, or about Hutchins, as to malign the President or Mrs. Roosevelt. It may have been that specific irritant which finally decided Field. At luncheon with his fellow trustee William Benton in early 1941, he suddenly said, "Bill, Chicago needs a liberal newspaper, and I've decided to start one. How do I do it?"

Benton was not the first to whom Field had broached the idea. He had mentioned it to a few of his advisers, and had discussed it at length with Charles Cushing. Benton and Cushing now proceeded to work independently on it.

Cushing was well connected, and had not long before accepted an assignment from Field that made his fact-finding mission much easier. He was, oddly enough, in the employ of *PM,* a newspaper for which he—a conservative financial expert—had little love. *PM*'s reporting-in-depth had resulted in an accumulation of unused features and photographs. In the winter of 1940–41 Field had asked

---

* From which Mr. Walgreen withdrew his advertising.

† For about five years Hutchins was never mentioned by name in the *Tribune;* "the President of the University" was as specific as McCormick permitted. Hearst did the same to Orson Welles after *Citizen Kane.* Freedom of the press.

R. A. Lasley and Company (it was Cushing's suggestion) to survey *PM*'s situation and future possibilities, and one of the Company's recommendations was that the excess feature material, or "overset," be adapted to the purposes of a Sunday newspaper magazine section—the new and lumpishly genteel phrase for a Sunday supplement. Field knew that a substantial number of newspapers needed such a magazine, unable to use existing supplements because the syndicates considered them "secondary" newspapers and had promised their "primary" papers exclusivity. Cushing had joined Field's staff as a supersalesman for the magazine, of which he owned 10 per cent. First the name was cleared: "Parade" as a title was subject to tenuous claims by both Time Inc. and *This Week,* and was bought for Field through a dummy. In the spring of 1941 trial copies of *Parade,* thirty-two pages on sturdy white paper, were printed and distributed to small towns in New Jersey, with or without local mastheads and logotypes.

The response was good, barring one sad note that Cushing had foreseen: *Parade*'s association with *PM* antagonized several national advertisers, and a few of the trial newspapers complained immediately. A small town in southern New Jersey was no place for radical overtones. *Parade*'s management succeeded in convincing both advertisers and publishers that the connection was in name only, and that *Parade* would offer its own editorial matter.

Cushing's first sale was to the Nashville *Tennessean,* circulation 123,853. The *Tennessean*'s owner and publisher was a man named Silliman Evans, an old war comrade of Cushing. Their talks, in the spring of 1941, had been on two topics: the supplement, and Marshall Field's plans for Chicago. Even before Evans bought the services of *Parade,* he had sold his own to Marshall Field.

Benton had meanwhile scouted the Chicago *Times,* going directly to his friend Samuel Emory Thomason, who was also the University's friend. Thomason was highly respected by Chicago's newspapermen, a man of energy and courage, a remarkable boss to his own staff. He and Colonel McCormick had been classmates at Northwestern Law School and had set up shop together as McCormick & Thomason; eventually the latter became general manager of the *Tribune.* His break with the Colonel was said to have occurred at contract time, in the late 1920s, the dialogue approximately this:

Thomason: "I've got my new contract. I've left the salary and duties blank."

McCormick: "Why blank?"

Thomason: "You're the boss; you have a right to fill them in."

McCormick: "A quarter-million all right, as usual?"

Thomason: "Fine. And the duties?"

McCormick (eyebrows Gothic arches): "For two hundred fifty thousand dollars a year you'll do as you're told."

Thomason rises, tears up contract, walks out.

He went on to establish the *Times,* an afternoon tabloid that tried to be liberal and often succeeded. His employees' affection was deep, and was a response to his warmth and probity; he and the staff were on a first-name basis (*both* ways). That relationship was severely tried during the Depression, when there just wasn't enough cash on hand for payrolls; the unions, including the printers' chapel, agreed to accept part cash, part shares in the newspaper. The arrangement was rare, if not unique, and ultimately profitable to the staff.

Benton went to see Thomason, and announced Field's decision. "Well, that's the end of the *Times,*" Thomason said ruefully. "I'm just hanging on by a hair." But it was obvious to both men that the *Times* might be Field's answer. "He can get into the fight the first day," Thomason urged. "The only way to lick Bertie is with a morning tabloid. Then he can bid for the *News,* and he's got it morning and evening."

It was not so simple. Thomason owed the International Paper Company about $3,000,000, and thought he might be able to settle for a third of that if they were all discreet. The *Times* was represented by 90,000 shares of stock, much of it owned by those who had accepted his offer during the Depression; he would offer it to Field at $30 a share. The *Times* could be had, debt-free, for $3,700,000.

Benton and Thomason took the Century to New York and visited Field in his Park Avenue flat. Field listened. With the outline before him he said, "All right. This makes sense. But suppose I do buy the *Times*—how do I get the *Daily News?*" Benton had half an answer: he and Frank Knox were old friends. A trip to Washington might solve the problem. Knox was seventy years old, a Republican Secretary of the Navy under That Man, cordially disliked among Chicago's conservatives for having served the Democrats. He might jump at the chance to sell himself out of Chicago.

Benton boarded a train.

Meanwhile Charles Cushing had been hard at work. He had gone to see another friend, this one in Washington, George Allen, who was also friend to several Presidents, to John Nance Garner, and to Jesse Jones. Garner and Jones knew Evans and approved of him— they were all three Texans, for one thing, and Jones had been a guardian angel to Evans. Jesse Jones was head of the Reconstruction Finance Corporation,* which had accumulated reams and quires of the Nashville *Tennessean*'s commercial paper; when a thorough reorganization became inevitable, it was he who had suggested—and from him it was an instruction—Evans as owner-publisher. Cushing and Allen agreed that Evans would do well in Chicago; and Allen mentioned the plan to Jones, who also approved. Evans had proved himself a competent publisher, and Field would be glad to hear that the man was a Southern liberal: perhaps not the same as a Northern liberal, but not the same as that New York crowd either. More respectable. To Cushing, who cherished Field † but distrusted liberals, Evans was a perfect choice.

Secretary Knox was an old pro, and Benton's proposition interested him immediately. But he refrained from a yes or no. "I don't know whether I want to sell or not," he said. "I'll have to think about it. But if Marshall Field decides to come in with a new morning paper, I'll print it for him in my plant." Which was by no means a disinterested gesture of friendship: the *News* owned a good deal of real estate, and far more plant than it needed at the time.

Benton, returning to New York with a sense that he had done remarkably well in answering Field's original question—"How do

---

* And consequently one of the most powerful men in America for a decade. It was said that $50,000,000,000 passed through his hands and not a penny came unstuck.

† Some wondered if he was a hanger-on. He was not. His affection for Field was deep and abiding, and his services to Field were financially important.

I do it?"—then made what he later considered a serious blunder. Feeling that it would be presumptuous to offer Field direct financial advice—how to negotiate, how to interpret Knox's words—he reported his conversations with a minimal gloss. He was sure that Field would recognize Knox's response as the first round in what might be an interesting series of discussions, and was reluctant to belabor the obvious: that Knox had a great deal to gain from leasing his presses but would—if Field held firm and bargained hard—doubtless be willing to sell the *Daily News*. Benton might have been more forceful if he had known that Cushing was preparing alternate plans for Field; as it was, he left for a Florida vacation unaware that Field was contemplating an altogether new morning paper.

Field was in a hurry. The United States seemed to him woefully unprepared, materially and psychologically, for what the next five years might offer, and that impression had been strengthened by his attendance at a meeting of the Fight for Freedom Committee at the Town Hall Club in New York on the evening of April 30, 1941. Harold Ickes, Secretary of the Interior, was the speaker, and he devoted his talk to the measures taken, or proposed, by the administration "to meet foreign propaganda and to persuade our own people." The audience included Lewis Mumford, Robert Sherwood, George Fielding Eliot, John Loeb, Spyros Skouras, Stanley High, and Field's old friend James Warburg, among others. Ickes and Field chatted unmomentously:

Marshall Field was one of those at the dinner. I had never seen him before. He is a good-looking man of representative appearance, but he seemed to be very shy. While many talked, even if only to ask questions, he said nothing at all. After the meeting I told him that when I was a cub reporter I had on one occasion interviewed his grandfather. He remarked that he didn't imagine I had gotten anything out of him, and my reply was that I had gotten what I had gone for because it was just a conventional statement.

But Field came away more convinced than ever of the need for immediate action in the Middle West.

Within a month or so Cushing had drawn up a tentative program for the future newspaper. Silliman Evans was to be its publisher, and he was unprepossessing: short, rotund, energetic, a pragmatist;

a cigar mangler and a shrewd politician. But Cushing emphasized two points: Evans was a driving executive, and a new paper would need several such; and his reputation was that of a good Southern liberal, which Field would appreciate.

There was more to Evans than that—and less. He was the son of a circuit-riding Methodist preacher, devout, poor, and fiercely respectable; Evans had had to fight his way up from fearful poverty and provincialism. He had scrabbled for an education, not a good one but enough, and had elbowed his way into Southern politics with a sharp, almost primitive, instinct for the success or failure of the people he met. He made friends in a hurry and dropped some of them in an equal hurry. He ignored no possible advantage, no toe-hold, no fingerhold, in his struggle upward.

He made it. If he "got all the mileage there was out of his ticket," if he "had intense loyalties that he'd change at the drop of a hat," * he also knew how to run a newspaper, and he was accustomed to being in a hurry. If he had six months to show a profit, he'd show it. Or so it was believed.

As a liberal he was not so impressive.† He had won the reputation by leading a two-fisted campaign against Tennessee's poll tax. Uncritical liberals, responding to the phrase "poll tax" and seeking no further, approved, and Evans enjoyed their approval. But he cared not a bit, really, who voted in Tennessee, provided he could whup the tar out of Memphis's boss Ed Crump; and one powerful weapon was the enfranchisement of a large body of anti-Crump voters. In the late 1930s Silliman Evans was not the man to range himself on the side of the Tennessee Negro; but Tennessee was a poor state, and thousands of whites, too, were disenfranchised by even a modest poll tax; he became their champion, and if the outside world thought highly of him, so much the better.††

---

* Both phrases spoken by a man who had worked with him for some time.
† Northern liberals may make that statement too often about Southern liberals, unappreciative of the contradictions, personal and professional, that the latter face every day. But Evans was not really a liberal at all.
†† Tennessee was indeed poor; Grundy County was at one time considered the poorest in the United States. It was there that the Highlander Folk School, to which Field later contributed through the Foundation, began its nefarious work of educating workingmen to fight for their rights. The only rights they were interested in at the time were economic, and the School taught them to take a hard, unquestionably and unblushingly left-wing, look at the way this country's economy was

How much of this Cushing knew is moot; probably a good deal. But he did know that Evans could get things done. Cushing was very dubious of "the *PM* crowd," and unquestionably did what he could to move Marshall Field into Chicago's newspaper world with a competent, tested, nonexperimental, and above all nonradical, crew of journalists.

Benton returned from Florida in late spring, and a few days later read in *The New York Times* that Marshall Field had decided to invade Chicago with a brand-new newspaper of standard size, to be printed on the presses of the Chicago *Daily News*. Its publisher would be Silliman Evans.

Benton rushed to Field's office, possibly reflecting with Emerson that "no man has learned anything rightly, until he knows that every day is doomsday." Field had set the most difficult and expensive course possible, and Benton's alarm was obvious.

Field explained calmly. "After you left, Charlie Cushing took me to lunch with Evans; you know they served together in the war. They persuaded me that to go up against the *Tribune* with a tabloid wouldn't give it stiff enough competition. Cushing thought I ought to hire Evans and start from scratch with a standard size paper.* I told them about Knox's proposal to you, and we've arranged to use his plant." Benton, feeling that he had somehow let Field down, let the University down, let Chicago down, asked more

---

run. The School was also integrated. It was naturally called Communist. In October and November, 1939, Evans's *Tennessean* sent out a reporter in disguise who investigated the School. The newspaper then ran a series of vicious articles, full of wild distortions and outright lies, "proving" that the School was Communist. Field never knew about that series until much later. One of the stories circulated—of course untrue—was that only three portraits hung in the School's administrative office: of Stalin, Eleanor Roosevelt, and Marshall Field. In November, 1959, the state of Tennessee moved to close the School on the ground that it violated the state's segregation laws, but the School, with Mrs. Roosevelt's moral support, defeated the attempt. It was finally beaten in 1961, after almost thirty years of operation, on the ground that it sold intoxicating beverages without a license. It was a long way from the nearest tavern, where integrated drinking was not allowed anyway, and the students had bought beer by the case, dropping nickels and dimes into a bowl to pay for the next case. Academic freedom: Scopes to Highlander.

* What Field omitted here was that Roosevelt had passed along a request not to publish in tabloid size in order not to compete with the *Times*, which was the only newspaper in Chicago that supported the administration. But Field preferred a standard size in any case.

questions, but Field had nothing essential to add except that "Emory Thomason looked old and tired; Evans is young and vigorous."

So, in outline, was the decision made. Field had conferred with Richardson and Weitzel, his immediate financial advisers, and with Louis Weiss, his attorney and close friend; he had reviewed his brief experience with *PM;* he had listened to Cushing, considered Mc-Cormick, looked once more at Europe and America, weighed assumptions and possibilities, and then acted. He was pleased. This was to be *his* newspaper, he thought; but he was wrong. He brought to publishing that diffidence, that politeness, that patience which marked his dealings with all men. The Chicago *Sun* suffered not from the presence of a bumbling owner, but from the reserved modesty of its very capable owner. What the newspaper needed for the next ten years was not less Field, but more.

3

That was hardly obvious in the summer of 1941. When the Nashville *Tennessean* subscribed to *Parade* on July 13, Evans was already acting manager of the Chicago newspaper, considering policy, investigating circulation, and scouting for personnel. He was in charge of a crash program: he had been hired to build a newspaper out of nothing in six months. There were two primary pressures: winter and spring advertising schedules, and the midwinter peak of circulation. The advertising schedules were drawn up well in advance, and agencies had to be able to count on Evans's estimate of publication day—and of circulation—if the *Sun* was to begin with any sort of financial break. And there was a third pressure, remote, vague, always present, more important to Field than to Evans: news of the war was not good. England no longer stood alone, but isolationism was strong again after the invasion of Russia ("Let them destroy each other. It's not our fight"), and if Field's newspaper was to do what he hoped it might—prod the country into accepting its international responsibilities—sooner was better than later.

The newspaper needed a name, and Evans decided to make friends while finding one: he announced a $10,000 prize contest. Chicago was interested. (More than interested. That was the sum-

mer of a mass meeting in Orchestra Hall, technically proadministration but actually anti-McCormick, after which the *conférenciers*
went out on the streets and burned every issue of the *Tribune* they
could lay hands on.) Over 220,000 entries poured in. (Frank Knox
told Harold Ickes that 250,000 entries had been received, subscriptions accompanying most of them, and that he expected the *Sun* to
start out with over 200,000 paid-up subscribers and to establish itself quickly.) The suggestion Field liked best was "The McCormick
Reaper," but such levity was considered unbecoming. "The Chicago
Sun" won more votes than any other name, and the prize went to
Mr. Russell Trenholme, whose reasons were poetic: "Well, it seems
to me that when morning comes you look for two things to make
your world right: you look for the sun and sunlight, and you look
for your morning paper for the truth of what's going on in the
world." Mr. Trenholme could not have known that there were
cloudy days ahead.

All the early troubles of the Chicago *Sun* were a consequence of
the need for speed. Some blamed them on Evans; but he too was a
consequence of the need for speed; he had been hired because he
was presumed able to haze an infant paper to its feet before it had
any real muscle. The deal with Knox was not economical—far from
it—but there was no time for extended haggling. The staff was not
brilliant—with exceptions—but there was no time to pick and
choose. The news coverage was not complete—partly because the
Associated Press denied the *Sun* membership—and there was barely
time to establish a network of correspondents and photographers.
One thing—an audience of tough, boisterous Chicagoans who
might not be prolabor, proadministration, interventionist, but who
were at least several decades ahead of the Colonel in their political
awareness—Field thought he had; but it was a long time before he
could be sure of even that.

Evans tried hard, but he made mistakes. He hired several advertising agencies to handle the *Sun*'s promotions, feeling that more
information and opportunities would rise from a wider distribution
of the problems (and feeling also that more advertising might find
its way to the *Sun*). He was wrong on both counts, and the mistake
was extravagantly wasteful. Evans liked promotion, and seems never

to have understood Field's opinion that the best promotion was a good newspaper.

And apparently Evans never felt that the personnel—editors and reporters anyway—might just as well be on Field's side of the political fence. Hearst's morning newspaper in Chicago had recently folded, and in a period when newspapermen were generally scarce Chicago boasted a temporary surplus. So for an adamantly liberal newspaper, the *Sun* began life with a sensational collection—about half the staff—of Hearst hacks and reactionaries, spiced by a few rummies. (For months the *Sun* was referred to as "the Field Museum of Hearst Antiques.") Many of them were good, or even great, newspapermen in the old *Front Page* tradition (SLAYER OF EIGHT DIES PRAYING; 'HE WAS A GOOD BOY,' MOTHER SAYS), but had no business on a Marshall Field newspaper. Liberal or not, Field was intelligent, and persisted in the heresy that the public was, given half a chance, permeable by reason. Too much of his staff had been brought up on the old rules ("One is a murder; two, a sex-killing; three or more, a massacre"). The old-fashioned political map, an ideological Mercator projection on which islands of pride and prejudice loomed larger than continents of sense and sensibility, was slowly being emended by great circles of truth and thoughtfulness, circles that often crossed bleak stretches of self-revelation and honesty but were the shortest distance between man and man. Yet most of Field's staff was steering by rote, and not by the stars.

But—they could get a newspaper on the streets. And among those who agreed with Field were some of the best journalists available. Many of them left in the first two or three years, largely because of Evans; others, hopeful, replaced them. (Some of the best men were rarely in the Chicago offices: foreign correspondents and the Washington bureau.) All in all, it was several years before the *Sun* could boast a first-rate all-around staff.

Some welcome encouragement arrived about three weeks before publication day: a letter from the President.

November 12, 1941

Dear Marshall:

I congratulate you on the opportunity for constructive service to the public which is yours in launching a new newspaper in Chicago.

I am sure you will win the confidence and patronage of an ever increasing clientele. I think it is particularly fortunate that you have my old friend Silliman Evans as publisher. And I know your paper will have all the success which an honest newspaper deserves.

The very simplicity of your motto: "An honest newspaper" is appealing. In living up to that high ideal you will, in Mark Twain's phrase, "gratify some people and astonish the rest."

Very sincerely yours,
Franklin D. Roosevelt

By the end of November, 1941, the *Sun* was ready for its dry runs. These had to be complete newspapers, printed as if for immediate sale, run off in issues of a thousand copies. For all the staff except circulation, the *Sun* came out on November 24, a Monday, with the printing of Tuesday's early edition. The run was three and a half hours late (some of the delay was attributable to the need for publicity photographs of various stages of the work), but Evans declared himself satisfied with the finished product: he would have been willing to go onto the streets with it as it stood. A week of private printings followed, including a seventy-two-page Sunday edition (plus *Parade* and sixteen pages of funnies). Field was absorbed and happy. He was up half the night sharing the excitement with old hands. Chicago itself was excited. One of its young men who waited up on the night of December 3, and who put down his two cents with a deep sigh of real satisfaction, said later, "You have no idea how excited some of us were. We were half ashamed of Chicago all through the thirties, because of that son of a bitch [the Leader of the Opposition], and we hung around the newsstands that night like expectant fathers. Some of the candy stores stayed open till two, three in the morning. When the papers came the dealer could hardly get them untied—we were crowding around him for a glimpse of the front page, and he had to shoo us back. They went like hot cakes—do you know they sold 900,000 copies that night? Some of us didn't even have sense enough to be disappointed in the *Sun* for a week or two."

Which sums it up. The *Sun* was not a bad newspaper, but it was not a great newspaper either, and only a great newspaper could have fulfilled the expectations of the half-million* frustrated liberals who had watched through the night. Volume I, No. 1, Thursday,

---

* The figure allows for the many buyers who were simply curious.

December 4, 1941, carried the headline REVOLT GROWS IN SERBIA, in retrospect a rather archaic report, as if from the previous war. The lead was "Open revolt in the West Moravia River Valley of Yugoslavia has forced Adolf Hitler to send three of his sorely-needed divisions into a 'third front' in an effort to eliminate Serbian armed forces operating under Gen. Draza Mihailovitch." The sub-heads tried to sum up the war: Hitler Forced to Put Army on '3d Front'; Reds Reach Taganrog: Axis Holds Edge in Libya. The second big story, also headlined across the page, was LABOR TO ASK MURPHY OUSTER, an Illinois story (the Murphy was Francis Murphy, the state director of labor). Other headlines were ANTI-STRIKE BILL PASSED BY HOUSE; AIR RAID NET WILL GUARD CHICAGO; SEE RAY OF HOPE IN PACIFIC CRISIS—the story, by Turner Catledge, was far less optimistic than the head; [Mayor] KELLY BOOMS CITY AS '2D CAPITAL.' There were local stories, an index, an encouraging weather report (68°, unusual for the date). Many readers must have turned first to page 18 for the editorials. Under a masthead announcing THE CHICAGO SUN   MARSHALL FIELD, Founder   SILLI-MAN EVANS, Publisher   REX SMITH, Editor, they found

THE SUN: ITS CREDO

The Sun appears today before the public.

For us the day is one of pride tempered with a consciousness of the grave responsibilities that lie upon any newspaper.

Not the least of these responsibilities is the obligation to present the news, honestly and fairly, 365 days of the year. Now, especially, this obligation must be met. For the millions of citizens of the great Midwest whom we hope to serve faithfully, no less than their compatriots of the West and the South and the East, are deeply concerned by and in the kaleidoscopic march of events throughout the world.

We believe they will look to The Sun for that full and factual report without which no American would wish to formulate judgments affecting his own, his children's, and the nation's future.

Believing this, the founder and the publisher and the editor have pledged themselves to bring you daily the complete story of history in the making, confining opinion and persuasion to the editorial page.

Yet even there The Sun will wear the colors of no party or class. It will support men and nations and ideas which it deems to be working in the best interests of the people of Chicago, the Midwest, and all America.

The Sun believes the best interests of Chicago, of the Midwest, and of

America can best be served at this moment by the complete defeat of Adolf Hitler and everything he stands for.

The Sun does not fear that the people of this country risk losing freedom by fighting for it.

The Sun believes in the present national administration and will support it so long—and only so long—as it merits that trust.

The Sun believes in the American system of private enterprise.

The Sun believes in fair and faithful labor unions and in all the legitimate rights and privileges they have won.

The Sun believes with Grover Cleveland that a public office is a public trust.

The Sun believes in human freedom; in the four freedoms of President Roosevelt and in all the other freedoms vouchsafed to American citizens by the Constitution of the United States.

We intend to publish the best newspaper we can; the fairest, the most interesting, and the most complete.

The Sun was born in Chicago. It is as integral a part of Chicago as the railroads, the Loop, the stockyards, and the Art Institute.

The Sun is your newspaper—your friend.

There were three more editorials: Toward a Labor Policy, Pacific Showdown, and Busy Youth; and then this, which may have said as much about the *Sun* as the Credo did:

A Blind Man Sees

A man in New Haven, who had been blind for nearly five years, suddenly, and mysteriously, recovered the use of his eyes. He is amazed at the changes he sees—the difference in women's hats, in motor cars, the alterations time has made in the faces of relatives and friends. Changes in everything.

There are many people in the United States, blind now to the conditions confronting their country, their fortunes, their existence. No doubt they will be as much astonished as the New Haven man when they begin to see things as they really are.

Elsewhere on the page were several letters to the editor, covering the usual range of human interest. Many of them sounded fabricated, as those letters so often do; seven of the thirteen were signed by initials or pseudonyms (A Republican—Unashamed); and they all reflected one or another facet of the American Epistolary Style, in which pseudo-Victorian periods are looped about the reader until he strangles (if anacoluthon doesn't get him, zeugma will). There was a column on Chicago. Three editorials from other newspapers were reprinted; one, from *The Christian Science Monitor,* called for immediate price controls. A cartoon by Charles Werner (Pulitzer Prize, 1939) rounded out the page.

Colonel McCormick doubtless went through that first issue carefully; he was surely more annoyed than frightened, and could comfort himself that the *Sun* had a long way to go. The figure of 900,000 may have jolted him, not because it spoke well for the *Sun* but because it represented so many subversive defectors. He knew it would drop, and drop it did; within weeks the *Sun's* circulation was less than a quarter of that. But when the *Sun* showed no signs of expiration by the summer of 1942, the Colonel's patience snapped. On Sunday, July 26, he came out swinging with three patriotic editorials (headed by a box of sans-serif capitals: WE'RE GOING BACK TO BATAAN!). The first approved of a plan for universal military training introduced by Rep. James Wadsworth of New York (the *Tribune* had opposed Selective Service violently). The second decried excess profits in war plants. The third, compounding half a dozen lies in one hysterical outburst, stood as a milestone in the literature of the gutter, meriting wide circulation in medical journals:

THE WORD IS COWARD.

Ralph Ingersoll, editor of PM, has been shamed into entering the army as a volunteer after his draft board had refused to grant him a deferment requested by his boss. It remains to be seen whether Ingersoll's friends in Washington will obtain a commission and a nice safe berth for him. Whatever his value as an editor, and it isn't much, he has had a real value to his owner. The publicity given to Ingersoll as a draft dodger has detracted attention from Marshall Field as a slacker. Field is of age to volunteer. He cried for war before it came. Now that it has come, he lets men like MacNider and O'Hare do the fighting while he skulks in his clubs, night and otherwise. No one would suggest that he is indispensable to PM or to anything else. The term to fit to him and to all the herd of hysterical effeminates is coward.

It hardly seems possible; but that is what McCormick wrote. Field must have experienced a moment of utter disgust and dejection, but he never let it show. And he realized that the *Sun* had received a high compliment. His response, in the *Sun* of July 28, was this lead editorial:

EDITORIAL OF THE DAY
You are getting rattled, Colonel McCormick.

A more thorough response was made for him by an organization not noted for its grim attachment to liberal causes, the American Legion. They sent Field a fine letter on August 28; copies of it went to every newspaper in Chicago. Most of it appeared in a Voice-of-the-People column in the Chicago *Daily News* on September 8.

Dear Sir:

In a recent edition of a Chicago morning newspaper, an article appeared in the editorial column in which our comrade and friend, Marshall Field, was charged with Cowardice. The 122nd Field Artillery Post #236 of the American Legion, at its regular meeting held August 6, 1942, by unanimous vote, condemned this editorial and authorized a committee to write this letter repudiating this charge and expressing our confidence in the courage and loyalty of our comrade.

In 1917, although Marshall Field was married and the father of two children, he did not attempt to evade service, and, although he was well qualified, he did not seek a commission in the armed forces nor did he seek a soft berth of any kind, but instead enlisted as a private in the First Illinois Cavalry Regiment. This regiment reported for active duty on July 25th, 1917 as the 122nd Field Artillery and from that date until just a few days before the Armistice he was continuously on active duty with this regiment. He served as a private and sergeant in Battery 'B', and his comrades of Battery 'B' found him to be an excellent soldier and a regular fellow. About the first of January, 1918, he was commissioned a First Lieutenant and assigned to Battery 'F'. As an officer in Battery 'F' he was an efficient executive and a splendid instructor. At all times he was unassuming, patient, understanding and was genuinely interested in our welfare; we had complete confidence in him and on our arrival at the front in August, 1918, we had no misgivings as to his courage, ability and leadership. Such names as Rambucourt, Raulecourt, Siecheprey, Mon-Sec, and Monsard in the St. Mihiel sector; Avocourt, Cheppy, Cheppy-Wald, Very, Montfaucon, Epinonville, Romagne and Cierges in the Argonne sector, are as familiar to him as they are to us and to thousands of veterans of the A.E.F., many of whom are now in hospitals because of wounds received while in action in and around these places.

The letter was printed up to that point. It went on to praise his conduct under hardships and his industry in helping to reorganize the regiment after the war. It ended with a resounding endorsement: ". . . it is not only our duty, but also our privilege to inform the

public of the true facts regarding the loyalty, patriotism and courage of Marshall Field as a soldier, a man and a gentleman." It
pleased Field mightily; here was one class, at least, to which he was
not a traitor. He had made his own answer, and would not add to
it, though with his knowledge of psychiatry he probably made the
wry observation that anyone who shrieked so about imaginary de-
ficiencies of character must be reflecting a certain inner turmoil.
Field was relatively immune to personal attack by now; he might
marvel at the depths to which his critics would descend, but he was
not overly interested in defending himself. (On the other hand he
was violent in his defense of friends and employees—Ralph Ingersoll being one example; and his loyalty to Silliman Evans was excessive.) Self-defense was so rare in these situations that Ruth Field
never knew about the letter from the American Legion Post until
twenty years later. He had little personal vanity.

Field did not write many editorials himself, though that one-line
answer gave him special satisfaction. On August 25 he wrote another:

The Way of a Demagogue

If there is one material thing, with the exception of the home, about which
the hopes of the American family revolve, it is surely the automobile.

Emotionally, the sacrifice of the automobile will perhaps hurt more than
any material sacrifice that we shall be called upon to make. The reason for
the sacrifice will be a shortage of rubber.

Now, if you were a claptrap demagogue without any constructive ideas,
what better could you do than blame the administration that is trying to
win the war for this shortage which it could not control in advance, and
which it is making every effort to rectify? When people are hurt it is so
relieving to have some person or persons on whom to vent their spleen.

By a strange coincidence this is just what Mr. Brooks, our senatorial in-
cumbent, did in his keynote at the Illinois Republican Convention.

In that same week Colonel McCormick brought up the big guns.
He was quoted in *The New York Times* (August 29):

The *Sun* is not a legitimate newspaper. . . . It is part of an alien and
radical conspiracy against our republican form of government. It is subsidized by the government to the extent that its losses, running into millions
of dollars a year, are deducted from the owner's income tax.

It was an old charge, but it came from a new quarter, and Field decided to reply. It took him about three months, and his friends were pleased to see that he considered counterattack better than passive defense. In the *Sun* of November 25 there appeared a quarter-page editorial, set in two wide columns of large, well-spaced type, under a fat headline reading SUBSIDIZED . . . NEWSPAPER? The editorial began by quoting McCormick's words, and went on:

The Chicago Sun was started last December by Marshall Field, using Marshall Field's money.

Mr. McCormick, publisher of the only other morning newspaper in Chicago, does not approve of The Sun. He says that The Sun is subsidized by the government, and its losses are deductible from the owner's income tax.

If spending your own money in a new business can be construed as a government subsidy—Mr. McCormick forgets that The Tribune has often employed similar "subsidies."

The New York News, started by the Chicago Tribune in 1919, enabled the Tribune to deduct from its contemporary income taxes the amount due on more than a million dollars.

Liberty Magazine, a Chicago Tribune project, is reported to have lost $14,000,000 between 1923 and 1931, when the Tribune got out from under. Liberty's losses drew loud complaints from minority Tribune stockholders, who apparently did not realize they were being "subsidized" by the government.

The Detroit Mirror, sponsored by the Tribune, is reported to have lost $2,000,000 in the seventeen months of its existence in 1931 and 1932—years when the government needed income taxes badly.

The Tribune's timber holdings and paper mill have undoubtedly resulted in deductions from the Tribune's income taxes at various times.

The radio station WGN was carried by the Tribune at a considerable loss for several years before it became self-sustaining.

The Washington Times-Herald, a consistently unprofitable personal enterprise, is still owned and operated by Mrs. Eleanor Patterson, whose income for the most part comes from Chicago Tribune stock.

So it would seem that all these Chicago Tribune enterprises in the last twenty years have been similarly "subsidized" to the extent of some $20,-000,000.

When The Tribune and its stockholders started and maintained publishing and business ventures in New York, Detroit, Canada and Washington, D.C. —it was assumed that such ventures were supported at the expense of their principals and not "subsidized" by the government. The Tribune and its stockholders merely engaged in commendable free enterprise, the inalienable right of every American.

When Marshall Field chooses to spend his own money in starting a new newspaper in Chicago, his venture is "part of an alien and radical conspiracy . . . subsidized by the government."

. . . Or does the devastating difference (in Mr. McCormick's mind) lie in the fact that Marshall Field spends his money in Chicago?

And that the new newspaper may be "subsidized" by some of the revenues that would have otherwise come to The Tribune?

This was lèse-majesté with a vengeance. McCormick was distinctly not amused, but he seemed to be running down. He hit back weakly in an editorial on January 6, 1943, entitled "The Pantywaist Press," with a glancing reference to "the cockroach newspapers conducted by Marshall Field to ingratiate himself with the family of his brother-in-law, the late John Hubert Ward, K.C.V.O." Poor Ward remained a man of mystery; he may have been a brother-in-law, but he was certainly not Field's. On January 15 there appeared in the *Tribune* Part Five of a rather shameful series on the New Deal's relations with the American press, by William Fulton. The burden of the series was that practically everybody in the government, and a majority of the nation's press, discriminated against the *Tribune,* our only truly American newspaper, whenever possible. An attack on Field was sandwiched between petulant complaints about Knox's *News* and a contemptuous dismissal of Thomason's *Times.* It was a botch: a rehash of innuendoes about *PM,* England, and Zilboorg. Field ignored it, and no more lances were tilted for some time.

If the very existence of the *Sun* provoked nervous spasms in the Colonel, he was not yet in any danger professionally. Silliman Evans had contrived, rather than built, a newspaper, and Chicago had not yet accepted it fully; the *Tribune* had been part of the city for three-quarters of a century, and was capable of repelling upstart invaders. The *Sun* could sustain losses, but not forever; and while it improved as a newspaper, hints of incompetence persisted. (At one point there was a column of astrology on the editorial page. Prof. Louis Wirth, the distinguished sociologist of the University of Chicago, reproached Evans for it. "The people like it," Evans said.

Wirth grimaced: "You'll need a much better reason than that.")
If the Colonel had been up against Field himself, with a Field-
dominated staff, he might have known serious trouble; but he was
up against Evans, too, and could count on confusion and contradiction in the enemy ranks. The big city, and big money, seemed to
have gone to Evans's head. He lived on a louder and more regal
scale than Field; his suite at the Ambassador East was larger than
Field's, and he was forever throwing parties in it. He drank too
much, and he drank more as time passed. He was at his best in a
fight, facing a challenge; when life was good to him he fell into irresponsibility, and ceased to be reliable. Without him the *Sun* would
have straggled onto the scene later, smaller, more modest; with him
it had burst from the wings in a blaze of brassy fanfare, and then
forgotten its lines.

But behind Evans stood Field, and Evans's mistakes were clearly
Field's responsibility. Field was once more in that old, uncomfortable situation: he had delegated responsibility, and he would not
meddle. Some timely meddling would have improved the *Sun*, and
saved Field a lot of money; but when there was conflict, Evans won
out. When Field disagreed with Evans, he deferred to the professional; when someone else disagreed with Evans, Field backed
Evans.

The brief Chicago career of Turner Catledge, who was the kind
of editor Field needed and should have hung onto even at the cost
of Evans, illuminates the complexities that Field failed to unravel.
Catledge was with the *Sun* from its first day. In the fall of 1941 he
was completing his twelfth year with the Washington Bureau of
The New York Times; his boss was Arthur Krock, which set a
natural limit to Catledge's possibilities of advancement. Evans knew
Catledge well, and so did Jesse Jones, who mentioned to Krock
that an editor would be needed in Chicago. Catledge was dining at
the Mayflower Hotel with Senator George—he probably knew more
luminaries in Washington than Evans did; another asset that Field
later failed to take proper advantage of—when Krock telephoned
to pass on Jones's bit of news; Catledge was interested. The salary
offer was quite good, and Krock, who had an extremely high opinion of Catledge, urged him to "take a fling at it." Discussions
followed, with the busy Mr. Jones an occasional and informal in-

termediary. Finally Evans called to suggest that Catledge meet him in New York—and to inform him that Rex Smith, formerly of *Newsweek,* had just been hired as the newspaper's editor. Catledge was naturally disappointed, but Evans made another offer: Catledge could come in as chief political writer and roving correspondent. It was a good offer, if not the best; but Catledge wanted to meet Marshall Field before accepting. Field was in Washington shortly afterward, and they met at the Mayflower for breakfast.

Catledge was not impressed at that first meeting; in such introductory chats Field always seemed preoccupied and inattentive. But the newspaper sounded good, and Field would obviously be a sensible boss. Catledge accepted the job, and left for Chicago soon after.

He survived a moment of extreme chill when he saw what was happening. The staff seemed a strange collection of odds and ends; Evans was superimposing a newspaper on Chicago, and not building one into the life of the city. But it was not Catledge's job to criticize his publisher. He went off to Canada to cover Churchill's visit, and then went south to an inter-American conference.

By late January, after only sixty days, it was obvious that the *Sun* had been oversold. Excuses were offered, but they were not valid: that the association with *PM* had tainted, or jinxed, the *Sun;* that McCormick had terrorized newsdealers into ignoring the *Sun.* Also, people agreed solemnly that Pearl Harbor had brought the *Tribune* back into the United States, so that the *Sun*'s corrective influence was no longer necessary. That was simply not true. For a month or so the *Tribune* relaxed its criticisms of the government, but as soon as the first great wave of patriotic anger had ebbed, the paranoid carping resumed. Roosevelt was running the war badly, and should give the generals more power; union activity was fatal to the war effort; the task before all Americans was to win the war without government intervention, or alternatively to invite General MacArthur home from the Eastern provinces to assume the purple. Our democratic allies were only waiting for the chance to do us in. Roosevelt and his striped-pants clique were favoring Europe, where we might better let the powers exhaust one another, and neglecting the Far East, where Russian influence had to be countered vigorously. And so forth. The *Sun* still had a corrective function, but its performance was mediocre.

It began to improve even in the first year, with some wholesale editorial changes. Many of the Hearst veterans left.* When Rex Smith, the *Sun*'s first editor and not a bad one, left for the Air Corps, Catledge was asked to take over as acting editor. He did, but with misgivings: the office intrigues were already Florentine. But the staff was cheered by his promotion, and by the arrival of Robert Lasch, whom Catledge asked to join the *Sun* as an editorial writer. Lasch had been with the Omaha *World-Herald* † and was just returning from a year at Harvard on a Nieman Fellowship. Another addition to the editorial page was Willard Shelton, formerly of the St. Louis *Star-Times*; editor of the page was Frank Smothers, who had come over from the Chicago *Daily News* foreign staff. Those two and Lasch composed perhaps the strongest editorial phalanx in the country in support of President Roosevelt. The *Sun*'s morale rose perceptibly, as did its circulation, which edged toward 250,000. Catledge, Field, and Lasch became good friends and worked well together. Hindsight confirms what the two editors felt at the time: when the editorial direction was in the hands of men who felt as Field did politically, the *Sun* became a better newspaper; when those men were replaced by, or subordinated to, the politically indifferent, the newspaper lost energy and flair, as in 1946, when Smothers and Shelton were dropped in a great shake-up. It was not necessarily that liberals put out a better paper, but that harmony between editors and owner gave the whole organization purpose and momentum.

It was a sharp surprise to the whole staff when, in the spring of 1943, Evans announced that his new editor would be E. Z. Dimitman, formerly executive editor of the Philadelphia *Inquirer*. Cat-

---

* One of those veterans was fired but paid off—with a single huge check—for the several months remaining on his contract. Check in his pocket, he repaired to Paddy Bauler's saloon. (Bauler was the man who first said, after one of the many futile attempts to beat the Chicago Democratic machine, "Chicago ain't ready for reform," which became a post-election byword.) There he sat for hours, drinking grimly, plotting revenge. At two in the morning he knew what he had to do, and he acted without delay: got up, went to a phone booth, called the *Sun,* and canceled his home subscription.

† The famous editorial about the placement of European children was not his work.

ledge was sufficiently nettled to compose a memorandum to Evans, in which he pointed out that Chicago had its own identity and could not be conquered by imported techniques; that the paper must be given time for natural growth; and that Marshall Field, with a Chicago name and identity, should be the newspaper's editor and publisher. Evans appeared to be impressed; he conferred with Catledge a few days later, thanked him, and announced that he did not intend to show Field the last paragraph of the memorandum. But Catledge had already lunched with Field and discussed the problems frankly, assuming that Evans had shown him the whole memo. Field was upset and uneasy on two counts: Evans had withheld information, and Catledge was leaving the *Sun*.

Here Field might have cut through the tangle with one Alexandrian chop. A newspaper with Catledge as editor, Lasch as editorial writer, and Milburn P. Akers (a knowing State House and White House reporter who had been with the *Sun* since the beginning) as chief political writer would have been very close to Field's ideal. That week Field should have taken off his jacket, sent Evans packing, and become a shirt-sleeves publisher. He did not. He deferred to Evans entirely. Catledge went back to the *Times** and Dimitman (tough and competent, but indifferent to Field's political ideas) took over.

Catledge was with the paper only a year and a half, but his career was symptomatic. He wanted Field in charge; he could not trust Evans; he resented the substitution of hoopla for good journalism; and he was totally discouraged by Field's obvious refusal to override his "experts." That was Field's great mistake. It was almost fatal: if Field's fortune had been any the less the Chicago *Sun* might have died a tragic death.

Field was aware of the undercurrents. His refusal to take charge was, once more, a function of his Whiggish diffidence. He was perennially optimistic—liberals have to be—and his faith in the *Sun's* philosophy, a faith necessary to the very existence of the newspaper, may have led him into a kind of professional accidie: hands off, go slowly, don't dispute the experts, all's well that ends well. He expressed his optimism in a "Statement by Marshall Field, Founder

---

* Of which he later became managing editor.

of the Chicago Sun," on January 17, 1943, in three columns. In it he answered charges of special interest (intervention; the Democratic party); went on to discuss the dangers of monopoly, pointing out that Los Angeles and Philadelphia had two morning papers each, Boston and New York four each, and Chicago—before the *Sun*—no choice. "Since last July," he wrote, "The Sun's circulation has increased every month. *This record of first-year growth has never been approached by any newspaper in the entire history of American journalism.*" There he was at best putting a good face on matters, at worst whistling in the dark. The fact was true enough; but the *Sun* was losing over $100,000 a week just the same, even though "The Sun stands today *eleventh* among all the 356 morning newspapers in the United States." He did point out toward the end of the piece, after a discussion of news and editorial policies, that "We established The Sun on fundamental business principles and after a reasonable initial investment we expect and know that the paper, like any other successful business enterprise, will show a profit." The statement ended, "We aim to help tomorrow be a better day."

Tomorrow *was* a better day. Slowly the *Sun* took on personality, grappling daily with the imponderables that mean life or death to a newspaper. The editorial conferences reflected the struggle; even there Field hesitated to assert himself. Phil Hanna, his financial editor, formerly of the Chicago *Journal of Commerce* and a conservative Republican, invariably embroiled himself in loud arguments with the others. He and Clifton Utley once had at each other so bitterly that they ended by calling time on each other, sliding a watch fiercely back and forth across the table. During one meeting Robert Lasch delivered a spirited obituary of the gold standard, which Evans and Hanna were insisting should be restored. Field remained silent, and only after the meeting made a point of going directly to Lasch and saying that he agreed entirely and had been glad to hear Lasch speak out. The idea of replacing Hanna may have crossed his mind; he rejected it as Evans's business.

The conferences were often funny. The classic anecdote about Evans concerned his reaction to the suggestion that an editorial be run on the Non-Partisan Council to Win the Peace, which was about to open a Chicago branch. Evans chomped on his cigar and said, "Tell me more about this outfit. It sounds suspicious. Who's behind it?" The names on the letterhead were read off; "That's what I thought," he interrupted. "Do-gooders." The list went on: Raymond Clapper, Mrs. Dwight Morrow, Marshall Field. Evans harrumphed, nodded vigorously, and said, "Don't misunderstand me. There's a lot to be said for some of these organizations." Field never cracked a smile. In late 1943 he made an unusual speech at one of the conferences. Wickware's article in *Life* magazine had just come out, and among the errors and balderdash was some biting criticism of Evans. (Wickware even hauled out the chestnut that ends, "the first time he had ever had his hand in his own pocket.") Field assembled the *Sun*'s executives, stood at the head of the table with Evans beside him smiling faintly, and proclaimed his complete confidence in his publisher, who, he said, had come to Chicago at great sacrifice and risk to his Nashville property. Several of the editors had the distinct impression that the speech had been Evans's idea.

But in general he spoke little. Most of his staff admired him greatly, and basked in his frequent "Oh well done you!" That was his somewhat British accolade, and it became a catchword of praise in the offices. (Another of his phrases, when he passed along a compliment, was "Here is a nice trader for you.") But they would have preferred a more active direction. They got it, finally, when Evans left in 1944; but in 1942, when Lord Beaverbrook asked Field's cousin, Ronald Tree, in London, "Does he love his newspaper? Sleeping and waking? Does he eat and drink and breathe newspaper?" Tree's answer was a regretful no. Field was committed to too much else, and not merely as a name on a letterhead. There was *PM*; there was child welfare, to which he gave a great deal of time; the U.S. Committee for European Children; a dozen trusteeships in mental health, race relations, community welfare, cultural organizations; a couple of dozen directorships; another couple of dozen advisory positions; another couple of dozen assorted memberships. He served on committees, made speeches, traveled. He loved to spend time with his family. He was simply spread too thin to become a shirt-sleeves publisher.

Most of his friends were aware (some impatiently, some sadly and sympathetically) that Field had been trapped by his own modesty. Years later Sen. Paul H. Douglas wrote about him:

I first met Marshall Field as he was starting the Chicago *Sun* in late November, 1941. He offered me the position of political editor, but since I was in the City Council at that time and was being talked of for United States Senator, I thought I ought not to accept.

After the publication of the *Sun* got under way, I came to know Marshall Field very well. From time to time, I had conferences with him on civic matters. I found him always to be anxious to help the underdog, kind and generous in all his activities, and one of the strongest forces for good that we have ever had in Chicago.

I shall never forget the night when the *Sun* first appeared. . . . It was uncertain up to the very end whether or not the sluggers who were believed to be around [and held] in readiness by a rival paper would succeed in preventing it from getting on the stands. It was not certain what the attitude of the police would be in this matter up until almost the very last hour. I was Alderman of the Fifth Ward and patrolled the Ward to see that the *Sun* got circulated and that the people had a chance to buy it. The crowds and excitement were enormous. . . .

In my judgment, Mr. Field was misused by many of the editorial and business staffs whom he hired for large salaries, but whose heart was not really in the job and who ran up costs and did not have his interests really at heart. It is regrettable that he had such bad luck with some of the staff of the *Sun*. . . . On the other hand it should be said that there were a great many . . . who were absolutely loyal and who made great sacrifices to come with him.

Mr. Field was one of my strongest political backers and I doubt whether I would have been nominated or elected United States Senator if it had not been for his aid. He never asked anything for himself. He was always interested in the general good. He gave one the impression of modesty and indeed of shyness.

(That last paragraph, incidentally, politely ignored a charge by the very perceptive and accurate writer Milton Mayer, in a critical article on the *Sun* in *The Nation* of March 7, 1942: that the *Sun* had declined to support a genuine liberal like Douglas for senator in 1942. Mayer's charges against the paper—whimsey, exaggeration, bad news balance, lack of taste—were true. To headline a story about a man nearly killed by a falling pile of salt, WORKER NEATLY SEASONED UNDER FIVE TONS OF SALT, was appalling flippancy. But Mayer's judgments were made early—the paper was only ninety days old—and probably reflected a general disappointment of high hopes.)

Robert Lasch, too, sketched a brief portrait of Field later on, in which what-was and what-might-have-been came through clearly and poignantly:

Marshall Field was one of the few rich men I have ever met who did not think that his wealth gave his opinions a special value. In the daily editorial conferences at the Chicago *Sun*, my colleagues and I could never quite adjust ourselves to his genuine modesty. Here was the man who was paying for the enterprise, and paying in a handsome way, yet he deferred constantly to those around him and chose to solicit the judgments of others instead of imposing his own. Somehow it did not seem properly publisher-like.

One of my sharpest memories is of how seriously Mr. Field wanted the *Sun* to make a strong, meaningful and progressive contribution to Chicago municipal affairs. The transit situation was in a mess. He authorized me to make a study of it with a view to writing a series of articles which would come to an editorial conclusion as to our proposed solution. The series was published in pamphlet form as well as in the news columns, and we began an editorial campaign for unification of the transit companies under public ownership. Mr. Field made an important speech at the City Club explaining and advocating our position, and backed up the campaign at every stage. The establishment of the Chicago Transit Authority, which now operates the transit system, was a direct result of the campaign. It was, in my opinion, one of the major accomplishments of the *Sun*.

Mr. Field also took a deep interest in the *Sun*'s continuing campaign for better housing. We came out strongly for a large public housing program at a time when the real estate interests had pretty well convinced the Chicago business community that this form of subsidy was "socialistic" and destructive. Mr. Field was always anxious that we should fight every day for urban redevelopment and the remaking of Chicago into a fine community in which to live. We had countless conferences with architects and city planners on redevelopment schemes. We campaigned just as hard for better public schools.

He was also from the beginning deeply interested in every aspect of race relations. The *Sun* fought against racial discrimination in every form in which the issue presented itself. I thought it one of the bitterest ironies of the paper's history that our devotion to the Negro's cause brought us little mass support from the Negro community. Although their intellectual leaders appreciated Mr. Field's work, the Negroes as a body went right on buying the *Tribune* and the Hearst paper. . . .

The strongest quality that came through . . . was Mr. Field's intense compassion. I think this was at the root of his liberalism. He had intellectual convictions, yes, but he also had a deep feeling for anybody who had not had all the luck in the world. This was more than a rich man's sense of duty or "noblesse oblige." It was a genuine sympathy which found expression in unusual receptivity to the aspirations of working men, Negroes, farm laborers, Hottentots, or anybody in the world who faced tough going. He responded emotionally to other people who shared this compassion—to Mrs. Roosevelt, for instance, and to people like Saul Alinsky who worked with underprivileged groups.

Nobody was sadder than Mr. Field at the failure of the *Sun* to become a solvent property. It hurt him deeply when each successive reduction in staff made the paper a little less able to carry out the ideas for which the paper was founded. I have always felt that the *Sun* would have had a better chance if he had placed more confidence in his own instincts. But he regarded himself as a non-professional in the business who had to trust the professionals he employed to carry on the actual work. So the *Sun* went through a rapid succession of managements none of whom really grasped what he wanted to do or how to do it. . . .

What effect did the *Sun* have on Chicago? These things are hard to pin down. I can remember expressing some discouragement to Mr. Field, or perhaps impatience, at the unfriendly soil which Chicago seemed to present for liberal ideas. He told me with serene confidence that the ideas which the *Sun* stood for were bound to have a long-run influence, building up gradually with cumulative impact.

Field wanted a great newspaper. (He once said that he had hoped to bring to Chicago a newspaper as good as the St. Louis *Post-Dispatch*.) He also wanted it to show a profit, and he worried about that more than a casual observer, thinking of him only as a man of vast wealth, could have known. He was in no danger of going broke, but money—or the basis and disposition of his resources—ranked high among his problems. (In February, 1946, he visited Winston Churchill in Miami Beach, in order to dicker for publication rights to the great man's memoirs. He came home empty-handed, and his rueful comment to his wife was "That man knows a buck when he sees one.") His concern was reflected in periodic staff reductions at the *Sun*, and in the only flat order he ever snapped impatiently at any of his executives: by 1943 he disallowed the advertising department's complaint that the *Sun*'s association with *PM* was making advertisers reluctant, and said bluntly that he never wanted to hear that excuse again. But those were relatively minor points. In the early 1940s three major events bore directly on the future of Marshall Field and the Chicago *Sun*—the final transfer of the Estate to Marshall Field; the passage of the Danaher amendment; and the antitrust suit brought by the United States against the Associated Press.

4

In 1941 the Associated Press was a nonprofit cooperative news and photograph agency, commonly called a "wire service." Its member newspapers contracted for the right to use AP material and agreed to make available to the AP all the local news they gathered. The effect was of a vast pooling of resources, so that the AP could advertise "a staff of 7,200, augmented by the staffs of member newspapers and affiliated news services in foreign countries—a total of approximately 100,000 men and women contributing, directly or indirectly, to each day's effort—a staff many times larger than the staffs of *all other American news agencies combined*." The italics are the AP's, who must later have regretted them; the phrase was crucial to Marshall Field's formal complaint against that organization.

Of 373 daily morning English-language newspapers published in the United States, with a total circulation of 16,519,010, no fewer than 302 with a total circulation of 15,849,132 were obliged by their contracts to furnish local news items of spontaneous origin *exclusively* to the AP.

Of a total of 1,480 evening newspapers with a combined circulation of 25,561,381, no fewer than 877 with a combined circulation of 18,812,988 were similarly obliged.

The AP had similar rights to the news gathered by over 90 per cent of the English-language newspapers of Canada, representing over 95 per cent of the total English-language circulation.

A monopoly?

It was a vast and powerful organization, and the availability or denial of its services might make or break a large daily newspaper. Its bylaws provided that any application for membership could be vetoed by a member paper in the same city; a four-fifths vote of the membership was necessary to override the veto.* Even then, the applicant would not be admitted except upon payment of "a sum equal to 10% of the total amount of the regular assessments received by the Corporation from members in the field (morning, evening, or Sunday) in the city in which the applicant has been elected to membership, during the period from October 1, 1900, to the first day of the month preceding the election of the applicant." (Not 10 per cent of the *annual* assessments; 10 per cent of the *total cumulative* assessments.) There were other and more complicated bylaws, but these alone presented Marshall Field with an almost insuperable problem.

First, the *Sun* could be excluded from the AP by a protest from Colonel McCormick.

It would then be necessary to seek the support of four-fifths (later, a simple majority) of the member newspapers—all of whom had paid for their exclusivity and were not likely to jeopardize either their privileged positions or their relations with the 99 powerful newspapers that controlled 80 per cent of the voting power.

And even if Colonel McCormick, a proud believer in free enterprise and competition, were consistent enough to welcome the *Sun*'s application—a fantastic notion—the *Sun* would have to put up $334,000, over and above its annual assessment.

Field applied for AP membership for the *Sun* in mid-1941, by which time, as he wrote later,

the AP had established its members as a privileged class, with tremendous power and exclusiveness. Through this agency, papers with 95.5 per cent of the morning daily newspaper circulation in the country had committed themselves to the pooling of their news-gathering resources internationally and domestically, had effectively prevented their competitors from having access to the news so gathered, and had worked out a program which was intended to prevent their reporters and photographers from doing even part-time work

---

* When the Department of Justice showed signs of moving against it in 1942, the AP reduced this to a simple majority.

for a competing paper or agency. In addition, the AP had cartel arrangements with certain foreign news-gathering agencies, such as Canadian Press. The AP had thus closed the door very tightly.

On the eve of the launching of the *Sun* and because of the delay which threatened, I again wrote to the AP as follows:

"In view of the fact that I propose to begin publication of the new paper within the next few weeks, such a delay entails the most serious consequences. To begin publication and to seek the support of the public without the benefit of Associated Press facilities is perhaps to risk the entire future of the enterprise, since the initial reader reaction to a newspaper may well be determinative of its situation over a long period. Moreover, when I announced the publication of this paper, I led the people of Chicago to believe that it would be in all respects a standard and complete newspaper; my performance cannot and must not fall short of my promise. Finally, the postponement of action on the application until April, 1942, may well constitute more than a postponement; there is no assurance under your by-laws, as I understand them, that I will be elected to membership at that time and consequently I cannot at the outset or at any time assure my readers that in due course the paper will have the benefit of all the standard press services available to other papers. It is these factors, among others, which have been causing me such grave concern."

Of course the AP gave him no satisfaction, and the *Sun* began life without membership. The International News Service was not available; it was a Hearst organization, and in Chicago only the Hearst *Herald-American* had access to it. (The *Herald-American* also had AP membership, and barely used it, but refused to give it up in Field's favor.) The *Sun* relied on the United Press, Transradio Press, and Reuters; on its own bureaus and photographers; and on a number of minor agencies.

We discovered . . . that the AP control over local reporters and photographers was very real and all too inclusive. As a result, the charges paid by the *Sun* in the single year of 1942 for news and pictures were rather staggering. It paid the UP under contract within a few dollars of $110,000. The amounts paid for photographs—not including expenses in connection with pictures made in Chicago by the *Sun* staff itself—exceeded $63,000. Beyond these items, the *Sun* in the year 1942 alone paid for news services, extra materials, bureaus, correspondents, and other arrangements a sum in excess of $425,000.

Some of these expenditures would have been incurred whether or not AP services had been available to the *Sun,* as part of a natural need to develop competitive advantages. But the major part of the extra expense could have been dispensed with if the *Sun* had been able to procure the services of AP, and the basic AP charge to each of two members in Chicago would be, I am informed, approximately $50,000 a year. . . .

These problems threw extra burdens upon the *Sun's* sports, financial, national domestic news, regional news, and news pictures departments. The necessary diversion of time and energy, as well as the expenditure of large additional sums of money, which resulted from our inability to obtain AP service, were among the obstacles we had to overcome in providing Chicago with a first-class morning newspaper.

Field consulted Louis Weiss. There was obviously more at stake than his own membership. Weiss in turn asked attorney Carl S. Stern to determine whether there was a basis for a claim that the AP was acting in violation of the Sherman Antitrust Act. Stern reported that in 1915 the Department of Justice had ruled that the AP was immune, but that the AP's position and function had altered since, and there had been a great "development" under the Sherman Act since—meaning that attitudes, interpretations, and the nature of society had changed. He prepared an opinion in support of his conclusion that the AP was vulnerable; Weiss modified it slightly, and signed it. The AP ignored it. Weiss and Stern then prepared a formal complaint to the Department of Justice, on the basis of which the United States brought suit against the Associated Press.*

The Department of Justice moved for summary judgment: that is, it proceeded on the assumption that the important facts were not at issue, and that the only question was their interpretation in law, so that a trial was unnecessary, and the case could be heard on affidavits and other written documents. Broadly, the AP was accused of restraint and monopoly of interstate commerce; specifically, the AP and the Chicago *Tribune* were accused of having conspired in such restraint and monopoly.

The ethical and Constitutional issues were more important than the fate of one newspaper; as usual, a major social conflict was

---

* It was generally assumed, inaccurately, that Field had pulled strings or engaged in political maneuvering to inspire the suit. That was unnecessary. Field had many friends in Washington, but any citizen may place a complaint before the Department of Justice.

symbolized by the specific legal action. The AP could claim immunity on two counts: that it was not the only wire service available, and was therefore not a monopoly; and that any regulation of it was an infringement of freedom of the press. The government countered that the AP's pre-eminence in the field made it in effect the only one of its kind; and that freedom of the press presupposed that the press was a public service, operating within the general application of the laws of the land. The AP pointed out that if membership were unrestricted, and everyone joined, the organization would indeed become a monopoly; the government countered, and the majority decision stated, that "if AP were open to all who wished the service, could pay for it, and were fit to use it, it would be no longer a monopoly: a monopoly of all those interested in an activity is no monopoly at all, for no one is excluded and the essence of monopoly is exclusion."

Beneath the arguments lay an ancient conflict: that between property rights and human rights. Essentially the AP and its member newspapers were trying to protect a commercial advantage, claiming the sanctuary of the First Amendment. A logical extension of their arguments would have created a kind of journalistic extraterritoriality, exempting any publishing organization from the common law: a murder, for example, committed in the Tribune Tower, would not have been punishable by civil authorities. And the arguments begged the major question: just how was unrestricted membership harmful to freedom? But the press approved of the AP's stand. *Editor and Publisher,* the trade journal, called the case "one of the most momentous crises in the history of journalism." The Cincinnati *Enquirer,* in an editorial typical of many, said that the "government's remarkable suit against the Associated Press, on the grounds of monopoly, is a threat to the freedom of the press itself." Colonel McCormick went further, and possibly revealed more of the basis of the AP's action than he meant to, in his statement about "an alien and radical conspiracy" and "tax subsidies." (It was that statement which *The New York Times* quoted on August 29, 1942, and which elicited a bristling answer from Field in the *Sun.*) A lot of propaganda was circulated, much of it in *Editor and Publisher,* harping on "the freedom of the press." The government could do nothing about that—the press was free, after all—but consented to Weiss's and Stern's explaining the circumstances to Prof. Zechariah Chafee of the Harvard Law School, the most distinguished authority in the United States, and probably in the world, on the freedom of the press. Chafee was disturbed, and wrote an impressive letter. His letters-to-the-editor were prized, and always presented with respect and pride; but not this one. Panic must have been extreme. *The New York Times,* exercising freedom of the press, refused to publish it. So did the *Herald Tribune.* As Stern wrote later, "Mr. Meyer of the Washington *Post* regretted his inability to publish it." It was finally printed by the Providence *Journal* on Sunday, April 18, 1943, after which the metropolitan newspapers reprinted parts of it.

Suppose a city has only one newspaper [Chafee wrote], and the citizens who would like another editorial policy must go without because nobody can afford to start their kind of newspaper in this city. Obviously the city lacks many advantages of a free press although no law forbids the establishment of a new journal. The situation differs from this only in degree when one newspaper is able to give its readers abundant news while any rival is denied access to the best source of national and international news.*. . .

Liberty of the press is commonly said to be endangered by the pending Sherman Act suit against the Associated Press. Innumerable editorials in member newspapers have denounced the suit as a senseless and malicious attack on this cherished constitutional right and as an effort to undermine the efficiency of this great organization. . . .

As a longtime advocate of free speech, I have tried to learn what all the shooting is about. I have no opinion whether the AP is violating the Sherman Act or not. That question can safely be left to the able Federal judges in New York and eventually to the Supreme Court. The purpose of this article is to show the unsoundness of the prevailing opinion that liberty of the press will be promoted by the retention of the present barriers against the admission of new members to the AP. On the contrary, it is these by-laws which abridge liberty of the press. . . .

Ever since Justice Brandeis' opinion [a dissenting opinion in 1918, in which Brandeis said that "news should be protected against appropriation only if the gatherer assumes the obligation of supplying it at reasonable rates and without discrimination to all papers which applied therefor"], I have hoped that the AP would voluntarily abandon its restrictions on mem-

* *Editor and Publisher* had run a statement to the same effect on December 31, 1938.

bership and throw its service open to all reputable newspapers that will pay the price. I still hope so, whatever the outcome of the present suit. That organization would be living up to its high traditions and rendering a notable service to the development of sound public opinion in our democracy if its members would now of their own accord do away with the existing barriers, which make it almost impossible for a new daily journal to give its readers the benefit of the magnificent achievements of the Associated Press.

The District Court—for the Southern District of New York— ruled in favor of the government, two to one, on October 6, 1943. Learned Hand and Augustus Hand were the majority; Judge Thomas Swan dissented. The decisions abounded in precedent and technicality, as usual, but included striking paragraphs:

> However, neither exclusively, nor even primarily, are the interests of the newspaper industry conclusive; for that industry serves one of the most vital of all general interests: the dissemination of news from as many different sources, and with as many different facets and colors as is possible. That interest is closely akin to, if indeed it is not the same as, the interest protected by the First Amendment; it presupposes that right conclusions are more likely to be gathered out of a multitude of tongues, than through any kind of authoritative selection. To many this is, and always will be, folly; but we have staked upon it our all. . . .

> Suppose the only source of information about momentous events in some remote region is a single exceptionally gifted correspondent: must any paper which engages him agree to admit all others on equal terms? Consistently, must we not recognize the overriding public interest in his reports, particularly since in such a case his employer will otherwise have a monopoly? The answer to such questions need not embarrass us: their pertinency presupposes that whatever is true in small matters, must be true in large; and the greater part of the law is founded upon a denial of exactly that; for in law differences in quantity again and again become decisive differences in quality. We need not therefore say how important the control of news in any suppositious case must be in order to demand relief; it is enough that in the case at bar AP is a vast, intricately reticulated, organization, the largest of its kind, gathering news from all over the world, the chief single source of news for the American press, universally agreed to be of prime consequence. Wherever may be the vanishing point of public concern with any particular source of information, that point is far beyond this service. . . .

> In conclusion it is perhaps proper that we should say a word about the freedom of the press, since that question has been mentioned in the briefs.

The effect of our judgment will be, not to restrict AP members as to what they shall print, but only to compel them to make their dispatches available to others. We do not understand on what theory that compulsion can be thought relevant to this issue; the mere fact that a person is engaged in publishing, does not exempt him from ordinary municipal law, so long as he remains unfettered in his own selection of what to publish. All that we do is to prevent him from keeping that advantage for himself. . . .

The decision was a victory for the Chicago *Sun;* also, to Field's way of thinking, for the open society over the closed. (It was incidentally a victory for Marshall Field over Colonel McCormick; Field was not above a large measure of personal satisfaction.) The judgment—instructions and court orders—was handed down on January 13, 1944,* and the AP appealed, but Field was confident that the Supreme Court would uphold the government.

The Supreme Court did so, in the October term, 1944. Weiss, Stern, and Blanche L. Miller filed a brief as *amicus curiae* on behalf of Field Enterprises. (With the consent of all parties, *amicus* briefs had been filed by the American Newspaper Publishers Association and, disappointingly, the Chicago *Times* in behalf of the AP and the *Tribune;* but the AP and the *Tribune* refused consent to Field Enterprises, which had to appeal directly to the court for leave to file the brief.) The District Court's decision was upheld by a vote of 5 to 3. Justice Black delivered the majority opinion, and was joined by Justices Douglas, Frankfurter, Reed, and Rutledge. Justices Roberts and Murphy and Chief Justice Stone dissented. Justice Jackson took no part in the case.

The Associated Press was open. Colonel McCormick was discommoded. The threatened disintegration of the social structure of the United States, the threatened sovietization of the press, the threatened disappearance of personal liberty, failed to materialize. Field was reminded of, and quoted, an editorial from the Milwaukee *Journal,* in 1934, after the American Society of Newspaper Editors had predicted the end of Western civilization if the National Industrial Recovery Act were applied to the newspaper business, and had rejoiced publicly at the firm resistance put up:

---

* Debate on the Danaher amendment opened two days later. One of the government's charges against the AP was, incidentally, dismissed: the AP's acquisition of Wide World Photos, Inc., was ruled perfectly legal.

The Society has not placed the press of America in an enviable light by trying to bolster the farcical behavior of a few Tory-minded publishers. In fact, the whole shameful affair may have done the press incalculable harm. It is not impossible that as the struggle against adverse economic conditions develops, America may find itself forced to pattern its government more closely after the dictatorships into which European nations have been thrust. Then, indeed, might there be an issue of freedom of the press to carry to the people. Then, indeed, might the press need the support of the public. And then would the people, deceived, as they have been, by the cry of "Wolf! Wolf!" respond?

The emotions that swirled about the AP case were familiar. Almost every extension of democracy in America follows the same pattern. A step is taken to diminish privilege; its opponents insist that it will mean the end of our way of life; it succeeds; our way of life is greatly strengthened. After all the *coups de grâce* to the American Way in Field's lifetime—the income tax, the Wagner Act, Social Security, unemployment insurance, relief and public works, price controls (or their removal), integration, foreign aid, dozens more—the United States remained the healthiest, strongest, and richest country in the world. We had even begun to reckon with the interesting possibility that our strength existed not in spite of, but because of, our progress toward a liberal society; that perhaps it was true after all that the best corrective for the ills of democracy was more democracy.

Field's comments on the case were a defense of competition:

As a matter of fact and of democratic policy, no unregulated organization in a democracy can be permitted to become so large, well organized, efficient, exclusive, and protective of the interests controlling it that it makes the creation of competing units economically expensive. When organizations get to be overwhelmingly large and self-protective—whether they be news-gathering combines, medical associations, steel companies, trade-unions, or any others—they gravely threaten democratic liberties in areas of our national life and, when large and powerful enough, the whole democratic framework. As I see it, the AP is one of several factors in the daily newspaper industry that now [early 1945] represent such threats. Whatever contribution the *Sun* and I have made to the precipitation of this issue has been made alike in an effort to solve our own Chicago problem and to help relax one of the basic restraints against freedom in American life.

5

On September 28, 1943, in Chicago, Marshall Field celebrated his fiftieth birthday. He rose at 7:30 in his suite at the Ambassador East. He bathed and shaved. (He shaved himself almost always, with an ordinary safety razor.) He must have stared into his mirror for at least a few seconds, perhaps searching wistfully or whimsically for the features of the boy, the university buck, the socialite financier, in the smooth, squarish face of the publisher and philanthropist. That face was firmly fleshed, the nose and jaw strong, the hazel eyes set wide and quite clear. His brow was high and not wrinkled; his hair was altogether silver at the temples and graying rapidly above.

He dressed, choosing a dark gray double-breasted suit, with the wide lapels and padded shoulders of the decade, and a darker tie, also wide. By then breakfast had been served. He joined Mrs. Field at the table; they ate in great good humor, chatting and leafing through the usual newspapers: his own, Colonel McCormick's, and *The New York Times*. At 8:45 he kissed his wife and went downstairs to meet Louis Weiss and Howard Seitz, Weiss's associate and Field's friend, in the lobby. Field's car was brought around; he used it as little as possible during the war, but today he had guests, and the occasion was special. The three men stepped out into a fine fall day, slightly breezy. Almost the first thing they saw was a Chicago *Tribune* truck idling at the curb; two handlers at the tailgate looked up, one of them said, "Hey," and they shouted in unison, "Happy Birthday, Mr. Field!" Field grinned broadly, waved and shouted, "Thank you," and stepped into his car. He chuckled on and off all the way to his office; Weiss and Seitz shared his pleasure. A Roman would have been delighted: it was a poetic omen on an important day, like an eagle on the right hand.

At the offices in the Field Building the three joined Col. George Richardson and Carl Weitzel at a conference table. They made themselves comfortable. Weitzel offered a document which was briefly examined by all of them. Field, sitting square in his chair, an unlit pipe in his mouth, spread the document flat before him, picked up a pen, and signed it.

With that signature the Estate of Marshall Field I passed out of existence, and Marshall Field III assumed sole control of something over $90,000,000. But when he said later, "I came of age today," he was not thinking of money. He meant that the name, quality, and fortunes of the Fields were now vested in him. He had been the beneficiary of wealth, a tradition, a position; he was now the lone steward of all three. Never again, almost certainly, would such a social and financial legacy be passed on intact, so great a harvest of one century transferred at the stroke of a pen to a citizen of the next. He might have felt acutely English for a moment: the coronet—and with it the demesne and the obligations—had passed to him. He was the Field.

He must also have thought of his children, particularly his son. Marshall, Jr., was a long way from Chicago. He had been graduated third in his class, and its president, from the Law School of the University of Virginia, in June of 1940, and had become clerk to Judge A. M. Dobie of the Fourth Circuit Court of Appeals, with the intention of going on to clerk for Justice Stanley Reed of the Supreme Court. Pearl Harbor intervened. Marshall enlisted immediately, went through a ninety-day officer candidate course at Northwestern University, and was assigned to the U.S.S. *Enterprise* as a gunnery officer. The *Enterprise* fought what almost amounted to a private war for the first year or so. For several months she was the only American aircraft carrier operational in the South Pacific; in addition to fighting she had to pop up at odd spots in that vast ocean in an attempt to confuse the enemy—which she did so well that the Japanese not only claimed to have sunk her three separate times, but also identified her as six separate carriers. During the Battle of Santa Cruz, the naval battle that kept the Japanese from reinvading Guadalcanal, the *Enterprise* was the nucleus of an American fleet far less formidable than the Japanese were permitted to know. The carrier suffered their concentrated attentions for weeks. On October 26, 1942, Marshall was blown out of his gun turret; he was unconscious for an hour, but not severely wounded. From that first desperate summer of 1942 to the fall of 1944 he survived twelve major engagements in the Pacific, serving on three different ships, enjoying a stateside leave, and emerging with a Purple Heart and a Silver Star. His father reacted precisely as other fathers reacted everywhere: he worried, was relieved, was proud, and bragged a little.

There was no formal gathering of the younger generations to honor Field's birthday. "Generations," in the plural; an outsider might have been pardoned confusion watching four-year-old Barbara Bliss play with her aunt, five-year-old Fiona Field. Bettine, the youngest of Field's first three children, was twenty; Field's stepsons, Harry and Bobby Phipps, were twelve and ten; his daughters, Phyllis and Fiona, were seven and five; his granddaughter Barbara was four; and young Marshall's children, Marshall and Joanne, were two and one. They were rarely together at one time; they were growing up in a world at war, and their elders were too busy for many of the light entertainments they might have enjoyed five years earlier. *Corisande II* had been turned over to the Coast Guard (for $1 a year). Caumsett itself had been offered to the government, which had accepted it (also for $1 a year) and turned it over to the Office of War Information for the training of Psychological Warfare teams. (George Gillies, the horticulturalist, reported later that the OWI had not been as respectul of the buildings and grounds as had the former occupants.) The gesture was naturally upper-class—only the upper classes had estates to offer—and it was reminiscent of the English, whose country estates, placed at the service of the Crown in time of crisis, became hospitals, rest camps, training areas, depots, and homes for harried urban children.

Field was too busy for Caumsett anyway. He spent half his time in Chicago, though he never established a legal residence there; it would have subjected him to double taxation and complicated his corporate bookkeeping inordinately. He gave up none of his directorships or philanthropies in New York, but became more intimately involved with his private and public obligations in the Chicago area: the *Sun,* the department store, St. Luke's Hospital and Provident Hospital, Hull House, the Illinois Children's Aid Society, the University of Chicago. He did not find these responsibilities tedious; he was enjoying life, more active than ever, making more friends than ever, and feeling more useful than ever.

He performed, very quietly, one service to Illinois for which the whole state was grateful. The Illinois State Historical Library was then headed by Paul M. Angle, and Lloyd Lewis, managing editor of the Chicago *Daily News* and Field's friend, was one of its three trustees. The Library had been offered a holograph copy of Lincoln's Gettysburg Address, and was desperately trying to raise the necessary $60,000. One-third of that amount had come in from various sources when the campaign stalled; Lewis learned that Field was interested, and arranged a meeting between Field and Angle. It was brief.

"How much money do you need?" Field asked.

"About forty thousand."

"That's a lot of money."

Angle agreed that it was.

"If I promise you half that sum," Field asked, "do you think you can raise the rest?"

Angle thought they could.

"All right," Field said. "You can have it." He sent his check along in a few days. Angle was struck by another sort of generosity Field demonstrated: when the *Daily News*—stiff competition for the *Sun*, in 1943—initiated an extensive campaign among schoolchildren for nickels and dimes to swell the fund, he supported it wholeheartedly despite its promotional overtones. (In the end the Library was so successful that it was able to return about $3,000 of Field's contribution.)

6

And Field the businessman was busier than ever. The passage of the Danaher amendment, intended to put a stop to his insidious revolutionary activities, led instead to a salutary reorganization of his holdings. To incorporate any of them, and thus to glide outside the purview of the amendment, was simple enough, but it was immediately obvious that a cluster of independent corporations, each worrying individually about profit and loss, each paying taxes on the basis of its own performance, was unnecessarily cumbersome; and the *Sun* could best be made financially secure by incorporation into a larger body of enterprises. Consolidation was the answer, and it was accomplished speedily in August, 1944, with the establishment of Field Enterprises, Inc., chartered as a Delaware corporation. The enterprises, with the exception of Pocket Books-Simon and Schuster, Inc., acquired later that year, were wholly owned, and their assets and liabilities were transferred outright to the new corporation, though of course they continued to do their own internal bookkeeping. The Delta Manufacturing Company, bought originally as a strong source of revenue (in the days when the *Sun*'s losses could be written off on Field's personal income tax) had been sold off; so had the Hudson Press, a small printing establishment in Hudson, New York. *PM* was never a part of Field Enterprises. *Parade* was fully consolidated only in 1949. So what Field actually established in 1944 was merely a nucleus, around which present and future holdings could agglutinate. And the nucleus was, for the time being, losing money. Field's major undertakings for the next five years were two: to add to the nucleus, and to put Field Enterprises in the black. The additions had to be "cousins" of the *Sun;* that is, holdings in the area of communications, related in function to the newspaper: publishing organizations, radio stations, media of information or culture. And the financial improvements could be achieved only by the rigorous application of sound business practices.

Field may have considered, briefly, cutting his losses—but where? The Chicago *Sun* was his own creation and of all his holdings the most important to the country. *PM* was struggling into the black; Field was changing his mind about its advertising policy, but having supported the idea of *PM* for four years he had no intention of letting it drop when it showed signs of possible success and independence. *Parade,* while still in the red, had an obvious potential. Starting on July 13, 1941, *Parade* had within six months been sold to twelve newspapers with a combined circulation of 1,760,000. The outbreak of war slowed progress; publishers waited to learn how much newsprint would be available, and were not eager to assume new features under contract. They were wise to wait: the government decided that the newsprint used in supplements should be debited from the quotas of the newspapers themselves; the quotas were to be based on the previous year's consumption, and frozen. *Parade,* as a new publication, suffered under those regulations; the government relented after formal hearings, and adjustments were permitted. Even so, six newspapers were forced to drop the supplement in 1942 and 1943; eight others picked it up, and the net gain was over 400,000; but that was slow, and there was no indication that matters would improve. Technical adjustments helped slightly (twenty-eight pages instead of thirty-two; a lighter-weight paper; a smaller page size), but by the end of 1944 *Parade*'s circulation was only an unprofitable 2,000,000 in fifteen newspapers. Advertising revenue rose consistently, though, and *Parade* was a good bet for the future.

So cutting losses was out; the alternative was to acquire profit makers. True, the losses of Field Enterprises were deductible (Colonel McCormick continued to gnash his teeth), but Field had not inherited his grandfather's empire in order to preside over its dissolution. He was a businessman, and wanted profits; he was a philanthropist, and needed resources. More important, he knew that his liberalism was on trial. Anybody could back liberal projects if he had the money; what counted was to prove that a man could be a liberal, managing liberal concerns in a liberal way, and survive in the marketplace. Again that insistence on the organic relationship: Field Enterprises had to be a part of American life, and not a subsidized sport. In the conception, management, and goals of Field Enterprises the liberal and the capitalist coalesced. They had to succeed together. The liberal could succeed by accepting losses, the capitalist by abandoning ideals—but that way lay failure. Each had to survive on the other's terms; only that, to Field, was success.

His two major acquisitions in 1944 and 1945 were publishing organizations. The first was Simon and Schuster and Pocket Books combined. The second was called the Quarrie Corporation; its principal products were the World Book Encyclopedia and Childcraft, a series of edifying and entertaining children's volumes.

A cute, and not very bright, little story grew up about Field's purchase of Pocket Books. He is said to have noticed, one day in the early 1940s, a rack full of small, low-priced paperback books in a drugstore, and to have realized in a moment of white-hot insight that they were "a good thing." Nonsense. Paperback books had been on the market since the early 1930s (the British Penguins led the way), and Field had been haunting bookshops on and off since 1936; it is hardly likely that he would have put five or six years into noticing the existence of paperbacks. What he noticed in 1944 was that he needed to buy up a few profitable enterprises. He was obviously not averse to combining that need with cultural improvement, and even those who criticized the intellectual level of many paperbacks admitted that it was *something* just to get so many books into the hands of so many people. Field approached Pocket Books, Inc., both because it was flourishing and because it was closely affiliated with Simon and Schuster. He and Max Schuster had served together on the board of *PM,* and Shimkin had occasionally sat in for Schuster; it was Shimkin's report, suggesting in 1940–41 that *PM* would not succeed, that Field had felt obliged to disregard for the sake of the idea. Field and Schuster had become casual friends; even before *PM* Schuster had clipped a newspaper article in which Field was quoted as saying that he was happier not being thought of as a symbol, and that he wanted to put his money to work constructively; Schuster had written to ask if Field wanted to write a book about his beliefs. Nothing literary came of it, but it was an introduction, and later the two discovered common interests: in music, chess, liberalism. (Also aphorisms. Schuster was an enthusiastic collector and quoter of them, and delighted Field one day with the Talmudic proverb, "It is better to be rich than sick.") The two talked seriously about publishing as both a profession and a social force, and decided that what they were *against* was Lord North's view: that crusty Prime Minister had, in the 1770s, financed an edition of Plato, limited by his stipulation to fifty copies, "lest it fall into the hands of the vulgar." (Too late; the damage was done; in that same decade most of his lordship's American possessions fell into precisely those hands.) Field and Schuster wanted to put as much reading matter as possible into the hands of the vulgar: "Better and better books for more and more people at lower and lower prices."

But Field did not communicate his interest directly to the publishers. John Wharton mentioned it to Richard Simon. Meetings followed, with the details of price, conditions of transfer, and future management ironed out by Wharton, Louis Weiss, and Shimkin, the last of whom worked out a twenty-year transfer plan, the price to be on a sliding scale tied to profits. That would provide both continuity of management and incentive. But it soon became apparent that the separate sale of Pocket Books would be uneconomical: the parent corporation would have to pay taxes on its profits, and the owners would then have to pay taxes on the net when it became personal income. The way out was obvious: sell the whole corporation to Field, taking capital gains. Simon and Schuster were momentarily disturbed; as Schuster said, it was one thing to see a nephew leave home, but another thing entirely to lose a son. But Field reassured them: he had no desire to change the firm's management. The twenty-year variable price could be kept; ownership would pass to Field; management would continue unchanged; profits would be split. It was a generous arrangement, and efficient: no changes in policy or personnel, not even a momentary commercial dislocation. So on October 1, 1944, Simon and Schuster, Inc. and Pocket Books became Field enterprises. For all the principals the sale and subsequent expansion of the firm were an absorbing adventure; for Louis Weiss, Wharton, and Shimkin, who had to agree on the fine print, it was heavy going. The formalities and protocol of corporate relationships, the minutiae and split hairs, could scarcely engage the full enthusiasm of the three principals; but to Wharton and Shimkin they were matters of prime importance. Two attitudes had to be reconciled. Businessmen must take risks; lawyers, acting for and protecting clients, avoid risks. Field wanted to risk some capital on expansion. Simon and Schuster were in a happy position: with Field's support they were able to consider and implement projects that might take a good deal of time and money to launch—Golden Books, for example, which required an extensive grass-roots distribution from greeting-card shops through drugstores to food-store chains, and which had to be produced by the millions to be at all profitable. Field liked the idea of Golden Books—the association of parent, child, story, reading aloud, even the hard covers—and was willing to put money into the difficult time of planning and production and laying out patterns of distribution without immediate profit. Shimkin too favored expansion, but his sympathetic understanding of Wharton's cautious gradualism served more than once to bridge the gap between enthusiasm and real possibility. (It was a two-way bridge. Later on, when he felt that the lawyers were *too* careful, Shimkin would discuss a project privately with Field; when it was broached at a board meeting Field, thoroughly briefed, would approve vigorously, which dissipated much initial opposition.)

Field's ownership imposed certain unforeseen obligations on management. The accounting, which had always been good, must thenceforth be perfect. Any reasonable doubt in matters of taxation had to be resolved in favor of the government. (That was a dictum to which Field subjected all his business associates.) Field refused to meddle in editorial policy, but as a newspaper publisher he felt accountable to the public for lurid paperback covers—he was not anonymous, like a Co. or an Inc., and he was ultimately responsible for everything produced by Field Enterprises. (He was amused by the problem of lurid covers, and once wondered: if you publish a racy book in a bland cover, are you deceiving the public? The portrait of a naked lady at least identified books for those who didn't care for that sort of thing.) His criterion for the artwork was necessarily evasive—"good taste"; but he asked Shimkin directly to exercise discretion even at a sacrifice in profit. (Once, and only once, he intervened directly; it made a charming anecdote, in which a poet might have seen a true distillation of Marshall Field's beliefs. He flatly prohibited the use of a nude on the cover of *Lust for Life,* a biography of Van Gogh; not, of course, because he had anything against nudes, but on the unassailable moral ground that Van Gogh had never painted a nude.) Pocket Books became discreet; and there *was* a small dip in sales. One distributor grumbled, "You better get grandma off the board." But Pocket Books survived.* And Field never attempted to criticize or censor any text. Shimkin once asked him to read a book they were considering (Nelson Algren's *A Walk on the Wild Side,* thought very daring), and Field was flattered and delighted. He didn't care for it (his primary allegiance, after 1936, was to Trollope), but told Shimkin he thought it was a serious book that should be reprinted.

Field's satisfactions in book publishing were obvious. He was seeding some sort of culture, putting more books (of whatever kind; the habit was more important than the individual title) into more households; he believed that an enlightened people would be a

---

* By the late 1950s a large part of the paperback industry had followed Pocket Books' lead, and it became possible again to distinguish between a bookstore and a private collection of Port Saïd postcards.

liberal people, and was acting on that belief. He was also making a profit, and every penny he collected from any of his enterprises helped to keep the Chicago *Sun* alive.

But the publishing house drew on Field, too. For long-range resources, and also for a kind of understanding and support that was not common. Freeman Lewis, director of Pocket Books' editorial operations for many years, wrote later:

> I don't think any management group in a publishing company ever received more consistent support or more real understanding than we at Pocket Books received from Marshall. The result showed not only in business terms, even though those were notable, because during the years in which he headed the management team here the company grew to be the largest publisher and distributor of books for the whole family in the history of the book publishing industry. Less visible, but equally important, was the happiness of the organization and the sense of security which came to such a large degree from his understanding of our ideals, our ambitions, and our problems. Mass market publishing is a peculiar kind of tightrope, in which the sales pressures all too often tend to suggest publishing policies which are less than ideal. Marshall played a consistent and continuing role in helping us to keep our balance.

Field was not as intimately involved with the Quarrie Corporation, acquired on December 1, 1945. It had been spotted, investigated, and recommended to Field by his good friend Joseph Carroll, an investment counselor who worked with George Richardson in Field's office and to whose observations Field always gave full attention and great weight. Quarrie was a specialized company: both Childcraft and the World Book Encyclopedia were strictly educational, and there was no trade book division. Quarrie was not large, but its profits were consistent, and Field had a hunch that it was potentially a big earner. It was also a "cousin" to Field's other enterprises. Its social usefulness was evident, but Field's motives must not be idealized: he wanted a large moneymaker. Always he came back to two goals: a financially independent and secure liberal newspaper in Chicago; and a body of healthy, competitive business concerns to pass on to his son and grandsons. That last was a motive that the public rarely ascribed to him; overimpressed by his liberal works and the publicity given them, too credulous of the myth that Field was "a bad businessman," and aware that he refused to exercise high-handed editorial control of his newspapers, people rarely gave him credit for his genuinely sharp business mind.

His hunch about Quarrie was supported by a report that Leon Shimkin drew up for him, and he bought the organization outright. The encyclopedias were sold primarily by door-to-door salesmen, and were bought primarily on the installment plan. The new board of Quarrie noted a consistent ratio of sales to calls, and deduced that more calls would result in more sales, and ultimately more profit. Here again Field's resources were an advantage: to expand the sales force required a capital investment; and to pay for the consequently greater number of books sold—when the consumer could defer his own payments for a year or more—required an even larger investment. A temporary paradox: more sales required more capital. Quarrie needed money if it was to achieve its potential, and the money was available. The risk proved eminently justified. In fifteen years Quarrie had expanded to about twenty-five times its original size, and its annual net profits were higher than the price Field paid for the corporation. It was probably the best investment Marshall Field ever made.

Again, he restrained his editorial instincts. The Childcraft series was aimed at young children and their parents—a project in education-at-home. Its volumes had titles like *Exploring the World Around Us,* and *Life in Many Lands,* and *Creative Play and Hobbies,* and *Your Child Goes to School.* Some of them could be enjoyed by the young reader alone; most were expressly designed for the use of parent and child together. Any less impartial owner might have been tempted to inject political or social indoctrination; Field never dreamed of it. The World Book Encyclopedia was aimed at students generally, but it did not compete with the Encyclopædia Britannica; its articles were accurate, but broader than they were deep, and not technically complex. They might strain the intellectual equipment of an eighth-grader, but to a college student they would be of limited value. In the hands of a partisan editorial board, however, they might have become an effective weapon of indoctrination rather than of research. Field *never* offered an editorial suggestion. His restraint reflected his probity, but it was also wise policy. When the World Book was attacked in Appleton, Wisconsin, two years later, not for anything in it but for Field's presumed political sins, he was able to write to the Rev. William H. Grace of St. Mary's Church in that city:

> . . . I have never in any way interfered with the contents of the WORLD BOOK. WORLD BOOK was an organization in which I became interested because I believe it an excellent medium for the distribution of objective knowledge. It is presided over by an extremely eminent editorial board, who would not for a moment tolerate interference with objective information eveh if I would have the temerity to attempt it. . . .
>
> You will perhaps realize, Father, that I am subjected to extremely bitter competition in many of my enterprises, that this competition is not always scrupulous, and will very often use any means at hand to vilify me or my interests.

He did not bother to state his firm belief that truth was always beter than *Tendenz*.

Six months after the war Field was head of one of the largest privately controlled corporations in the country. The future of Field Enterprises depended in large degree on the future of the country; if, as everyone hoped, demobilization was to be followed by a new prosperity, the potential of the organization was almost unlimited. The *Sun* looked healthier; *PM* was temporarily in the black; *Parade* was on its way, and a sure winner; Quarrie, Simon and Schuster, and Pocket Books were making good profits. No one was quite sure what would happen, but Field stood with the majority, who felt that a new world was in the making. The next four or five years were the happiest and most hopeful of his public life. The war had accomplished certain revisions in the American political and economic outlook, and the shifts of emphasis were to Field's liking. Reaction was unpopular (or perhaps only dormant), and traditional liberal "threats to the American way of life" were firmly mortared into the social structure of the most powerful nation on earth: Social Security and collective bargaining, for example. More threats were gathering force: health insurance, integration, accelerated aid to education. To a liberal the portents were good. Field did not know that the spread of communism and the natural growth of Soviet power would, by the usual unnatural and illogical association, rejuvenate American reaction by supplying it with irrational public fears and fanciful liberal targets. But he had come to believe, and he was right, that the American people were conservative about change but liberal about humanity: that change would be slow but generally in a "good," that is, liberal, direction. Eleven million Americans had been displaced, shifted about the world by the exigencies of war, and even the stay-at-homes had been exposed to an intensive course in world geography and political science. On the other hand, life had been cheapened by the years of carnage and the atom bomb; there had been an indefinable and worrisome shift in the basis of human morality. A worldwide revulsion at misery and death was possible; equally, a shrugging acceptance of brutality and horror. The world's momentary stability at the war's end masked a moral stasis, with—in the ancient terms—the prevalence of evil opposed to the desire for good; with "Not to be born is the best for man" trammeling "We are here; what do we do about it?" Field felt that optimism would defeat lassitude—but not without a struggle. He thought the United Nations would mature—but after a difficult adolescence. That want and fear would be reduced, if not swept away—but against the resistance of property and prejudice. That democracy would thrive—but not everywhere, and nowhere without education, enlightenment, ideas. His attitudes were simple, and easy to characterize as naïve; they sprang from the old liberal hopes of a New Deal for the world. He found that the public approved of those ideas in the black-and-white oppositions of war, when their application had to be deferred, but was chary of commitment in the confusions of sudden peace. The Atlantic Charter and the Four Freedoms supplied handy slogans to the embattled; two years after the war they were quaintly historic. But Field took them seriously. If he had one article of faith, it was that a better world *could* be built. "The whole history of our country is a testimony of this fact," he wrote in 1945:

But what we have accomplished has been accomplished only by blood and sweat, by the utmost efforts of men and women who believed in their dreams and who got out and fought for them, figuratively and literally. That is why we must all join together to promote freedom *actively*—by becoming tough enough to move in a new direction when old methods fail, by giving all our countrymen the rights we ourselves want to possess, by preparing our children to be able to think for themselves, by supporting freer access to facts in every field both new and old, and by working for a peace that will give all nations the chance of eventually joining in a free world community.

It is a tremendous task that lies ahead of us, and it must not be minimized by any desire on our part to have an immediate or material advantage. Only in the faith of Jefferson and Lincoln can we find the spiritual drive that will keep America and the world on their course toward greater opportunities for greater numbers of people, greater free enterprise in the real sense of that expression.

Freedom is more than a word. Freedom is action, for the foes of freedom never hesitate to take action when they, in their toughness, think that free men are weak. The days ahead will always be filled with peril for freedom, but we can keep freedom if we want it and are vigilant for it. "We, the people" must be a living force, not just a phrase to beguile us at political rallies. Man has little stature set against a Norris Dam or measured against a Flying Fortress, and he will indeed be a small thing unless he decides that his spirit can master the engines of his creation so that his State will be a living force concerned with the freedom of every individual.

CHAPTER EIGHT

There is nothing of permanent value (putting aside a few human affections), nothing that satisfies quiet reflection, except the sense of having worked according to one's capacity and light to make things clear and get rid of cant and shams of all sorts.

—T. H. HUXLEY,
Letter, 1890

The secret of happiness is this: let your interests be as wide as possible, and let your reactions to the things and persons that interest you be as far as possible friendly rather than hostile.

—BERTRAND RUSSELL,
The Conquest of Happiness, 1930

O N JUNE 9, 1941, a few months before the United States entered the war, Marshall Field made the principal address at the commencement exercises of the University of Virginia. His thought had crystallized to a surprising degree, and he never significantly altered any of the beliefs and warnings he expressed that day. He aligned himself with Thomas Jefferson, founder of the University, and he made it clear that the United States was already engaged, in all ways short of combat, in the struggle for survival called the Second World War. He was modestly dubious about his own generation's right to preach. Speaking of another commencement long before, he said, "We were free without knowing it, prodigal of that freedom, and in our prodigality utterly casual and wasteful in the uses we made of it." Later in the speech he said:

Perhaps many people would wish you success. . . . I know definitely that what some of the world considers success I would not wish for you. I have known some men that the world considers successful. Well enough to know that . . . they are racked by regret for what it has cost them—the loss of ideals, the lack of identification with their fellow men. . . .

With Ortega, I believe in this definition of the nobleman: that man who makes the greatest demands upon himself. Such a man will never achieve success. While there is one disease that is not cured, one injustice that remains unrighted, one dark patch of ignorance unlit, such a man will never consider that he is successful.

. . . What then are my wishes for you?

I very deeply wish you, for one thing, an open mind.

You have learned many things in this university. I know that nobody will agree with me more readily than your teachers when I say that you will have learned many things that are not so; many things that are true today will not be so in the years to come.

Truth is, as you know, a maddeningly elusive will-o'-the-wisp. Take the pattern of your search for it from these same teachers who have worked with you and shown you how the search is made. If you are diligent, and lucky, you may find parts of it here and there.

You will certainly find nothing unless your minds are open when you leave here and remain open despite all the pressures to close them. . . .

If you are to keep open minds in the hard years ahead, if you are to continue in the great tradition of free inquiry amid the forces that will surely oppose it, you must also have tolerance.

So I wish for you tolerance. Your intolerant person is, you may be sure, a deeply insecure person. The man who is secure in his search for truth will not be intolerant of others no matter how radically he disagrees with them. I can see no excuse for the kind of intolerance which makes one group of people look down on another group, or hate them. That kind of assumption of superiority comes from fear and insecurity.

You have learned during these four years some scientific facts about superiority. You know that no ethnic group is inherently superior to any other. You know that no race is inherently superior to any other. You know that no nation is inherently good and any other nation inherently bad. You know that no economic class is better, per se, than any other. You know all these things, and you will never let anything but scientific fact persuade you otherwise. So you will be intolerant of those who try to move you to intolerance. . . .

For perhaps a long period, possibly longer than many of us realize, you will make of this nation a repository, to hold in trust for the future all that civilization has won at so great a cost over the centuries. Some of you will fight sickness and disease; some of you will fight for human justice, and some against ignorance.

I cannot wish for you peace, gentlemen. You will have peace . . . when you are dead, and you will be a long time dead. . . .

That was fairly strong stuff for the time, allowance made for the customary rhetoric. It was more accurately prophetic than most such orations. And to tell an audience of Virginia gentlemen (some by adoption) that they were intrinsically no better than Negroes— even if the latter were not mentioned specifically—and would do well to remember it, was not the usual bland expression of homiletic gratitude for the privilege of the podium. Nor was the call for a frankly international outlook, or the insistence that moral health presupposed change. Field delivered the speech gently but with confidence, and it was received with unusual warmth.

Six months later we were at war, and at the war's end in 1945 we were unquestionably the most powerful nation on earth. Our energies had been bent to one task for four years; never in history had we experienced such unity of effort, such concentration on a single goal. (If our national force were ever brought so fully to bear upon William James's "moral equivalent for war" we would make a brave new world indeed.) Victory brought us power partly because we were unscathed. Twelve and a half million Americans had served in the armed forces; 325,000 had died, 700,000 more had been wounded; immitigable sorrow had struck half a million homes. But no bomb had fallen on the continental United States; * fire storms had not swept its cities, nor epidemics its population; none of its industrial plant had been damaged; its highways and harbors were intact; food was abundant; † postwar prospects, symbolized by an unquenchable gleam in the consumer's eye, were brilliant.

The domestic history of the time was a history of abeyance; not total, but remarkable. Labor and management, buyer and seller, liberal and conservative, went on jawing at one another but in prac-

---

* A Japanese submarine shelled an oil refinery near Santa Barbara, California, on February 23, 1942; another shelled the northwest coast on June 21. There were no casualties.

† There had been shameful complaining about shortages (sugar, meat, gasoline), but to any other country in the world our state of shortage would have been *peacetime* luxury.

tice yielded to the community of interest. Strikes were unpatriotic, and for the first time since 1932 employers could snarl at workers without trepidation—but if wages were frozen, so were prices, and the seller's market in consumer goods was limited to marginal items. Taxes were high, but so (after the first year) was morale, and everyone assumed (unfortunately with the usual maniacal American optimism) that taxes would drop sharply after the war. Part of the fine mood was induced by affection for our noble allies, including Russia, and a concomitant delusion that the last real enemy of mankind was about to be extirpated. Part of it was a proud reaction to the show of national strength; the decadent democracies, in spite of their mawkish liberalism, were doing well. Part of it was a sort of traveler's exhilaration: perhaps a third of the population was, at one time or another, on the move, entering the armed forces, following defense jobs, seeing new countries and new cities and new kinds of people. And with the success of the armies of democracy came a new approval of the ideals of democracy; temporarily a great many Americans took the Four Freedoms seriously, and if they forgot about them as soon as the war ended, the effect lingered nonetheless. Anti-Semitism became unfashionable; men who had worked beside Negroes had learned at least to think of them as workingmen rather than just Negroes; union labor won some respect when it refrained from taking advantage of the emergency; the lunatic-fringe right wing, while it never experienced the full severity of the law, was discredited; the Russians put up a hell of a fight, and radical thought seemed, for the moment, less dangerous than ever; * technological surprises, culminating in the atomic bomb, restored professors to some prestige, and led to much loose and cheerful talk about the push-button world of the future.

America was, in other words, buoyed up by the optimism that must inform great enterprises. We had always had problems, but Hitler seemed a problem of a greater order of magnitude altogether, and we were persuaded that success against the great enemy would leave us only small, easy, mopping-up operations on the way to a

---

* When the winner of a Distinguished Service Cross—awarded for extreme valor, and not simply devoted attendance—was asked what he did in civilian life, and answered, "I was an organizer for the Communist party of Ohio," there were no howls of rage. A few years later he was convicted under the Smith Act—for what might loosely be defined as organizing for the Communist party—and jailed.

middle-class Utopia. Provided, of course, that Russia proved amenable.

All that is vastly overgeneralized, as descriptions of a "national mood" must be. It might be easier and more accurate to say that we were too preoccupied with international psychoses to devote much attention to national neuroses. But all through the war there were men whose position, or whose intelligence, or whose political experience, required them to see the war as an episode in history; as a battle, perhaps, in a longer war. Some were convinced that Russia was the great enemy, and that we should not be lulled by a victory over Hitler. Some were uneasy about the old "yellow peril" in a larger sense than Japanese aggression. Some feared an orgy of democratization after the war that would end in anarchy and license. Some saw the government's unprecedented and vast control of business as a permanent change in the American Way—as indeed it was. Others, less defensive and pessimistic, worried nevertheless about postwar power vacuums, foreign and domestic: who would rule Germany, and how? what about economic controls and inflation at home? how deeply, and how far from our own shores, should we commit ourselves to military government? should we support or suppress revolution? who were our friends in the world, *really?* did the United Nations mean anything? what was this talk of world government?

And off in a corner someone might be muttering gloomily that sharecroppers were still hungry, old people were still poor and sick and lonely, we needed schools and teachers, race riots were on the way.

Marshall Field took no direct part in the war. He was not invited to Washington to be a munitions czar or a price administrator or a strategic planner. He was not sent abroad to create good will. If he had been offered any but the most urgent assignment, one for which he was uniquely fitted (and it is hard to imagine what that might have been), he would have declined. The Chicago *Sun* was far too important, both to him and to the President. As its publisher he could exhort, criticize, review, suggest; he could provide support and publicity for Roosevelt's decisions; and he could remind his readers that the war would end someday, that the problems dwarfed by it would resume their ancient importance.

Field had been approached by William Benton and Paul G. Hoffman in 1941, when the latter two were trying to organize an "American Policy Commission"—a small assembly of "literate businessmen" who would meet four or five times a year for two- and three-day sessions at which they would examine public policies and make public criticism of them, relying upon academic experts for specific reports and memoranda. The group would have a symbolic as well as a critical function: businessmen behaving like professors could hardly fail to interest the press and a fair portion of the general public. The organization of the group was interrupted by Pearl Harbor, after which its proposed activities became "postwar planning." The Department of Commerce, in the person of Jesse Jones, took a natural interest; so did the National Association of Manufacturers and the U.S. Chamber of Commerce, defenders of competition who, like others, brooked it badly. These organizations displayed more restraint than enthusiasm; they admitted that no existing group could cope with the problem of postwar employment, and that a return to the dangers of the 1930s would be madness— but they resented the birth of a new, and possibly liberal, business organization, and compacted quietly with Jones to support it only for the duration of the war. After that Jones took over the whole program. He was an ideal organizer. He was respected by businessmen everywhere (conservatives suspected him of being a New Dealer, and New Dealers suspected him of being a conservative, which suspicions canceled each other neatly), and could accomplish more by telephone than most officials could by personal appearances.

From the list of proposed trustees submitted by Benton and Hoffman, Jones struck the name of Marshall Field. He never offered reasons. He also declined the services of Henry Luce, less liberal than Field (though the Chicago *Tribune* despised them equally) and a more influential publisher; and rejected Ray Rubicam, the advertising executive. Jones's motives remain obscure. Perhaps it was a matter of avoiding friction with Congress; perhaps simply personal preference. But Field would have liked the work: the organization, finally named the Committee for Economic Development, was a serious effort to educate the big businessman.*

There were other possibilities that never worked out. As a heavy contributor to the Democratic party since 1936, Field had been mentioned as ambassadorial material. He had all the traditional attributes of the prewar ambassador: a gentlemanly manner for diplomacy, money for entertainment and travel, and a good name. He had more, of course: some knowledge of the world, a concern for its future, friends in Europe, a liberal and not provincial outlook. But there were drawbacks. He was perhaps too liberal; the owner of *PM* might have struck a jarring note in the State Department. When Joseph P. Kennedy returned from London, Roosevelt was asked if Field might replace him, and answered, "No. If Marshall Field is interested in an embassy, I can offer him Mexico." (It is almost surely not true that Roosevelt "threw back his head and laughed" as he said it—a later embellishment to the story. He was too good a politician; even if he had thought the idea funny, which it was not, he would not have been so impolitic as to insult both Field and Mexico with unseemly levity.) But Field was not at all interested in an embassy at the time. He might have been later on. In 1944 former Ambassador to Russia Joseph E. Davies suggested the Moscow position to Field; Field indicated some interest, but said that his commitment to the *Sun* would make it impossible. The decision was of course not Davies's, and nothing came of their brief talk. Other suggestions, after the war, were equally fruitless: that he take a high executive position in the Red Cross, or that he lend his experience to various international banking commissions.

The course of Field's life, which had led him ever deeper into public service, had paradoxically unfitted him for political functions. American politics is compromise, and many influential Americans still resented the "traitor to his class." There is no evidence that liberals continued to harbor lingering suspicions of his wealth; but on the higher levels of government and journalism there may

---

* As such, it got a bad press. Conservatives thought it infiltrated by liberals, and disapproved of that kind of education; liberals thought it no different from the N.A.M. or the Chamber of Commerce—i.e., ineducable.

have remained understandable confusion about a man who had
been so aggressively on both sides in one lifetime—first the complete
upper-class sportsman, then the confirmed enemy of privilege.

So he remained a private citizen. His personal concern, like anyone's, was his family and friends in combat; his general concerns
were those of the liberal, the publisher, and, in the old-fashioned
phrase, the man of sensibility. Marshall, Jr., was in the Pacific; like
all parents, Field could only wait, praying for good news. Ronald
Tree, Field's cousin, was serving as an undersecretary in the British
Ministry of Information, advising on American policy. With his
wife Nancy (Henry Field's widow), he played a more exciting part
in the war: Winston Churchill's estate, Chequers, was considered
unsafe, a prime target, on weekends of full moon, and on those
weekends the Trees extended to the Prime Minister—and to those
of his friends and associates whose presence he required—the hospitality of their own home, Ditchley. Field's old friend Oliver Lyttelton, who had become one of England's most knowledgeable and
powerful authorities on the production and use of metals, was named
Controller of Metals in 1939, President of the Board of Trade and
Foreign Plantations in 1940, member of the War Cabinet in 1941,
and Minister of Production in 1942. His meetings with Field were
infrequent, but the two remained friends. Lyttelton even found the
opportunity to strike a glancing blow for Field, at the Rainbow
Club in London in 1943. He was with a group of British and American officers; one of the latter offered the old, silly reproach that
the British lacked a sense of humor. Lyttelton answered him, "I
admit we have nothing as funny as the Chicago *Tribune.*"

Through those men, and through dozens of friends and employees who had gone off, Field was personally tied to the war. But
during the war years he remembered peace. The future meant as
much to him as the present. He was one of the caretakers. Most of
the world was out defending freedom; Field was mindful of the day
when extending it would once again be the primary task.

2

In the fall of 1944 Marshall Field wrote a book. It was called *Freedom Is More Than a Word,* and was published by the University

of Chicago Press in the spring of 1945. It was a small book and a short one; as one reviewer pointed out, for a book that meant to get to the people, and that talked about economic democracy, it was overpriced at $2.50. The reviews were generally favorable, and the book sold over 14,000 copies. It was a very personal document, though it dealt with society; but Field had not immured himself in an author's den; he had asked for and received the help of several people, including the editorial staff of the *Sun,* who were free with suggestions. His chief assistant was Prof. Alfred McClung Lee, whose "knowledge of the history of the newspaper business and whose research," as Field pointed out in his acknowledgments, had been invaluable. The three friends who examined both his ideas and his manuscript, who suggested revisions and who sharpened a phrase here and there, were Max Lerner, Louis Weiss, and James Warburg. Field was not shy about acknowledging their help; the book was not an act of auctorial vanity, but an active defense of democracy. The writing was not bad—comfortable and educated and less turgid than most political prose. Field wrote out of personal experience and personal conviction in about equal parts, so that every platitude about liberalism (it was, as it remains, almost impossible to discuss liberalism without platitude; the best political stylists have always been attackers and not defenders) was backed by an event at Eton, or a citation from Colonel McCormick, or a discussion of the AP case or *PM.* The historical references were appropriate, peppery, and edifying, and ranged from Abigail Adams to Thorstein Veblen (Peter Zenger would have rounded them off better) by way of Karel Capek, Galileo, John Milton, and Lincoln Steffens. But the ideas were more important than the style, and in his quiet way Field was blunt and forceful. He mentioned, and then avoided, the dangers of excessive courtesy:

But, on the functional side, freedom of expression has suffered, for all the lip tribute we pay to our democratic heritage and for all the copybook maxims about the value of freedom, free enterprise, and democracy that we reiterate. Our infernal gentlemanliness is a part of the trouble. Once many Americans felt vehemently that controversial discussions had merit. Today we have more and more precise notions about the "proper limits" to "constructive discussion," and we face a constant diminution of competition—a constant rise in local monopolies and in monopolistic national and international agreements—in all the major media of discussion. We are in grave danger of forgetting the great truth uttered by Edward Beecher concerning the mob-killing of the abolitionist, Elijah P. Lovejoy, in Alton, Illinois. "We are more especially called upon," Beecher said, "to maintain the principles of free discussion in case of unpopular sentiments or persons, as in no other case will any effort to maintain them be needed."

That stated, the message of the book was made clearer: it was not only a defense of democracy, but also a plea for real competition. "For goodness' sake, let us have more and better 'crackpots,' " he wrote at one point, which was his way of taking an absolute position on freedom of speech. His faith was in the consensus—but only in the *free* consensus; and nothing, he realized, was easier to obfuscate than freedom. The press was guiltier than most; discussing some rather dubious conclusions by Dean Mott of the University of Missouri School of Journalism, Field wrote:

> But, despite what he says about "correlation," let us look at what Mott concludes has been the relationship between newspaper support and the election of specific presidents. His list of presidents whose candidacies were opposed by a majority of the press includes Thomas Jefferson, Andrew Jackson, Abraham Lincoln (first candidacy), Woodrow Wilson, and Franklin D. Roosevelt. Those aided in their election by a majority of the press have been, among others, U. S. Grant, Grover Cleveland, William McKinley, Theodore Roosevelt, William Howard Taft, Warren G. Harding, Calvin Coolidge, and Herbert C. Hoover! In other words, Mott unaccountably finds nothing of significance with which to correlate the fact that the majority of the newspapers have supported our greatest presidential protectors of vested privilege and have opposed our greatest liberal presidents!
>
> . . . Perhaps the matter might be stated rather simply thus: Wherever there is a striking issue between property rights and human rights upon which the people are permitted to pass judgment, the majority of the press has aligned itself on the side of property rights. Sometimes, when the issue is confused, the press has carried the people with it. But when the issue has been clearly enough defined between the partisans, and the facts have reached the public, the majority of America's voters have ignored the special-interest pleas of the publishers.
>
> . . . The situation in a truly competitive daily newspaper market is obviously different from that in a monopolistic setup. Here the dynamics of competition for group representation force the various existing papers to represent different groups in order to continue.

. . . Only in a competitive field, a field in which newspaper competes *in news and views* against newspaper, magazine against magazine, radio station against radio station, and the various media against each other, can there be some approximation of popular representation that will remain effective over a period of time. Only in real competition, with a number of different points of view to compare and to choose from, points of view actually presented and advanced, can there be said to be some real substance to the freedom of expression and discussion offered.

The book focused primarily on freedom of the press, but through that prism the light of Field's argument was scattered across a wide spectrum: freedom of speech and assembly and religion; Jim Crow and Negro ghettos; anti-Semitism; monopoly; the cruelty of the "nice, polite" white Christian majority; labor and management; war and peace; productivity and depressions; Maimonides and Manchester, the Mills and Mussolini; Hamilton, Harding, Hearst, Hitler, Holmes, Hoover, and Robert M. Hutchins. Even the book's table of contents defined Field's thinking: I. A Society of Free Men (The Individual and the State; The Disinherited; An Atmosphere of Freedom); II. Freedom of Expression (What Is It? What Gets in Its Way?); III. Efforts to Promote Freedom (*PM;* The Chicago *Sun;* The AP Case; Toward Better Access to Facts); IV. A Faith in Human Possibilities (A Peoples' Peace; The March Forward). "A Peoples' Peace," "The March Forward"—awful clichés, like "freedom" itself, but they stood for ideas and conditions never fully realized, which were to Field the only ideas and conditions that would achieve for Americans (and ultimately, he could hope, the world) the kind of society they had always wanted and had too often been led to believe they already lived in. Underlying the whole book was the old utilitarian concept of "the greatest good for the greatest number," qualified drastically by the difficulty of defining that good. It was not, Field warned, "something that any one man or any group of men can possibly envisage or claim to know. The greatest good can only be arrived at by discussion, conflict of opinion, and group decision. It cannot be planned, nor can it be imposed from above." Not even by the New Deal, whose mandate was either from the people, renewable and revocable, or no mandate at all. "Anyone who labors under the delusion that it can is either a prospective

tyrant or is in danger of throwing away his freedom to a demagogue."

The great danger was unanimity, of which suppression was the
first instrument. The need, the salvation, the hope for the future,
was competition. And of course there was more than one definition
of *that*. Field liked the one that had appeared in *Editor and Publisher* in 1938:

> The American system thrives best when ideas strike sparks and opposites
> rub each other into usable size and shape.

There were few enough sparks in the newspaper world. Its tendency
toward monopoly—the "one-paper town"—was already dangerous,
and much of Field's book was a warning about that. Once again he
had come out for competition, and warned that those who talk most
about it do most to stifle it.

The book's publication led to a radio appearance: Field was invited to be the Author, or sacrificial lamb, on *The Author Meets
the Critic,* one of the more popular egghead programs of the time.
The date was June 11, 1945. The moderator was John K. M. Mc-
Caffery; the Critics were Henry Hazlitt, then of the *New York Times*
editorial department, and Dr. J. Raymond Walsh, head of the Political Action Committee of the CIO. The program was not overly
enlightening. The principal points of the book were neglected in
favor of a discussion of *PM,* and Hazlitt, particularly, showed a
strong desire for autobiography: how and why had Field transformed himself into a liberal publisher? Dr. Walsh defended the
book and its theses, though his colleague and their moderator felt
impelled to point out that he represented a special interest, the
PAC. The program was really a cautious attempt to argue the lib-
eral-conservative question without identifying it as such, and the
conversation was consequently weighed down by circumlocution,
inability to get to the point.

Field handled himself ably, but ten minutes or so of radio time—
with interruptions, false starts, and choral interpolations when everyone spoke at once—was hardly sufficient. He managed to say a few
interesting things, and drew applause three or four times. "I'll have
to try to take the criticisms more or less in order," he said, when he
had the microphone. "In the first place I don't think that my edu-

cation, or how I arrived at what I think, is in the least important."
(He was wrong; but he had come prepared to discuss the book, and
was not ready for the digression.) "To generalizations, perhaps I
must plead guilty." He had been forced to generalize. In explaining
PM and the *Sun*, "which had been very much criticized in some
quarters," he had had to go into his "beliefs and feelings about the
world in general, freedom in particular, and what democracy meant.
I have the greatest faith," he went on, "that the American public,
if they are given the facts and all the facts, will be able to make up
their minds to their own best interest." Of pressure groups he said,
"The effort to stop them would be far more dangerous than the
pressure groups themselves. Sometimes we like pressure groups,
sometimes we don't. I do not see how you're going to have a democracy function and avoid pressure groups." (He reminded his
hearers of the constant presence of pressure groups even in Jefferson's time; and incidentally showed a good grasp of the concept of
"countervailing forces" later developed by J. K. Galbraith.) "The
danger is that in trying to eliminate them you will put a great burden
and stop on free speech—which I think is extremely dangerous."
A bit later he said, "I don't think to start with that *PM* needs any
defense from me," which drew applause; he went on to point out
that he was the major stockholder but had no editorial voice at all.
Asked if he were similarly reticent in Chicago, he said, "No"; asked
if he determined the *Sun*'s policies, he repeated, "No," and added,
"I do not determine them. They are arrived at by consultation;
consultation at which I am present, and in which we arrive at a
unanimous opinion on the editorial staff." When he repeated that
he exercised no control over *PM*'s policies McCaffery was moved
to remark, "This is the most wonderful attitude toward an editor
I've heard of, Mr. Field," but when Walsh cut in immediately, "Why
do you call it a wonderful attitude? Aren't you admitting Mr. Field's
thesis [that editors were too often under the control of vested in-
terests]?" McCaffery declined gracefully to be hoist on anyone's
petard, and let Field go on to say that he had always hesitated to
impose his will on professional newspapermen who had seen more
of the world than he. Hazlitt probed Field's reasons for going into
publishing. "I've been in many businesses," Field answered, "and
this is the business I like best." Reminded that he had come to it

late, he said, "I certainly did. I wish I'd discovered it a long time ago; I should have been, undoubtedly, a happier and more constructive man if I had."

Walsh then turned the talk to the tendency toward monopoly in the newspaper business, much discussed in the book. McCaffery then asked what would happen if John Lewis, *PM*'s editor, were suddenly to take a conservative line. Field said, "I don't think he'd get his staff to go along with him. That's a real point." It was a point that occasioned some surprise on the panel, perhaps more accustomed to the conventional journalistic chain of command. Hazlitt asked if Lewis could hire and fire absolutely; Field reminded him of the Newspaper Guild, which had a good deal to say about such matters, and then made it clear that Lewis discussed even hiring and firing with his staff. The real answer, Field felt, was that people who disagreed with the policies of a staff-run newspaper generally left of their own accord. Mildly rebuked for implying that a newspaper should be staffed by people who agreed with its policies, he was firm: "I don't think you can ask any newspaper to *be* a newspaper, and to be any good, unless the staff pretty much agree with each other. It would just completely lack character." Hazlitt then asked why Field and Walsh talked as though *PM* and the *Sun* were "unique among the thousands of newspapers in this country." They had never said anything like that, but he insisted that "the discussion has taken that implication." "I don't claim for a moment they're unique," Field said, "but I do claim that they're performing an important function." At which point the bell rang, and the program ended.

Field's voice was pleasant, well modulated and with that point of Britishness to it, though it was less broad than in his youth. He made a good impression on his audience, many of whom must have wondered with Hazlitt how so rich a man came to be in liberal journalism, but most of whom must have given his motives the benefit of the doubt. The program, like most such, would have been more meaty with more Author and less Critic. The Critics were not using their air time to demonstrate private theses, and it was their assigned function to nag at the Author; but Field would have preferred to ramble a bit, discuss, quote, explain. It was a decent program, had little effect on sales, and left the Author feeling rather frustrated.

3

Field's life in Chicago was compound of the old and the new—upper-crust friends from the 1920s and post-New Deal professional friends—but the emphasis was on the new. He was not a publisher who had been successful enough to become a civic leader, but a philanthropist and man of affairs who had chosen to become a publisher. The difference was vital. It was the answer to Beaver-brook's question, and it meant not only that Field could not be a full-time professional publisher, though he came close to it after 1944, but also that he had accumulated a body of obligations, a series of commitments, that he could not go back on. Pleading the pressure of business would have amounted to breaking his word. He was committed to child welfare, to community improvement, to clean government—in short, to social action. When he moved back to the Middle West he added even more to his extraprofessional burdens. He did so cheerfully. If he felt a conscious choice between publishing and social action, he chose to act in as many areas as possible, and to rely on professional newspapermen to take up any slack at the *Sun*.

He found in Chicago, as he had in New York, that the men with whom he worked became his friends. Not intimate friends—if Damon had a Pythias it was Louis Weiss and no one else—but close friends, who shared his purposes and outlook. (A few of his older friends did not; they were his friends nonetheless.) He spent a large part of his day at the newspaper, where men like Milburn Akers, Turner Catledge, Robert Lasch offered him talk, thought, and working companionship. Outside the office were old friends like Charles Cushing, or Robert Straus, an intelligent banker, or Hughston McBain, president of Marshall Field and Company; and newer friends like Bishop Bernard J. Sheil, James Brown IV, adviser to the University of Chicago on the legal aspects of child welfare, or Saul Alinsky, a brilliant, rough-and-tumble neighborhood planner. Field's life in Chicago was refracted through the lives of his friends to an extraordinary degree; the city was not quite home to him, and there was an odd note of the perpetual transient in his four-day-a-week hotel suite existence. That was perhaps indicated by a new habit he fell into: when Ruth Field was in New York, and he had no meetings, luncheons, or dinners scheduled in Chicago, he saw an appalling number of movies. The content was unimportant: love story, shoot-'em-up, war epic, white-telephone comedy—he put down his dollar and a quarter, bought a bag of peanuts, and sat in the gloom, anonymous, relaxed, and oblivious to the outside world. The movies may have been a needed relief: he could empty his mind for a couple of hours, and become not Marshall Field but Row G Seat 21. How often in his life had he sat in a roomful of fellow citizens not one of whom knew who he was—or cared? When he was alone in Chicago he sought their company, or noncompany. When he was not alone the aspects of his life, in both Chicago and New York, could be defined by the friends who shared it.

Those friends ranged from his chauffeurs in New York, James Haslam and Albert Risebrow, to the New York Philharmonic Society *in toto*. Haslam and Risebrow were devoted to him, and both were with him for many years, though occasionally he drove the car himself. Field's manner with them, as with everyone, was gracious —the most severe stricture they received from him was a wartime order to stay within their gasoline allotment and *never* to finagle, either for extra fuel from the pump or for extra coupons from the banditti of the black market.

Field's functions with the Philharmonic were more complicated. He had been elected a member of the board in April, 1923; vice-president in May, 1928; president in October, 1934; chairman of the board and president in May, 1939. He had many friends on the board, of course, but his closest working friend was Bruno Zirato, who had served as the Society's liaison with Arturo Toscanini for two years, and who later became its managing director. Field endeared himself to Zirato not only by confessing his relative ignorance of music, but also by doing something about it: in the 1930s he subscribed to a series of lectures offered by Mme. Olga Samaroff, and—few of his friends knew this—studied theory and piano with her. (He was never very good at it, but he had fun.) In 1934, during a strenuous campaign to raise $500,000 for the Society, he underwrote $18,000 in expenses; over a period of years his contributions exceeded $100,000. Once he invited the orchestra to

Caumsett for a pheasant shoot, and a few accepted. When Artur Rodzinski was musical director, and the Society wanted to celebrate his birthday with a fine gift, Field supplied it. Rodzinski had a small dairy farm in the Berkshires, and indicated that he would be molto allegro if they offered him a registered Guernsey. Field had a hundred of them at Caumsett; in a ceremony there, the conductor got his cow.

In 1942 the Society celebrated its centennial, and hoped to be honored by the guest direction of Serge Koussevitzky. The Boston Symphony was not unionized, however, and the Philharmonic was; James C. Petrillo, the famous and fiery head of the American Federation of Musicians, refused to allow Koussevitzky's appearance. Field went to see him, conscious that Petrillo was quite justified, and that he himself was asking a special favor. Petrillo yielded immediately:

This afternoon I received a personal appeal from Marshall Field 3rd. Mr. Field is a man for whom I have great respect. He is one of the leading merchants and one of the most influential men in America, but in spite of that he is a GREAT HUMANITARIAN WITH A CIVIC CONSCIOUSNESS and regard for the social rights of labor, which I admire and respect. In my desire to show my appreciation to Mr. Marshall Field, and to cooperate with him in any endeavor in which he is concerned, and in recognition of the position he is placed in, having announced that Dr. Koussevitzky would conduct, I am giving permission to the union musicians who are members of the New York Philharmonic-Symphony Orchestra on this special occasion to play under the leadership of Dr. Koussevitzky.

Toscanini had conducted the Philharmonic for several years, up to 1936. He and Field were friends, and Field thought the maestro's presence essential during the Centennial. The two met several times, and Toscanini finally straightened out his schedule. This was his formal acceptance:

My dear Marshall Field:

You cannot doubt that I have the greatest respect, regard, and happy association of memory with your Philharmonic-Symphony Society and I would have answered months ago to your kind invitation but there have been complications that have made it difficult for me to determine the course I wished to pursue.

Today I write you to say that I will be very glad to finish up the Centennial Season with the Philharmonic for such time as you may allot, not to be over two weeks! It would be much to my preference to start the season with you in 1942 (so important this Centennial one) for say two weeks.

However, though, I leave the matter in your hands, and with my best wishes, I remain,

Yours sincerely,

Arturo Toscanini

At board meetings Field's proposals were thoughtful and were usually accepted. One of the first, when he became chairman, was to vest in the full board all powers that had formerly been exercised by the small executive committee. He stood by the musicians in everything from salaries to new music stands. Music naturally needed a public, but Field seemed to think too that the public needed music; he often introduced or supported proposals to broaden the Society's audience. (For many years he hoped that the Society would be able to buy Carnegie Hall for its own use, and he was quite disappointed when the talks fell through. In 1946 he supported a project for a new building, to house both the Metropolitan Opera and the Philharmonic. That too proved impossible.)

Field was not a musicologist, not a historian, not a technician, not a performer. He was an old-fashioned dilettante: he *enjoyed* music, and wanted others to. He may not have known a mordent from a pralltriller, but he liked much of what he heard, and gave his soul to it without critical reservation. Of course it was worthy work he did, bringing the noblest of man's creations to the many and not to the few; but he would have scoffed at such pretentious sentiments. He liked music; it brought him peace and happiness; he wanted others to have it. He was no Esterhazy, patronizing Haydns; he was Marshall Field.

In Chicago he heard less music. The *Sun* kept him busy; and he was also a director of Marshall Field and Company, St. Luke's Hospital and Provident Hospital, and a trustee of the University of Chicago, Hull House, and the Illinois Children's Aid Society. In Marshall Field and Company he bore no more responsibility than any other director, and less than many. He was faithful about board meetings and his comments were heeded: he was a major stockholder and a man of importance. But his concerns were social and financial rather than mercantile. The store and the land it occupied had been sold to the management by the Estate in the 1920s (it "went public" in 1930), and Field was no less diffident with merchandising experts than with newspapering experts. He *was* concerned about fair employment practices, and had begun to agitate for "Negroes behind the counters" in the late '30s. Expansion— shopping centers and suburban outlets—interested him as a postwar possibility.

Of his friends on the board the closest was Hughston McBain, who had joined the firm almost directly after college, in 1922, and had risen steadily; he became first a director, then vice-president, then (in 1943) president. His accession, following a probably unique line of brilliant merchants (Harlow Higinbotham; Harry Selfridge, who left after a dispute with the old gentleman and founded the famous London department store; John Shedd; James Simpson; John McKinlay; James McKinsey), marked the completion of a change in the company's character. Until around 1910 much of the annual income had derived from wholesaling: the company owned mills in the South, and supplied dry goods to retailers all over the country. But with the rise of clothing chain stores, wholesaling became less necessary, and finally unprofitable. By 1930 the company's retail stores were making good profits, and the company as a whole was losing money. It was Field who suggested to Simpson that they call in a management consultant. They selected McKinsey, who did his work so well that he was asked to come in as chairman of the board. He began a streamlining operation that consisted essentially of trimming the wholesale side of the business, and resulted eventually in the sale of the mills and total concentration on retailing. When McBain became president he carried the reformation a step further, improving the physical premises, amalgamating departments, and extending the store's appeal both up, to the swank, and down, to the bargain basement. He and Field were close. McBain did not call himself a liberal (and Field did not require his friends to do so), but his first step as president was the inauguration of a pension plan, with a ceiling of $12,000 a year to forestall the criticism that it was a plan to enrich the executives. (Under McKinsey, in 1938–39, the store had established a health insurance program for its employees. That was long before the threat of "socialized medicine" made private health insurance respectable.) Field liked McBain's competence, integrity, and generosity. McBain, who saw Field in a more businesslike context than most of Field's friends, realized that he was a more complicated man than appearances suggested, and respected him for the depth of his convictions. "Field was not in the least anticapitalist," he said later on. "He was very much against the suppression of competition. He believed in competition as much as any man I ever knew. After the war a lot of State Street stores agitated for legislation against discount houses—they were the new thing, and a real threat. Field fought the legislation, and the board agreed with him when he said, 'If you believe in competition, you've got to stand by that belief.' It was something his grandfather—a real free-trader—might have said." (The legislation was defeated.)

The question of "Negroes behind the counter" bothered Field more as time went by. The company had always employed Negroes in its stockrooms and trucking, but successive boards had felt that the customers would object to personal contact. The cruelty in that blithe assumption was not theirs alone or, it should be said, entirely to their liking; when the question came up they experienced the vague, but not really painful, discomfort of men making important decisions on shifty moral grounds. They were not more prejudiced than others of their station—prejudice was not seriously attacked in the United States until the 1940s and 1950s; their real mistake was underestimating the customers' indifference to that aspect of shopping. Frederick & Nelson, the great Seattle store bought by the Company in 1929, employed Negroes behind its counters, and no one seemed to care; but the lesson came slower in Chicago. When the Chicago *Defender,* a Negro newspaper, attacked the store's policies, McBain could refer to photographs of himself in South Carolina violating that state's cherished traditions at a thoroughly mixed sit-down luncheon in one of the mills; still, that begged the question, proving that McBain was a good fellow but not that the store's policies were reasonable, and ignoring entirely the fact that Chicago's Negroes spent a good deal of money with Marshall Field and Company. Ultimately (a word that seems always to be necessary in talking of this sort of progress) Negroes were employed as clerks, beginning in 1949, but even then there was a note of caution: Carson, Pirie, Scott had broken the color line some years before, and some of their Negro employees had not "worked out" (some of their white employees, too, without doubt). So Marshall Field and Company screened its applicants carefully, and took on only those it felt were potential department managers. A double-edged attitude: Negroes could hope to become department managers, which was not true in many stores; but white employees were not required to display such promise.

On balance, Field was very pleased. So was McBain. The latter had already proved himself a sterling executive, and had become one of Chicago's first citizens. Field respected him thoroughly, and supported him in the great postwar expansion of the Company. There had been three branches since 1929, in Evanston, Oak Park, and Lake Forest; but they were only branch stores, and not the large out-of-town shopping centers of which so many sprang up in the 1950s. (Filene's, in Boston, led the diaspora.) Marshall Field and Company moved slowly, inspecting every major shopping center in the country. The board insisted on caution. (The board was, in fact, so cautious that a legend sprang up to the effect that McBain purchased various pieces of land behind their backs, and wriggled out of the predicament by taking each board member to luncheon afterward and persuading him that they *ought* to buy. There was no truth in the story. The board approved all purchases.) In 1956 the Company opened a small store (140,000 square feet) in a Park Forest center; they decided to do it "for the experience," and the experience was profitable. Another, larger (300,000 square feet), was opened later at Old Orchard, outside Chicago; in 1959 Frederick & Nelson opened one in Bellevue, a suburb of Seattle; in 1962 the Company added another, near Oak Brook Terrace at the western end of Chicago's new Congress Street Expressway. They were all successful, and they were due to McBain as much as to anyone.

McBain also had the gentle touch. He often answered his telephone without benefit of secretary, and one day found himself talking—or listening—to an irate lady who had ordered a tricycle for her boy's birthday. The birthday had arrived, and the tricycle had not. Gravely McBain assured her that the merchandise would be delivered on time. He sent for a tricycle, lugged it aboard his Cad-

illac, and gave his chauffeur the address; in half an hour the lady
was thanking a most urbane, impeccably groomed delivery boy,
and squinting around him at his shiny car. She did not offer a tip.
McBain retired in 1958, leaving a highly solvent little shop behind him.

In the history of the store the problem of Negro employment was
a minor contretemps with a happy ending. But Field himself felt
it deeper; he could not live a life half principled, and, also important, he was as a publisher vulnerable to personal criticism. The
store had not suffered from his identification with *PM*—something
like three complaints in five years—and it did not suffer when it
accepted his reasonable view of employment practices. The Chicago
Defender had of course backed him on the issue, and had refrained
from sniping at him. More than that: it had published a meaty and
approving interview with him on Page One of its magazine section
for July 23, 1945, by Earl Conrad, in which Field's forthright honesty was exemplary. So was Conrad's:

Marshall Field, America's unique liberal-philanthropist-capitalist, bluntly
said: "Perhaps after the peace the most pressing problem in this country
today is the Negro question. . . . You can't read Gunnar Myrdal's 'American Dilemma' without realizing that. All you have to do is look about you
to see how vital it is."

That is strong realization, coming from a man with the social and economic background of Mr. Field. It would be a sensible reaction in a practical neighborhood politician or in a white workingman, or among liberal
and left-minded people. Often you won't find such accurate realization in
these quarters, so it's doubly significant when one of the richest men in the
country tells us so. . . .

Without any specific question from me, Mr. Field happened to remark:
"I think the restrictive covenant . . . stinks."

I asked Field whether he read the Negro press, and he declared he was a
regular reader of the Pittsburgh Courier and the Chicago Defender.

"The Negro press provides one of the best means I know for educating
whites. It's important to get this press to the whites. That's the part of our
society that needs the education."

Along the same line, he said, "The Negro Digest is a very well done job.
I admire that magazine and its editor very much."

In the last issue of that magazine, Mr. Field answered the question, "If I

Were a Negro." I told Mr. Field I thought he had given a pretty good answer, especially showing restraint in his concluding statement which was in effect that a white person couldn't possibly appreciate the full meaning of what it was to be a Negro in America. . . .

On another fundamental question, whether change should be immediate or gradual, he said: "I have a great sense of immediacy on this. You also have to approach it on a basis of the present state of public opinion. You can't approach it too quickly to please me. And I have no feeling for those attitudes which say, 'It'll take a hundred years.' It's a question of changing our education. Take a youngster, he has no natural antipathy. Something in his education gives him that. That's what we have to change."

. . . Mr. Field has pretty pronounced views on social freedom between the two groups. He has met many Negroes, mostly educated individuals. Replying to a question on the Negroes' demand for integration, he said:

"That's what you have to look for. Wherever whites have a chance to come into contact with Negroes, they get a different view. It's appalling how few whites have ever met well-educated Negroes, owing to their fear of meeting any. And Negroes are missing as much as whites by this failure of people to get together. I always welcome such association when I get the chance."

. . . Newspaper discussion brought him around to the Negro press again and this time he said that he viewed the Negro press as a kind of "special purpose press, somewhat like a union paper." He suggested this press could improve itself by acquiring a world point of view. "It should get a little more the feeling of being a general part of the public." As an example, he said, if the Negro press got behind the Murray Full Employment Bill, which in the long run affects the Negro, with the same zeal as it supports the FEPC movement.

Asked about whether people in powerful places discussed the issue of white supremacy fully, adequately, or not at all, Marshall Field said that it was a kind of "gentlemanly custom" to avoid controversial subjects. "So I generally bring them up."

. . . Marshall Field discusses any and every phase of the Negro-white relationship with the greatest of ease. I have no doubt that he makes a sincere attempt to "work at it" in order to "do the job."

Fifteen years later Field's attitudes were fashionable, like expensive books on coffee tables; in him they dated from the 1930s, when it was not so easy.

One of his closest old friends in Chicago was Robert Straus, a banker and a very gentle man. He and Field never did business together; they were just good companions. Straus had met Field through Charles Cushing in the 1920s. Cushing and Straus had been competing for a client, met at a country club, and decided to join forces. There followed small jokes about whose name should come first in the advertisements—a game of squash decided the point in Cushing's favor, but he claimed not to care—and then friendship. Straus then met Field, but they became close friends only in the 1930s.

What attracted Straus particularly was Field's sense of enjoyment: he took vast pleasure in work, play, philanthropy, conversation—and did all four well. (He and Straus played bridge often in Chicago; in one game, among experts, it was suggested that Field, only a good amateur, let his partner carry him. Field murmured politely, "I think perhaps I can carry myself.") Now and then Field discussed a project with Straus, who listened with understanding and detachment and occasionally offered a bit of advice. "I never knew a kinder man," Straus said of Field. "The only problem he ever gave me was that I cringed at the advantage people took of his kindness; not that he was stupid—he was just so gentle. He paid more for some of his enterprises than they were worth, but when he had losses they were always offset by profits somewhere else. A good thing, because he was a liberal, and he stayed a liberal. He thought liberal causes were best for the country in the long run; that they'd preserve the country and its values better than the conservative. But he was a *good* businessman." Straus visited Caumsett several times, remarking later that "Marshall and Ruth remained quite simple in formal surroundings," but remembering too that one evening he proved to be the only guest without a smoking jacket and petit-point slippers! Of his first visit, he reported, "I was late getting out there, and drove to the most elegant building in sight. It turned out to be the barn." He noticed, as so many of Field's friends had, the affection for Field demonstrated in small ways by the staff. But he also noticed a good reason for it: the only time he ever saw Field furious was when some of his employees were criticized by an outsider.

Most of Field's closer friends were more actively engaged with him in his good works, but Straus was the sort of fellow—there were few—with whom he could be quiet, comfortable, relaxed. It was to Straus that he might volunteer his decision that the name of the

Field Museum be changed to the Chicago Natural History Museum, or that he was about to give the Pittsfield Building to the Museum, or that he was thinking of buying the Chicago *Times,* or that Lloyd and Kathryn Lewis were coming over for dinner, and Straus might enjoy seeing them. There was never any strain between the two, never any urgency. Straus noticed early in their friendship that Field was a shy man, but the shyness wore off in time; as it did not with others. Field let himself relax with Straus, Louis Weiss, Charlie Cushing, George Richardson, James Warburg; with most other friends he was at once more purposeful and more reserved.

Of his friends in Chicago James Brown IV was probably the youngest. An affinity bound them: both had hopped out of a fore-ordained rut. Brown was a "fine young man of good family" who might have glided smiling through the social pleasantries of life as junior, and then senior, executive. But during the early Depression he did volunteer work with a private relief agency, and when he later took a job with the Gulf Refining Company he found that the joys of management and commerce were fleeting. He quit to go back to social work; realized that social work without knowledge was merely condescension; and enrolled at the University of Chicago, where he completed the wide variety of courses and projects that led to doctorates in the social sciences. Grace Abbott was head of the department of child welfare; when she died, near the end of Brown's studies, he was already marked as out of the ordinary, and was asked to take over her courses. All in all he was with the University for ten years, from 1939 to 1949, teaching and advising.

He and Field became friends in 1943, when Brown served on the U.S. Committee for European Children, and their talks quickly took them beyond the immediate task to child welfare in general. With others Field had to begin by restating the need for welfare, or by justifying it, defending it against the suspicions and doubts of a public brought up on *Oliver Twist* and assuming that more oatmeal was the answer. With Brown he could take for granted the political-social basis of the work, and go on to specifics. He learned from Brown, who had history, statistics, anecdote at his fingertips. Brown in turn admired Field's mind, saying later that he was "probably the best-informed layman in the country," and writing of him as "a person with a sympathetic point of view and extraordinary knowledge of social welfare. Although he never used it to impress, he had an almost professional knowledge of child welfare."

Field and Brown agreed on two points: that the old-fashioned "orphan home" solution, financially feasible anywhere in the United States, was obsolete; and that the paramount deficiency in welfare programs was emotional care for the disturbed individual child. These points were contested from two quarters: enemies of all welfare, whose position was obvious and whose resistance became ferocious when psychiatry was added to the program; and those who felt that psychiatry only treated symptoms when the disease was society itself. Field was patient with the latter group, and tried to ignore the former. He and Brown became trustees of the Illinois Children's Home and Aid Society, which, with the Jewish Children's Bureau, was the most advanced of welfare agencies, in thinking and technique, in the Middle West. Field's contribution to the Society was not money—up to 1949 it had received less than $6,000 from the Field Foundation—but ideas, speeches, suggestions, and administrative work. Where the Society was limited by purpose or geography, Field could apply his ideas—many of which came out of his work with the Society and his talks with Brown—elsewhere. Through the Field Foundation he provided support for Anna Freud's program of teaching and research at the Hampstead Child-Therapy Course and Clinic in London, and one thing led to another:

> The most important "night school" course in Chicago may well be the four-year course in psychoanalytic child care that stems from Anna Freud's training of non-medical psychotherapists for children.
>
> Helen Ross of the Chicago Institute [the Institute for Psychoanalysis] visited London in 1949 at the [Field] Foundation's request and on her return the Institute established this postgraduate course adapted to American needs —teaching psychoanalytic principles of child care to non-medical professional persons working with children. It serves as an American model for advanced education in child care.
>
> Eighty students have graduated [this was from the Foundation's Report in 1959], eight are almost ready to graduate, and the "freshman" class numbers 20. Fifteen are social workers employed in family agencies, children's agencies, clinics and schools. Three are teachers at the nursery and primary

grade levels; one is an occupational therapist; one is a nurse in a teaching and research position. A special student, a minister who is an outstanding Biblical scholar, was admitted to the first year.

In the late 1940s Field made frequent speeches; he was by then eloquent and confident on a platform, and his ideas in welfare were known to be advanced. He and Brown often discussed his talks beforehand (they later wrote one speech together that became famous within the profession). Field's best address of this period was probably his speech in 1949 on the final day of a series of conferences at the Menninger Foundation in Topeka. This was not a pleasantly hortatory allocution for the easy benefit of potential contributors: it was a professional discussion of ideas, goals, and techniques, addressed to professionals. For three days, October 18–20, those professionals had been hearing and delivering reports of considerable sophistication and complexity. To have climaxed the three days with a dinner meeting at which the final address was a genial babble of inanities would have been catastrophic. It was a high compliment to Field that he had been chosen. He graced the occasion with compassion and insight.

Like many of Field's friends Brown ceased very quickly to think of him as just a rich man. Few of Field's friends ever picked up a dinner check, and many worked with him on projects that required money; but he was lucky enough to spend the last fifteen years of his life with a good number of people who despised high-class mendicity. Probably it was not luck: people who spend their lives trying to improve society—from the bottom up—tend to shed avarice, except for their causes, and manage better than most to submerge personal ambitions. Which is not to say that Field was free of accomplished beggars, but that his friends enriched him because they were the kind of people who *gave*.

Brown witnessed in Field a growth, a process of education, that accelerated constantly after 1940. With it came a new confidence, and even a new impatience, once impossible to the Perfect Gentleman. He and Brown were talking business one afternoon at the Tavern Club when a lady who had met Field once socially insisted on hovering, making it rather more clear than necessary that she would be gratified by the offer of a drink in such company. Field took it for a minute or two, and then said wearily, "We're awfully busy here. Why don't you run along?" Brown came east from time to time, and was made welcome at Caumsett. In return for what he taught Field, he learned much about the management of large foundations—knowledge he put to good use when he became an executive in the Chicago Community Trust, which administered ninety-six separate trusts left to it over a period of forty-five years, and was operated with extreme flexibility. It was the largest foundation in Chicago; in general it attacked obsolescence through grants to responsible organizations; and it had the power to redirect its income to contemporary purposes. It was Fieldian in intent, and even broader in scope. Field's impact on welfare was greater than he knew, and was an impact of ideas and attitudes, not of money; people who worked with him are still inclined to ask themselves what he would have said or done in a given situation. Writing about him later Brown summed it up:

The history of American philanthropy is not very long if limited to the story of those who have expressed their love for their fellow men by giving or bequeathing princely sums of money. Stephen Girard, who became the first American millionaire, did not die until 1831; the first American foundation, the Peabody Education Fund, was not created until 1867.

Thus far—and fortunately—the American philanthropist has been permitted to range over a wide area, and his giving may be a reasonably personal expression of interest and enthusiasm. . . .

Marshall Field's giving set an example for those who want to preserve this freedom of expression in philanthropy. He believed in and defended the right of the public to have an accounting of the way in which tax-exempt funds are spent. . . .

He also believed that the giving away of large amounts of money was a responsibility which should be shared with informed outsiders, and thus he established the provision . . . that the non-family members of the Field Foundation should always be in the majority.

Unlike Stephen Girard and some more recent philanthropists who impose rigid restrictions on how their money may be used in the years to come, Marshall Field made no effort to outguess the future or to inflict his convictions on coming generations. He knew that to do so keeps the money from being of maximum usefulness and is a certain invitation to legal proceedings which waste it.

Finally, he also believed that foundations should live a little dangerously and should be willing to take a chance on an individual or a new idea. This might be called gambling with philanthropic funds except that he always insisted that there be careful investigation of the individual or the idea by experts in the field before the bet was placed. Once this was done, he was willing to sit back like the sportsman he was and take the failures along with the winners.

Another of Field's friends was Bishop * Bernard J. Sheil, who had met him through Eugene Meyer, owner of the Washington *Post,* and again through a word from President Roosevelt, who, as Sheil recalled later, "admired Field before the *Sun.*" The bishop was an early member of the U.S. Committee: he was their "last resort," in that he accepted children for whom no care could be found elsewhere. He consequently found himself guardian to a few memorably uninhibited savages, but his infinite patience, real love of children, and probably even his athletic talents (he had been a semipro ball player before entering the Church) pulled him through. His affection for Field was real, disinterested, and unqualified. "He wasn't a slugger," the archbishop said later, "and he didn't care for brawls. He was what I'd call a 'witness': the force of his own example, and a good brain, were his weapons." (Sheil, who lived in a tradition of personal humility, refrained from pointing out that he too was a "witness" and, in his own context, as much a maverick as Field.) Field made no secret of his affection for the bishop. Curiously, the two never discussed religion. Perhaps Field preferred not to explain his lapse from faith; the bishop respected his privacy. Sheil's breadth of mind seemed to Field remarkable; the bishop's faith buttressed, and did not limit, his tolerance and understanding. Probably no one else could have induced Field and Colonel McCormick to sit together, for the benefit of photographers, at a great rally in Sportsman's Park for Chicago's combined charities; and when someone remarked, "That was sporting of Field," probably no one else would have answered, "Pretty sporting of the Colonel, too." But if he could see temporal difficulties under the aspect of eternity, he could also see temporal solutions to them, and in fact made a name for himself (several names, and not all of them complimentary) by his

---

* Later Archbishop.

concern for Chicago's workingmen, their children, their labor unions.

The deepest bond between Field and Sheil was a hatred of suppression. Field, the great capitalist, and Sheil, the Roman Catholic bishop, were adamant: the great moral obligation was to fight suppression. (Each, consequently, suffered criticism from his peers.) That was a sufficient community of belief for a lifetime of friendship; it brought them together in child welfare, charities, the defense of civil liberties, the Industrial Areas Foundation. The two saw the world from vastly different eminences, but somehow they both saw it at ground level. They did what they could for it, and each took heart from the other.

The Industrial Areas Foundation was the creation of a man named Saul Alinsky, who was as different from Sheil, or Brown, as he was from Field—except for the battered old conviction they all shared that man could shape his own ends. Alinsky was a native Chicagoan, the son of Jewish immigrants. It would be easy here to romanticize second-generation American Jews, marking how many of them supplied point, dignity, commentary, impetus to the great social changes of the twentieth century; it would also be necessary to ignore the millions who did not. No one has a monopoly on political morality. But a certain number of them—many through the New Deal—succeeded in transforming a traditional concern for justice and learning, and a traditional capacity for endurance, into an active, even truculent, genius for social reform. Alinsky was one of them. He had come out of the University of Chicago in the early 1930s with a degree in archeology. "I just wanted the world to let me alone with my shovel," he said later, "but the only shoveling jobs were on the WPA." He was granted, out of the blue, a fellowship in criminology; hung around with the remains of the Capone organization trying to learn something; and when he was twenty-two was hired by the state of Illinois as a criminologist, working at Joliet prison. Twenty years before it became parlor conversation, he narrowed down on juvenile delinquency, and came early to a conclusion about crime in general that he saw no reason afterward to change. He stated it clearly before a United States Senate subcommittee in 1955, when delinquency had finally become a major concern:

The trouble is that we shy away from doing what we know must be done. We persist in programs of cosmetic coverups, instead of the required social surgery. It is almost impossible to find the criminology study or textbook which does not begin and end with the findings that in the main delinquency and crime arise out of inadequate, substandard housing, disease, economic insecurity, inadequate educational facilities, discrimination, and a series of social ills which combine to foster and relate to each other in a vicious circle with each feeding into the other so that frustration, demoralization, and delinquency mount.

And what do we do about it? Do we attack the causes? Do we do as the medical profession did when they discovered the etiology of malaria, drain the mosquito-breeding swamps? We do not. We avoid the causes and go in for supervised recreation, leisure-time activities, handicraft, summer camps, and something mysterious called character building. These approaches may be good in themselves for whatever their objectives may be, but they certainly are not aimed at coming to grips with the recognized major causes of delinquency and crime.

By then there were many who agreed, but twenty years earlier everything was blamed on the Depression, and no one did much thinking about the kids because Daddy himself was out of work. Precocious, brash, Alinsky was also right when he decided that criminology as then practiced was a kind of condescension, much like old-fashioned charity: the Criminal Element was lectured, exposed to Higher Morality, urged to do Useful Work, and expected to Go Straight, while the causes of crime remained comfortably obscure. Controversial issues, like the fine line between a bank robber and a slumlord, were ignored; and the noncontroversial issues were merely silly. The result was a largely futile attempt to reform individuals, bringing balm and heart's ease to the reformer and no lasting result at all to anyone else.

Alinsky kept reaching out, and out, toward society itself. The late 1930s—Depression, Spanish War, CIO, New Deal—accelerated the process. He was offered a job as chief of probation and parole in Philadelphia, with a good salary, a good social life, and a chance to teach part-time; but Hitler, in a manner of speaking—all the major evils of the time—kept him from taking it. He met John L.

Lewis, "fell in love with the CIO," met Roosevelt. By 1939 he was considered a professional antifascist, an epithet that pleased him greatly. He considered himself a left-winger of some sort but, as he put it later, "a well developed sense of humor" kept him from joining any political group. (It was more than that, he added: it was a deep detestation and fear of people who believe that their own dogmas and creeds are The Truth.)

By then he had come to believe that mass organizations were necessary, to give purpose and direction to the apathetic, the unconsulted, those who were "ruled" even in a nominal democracy. People had to face real issues, like the function of labor and the need for housing and the insanity of discrimination and prejudice— they had to face those issues *personally,* and not through a ward heeler.

Easier said than done, of course. Hardly to be done at all on a large scale, or in the complacency of a "good neighborhood." To Alinsky the evils of his century seemed concentrated in the slums and exaggerated among the dispossessed: miserable housing, rotten sanitation, violent parochialism and prejudice, total lack of purpose and hope, and no political existence at all. Chicago's worst slum was in the packinghouse neighborhood: it was Upton Sinclair's jungle, bordered by Studs Lonigan's turf, and time had not improved it. It was full of Silver Shirts, Bundists, and Communists. The infant mortality rate was 10 per cent. Base pay in the stockyards was 35 cents an hour. Poles hated Mexicans hated Lithuanians hated Hungarians hated Negroes hated Slovaks; about the only emotion that united them was hatred of the Irish. Street gangs ran wild; racketeers were folk heroes. The police were discreet, and little inclined to risk mayhem for the sake of people they despised. The history of the neighborhood was an unbroken chronicle of poverty, disease, grime, bitterness, hatred, hopelessness. Migrants arrived in waves, as the packers found new groups of the underprivileged to underpay; each new wave broke against a solid wall of hate. (The Negroes, for example, had arrived back in 1919, hired to break the great strike of that year. They were poor ignorant Southerners, and maybe one in twenty had any notion of the issues; those who knew what strikebreaking was probably figured it was the noblest profession to which they had yet been called—weren't they on the side of the Swifts and the Armours? Their impact on the neighborhood was disastrous for a generation, but that was their worry, and not the packers'.)

But by 1939 there was a ray of hope. Alinsky found two effective pressure points. The neighborhood—Back of the Yards—was 90 per cent Roman Catholic, and while the priests were not *prêtres-ouvriers,* they were not unctuous tranquilizers either. And most of the neighborhood had joined the CIO. Here were two existing organizations, both powerful, to work with. Beyond that, there were the local leaders, and Alinsky's definition of them was simple: if you had a following, you were a leader.

He talked to Bishop Sheil. Many Catholics opposed the CIO, and the local CIO leader was a Communist (it was legal then). Sheil believed that the Communist party in America could never stand up to Christianity, and that the risks of a confrontation were far graver for the Communists. Alinsky also talked to Joseph B. Meegan, a native of the neighborhood, who was recreational director in Davis Park Square, the nearest thing to a playground in the area. With the support of his two friends Alinsky called a community congress for July 14, 1939. It did not cross his mind that this was the 150th anniversary of the fall of the Bastille.

Three hundred fifty people, including the bishop and the Communist, attended. They experienced certain shocks, perhaps symbolized by the revelation that the president of a Holy Name Sodality was also an officer in the union. When they got busy arguing about labor, housing, health, and the kids, they found—over a period of a few hours—that there was time to get things done, or to run each other down, but not to do both. They got things done. This was the first time anyone had suggested working on the jungle from inside, and they were so relieved at the absence of reformers with fancy vocabularies that they went right to work. Which is not to say that it was a love feast; but when they passed a resolution overwhelmingly, in support of the CIO's demands in a strike scheduled for two days later, they suffered a new emotion, and it hit them like the flu: solidarity.

The Back of the Yards Council was in business. Meegan became its executive secretary. Its business thenceforth ranged from bucking Mayor Kelly's machine (which it did successfully) to investigating the charge that a waitress had refused to serve a Negro (which was true; the restaurant manager apologized, and then took the Committee and the Negro to lunch). The story is necessarily skimpy here. Stated broadly, and omitting inevitable frictions, it was this: in a period of five years the jungle became a flourishing piece of America. The Back of the Yards Council represented *all* its people. It got them to clean up their streets and houses; it brought in sanitation and a station of the Infant Welfare Society. It rented a three-block recreation center; it sent 300 kids to camp in summer. It established a Senate (185 members, meeting monthly) in which a street athletic club of fourteen boys could argue with a union representing 15,000 men. Schoolchildren took home questionnaires about violations of health and fire regulations: a list of 3,600 such violations was sent on to City Hall—where it languished until the Council newspaper reported the facts, mentioning the number of votes in the neighborhood. Lutheran children sold tickets to Catholic raffles—because everybody went to everybody else's festivals. Anti-Semites came in with soapboxes and went out an hour later with black eyes, administered by good Christians. A Council representative made an anti-Negro speech and was thrown out of the meeting.* When the city contributed building material for the recreation center and offered to send on a night watchman, a Council member asked why, and was informed, "You people carry off park benches and fences, you know." After a moment of silent shock a teen-age boy summed up the neighborhood: "Nobody's going to steal from this recreation center. It's *ours*."

---

* The charge that Back of the Yards remained lily-white, while not strictly true, is true enough to require answer. The answer lies in a problem still unresolved. When Negroes moved into white neighborhoods, the whites moved out; not necessarily because they disliked Negroes, but because each family was afraid that all the others would run, and that it would be left as the sole white family in a Negro neighborhood. Alinsky did not know how to solve this problem, but he did know that Back of the Yards could be destroyed by it. Alinsky made many enemies pointing this out, but he refused to let people delude themselves, cling to ideals he knew they would abandon when the chips were down. He was in an awkward position, but as he saw it the alternative was the kind of sentimentalism that urges total integration and then clucks dolefully when the result is not an integrated community but an expanded Negro ghetto. Fifteen years later he tackled this again with an explosive proposal that made him even more enemies; see page 363.

But back in 1939 when it all began Alinsky had, in his own words, a bull by the tail and no job. (He got no pay for his work with Back of the Yards.) John L. Lewis, who had originally opposed the Back-of-the-Yards concept, but was shortly converted, called to offer him a job organizing and heading the CIO's public relations. Alinsky declined, feeling that he had to remain uncommitted—that "auspices" would hamper his work. Roosevelt offered him a job with the National Youth Administration (Alinsky had in a few short months become a national figure, jumping from a paragraph deep within the daily papers to a story in the national affairs section of *Time*); Alinsky declined again, because the job was partisan and limited. Bishop Sheil mentioned Alinsky to Marshall Field, who sent off a note asking Alinsky to call him. Their first meeting, with the bishop present, took place in the fall of 1939 at the Waldorf in New York, a long way from the jungle. It was brief and general: they ran over the basic idea, dreamed a bit about millions of democratic communities all over the world, and acknowledged that the idea would have to be implemented as part of the world that was, and not as a Utopian ideal. Alinsky's enthusiasm for Field was limited: here was a very rich man, refined, restrained, almost bland, the perfect English country gentleman—who probably didn't understand at all. Still, it was nice of him to show interest, and the meeting broke up with friendly expressions of good will.

A few days later Field asked Alinsky to lunch, and the latter revised his opinions. Field peppered him with questions: where else could this be done? was Alinsky sure, or just hoping? did he have statistics? did he need a board of advisers? did he want to hire sociologists or political scientists or cheerful liberals or what? had he thought of a foundation, and if so how much power would he be willing to vest in the trustees? The two focused on ways and means, rather than ultimate goals. Alinsky hesitated to use a foundation, feeling that all foundations were products of the status quo, over-cautious in approach and scared to death of firebrands; the trustees, it seemed to him, were inevitably men of substance with a stake in inertia. Field made a suggestion: if he limited contributions he could also limit power, and keep the direction more in his own hands. Alinsky was, in the end, much impressed and much encouraged. Field seemed to mean what he said, and unquestionably understood what Alinsky was after.

In February, 1940, the Industrial Areas Foundation was established, with Alinsky as its executive director (incidentally at a salary of $7,500 a year, including expenses; he was later accused of making a good living, a charge that made him wistful). Its board comprised Alinsky, Field, Sheil; G. Howland Shaw of the State Department (acting of course as an individual, and not ex officio); Kathryn Lewis, daughter of John L.; Adele Levy, daughter of Julius Rosenwald; Theodore Rosen, judge of the Juvenile Court in Philadelphia (and holder of the Congressional Medal of Honor); Stuyvesant Peabody, the coal magnate; Britton Budd, then president of Northern Utilities; and Mrs. Valentine Macy, wife of the owner and publisher of a chain of newspapers in Westchester County, New York. Two questions had to be answered during a trial period, after which the fate of the Foundation would be finally determined. First, was the Back of the Yards successful mainly because of the timing, and not because of Alinsky? Second, the program had succeeded with Catholics and the CIO; how would it do with Protestants and the AFL?

The total capital was $15,000—half of it Alinsky's pay and expense money. The board held informal meetings every few weeks. At one of them Field expressed curiosity: how did Alinsky manage with no suite of offices and no staff? Answer: he was in the field almost all the time. One result of that field work, over the next five years, was the establishment of neighborhood councils in Kansas City, Omaha, South St. Paul, and Los Angeles.

Another, quite natural, result was the emergence of Saul Alinsky as a threat to American institutions. Field loved the anecdotes he brought back from his trips. At one board meeting Alinsky described his career in a Kansas City jail. A police captain there named Beatty was strongly antilabor, and Alinsky, considered an advance man for the CIO, was jugged periodically. It offered him his only spare time, and he improved each shining hour by extensive reading. Beatty was literate, and became curious; during the long evenings he and his prisoner debated; the captain mellowed, and for a time Alinsky was not sure whether his incarceration was injustice or flattery. In the end the captain was converted; but then he missed Alinsky's company, and the dogwatch became tedious. After that Alinsky dropped in socially whenever he was in Kansas City. Field roared in delight at all this while the rest of the board, unversed in the arcana of crime and punishment, smiled weakly.

Alinsky's difficulties were not all local. The FBI, always sensitive about democracy, interviewed him several times. Field once called to say that they were in his office, and had just told him that Alinsky had raised $150 for the Spanish Loyalists. "That's a lie," Alinsky asserted hotly. "I raised at least twenty-five hundred dollars." Field later commented, "They really go around running people down," but then Field was also a suspicious character. The two were on common ground here. What each valued highest—democracy—seemed to be all things to all men, and Field and Alinsky, who saw it as *one* thing to all men, were in a distinct minority. But they complemented each other. Field had, despite his critics, great respectability. He also had an intellectual generosity that Alinsky would not have found elsewhere. And Alinsky was a fulfillment—precisely what Field had hoped for when he expressed the desire that the Field Foundation would contribute to work "in areas of great tension and controversy."

Field was quite informal with Alinsky,* who was as charmed by the man's casual sense of humor as by his stubborn liberalism. The two dined together in Chicago one night, and then started for the Back of the Yards; unable to find a cab, they stopped a *Sun-Times* truck (this happened after the two newspapers had merged) for a lift. Field identified himself. The driver was not amused: "O.K., Napoleon," he said. Field guffawed. On a less funny occasion Field and Alinsky were dining at the Tavern Club when a Democratic leader, beaten after a brisk campaign against him by the *Sun-Times* (that is what "independent" means), came up to their table and slammed a sheaf of papers down on Field's steak platter, saying loudly, "You son of a bitch, I'm going to sue you for ten million dollars tomorrow morning." Field suddenly seemed very tough and very cold: "Sue and be damned," he said, "but there's no need to get gravy all over me." Field's greatest importance to Alinsky may

---

* When Alinsky suffered a deep personal tragedy Field dropped everything to offer him strength and comfort.

be summed up in that "Sue and be damned." The Industrial Areas Foundation was no haven for the timid.

Alinsky wrote a book called *Reveille for Radicals* that came out in 1946—a good, solid, inflammatory handbook for people who wanted to make industrial democracy work. Field scheduled a literary cocktail party at Marshall Field and Company, where there was an excellent book department, but a letter from the store's management arrived shortly pointing out that the book was highly-controversial, not at all the sort of thing the store wanted to give an appearance of supporting; and that there would be neither party nor publicity on the premises. Field was furious, and threatened to throw his weight around—violently out of character—when he talked it over with Alinsky. But Alinsky reminded him that good billing was on the way: first printing from the University of Chicago Press was 32,000 (incredible for a university press), and there would be plenty of advertising and discussion in the news columns. The store, he felt, would look foolish *not* carrying the book. Field took his advice and calmed down, and the event justified the optimism: 16,000 books were in the shops in Chicago on publication day, and sales were brisk from the first hour. And on the third day the Chicago *Tribune,* no less, ran an advertisement in which Marshall Field and Company presented *Reveille for Radicals* to its public. The combination was too much for Field; all he could say was "Well I'll be damned. Let's not even talk about it."

Alinsky was called everything from Communist to fascist, but none of the labels really stuck; he was too various a character. It was hard to persuade people that a man was a Communist when so many parish priests worked with him and spoke out hotly in his defense; or a fascist when the United Mine Workers made a large contribution to the Foundation. (After 1949 the Schwarzhaupt Foundation in Chicago also made large grants.) One reason for the irritation he engendered was his firm belief that until every participant in any project had sat down and faced his own prejudices, doubts, and reservations, the work would not be valid. Lip service to ideals was no goal at all; and no man, or group, could beat an enemy that hadn't been identified. The truth was often bitter, sometimes agonizing, but it was the only basis for action. Much later, in 1959, Alinsky flung a bombshell into the hearings on housing integration of the United States Commission on Civil Rights, and no man who could say what he said then would go through life without bitter enemies. He was a man without a trace of racial prejudice, one of whose goals was a world so integrated that the word itself would fall into disuse, but when he cut through the snug coating of treacly idealism in which so many people feel comfortable, he was called names too fierce to mention. Bluntly, his proposal was to avoid the customary exodus of white families by integrating *all* neighborhoods on a quota basis—the quota to be determined by whites and Negroes acting together. It was at first hearing a horrendous idea, and the roof fell in, but he stood firm, claiming that the alternative would be what it had always been: an expanding Negro ghetto with no advance in the sympathy, friendship, or comprehension of whites. He felt that a quota would guarantee an integrated neighborhood—which no other proposal had achieved. And in time—five years, ten, a generation—whites accustomed to Negro neighbors (and friends) might forget about color altogether, at which point they could also forget about quotas.

Alinsky wanted to *get something done,* and it was possible that if he had made his suggestion in 1940, and it had been followed, results would already have been apparent. He was, of course, acutely and wearily conscious of the irony in a Jew's arguing for quotas; and in addition to the protests of liberals he had to suffer the approval of a few groups he had no use for. He delivered his arguments with savage frankness:

... But the same academicians who are saying the statistics show the problem is taking care of itself have another set of figures that show Chicago has become more segregated with each passing decade.

There are several reasons for this. One is that no white Chicago community wants Negroes, and that includes the Back of the Yards. Let there be no mistake about it: no white Chicago community wants Negroes, and that also includes those communities which publicize themselves as interracial. The only places in this city there is even consideration of an integrated population [are] where the Negro ghetto has rushed in on the whites who, for various financial reasons, are trying to stick it out. In these instances integration is just a desperate adjustment to a fait accompli.

All that was after Field's death, but it indicates the kind of damn-the-torpedoes honesty that he cherished in Alinsky. Whether or not he would have agreed with Alinsky's thesis is impossible to say. He knew that Alinsky wanted—passionately and without rationalization—total integration and total democracy; and he knew that right or wrong Alinsky and his Foundation called the truth as they saw it, and would work with nothing else. If liberals wanted to wait for Abie's Irish Rose to set things right, Alinsky wished them a patient old age; meanwhile he had work to do, and while he lived Marshall Field helped him to do it.

4

At various times Field was closely connected with five institutions of higher learning. He was a student at Cambridge University; a trustee of the University of Chicago, the New School for Social Research, and Sarah Lawrence College; and a member of the advisory board of Roosevelt University in Chicago. Of the last four, Roosevelt University owed him most: it might never have existed without him. It was founded in a storm, and Field was often warned away from it. But in it he found another example of ideals misunderstood, of marchers to the sound of a different drum.

The drum-major was Dr. Edward Sparling, a Christian idealist whose experiences on the family farm, in college, with the YMCA, in the early air service, at Columbia University and Long Island University and the Union Theological Seminary, in settlement houses, at Hiram College in Ohio where he had been dean of men, and at the YMCA Central College in Chicago, of which he had been president, had developed in him a compulsive sense of equality and social justice. He had come to YMCA Central in 1936, and by 1945 he was embroiled in a fierce battle with the trustees. He had improved the college greatly, adding distinguished professors from Europe and changing an alarming deficit to a healthy surplus; but in the process he had seen to it that admission was based on merit alone, with the result that where the student body had been 4 per cent Negro, 25 per cent Jewish, 20 per cent Roman Catholic, and the rest white Protestant in 1938, by 1945 it was 5 per cent Oriental, 25 per cent Negro, 35 per cent (and 90 per cent of the scholarship students) Jewish. The board had demurred, and had asked him to reduce the number of "minority students." He refused flatly.

It was easy enough, and perhaps morally obligatory, for liberals to side with Sparling. He was right. But the uncompromising man faces special difficulties, one of them being that he can't convert everyone all at once, and may consequently find himself alone at the end of a limb. The YMCA was an old-fashioned service organization, a product of the nineteenth century, Christian and moral, vulnerable to criticism and jokes (about "cold hip baths and lectures on 'hygiene' "), stodgy and humorless; but it was firmly rooted in a tradition—the tradition of Marshall Field I—that would die hard. Sparling underestimated the dismay of a board of Christian gentlemen informed that 65 per cent of its student body consisted of people who were not, by the classical definition, Christians at all. Sparling might say that he was the better Christian; but the gap between profession and practice was also part of the old tradition, and no educator could bridge it with one leap. Sparling tried, asking for help—money—from the Carnegie and Rockefeller Foundations, and was urged to compromise: he still had more minority students than other schools. But tact had never seemed to him one of the supreme virtues; he declined to compromise. So did the board. Neither yielded an inch, and both were trapped in the ancient conjugation of the verb "to persist"—I am principled, you are stubborn, he is pig-headed. There matters stood for some weeks.

Sparling turned to Field, whom he had met in 1943, for help in the *Sun*'s columns. (The *Tribune* naturally opposed Sparling.) John McGrath, the *Sun*'s education editor, investigated, and wrote a report that favored Sparling's stand. Field, hoping to salvage a good college, offered financial support for YMCA Central if an accommodation could be reached. But when the board met on March 26, 1945, and a member rose to ask if Marshall Field were trying to blackmail the YMCA, Sparling knew it was the end. The board resolved that Sparling was stubborn and insubordinate (which was true but evaded the issue), and on April 13 asked for his resignation effective the 16th. Sparling complied.

On the 17th Sparling sent $10 to the state of Illinois and incorporated Thomas Jefferson College, housed in three rooms at 11

LaSalle Street, rental $120 monthly, with desks and four chairs. The newspapers made tumult. Sparling issued a statement giving his side of the story. His former faculty backed him 62-1, and petitioned the board to yield; when the board held firm, the sixty-two resigned. By now Sparling had a new board, for his new college; its chairman was Edwin Embree, the financially conservative, politically liberal head of the Rosenwald Fund, whose primary social concern was race relations. He was Field's friend, and the two conferred on the problem within a few days. They decided that their Foundations would each put up $75,000 in support of Sparling's new college. On April 24 the college was renamed in honor of Franklin Delano Roosevelt, who had died on the 12th.

(While Sparling waited for the various governmental rulings that would confirm his college's tax-exempt status, and for the contributions he could then expect, he faced a somewhat more immediate problem: he needed $500 with which to open a checking account in the college's name. Fittingly, he got $25 from a Hindu professor, $100 from a Jewish furniture dealer, $200 from a white Protestant M.D., and $175 from his own pocket.)

As soon as the Chicago *Sun* stepped into the picture, various friends and acquaintances had warned Field to keep his distance from Sparling, who they insisted was a "troublemaker." He was, of course, and Field approved; but Sparling did not have Field's gentle, refined tact, and often impressed people as a man of rather humorless inflexibility; one exasperated opponent described him as "the most illiberal liberal I ever ran into." But Field had read McGrath's report carefully, and had made his decision without reference to personalities—though he was abundantly pleased to find Embree on his side. The Rosenwald Fund advanced $50,000 to the college on June 8. Field was more circumspect, and notified Sparling that until the college's tax exemption was legally established, the Field Foundation would be unable to advance funds. In view of which, he added, he was sending along his personal check for $50,000, as a non-interest-bearing loan. In November the college's status was confirmed by the government, and the Foundation made over to it $75,000; the college immediately repaid its first major debt.

The history of the college since then is one of almost unique

growth and accomplishment. Within six months it was fully accred-
ited—something of a record. In ten years the student body rose to
almost 5,000; in fifteen it numbered 12,000 in regular courses,
auditors' courses, and summer sessions. In 1947 it bought and
moved into the historic ten-story Auditorium Building facing Grant
Park.* Thousands of individuals, business firms, and foundations
contributed to the college (the Field Foundation alone contributed
$175,000 before 1950); its capital assets rose in fifteen years from
Sparling's original nonsectarian interracial $500 to $3,500,000.
The Association of Founders and Friends of Roosevelt University,
numbering over ten thousand, raised over $4,000,000. A Ford
Foundation grant in 1955, for faculty salaries, was the University's
first formal endowment (the college had become a university in
1954). Meanwhile the list of board members had expanded impres-
sively; with and after Embree came dozens of men and women—
corporation presidents and executives, labor leaders, brokers, professors, management consultants, administrators. The board of advisers was illustrious. Field was one of the first, and he was followed
by Marian Anderson, Francis Biddle, Pearl Buck, Ralph Bunche,
Agnes de Mille, David Dubinsky, Murray Lincoln, Gunnar Myrdal,
Vijaya Lakshmi Pandit, Frances Perkins, Jacob Potofsky, Eleanor
Roosevelt, Adlai Stevenson, and James Warburg. Among the artists
and thinkers brought to Chicago by the University's program of
public lectures were Archibald MacLeish, Margaret Mead, Frank
Lloyd Wright, Chief Justice Earl Warren, Edward R. Murrow, Jus-
tice William O. Douglas, Marshall Field, Erich Fromm, Russell
Kirk, Thomas Mann, Nelson Rockefeller, and several of the ad-
visers, among them Mrs. Roosevelt, Miss Buck, and Governor
Stevenson.

The University expanded to five colleges or divisions: Arts and
Sciences, Business Administration, Chicago Musical College, the
Graduate Division, and the Labor Education Division. All these
offered a full range of courses; the last offered special courses for
union officials and members. The University's motto was "Educa-

---

* The building is one of the handsomest in Chicago. It housed the Chicago Civic
Opera for years, and was the scene of many political conventions. It was designed
by Louis Sullivan and Dankmar Adler; the detail drawings of their ornamentation
were rendered by a young draftsman named Frank Lloyd Wright.

tion for Freedom," and it educated well. From precarious beginnings, from a radical reputation, from what amounted briefly to dependence on Field and Embree, the University came to rank in quality with the best in the country. It did not move to the suburbs, embrace professional collegiate athletics, or dilute its first ideal—education for all on equal terms, and no nonsense about race, color, creed, provenance, bloodlines or preference in haberdashery.

This was surely one of the more successful "ideas that deserved a chance." No one even calls it radical any more, with all those capitalists on the board, and with that excellent business school. But it is as radical and as normal today as it was in 1945; it was not the University that changed, but the society around it. When it was three rooms and four chairs, Field and Embree saw what it stood for, whether or not it became large and distinguished. When Sparling was called names, it was Field who recognized, under the somewhat dogmatic manner, a working liberal. When Field's friends warned him off, he laughed wisely: he knew that if it had been a normal investment, if he had been able to tell them that a thousand now would be ten thousand later, they would have understood, and admired, regardless of the ideal; because it was an even greater investment, with an even greater return, they tried to tout him off it. Field was there, as in so many places, when it mattered—*at the beginning*. The University was part of what he meant when he hoped that "by experimentation a few ideas and social techniques may be helped to germinate which will eventually prove to be of enough value to be adopted by the community." Sparling said later, "Field was our greatest benefactor, and if someone gave us ten million dollars tomorrow, Field would still be our greatest benefactor."

Well, Field was a do-gooder. What motivated him to help Roosevelt University was what had motivated him to help *PM*, or disturbed children, or Saul Alinsky: an uncommonly firm conviction that everybody in the world was entitled to a fair chance. It was the sort of thing a city (or a country) never bothered to thank a man for, and at any sign of gratitude he would only have murmured an embarrassed acknowledgment and passed the credit along to someone else. But without him, without the quiet radiations of his liberalism that somehow got into people's bones in spite of themselves, Chicago would have been a different and far worse city—nobody to help Brown take care of the kids, or Alinsky work for the grown-ups, or Sparling teach the in-betweens; or to help the whole city get a decent morning paper, or to put in a good editorial word for tolerance and generosity and humor and affection and simple humanity.

The wheel came full circle in 1962, when the McCormick Foundation made a grant of $30,000 to Roosevelt University.

5

Aubrey Williams, preacher, Foreign Legionnaire, social worker, Federal administrator, printer and publisher, was also Marshall Field's friend, and was important in Field's life because he represented a Northern liberal's most considerable foray into the conservative (and reactionary) South. In its larger aspects the invasion failed, but as sometimes happens in liberal campaigns its victories in the minor skirmishes brought hope and a sense of dignity—not to mention food, shelter, and clothing—to a good many of this country's most hapless and hopeless citizens.

Williams himself was born one of those, into a miserably poor Alabama family. His grandfather had been a slave owner, and was ruined by the Civil War. His father was a blacksmith. Aubrey grew up on the lowest economic level of white Birmingham. He had six months of schooling at age seven, and none at all after that until he was twenty: he spent his youth as a cashboy in a Birmingham department store. The Williamses were devout Presbyterians, and Aubrey was rescued from a life of permanent despair and tribulation by his sanguine reliance on two animating beliefs: the Christian belief in equality, and the American belief in opportunity. (They got him into trouble decades later, when he entered public life: instead of simply affirming them he acted upon them.) At twenty he left Birmingham for Maryville, a college in Tennessee for mountaineer children; after three years there he went on to the University of Cincinnati, where he prepared for the ministry, taking courses also at a seminary. The president of the seminary had the unfortunate habit of delivering anti-German, pro-war speeches in Fountain Square (this was in 1916); sensing a certain contradiction, Williams challenged him publicly. That was the end of his seminary career, and the beginning of his doubts.

In some confusion, because the ministry had represented a "way up" for him and his future was now dubious, Williams went to France with the YMCA. He was appalled by the carnage—these were Christian nations—but he also felt guilty about behind-the-lines work while other men fought. Confusion and dilemma were compounded, but emotion won out: he joined the Foreign Legion Regiment of the French 33d Division in time to fight at Chemin des Dames, where thousands of men died first gaining and then losing nine kilometers. In the regiment were men of all colors from twenty-nine countries; Williams's commanding officer was a German named Schmidt, and his closest buddy a Negro from Virginia. Williams was a Southern poor boy, but the Virginian had thrown himself between him and a grenade, fortunately surviving with minor wounds; that settled the race problem for good, though Williams's Christianity had already solved it in the abstract. When the American armies arrived Williams left the Legion and enlisted (February, 1918); he became a general's orderly, then a lieutenant, then, because of his experience, an artillery instructor on French 75s. Later he was granted permission to attend the University of Bordeaux and the Sorbonne.

Home again, he realized that the church had failed him (or perhaps he it); he tried, going to a church near Cincinnati as supply pastor, but his sermons were far too social and immediate, and the Evangelical Lutheran hierarchy pronounced him heretical. His transition to social work was natural and easy. Jane Addams's influence was spreading; Grace Abbott of the University of Chicago drew 5,000 people for one lecture in Madison; Roger Baldwin, later of the American Civil Liberties Union, was another guiding star in the profession. Williams became secretary of the Wisconsin Conference for Social Work and stayed on for almost ten years, until he left in a policy conflict in 1929. Shortly afterward he undertook liaison between the American Public Welfare Association and the various state governments: it was during this period that he converted the Governor of North Dakota.*

---

* Page 123.

Williams was then lent by the Association to the United States
government, which needed a man to administer $1,000,000 of the
Reconstruction Finance Corporation's relief fund in Mississippi.
That was his introduction to political infighting, and he did so well
at it that in May, 1933, during the Hundred Days, he had a wire
from Harry Hopkins, who had just been appointed Federal Relief
Administrator, summoning him to Detroit to report on migrant
workers; but Hopkins's first questions were on the advisability of
letting private agencies administer relief money. Williams told him
they would make a grab bag of such large amounts; the government
had to administer its own program. Hopkins said the same in a
speech the next night, and made some powerful enemies. He also
asked Williams to come onto the Federal payroll as relief administrator for the Southwest. Williams did so, and fired five of seven
governor-appointed state administrators almost immediately; Sen.
Joseph Robinson of Arkansas hastened to the White House to demand that Williams be pulled out of his state and the local men
rehired. As a result Williams was invited to dinner with the President, who called him Aubrey immediately, asked him about a quotation from Jefferson he had used in a speech, and never got around
to discussing Robinson or Arkansas. Williams went back into the
field and found that cotton pickers were striking for 75 cents a
hundredweight (a hundredweight was a day's work); he approved
them for relief, which strengthened their position and further outraged local authorities. Hopkins thought that was just fine, and
asked Williams to make a full report to other field representatives
and interested parties. While he was in Washington Hopkins called
him into a conference about what people should be allowed to buy
with relief dollars. The administration thought they ought to be
limited to groceries. Williams protested bitterly—what about medicine, clothes, rent? The session, a noisy one, lasted all day; when
it ended Hopkins said, "You come with me, Aubrey." The two went
to Baltimore, where Hopkins made a speech; on the round trip they
talked privately. (Williams said at one point, "You know, Harry,
when you called me out of there, the others thought I was going to
be fired." Hopkins smiled: "Did you?" Williams said, "Well, yes.")
Shortly afterward Williams was made Hopkins's deputy, and did

much of the administrative work in Federal relief programs until 1935.

In June of that year the National Youth Administration was established by executive order, and Aubrey Williams was made its director. It administered work-relief and employment programs for those between sixteen and twenty-five, and provided part-time employment for needy students to help them go on studying. By the end of 1936 some 600,000 people were in those programs; in 1939 and 1940 about 750,000 students in 1,700 colleges and universities and 28,000 secondary schools received help. All that was in the face of a concentrated campaign of Congressional and corporate calumny: that a young man of twenty should be abetted in his study of Macedonian folkways, early Roman fibulae, or (worst of all) the dance, was beyond the understanding of the red-blooded. In 1939 the NYA became part of the Federal Security Agency; in 1942, of the War Manpower Commission. In September, 1943, it was terminated, and Williams was out of a job.

His first communication with Marshall Field was in 1940. Mrs. Mary McLeod Bethune, the redoubtable president of Bethune-Cookman College (in Daytona Beach, Florida, for Negro women), was also director of Negro Student Work in the NYA. She had come out strongly for Roosevelt, and several of her Republican benefactors had withdrawn support from the college. She needed money, and she asked Williams to call Marshall Field. (This occurred before Field assumed control of *PM;* his personal reputation prompted the plea.) Williams protested, believing he was a total stranger to Field; * then he yielded. He called New York, was put through, and explained Mrs. Bethune's difficulties. Field was friendly: "I don't know what I can do at the moment," he said, "but I'd always be glad to see Mrs. Bethune." Williams arranged an appointment; Mrs. Bethune went to New York. Field told her he was "overextended at the moment"—which people never believed possible, but which was true. But when she finished her story he said, "I have eight thousand dollars for you. You take it, and come

---

* Of course he was not. The press, shouting that he was infamous, had made him famous.

to see me again in six months." She did; and Field made frequent contributions to the college from then on.

So when Field and Williams met later that year at dinner in the White House,* they fell into easy conversation immediately, and felt almost like old friends. They saw each other rarely for some time. In the spring of 1942 Williams wrote Field with a suggestion: there were country weeklies all over the United States, some 11,000 of them, most struggling along on local gossip and chewing-tobacco advertisements; would it be possible to reprint features from *PM* and the *Sun,* run them off as supplements, and make them available at a nominal price? Field liked the idea, and investigated. His staff was discouraging. It would mean a diversion of resources and an addition to a very tired payroll. There was a newsprint shortage. Profits would be doubtful. *Parade* was already in difficulties. Not that the proposed supplement would compete with *Parade,* which was bland and commercial; but it was not, even potentially, a big winner that the staff would cheerfully pitch in on. In sum, nothing happened.

In early 1945 Roosevelt nominated Williams to be head of the Rural Electrification Administration—after much hesitation on Williams's part. The latter still bore an assortment of journalistic tags and labels, ranging, as he put it, "all the way from radical to Communist." The Communist label never stuck—the Senate knew better—but Williams was a political liability just the same. He warned Roosevelt not to send his name up until he, Williams, had spoken to Senators Bankhead and Russell—why risk an unnecessary political defeat? Bankhead approved; Russell made it clear that he disagreed with Williams on many points but had confidence in him as an administrator. Williams informed the President, and was duly nominated. The floor fight in the Senate was brisk and bloody; the newspapers attacked him viciously. (Possibly the end-of-war swing to the right, which culminated in the Eightieth Congress of 1946, had already begun.) When it became obvious that anyone who supported Williams would risk low accusations, Bank-

---

* Page 195.

head and Russell withdrew their support. The Senate rejected Williams, 37-41.

Williams moved up to New York City to rest for a while and look around, and while he was there he dropped in on James Warburg. The latter had been working for the CIO-PAC in 1944; had been dismayed by the poor, and sometimes nonexistent, coverage of labor, politics, international affairs, and even farming news in America's country and small-town weeklies; and had decided to do something about it. He had talked to Field, and together they had established *Cross-Country Reports,* a weekly four-column syndicated sheet in which Ed Leahy reported on labor, David Loth wrote from Washington, Ben Stone of the Farmers' Union discussed agriculture, and Warburg wrote on foreign affairs. The sheet went out at a very low price to any local newspaper that wanted it. Too few did, but it kept coming out. Williams was impressed by it, and he came to Warburg with a direct proposal of his own. He wanted to buy out a Southern farm weekly called the *Southern Farmer,* modernize it, and make it pay. The South needed a liberal weekly, but Williams was talking business and not ideals: he was sure he could make it very profitable. He could get it for $100,000.

Warburg was interested. Williams was too good a man to languish rejected because the New Deal was aging, or because Washington had no place for him. The South needed men like him. Warburg suggested that Williams see Field, and Williams smiled: he was off to Chicago shortly to be the guest of honor at a testimonial luncheon over which Field was to preside.

Warburg called Field and talked to him about it. Late in the morning of the day of the luncheon Williams went to Field's offices at the *Sun,* and in a little under an hour Field approved the project and offered support.

While waiting to begin, Williams popped off to Mississippi to do some organizing for the Farmers' Union. He then returned to Montgomery and set about buying the *Southern Farmer:* est. 1839, circulation—so its owners said—415,000. It was, by big-city standards, a horrendous journal. Beneath its name was the explanation (A PLAIN FARM PAPER FOR PLAIN PEOPLE), which was conscientious understatement. Page One consisted of twenty or thirty separate paragraphs of spot news, quotes from sermons and lectures, and fifty-word editorials running the full gamut of populist and fundamentalist opinion: anti-war, anti-Europe, anti-New Deal, anti-taxes, anti-relief, anti-automobile, anti-big business; Senator Bankhead, respected as the flower of Southern chivalry, was nevertheless referred to as Senator Bunkhead when he proposed legislation for agricultural control. The innards of the newspaper offered helpful hints on clothing the family cheaply, optimistic reports on new Italian grasses, accounts of free-flowing champagne at bankers' banquets in New York, pertinent quotes from Daniel Webster and Calvin Coolidge, and advertisements that erupted from the page: ECZEMA PSORIASIS FISTULA CHICAGO'S NEWEST HOTEL TRUSSES WOMEN! DELAYED? PELLAGRA SPECIALIST QUIT WHISKEY MARRIED SECRETS NOW QUIT TOBACCO MANHOOD LOSS? TRY DR. HOLLOWAY'S VIGOR TREATMENT and, should Dr. Holloway fail, 100 lb. TOMBSTONE $17.50. There were also classified advertisements and cash-prize contests, in the announcement of one of which the most pathetic statement—such was the temper of the times and the region—read, "The money to pay every prize is on special deposit in the **big, strong Des Moines bank.**" The newspaper was a going concern (although a circulation check revealed that its subscribers actually numbered only 200,000 or so) but its destination was unspecified. It had reached its peak of inspiration along about 1928 and got stuck right there.

Warburg and Field together were behind Williams, Field putting up the major share. They made their support contingent on the acquisition of enough newsprint to make expansion immediately feasible. Williams applied for it, and was still *persona* sufficiently *grata* in Washington to get it. During the negotiations Field's financial advisers hesitated; their polite phrases were translatable as "This is a crazy idea." But when the newsprint came through, Field drew the check, and Aubrey Williams became editor and publisher of the *Southern Farmer.*

His first vigorous step was promotion through a radio contest, with an automobile as first prize. On the first contest alone he picked up 96,000 subscriptions, and within two years he had 800,000; by the end of 1948 the figure was up to 1,300,000.

These were, apparently, satisfied customers. With reason: Williams had renovated the paper drastically. He expanded it from twelve to sixteen, and then to twenty-four, pages; cut the squibs about Samuel J. Tilden and Jefferson Davis; used large, clear, well-spaced type; added photographs and a political cartoon; scattered gag cartoons and comic strips throughout; and substituted for the hundred cramped notes on Australian wool production, etc., half a dozen long and instructive articles on farm techniques and policies. Some of the old column-inch advertisements remained, and remained fascinating; but by far the greater number of advertisements were for mail-order clothes or sewing instruction, and were lavishly and tastefully illustrated.

But the deeper change—and a change that made the gigantic leap in circulation rather a surprise—was in the newspaper's editorial policy, which was, under Williams, opposed almost point for point to the previous policy. Williams was anti-Tory, anti-white supremacy, anti-Klan, anti-magnolia; he quoted old Tom Jefferson on Page One, lashed out at Congressional investigating techniques, named those he considered reactionary in Southern state governments. He flayed the Southerners who bolted the Democratic party in 1948; he preached brotherhood, equality of opportunity, extension of Social Security; he was a peacemonger and a trust buster. He brought to the South an extreme Northern-liberal position; and circulation went up and up and up. By 1948 he was an object of solicitous attention from legislative committees of the state of Alabama, and all the old cries were raised louder than ever. But he confused the opposition expertly, and won another large batch of subscribers, with an editorial—front page, top—in October entitled "Come on Back Home, Henry," in which he blasted the Progressive party, the Republican party, and the Democratic bolters all at once, slashing as savagely at the House Un-American Activities Committee as he did at communism, and asking Wallace to repudiate his supporters. "This country needs a progressive party," he wrote, "but no progressive party can ever be built around the Communist-dominated clique which sits at the center of the Wallace movement." It was a sharp surprise to those who had forgotten, or had never known, that opposition to people like Herman Talmadge, or to the disgraceful promotion-and-publicity carnivals of investigating committees, was not quite the same as Bolshevism. Most of

Williams's subscribers had never been exposed to any genuine liberalism—they had at best been offered a choice of authoritarian
cliques, some of which may have called themselves liberal in comparison with the others—and they responded to it. Most of them
were miserably poor (a subscription to the *Southern Farmer* cost
$1 for three years), and often the very poor found relief in political
extremism. But not these. Many of them were doubtless politically
indifferent, and bought the paper for its farm advice and advertisements; but a majority probably knew what they were reading,
and approved.

Williams then decided on a bold step. With circulation high, and
the hope of job printing to come, he planned a new plant with new
presses. The future looked good; Field and Warburg backed him.
The plant was built; "the oldest Hoe press in the United States"
was replaced.

But Williams was wrong. The job printing never materialized,
and he had ignored one danger, one softness that had killed publications before and would again: major advertisers did not like the
Southern Farmer's politics, and distrusted its effectiveness. It entered
the homes of the very poor, to whom luxury advertising might have
been an insult (though more likely it would have evoked pleasant
daydreams); it went to small farmers, a vanishing breed. Buying
power lay with the middle classes, more numerous and richer every
day; and mail-order houses, who sold to the poor but invested heavily in catalogues, hardly needed the *Southern Farmer*. Nor did the
automobile industry, or even the farm machinery manufacturers.
Some who might have advertised were deterred by the name and
reputation of Aubrey Williams; some were still fighting Roosevelt.
The *Southern Farmer* did well with low-cost consumer items, like
breakfast cereals and baking powder, but the full-page, two-color
advertisements simply did not come in. And the newspaper could
not hope to survive if it raised its subscription price.

By 1950 Williams was compelled to retrench: revenue did not
cover paper and printing costs, which meant that the subscription
list had to be reduced to a manageable number. He pruned it to a
million by letting lapsed subscriptions stay lapsed; then to 800,000.
By 1952 Field and Warburg were suggesting liquidation or sale—
so had the mighty fallen. But no one would buy the *Southern*

Farmer. Williams's chief competitor, the *Progressive Farmer* (which was not at all progressive), never sought subscribers making less than $5,000 a year, and had no use for Williams's poor-white and Negro audience. In 1952 the *Southern Farmer* became *Southern Farm and Home,* a quarterly almanac. It was a shame.

Williams had many other interests, and Field occasionally helped him with them. With $30,000 put up by Field, Williams organized five small-farmer cooperatives in Alabama and Tennessee; they lasted only a few years, were never prosperous, and went the way of the small farmer. In 1949 Williams backed a low-priced housing development for Negroes in Birmingham, people for whom developers and banks had little regard, and who consequently found it impossible to escape from their shacks even when they were making fair wages. All the first mortgages were cleared by the Veterans Administration, and the tenants were sound; but down payments were hard to come by, and Williams needed about $1,500 per house in second mortgages. He was $45,000 short of his goal when the money ran out. He went to visit Field at Chelsea, told him about the project, showed him the figures, and left with Field's commitment. In the end Williams built 450 houses, sold them all, and had only five defaulters. He operated on a tight margin, and his customers knew it. For most it was the best housing they had ever enjoyed. By 1952 Field had been paid back in full, possibly to his surprise, but Williams had accomplished more than that. He had converted several white Birmingham bankers, who were rather upset by the preposterous fact that the Negroes' record of payment was markedly better than that of whites on the same economic level, and by the equally preposterous fact that the Negroes' houses and grounds were in far better physical condition after a year or two than the equivalent white housing. The example of those developments, Williams's only venture into housing, raised the level of Negro housing in the whole Birmingham area. Williams noted that banks, once convinced that an investment was sound, lent money regardless of color or politics, but he was discouraged that "it took so much longer to convince them when Negroes were involved."

Field's support of Williams was special. It survived even a great *gaffe* by Williams in 1949, when he was having his first real troubles with the newspaper and had asked Field for extra operating money. *Time* magazine interviewed him at just that moment, and in defense of his life's work Williams said, "As for changing men's minds, making money is a lot easier thing to do." Field was not amused; but his dry annoyance passed quickly. To a Northern liberal, the South had a long way to go, and if it could be led by Southerners it had a better chance of getting there. "Aubrey Williams is important to the South," he said once to Carl Weitzel; and Williams was. He was important to the Georgia Education Commission in the early 1950s; it had to have some nearby target in its desperate onslaught on integration. He was constantly important to the Alabama Legislature, for roughly the same reason. There were not many around whose lives had been so openly spent in the pursuit of democracy for others. And Williams, for all his difficulties with the local authorities, for all the attacks in the press, for all his friendship with Martin Luther King, for all the midnight harassment by anonymous telephone callers, had made headway. When the *Southern Farmer* was so sick that he had to diversify his business by printing up interminable address lists for the large mail-order houses, the job took him out among the store managers, many of whom knew who he was. Some argued with him; one, a noted dog fancier, reproached him for tolerance, but when Williams said, "You like dogs; I like people," he accepted the distinction thoughtfully, and gave Williams an order. Another would never have finished college without the National Youth Administration, and recalled Williams's signature on all his official communications. The managers talked honestly and calmly with him; they did or did not understand him, but regardless of the publicity and the political orations they accepted him as an honest human being.

It was Williams the symbol who provided a target for Fourth of July bombast; Williams the man was respected by other men. An editorial in the Montgomery *Advertiser* of August 18, 1954, pointed out that he was "one of the few authentic radicals we have known who was not a solemn, humorless ass," and went on to commend him for his courage in wearing walking shorts with knee socks during the hot weather: "our impression is that he is the only dirt farmer (as well as publisher) in Alabama with both the legs and nerve to do it." But on September 4 there appeared another editorial in the same newspaper, a remarkable piece of writing for the cradle of the Confederacy, entitled "Notes on an Incendiary." It reviewed his career and transgressions ("Some years ago . . . the lean and gentle Williams . . . told a throng of Confederate descendants in the City Auditorium that he did not believe in segregation and had had colored guests in his home"), but ended rather ringingly:

> But while deploring Williams' agitations . . . *The Advertiser* considers it fair to say that Williams behaves as he does out of conviction. He holds his views at considerable economic and social sacrifice.
>
> Williams and his like-minded associates act unwisely in our view. Nevertheless, if Williams were defending himself before a bar for opposing segregation he would not be without a brief. He probably reasons: "The United States Supreme Court says I'm right. The Democratic Party says I'm right. The Republican Party says I'm right. Adlai Stevenson says I'm right. Dwight Eisenhower says I'm right. A great element of the Protestant and Catholic churches say I'm right. Can you say I'm alone?"

Well, he wasn't alone at all, and among those who liked him, respected him, and trusted him was Marshall Field. If Field gave Williams financial and moral support, he got a return on his investment: the knowledge that a liberal Southerner was back among his people, and less alone every day.

6

Field liked most of those people; he cared about their work and was genuinely, deeply happy to have helped make it possible. With some he spent hours of his life; with others, minutes. But those with whom he spent his days were newspapermen, business advisers, foundation officials, welfare workers; and those with whom he spent his evenings and vacations were old friends, like Robert Straus— and these were people of all political and social shades.

He was particularly fond of Stanley Field's daughter, Katherine Rodman ("Cousin K."), and of her husband Clifford. They were Field's oldest and dearest friends in Chicago. (The Rodmans' politics were certainly not Field's, but neither they nor he ever imposed test oaths upon affection.) Mrs. Rodman was like a sister to both Marshall and Ruth, and with sisterly ferocity she defended Field against the attacks and sometimes sneering jokes of upper-class Chicagoans who ridiculed his internationalism and liberalism. The Rodmans were "family," but more than that: they took him as he was, and asked only that he be happy. There were not many who worried about Marshall Field's personal happiness; and serious as he was about the problems of society, much of his deepest affection always went to the old friends who tried to give him happiness by sharing his more carefree moments.

In New York his cousin Ronald Tree was one of those; later on he took a cottage at Caumsett in summer. (Another friend, who also had a cottage there, was Edward M. M. Warburg.) Tree shared with Field aspects of life that almost no one else close to him had experienced—the English background; and their friendship, interrupted by the war, was renewed in their easygoing summertime life at Caumsett. Field swam, played tennis, rode. (He was in fine condition, and seemed able to work himself back into his best form very quickly, even after a long layoff. Until the last two or three years of his life he remained a good horseman, and in a hunt kept up with the younger generation.) In the evening a quiet drink; over the weekend a party, at which the guests were neighbors, "socialites," intellectuals, business acquaintances, old cronies like Charles Cushing. Of course those parties were very different from the parties of the 1920s; they were more sober, the conversation was sometimes quite serious: the texture of the guest list, as well as of Field's life, was far richer.

But like all men he had a frivolous side; it had once, long before, predominated, and a talent for enjoyment dies hard. He liked gaiety, witty talk, sports and games, pretty women—and in that too there was an echo of the patrician Whig, the connoisseur, an earlier century, a guinea on the chestnut, pass the port, and gad sir a well-turned ankle. (At bridge one evening, with Charles Cushing his partner, Field persisted in bidding a minor suit—requiring more tricks for game—over Cushing's obvious preference for a major. "Marshall," Cushing complained in mild despair, "would you take an ugly woman out to dinner rather than two pretty ones?")

Field never gave up the comforts and distractions of his position, but now he enjoyed them most in the company of old friends, and he never made or broke a friendship for any but truly personal reasons. The notion that his friends should be liberal because he was liberal, or conservative because he was rich, would have shocked him. He was an affectionate and loyal man, and he knew that snobbery worked both ways. He might have said with William Penn that there could be no friendship where there was no freedom; or with Thoreau that the most he could do for a friend was simply to be his friend. And to the end of his life most of his closest friends were also his oldest friends.

CHAPTER NINE

Your lordship, though not clean past your youth, hath yet some smack of age in you, some relish of the saltness of time.

—Henry IV (Part II), Act I

What greater ornament to a son than a father's glory, or to a father than a son's honorable conduct?

—SOPHOCLES,
Antigone

FIELD LOST ONE FRIEND IN THE 1940s: Franklin Delano Roosevelt died on April 12, 1945. Field was in his office when the report came over the wire; he sat unbelieving, momentarily depleted by the total gloom that marks an irrevocable personal and historical loss. Then he walked into Robert Lasch's office. "I still remember the desperate anguish on his face," Lasch wrote, "as he tried to fathom the consequences." That anguish was political as well as personal: Field did not see how the country could maintain its greatness under Truman. Lasch reminded him of a more specific problem: the *Sun* had opposed Truman as the Vice-presidential candidate in 1944, preferring either Henry Wallace or Justice William O. Douglas. "We may pay for that mistake," Lasch burst out. Field rebuked him: whatever the editorial attitudes, Truman was entitled to great respect for the burdens he would assume.

But Field had deeper reservations than he would admit at the time. Most of what he had come to believe in since 1936 was symbolized by the New Deal. And the New Deal *was* Roosevelt: not since Washington had one American leader so thoroughly sensed —and directed—the national mood and the national resources.

Now there was national sorrow, but there was also a sharp, prickling anxiety, a fear that great institutions and projects, on the scale of humanity and not of precinct, were to be left to men who did not measure up to them. Liberals had for years relied upon Roosevelt's magic. He had protected them from the press, from their own Congress, from the vituperation of patriotic and veterans' organizations, from the assaults of the pious, from their own doubts, from the lingering insults of ideological myth and bias. In the hour of bereavement they underestimated themselves; it took them five years to recover their self-esteem. Which was weakness—a weakness that Field shared to some extent, and that made a political mess of Harry Truman's first term.

Truman was tough enough to survive it, and in the end to teach his own party a thing or two, but he took his oath of office handicapped as no President had been since Andrew Johnson. He was neither untalented nor weak, and he was honest; but because he followed one of the superlatively great Presidents the public—who knew not much about him to begin with—assumed that he was a nothing, a cardboard executive, a party hack who would suffice until a real election could be held. After 1948 it was a commonplace that Truman had "grown into the office"; in 1945 few considered that possibility.

Liberals had still another problem: even if Truman proved capable in office, he was not a liberal in the Rooseveltian sense. Not a molder, not a crusader, not the Great Democrat prepared to trust himself and his people in great enterprises, evoking trust in his allies and even in his enemies. That lack disturbed Field, who was a Democrat because he was a liberal, and not vice versa. In the bleak aftermath of Roosevelt's death Field's instincts rejected Harry Truman, and later events never transformed that rejection to full acceptance. Having grown up politically in an era of unrestrained liberal enthusiasm, Field would not submit himself to anything less. But enthusiasm has its dangers; insistence upon the best is often a disservice to the good. Thought, tolerance, and accuracy of observation characterized and informed most of Field's judgments, but in 1946 his distrust of President Truman culminated in enthusiasm for a proposal that was thoughtless, intolerant, unrealistic, and panicky. It was Field's one political foolishness, and it was a beauty;

it was his greatest political error, mitigated only by its genuinely, and almost desperately, liberal motivation.

When the Republicans took both Houses of Congress in the elections of 1946 Marshall Field proposed, in a signed front-page editorial, that President Truman resign:

AN OPEN LETTER TO THE PRESIDENT OF THE UNITED STATES

Dear Mr. President:

In our respectful opinion the hour has come for you to create a notable precedent in American history.

This opportunity comes to you as the result of the unmistakable verdict of the voters in Tuesday's elections. These voters have registered their belief that domestic progress and international tranquillity can be better won by the Republican party.

That we do not share this belief is beside the point—the people have spoken.

It goes without saying that the voters in this election have raised no doubt as to your honesty of purpose nor purity of motive. Their decision does not deny the fact that you have accomplished great objectives in the establishment of the United Nations Organization, the World Bank and the feeding of hungry populations.

But the fact remains that Tuesday's election gives your opponents control of national legislation and appropriations for the next two years. With hostile forces dominating the Congress and with you in control of the Executive Office, our foreign policy will be vacillating and our part in the pacification of the world come to stalemate. The acts of our foreign representatives will be questioned by the other nations of the world from now until the elections of 1948.

We believe that if at this time full responsibility be thrown upon the Republican party to develop and administer a national policy, the voters will have the issues cut clearly and intelligently for them in 1948. By then it is our fervent hope that a liberal Democratic party will have formulated progressive policies that will give the voters a clear choice.

Therefore, Mr. President, we urge you to ask the Republican members of the new House and Senate to suggest to you a man whom you will name Secretary of State, in whose favor you can resign your high office.

We can anticipate the pressure against this patriotic and courageous step that would be put upon you by dismayed Democratic officeholders and frightened Republicans, but your act would be in agreement with both the Constitution and the welfare of the nation.

MARSHALL FIELD,
Publisher and Editor,
The Chicago Sun.

The idea was not Field's alone; no less a Democrat than Sen. William Fulbright of Arkansas had offered the suggestion. At first glance Field's editorial is somewhat panicky, thoroughly naïve, and rudely lacking in confidence in the resiliency of either the Democratic party or its leader. There was slightly more to it than that—but not much. Even if it reflected the temporary demoralization of Democrats, even if there was some small point to the cry for liberal unity, the editorial marked the low point of the *Sun*'s political judgment, and was a grossly ill-considered repudiation of an elected official who needed all the help he could get. After 1948 hindsight made it easy to criticize the *Sun*'s brainstorm, but even on the day it appeared many ranking Democrats were furious, and many ordinary voters were thoroughly confused. (Colonel McCormick, on the other hand, was positively congested with pleasure.) The editorial was not a contribution to political clarity; nor was it the fruit of mature thought. It appeared on Thursday, November 7. Tuesday, the 5th, had been Election Day, but the returns—a Republican sweep—were not finally tabulated until Wednesday morning, and the editorial was written Wednesday afternoon and evening. Twelve hours' thought, interrupted by the labor of composition, scarcely justified the proposed radical transformation of a century and a half of political procedure.*

No one could have replaced Roosevelt. Field and the *Sun* knew that, but had hoped against hope that a miraculous transformation, an abrupt metamorphosis of Harry Truman, would inspire America to still greater heights of liberal achievement. When their wistfully simple hopes were denied, they fell back, apparently, on the old political maxim that things have to get worse before they can get better; if they could ease Truman out, and let the Republicans make mistakes, a new Democratic party would sweep clean next time.

---

* Robert Lasch, Field's chief editorial writer, was dead against the whole idea, and tried to dissuade his boss. Field's prose, which tended to be imprecise and loose, was not at its best in this letter: a further weakness.

They were wrong on all counts. Truman was not Roosevelt, and asked only to be judged as Truman. All kinds of flamboyant idealism were dormant in 1946, exhausted, resting. Even if Roosevelt had lived, the Congress might have passed to the Republicans— and would the *Sun* then have called for Roosevelt's resignation? Not likely. And there was no longer—would not be, for some time —a clear ideological difference between the two parties, even among the rank and file: the elections had revealed not Truman's failure, but the electorate's retreat from war, curiosity about the outs, and weariness with the ins. Field's suggestion that "frightened Republicans" would resist Truman's resignation was *naïveté* on the grand scale: far from fearing responsibility, they had thirsted and panted after it lo these fifteen years.

Many of Field's advisers had opposed the editorial, but Field was fortified by an experience the others lacked: his sojourn in England. What he proposed was not far from the Parliamentary system, and his enthusiasm for the forms, practitioners, and results of the governmental art in Britain surely helped to determine his attitude. He hoped for greater Cabinet responsibility, greater harmony between the legislative and executive branches, and a more direct executive responsibility to the people. All of which might have come to pass, if Truman had yielded to the whimsical proposal—but what an irony! The unique institutions of the world's oldest republic transformed in a burst of despair because a hero had died! Now, if ever, was the time for all good men to come to the aid of their party, and it is a fair conclusion that Field, with the best of intentions and the worst of judgment, preferred to lower the colors and fight another day.

True, Field was a liberal before he was a Democrat, and was not bound indissolubly to the Democratic party in all its forms. He was trapped by an excess of faith in the liberal movement divorced from practical politics: for twelve years Roosevelt had managed the politics and left the liberals free to effervesce. In 1946 the latter took a thorough drubbing—and with a most illiberal refusal to find out why they were licked, they made Truman their scapegoat, and asked him to pay for Roosevelt's greatness, for war-weariness, for the two-party system. Field's editorial was a reflex of alarm, and not a studied document. It was revolutionary, and hardly a response to the "consensus" he respected so highly. It was a "bright idea," and it was irresponsible. "Enthusiasm," wrote an eighteenth-century bishop of Gloucester, "is that temper of the mind in which the imagination has got the better of the judgment."

President Truman, reluctant to break a lease unnecessarily, ignored Field's advice and settled in for a brisk two years of politics. He fought a slow-motion battle with inertia, as embodied in the Eightieth Congress. The Republicans were unaccustomed to power, riven by faction, and handicapped by their legacy: the last Republican Congress, elected in 1928, had dedicated itself and its posterity to the proposition that the least legislation was the best legislation. The Eightieth did, however, pass the enabling legislation for both the Truman Doctrine and the Marshall Plan. The Truman Doctrine —unilateral military and economic aid to Greece and Turkey— came first. Congress did its work, the press voiced praise, and President Truman relaxed a bit. But the *Sun* struck again—this time responsibly and courageously.

The time was March, 1947, and the issues were two. Secretary of Labor Lewis B. Schwellenbach had proposed to outlaw the Communist party (he was encouraged by the establishment of a Federal loyalty program on March 21); and President Truman had proposed Greek-Turkish aid. Field objected to both proposals, and sensed a similarity of principle in his objections. He investigated. When Secretary of State Dean Acheson invited a group of publishers to Washington for a dinner and a briefing on the Truman Doctrine, Field was unable to attend; he asked if Lasch might represent him, and Acheson acquiesced. Field's tentative objection to the program was that it ignored the United Nations and our multilateral alliances: it was too obviously a swap of goods and guns for what might turn out to be the precarious friendship of reactionary governments, and it lacked the solidity of a program based on international community of interest. Nothing that Lasch heard in Washington induced Field to modify his position. Acheson left an impression of almost total disdain for international agencies, implying that UNRRA, purely a relief organization, was the limit of acceptability; reminded that the Food and Agriculture Organization had sent a mission to Greece, he replied that this was the sort of international mission he liked—all Americans but two. He seemed to feel that the public had deluded itself into a belief that the UN could solve any problem, and Lasch's conclusion was that Acheson wanted to base policy on what was "right" for the United States without regard for the wishes, or ultimate support, of other countries; at best, an imbalance of power in America's favor, and the Devil take the hindmost.* Both Lasch and Field were disturbed by Acheson's apparent scorn for international agencies, which scorn would inevitably exacerbate and not mitigate the incipient cold war.

The proposed combination of suppression at home and bribery abroad impelled Field to write out the best of his own editorials— which Lasch revised and lengthened, using Field's paragraphs, inspired mainly by Schwellenbach's surrender to fear, as an introduction to further discussion of the Truman Doctrine:

You Can't Outlaw Ideas

Secretary of Labor Schwellenbach wants to "outlaw" the Communist party. His outburst on the subject last week was a timely illustration of the confusion with which many of us approach communism as well as foreign policy.

Secretary Schwellenbach evidently hopes to suppress the idea of communism in this country by denying it legal political expression. But neither history nor common sense supports the notion that any idea, however unpalatable to the vast majority of us (as communism is), can be obliterated by force or legislation.

Christianity was not killed by the might of ancient Rome. The ideas of Locke, Hume and Montesquieu were not killed by the British tories who tried to "outlaw" the American revolution. The ideas of Plato and Aristotle which underlay the Renaissance were not smothered by the weight of the Dark Ages.

The only way to kill an idea is with a better idea.

* * *

President Truman's foreign policy is said to rest on the principle of "containment" of Russia. That can mean two things.

---

* It was ironic that Secretary Acheson should later have been a target of the lunatic right. He was a conservative Secretary of State with more faith in Adenauer's Germany than in England; and Secretary John Foster Dulles's policies, later so often criticized by Democrats, derived closely from Acheson's.

It can mean interposing barriers to an imperialistic expansion of Russian nationalism. In that sense the policy is entirely legitimate and thoroughly justified. It is to the interest of a stable peace, and therefore to our own national interest, that we join other nations in halting aggression against freedom wherever it occurs. The United Nations is built on that principle.

But containment can also mean an effort to stop *the idea* of communism, and eventually smother it, by the use of our financial and economic resources and our armed might. In that sense the policy, apart from being morally wrong, will represent in the end a tragic waste of effort, money, and possibly lives.

The best instrument, and so far as we know the only instrument, for stopping the communist idea is the counter-idea of a dynamic, functioning, American democracy that brings its people and all who freely adopt it a progressively higher standard of living.

*   *   *

The peril of President Truman's policy on Greece and Turkey lies not in what he says about it but in his failure so far to distinguish between containing Russia and containing communism.

When he says we must "help free peoples to maintain their free institutions and their national integrity against aggressive movements that seek to impose upon them totalitarian regimes," he is on unassailable ground. But Mr. Truman himself is not following that principle in Greece and Turkey unless he makes our aid—which should be economic and not military—conditional upon the emergence of governments genuinely representing the free wishes of the Greek and Turkish peoples.

Greece is ruled by a rightist monarchy which has ruthlessly suppressed civil liberties and attracted to it the dregs of fascist reaction. Turkey is governed by a quasi-fascist regime which could not be induced to support our side in the war until our victory was certain.

Backing such governments is not the same thing as backing the people of Greece and Turkey. No nation can go through what Greece has endured without developing a strong popular movement for basic social and economic reforms. The Greek monarchists are attempting to suppress the ideas behind that popular movement—not only communist ideas but progressive and democratic ones as well—by force. When we back the monarchists, we back this assault on the people's ideas.

If we enable reactionary regimes to war against their people in the guise of erecting a barrier against Russia, how can it be said that we are thereby "helping free peoples to maintain their own institutions"?

If we attempt to combat communism by imposing our own military domination in the Mediterranean, how can we object to Soviet military domination elsewhere?

If we impose our own national will in the Middle East, how can we insist on a United Nations collective will anywhere else?

The only way to beat an idea is with a better idea. We cannot beat the idea of communism with the idea of military imperialism. We can beat it with the idea of free democracy.

That was the sort of statement Field could originate at his best. He believed firmly that *it was never the presence, and always the absence, of liberals that bred despotism,* and nothing in modern history has disproved that belief.

It took more than ordinary courage to publish the editorial. The *Sun* was almost alone in its stand, and was attacked violently for its "Red sympathies." Circulation was not rising; Field had cut his staff drastically only a few months before; losses continued. But among the *Sun's* editorial personnel there was great pride, perhaps more than ever before. The newspaper had taken on Democrats, Republicans, and public opinion in an honest if futile attempt to prevent a further breach, in an atomic world, between East and West. When the Marshall Plan was proposed three months later, the *Sun* supported it. The Russians, who doubtless had reasons of their own for sheering off, made the not unreasonable assumption that it would be a major extension of the Truman Doctrine, in the guise of reconstruction, and declined to participate. The Cold War had begun.

2

Marshall Field took part in negotiations over two newspapers in the 1940s: peripherally, the Chicago *Daily News;* directly, the Chicago *Times.*

Frank Knox died in the spring of 1944. He and Field had not been close friends, and their political philosophies were far apart, but they shared certain views on public policy and certain professional intimacies: Knox had been Secretary of the Navy in an administration Field supported, their ideas on the war and on the position of the United States were close, and the *Sun* was still being run off on the presses of Knox's *Daily News.* Adlai Stevenson, a

Chicago lawyer and friend of both men, had been the organizer and leader, in the Chicago area, of the Committee to Defend America by Aiding the Allies, and had enjoyed the ardent support of both Knox and Field in the prewar conflict with powerful isolationist groups headed by the Chicago *Tribune*. As war approached, Stevenson had joined Knox in the Navy Department, serving as his assistant and counsel until the Secretary's death. Their relationship was close, and Stevenson was privy to Knox's hopes and desires for the future of the *Daily News*. And he knew well many of the newspaper's executives, in particular Lloyd Lewis and Paul Scott Mowrer, its editors. It was natural that after Knox's funeral the newspaper's department heads should ask Stevenson to form a syndicate to buy a controlling interest from Knox's estate.

Stevenson resigned from the Navy and spent that summer in Chicago reviewing the *News*'s financial structure and organizing a group of investors to supplement the meager resources of the employees. Among his first meetings were several with Marshall Field, whose printing contract was highly profitable to the *News* (and almost a matter of life and death to the *Sun*). The two agreed that Field should not buy the newspaper or even participate in the syndicate if the employees could swing it without him. Neither man wanted to arouse advertisers' worries about monopoly, or to provoke Colonel McCormick to a frenzy of competitive machinations, vituperation, and reprisal. But Field, among others, remained a potential (and congenial) source of financial backing for Stevenson and the syndicate.

Stevenson concluded, and his investors agreed, that Knox's stock was worth $12 a share. Knox's executors approved Stevenson's plans for financing and management, but wanted more money. Field offered to help, suggesting conditions that would exclude him from participation or influence in the paper's policies and direction. But on Stevenson's recommendation his group raised its bid to $13 a share without help from Field. That was Stevenson's limit: he was fulfilling Knox's desire for local ownership and continuity of management, but having decided that $12 a share was a fair price he could not in all conscience recommend bidding more than $13. The executors asked him, however, to match still higher bids; after explaining his position to Field, who remained willing to rescue the project, Stevenson withdrew from the bidding. He recommended that the executors accept an offer of $15 a share from John S. Knight of the Detroit *Free Press,* and they did so.

Field was disappointed. (He was also apprehensive about his expensive contract to print on the *News's* presses.) He had liked the idea of a friendly newspaper of high quality, staff-controlled and locally owned. It would have resolved a dilemma for him. To have bought another newspaper outright—which is what he finally did— would then have exposed him, in the wary and skeptical Chicago business community, to charges of monopolistic expansion, driving for power, and so forth. And mindful of the hazards of a second newspaper, Field was not eager to add major new obligations to the losses he was already sustaining. The *News* in the hands of its staff would have been a perfect solution.

Samuel Emory Thomason had died in 1944. His staff, including many who had accepted shares in lieu of cash wages during the Depression, kept publishing, but sale was inevitable: Thomason had owed money, and a newspaper needed direction. Field's purchase of the *Times,* in 1947, was so uneventful as to be almost unbusinesslike; no intrigue swelled the transaction, and no competitive pumping swelled the price. Field's reasons for buying were three: he wanted that second newspaper; John Knight had continued the traditional practice of the *Daily News,* and was overcharging Field for the office space and presses; and Field still needed some good business management, which he hoped the executives of the *Times* would supply. (He also needed circulation, and the readers of the *Times* were a loyal crew.) Among the personnel he acquired were Richard Finnegan, editor of the *Times,* and Russ Stewart, its managing editor. For a few months—September 30, 1947, to January 31, 1948—the new presses turned out two newspapers, a tabloid *Sun* in the morning and a tabloid *Times* in the evening; they were combined on Sunday, becoming the Chicago *Sun and Times.* That was uneconomical. Two newspapers proved, after all, to be a wistful fiction; and shortly the merger became complete, with the appearance, in March, 1948, of a morning tabloid called the Chicago *Sun-Times,* Finnegan its editor, Stewart its managing editor.

But on some levels of the old organization there was disappointment, even bitterness. The *Times* had always been stuffier than the *Sun,* and when its editors assumed control of the *Sun-Times,* the *Sun's* truculent liberalism was moderated. The very shift to a tabloid offended some of the *Sun's* veterans, and they were not alone. In October, 1947, one reader wrote to Field in blistering denunciation of his betrayal—killing the *Sun* to make way for a "small-bore tabloid"—and the best he could do for an answer was:

November 3, 1947

Dear Mrs.———:

I sincerely hope you feel better since getting your letter of the 30th ult. off your chest.

Yours truly,

MARSHALL FIELD

The psychological undercurrents were dramatic, if not melodramatic. The newcomers were good newspapermen and good businessmen, and Field welcomed their talents: Finnegan was as different from Evans, for example, as Bernard Baruch was from Bet-a-Million Gates. But they had not worked under Field, and did not share either his vision or his willingness to use a newspaper as an uncompromising instrument of liberal policy. They had fought McCormick independently, but had not worried the *Sun* through its early years; not suffered when it was attacked or rejoiced when it counterattacked; not experienced the pride of the forlorn hope; not gone up against the Colonel with a new, full-sized, eight-column, two-section, roomy and dignified journal, where a full spread of department-store advertising need not monopolize eight consecutive pages and crowd the news out. To the *Sun's* old-timers, reduction to tabloid size smacked vaguely of advertisements for chewing tobacco and false teeth, and they were repelled by headlines that seemed to occupy a quarter of the reading page. There was no question, either, about a swing toward the political center. In short, the old *Sun* was gone, in form and content, and its Praetorian Guard was restless.

But the old *Sun* had not made money, which rankled; and one side of Marshall Field insisted on a prosperous newspaper. He had backed a liberal experiment in New York, which was not yet over, with about $5,000,000; and his losses on the *Sun* and *Sun-Times,*

before they reached the black, would amount to something near
$25,000,000.* It was not a state of affairs he could tolerate forever.
Again, an irony: in the years of his most vigorous journalistic
liberalism, 1947 and 1948, he took the one step incompatible with
his original ideal, "a newspaper as good as the St. Louis *Post-
Dispatch*." A tabloid could be liberal and brassy, like the New York
Post; it could be conservative and brassy, like the New York *Daily
News*; or it could, with effort, be conservative and staid, which the
Sun-Times became; but it could not be liberal and dignified, because
liberal and dignified tabloids were invariably, and perhaps inevitably, sincere, earnest, jejune, and unsuccessful.

At any rate, the *Sun* was dead.

3

In 1948 the *Sun-Times* supported Harry Truman, but not before
making energetic overtures to Dwight D. Eisenhower in the hope
that he would turn out to be a Democrat. No one knew then just
where the General stood politically,† but his popularity was undeni-
able, and both parties hung around the front porch with candy and
flowers. (If the Republicans had nominated him, the *Sun-Times*
would have opposed him and stood by Truman.) Finnegan and
Field called on him when he passed through Chicago; Eisenhower
was flattered but rejected their suit. Field was, finally, in a position
to swap political anecdotes, and to appreciate Eisenhower's reluctance: Field himself had not long before turned down a suggestion
that he run for the governorship of Illinois. The matter had come
up in October, 1947, with a letter from Samuel P. Gurman, a Chicago attorney:

> In a recent conversation with several people, I found that every one
> seemed to be stumped as to who would be candidate for governor on the
> Democratic ticket, having in mind also that that would be a stepping stone
> to the Presidency. It has been suggested, and it was also my thought that you

---

* A. J. Liebling, who did the best writing in the world about journalism and
boxing, and some of the best about politics and food, put the figure at $100,000,-
000, which is inadequate if hyperbole and inaccurate if reporting. Perhaps he was
thinking of the gross outlay; but there *was* revenue.

† His own statements, public and private, implied that he had never given the
matter much thought.

would make an excellent candidate. You would lift the campaign out of "gutter politics". People would expect the issues to be on the higher plane on which you are known to hold views beneficial to the common man.

Of course, I don't know whether you have any political aspirations or ambitions, whether you're a liberal Republican or a New Deal Democrat, but I think it may not be a bad idea at all for somebody to start the ball rolling, of course, with your consent.

The proposal was startling, and so was the reluctance to classify Field, who, like Eisenhower, occasionally bemused the political taxonomists. Field was obviously enough a New Deal Democrat— but then he was also a very rich man. His progress through *Who's Who* was slower than his personal evolution, and may have confused admirers: until the edition of 1942–3 he had declared himself "Republican" and "Catholic," and only then emended the entry to the single word "Democrat." (He received a postcard in 1946, addressed to him in care of the information bureau of the Chicago *Sun,* asking about his religion. He answered: ". . . I was baptized in the Catholic faith, but, owing to personal circumstances, I am not an active communicant at this time, although I have the greatest admiration for the Church," which was barely an answer at all, though there was something in it to please everybody. He had told a friend in the early 1940s, "If I felt the need of organized religion again, I'd become a Quaker," and as early as the mid-1930s he had expressed, at a dinner party, extreme skepticism about one of the periodic "returns to spirituality" through which newspapers insisted the country was passing. By 1946 he was drifting toward, if not ensconced in, a tolerant agnosticism.)

At any rate, he answered Gurman:

I am very much honored by your kind letter suggesting I might be a candidate for governor.

However, I have no political aspirations of any sort, and am firmly of the belief that publishing newspapers and running for political office do not go together. In fact, I know of no better way of losing the objectiveness of a newspaper than having its publisher run for office.

I am sure when you think it over you will agree with my decision that I could not consider running for any public office.

Gurman persevered, in a letter that began "Dear Governor":

. . . Unintentionally, I seem to have become a one-man Gallup Poll. I have talked to a good many people, including some educators and teachers, about the possibilities of your candidacy, and I have also mentioned it to a judge who is very near the throne of the kingmakers. In each case, there was great enthusiasm and affirmation of the idea. I went further and talked to my ward committeeman about it, and I can hardly describe or overstate his enthusiasm. He would like to meet you, if you care to make an appointment, and he promises to get a great many more committeemen and to make a motion in the inner party circles that you be named as candidate. So now, you cannot blame me for feeling that there is a general draft moving in your direction.

But Field entertained no illusions, closing the correspondence on October 29:

I regret I must stick perfectly firmly to my policy as laid down in my last letter. While I appreciate your interest, I am afraid any further talk of this would cause me nothing but embarrassment.

That was the end of the Field draft. Field had his own ideas about the governorship of Illinois, and they centered on his friend Adlai Stevenson. The *Sun-Times* had a fine slate to support in 1948: Stevenson for Governor, Paul Douglas for United States Senator— and Harry Truman for President, which everyone thought mildly ridiculous. The *Sun-Times* supported Truman without reservations, and also without wild enthusiasm. But its vigorous support of Stevenson and Douglas served Truman well, and although few at the *Sun-Times* really thought Truman had a chance, it was one of the half-dozen newspapers in the whole country which backed him.

The election was a slam-bang affair, and subjected the American press to extraordinary stresses, strains, tizzies, and old-fashioned fits of the vapors. For Thomas Dewey, the Republican candidate, it was a personal tragedy exaggerated almost beyond bearing by the boozy confidence of the press, 95 per cent of which supported him overconfidently, while the other 5 per cent inclined to silent despair. For Harry Truman it was an hour of pure glory and pure exhilaration: he had beaten not only Dewey and the press, but also the Dixiecrat Strom Thurmond and the Progressive Henry Wallace, both of whom drew votes from him and not from Dewey. Thurmond and Wallace drew about the same vote, in the neighborhood of 1,160,000; if all those had gone to Truman his margin would have been 26,000,000-plus to slightly under 22,000,000—not much different from Roosevelt's victory over Willkie.

To Marshall Field the results were eminently satisfactory. Stevenson and Douglas won overwhelmingly in spite of numerous pre-election polls by the Chicago *Tribune* proving they had no chance; the free, "objective" press made an ass of itself; and Colonel McCormick suffered the famous embarrassment of rushing the *Tribune*'s early edition to the streets with headlines proclaiming a Dewey victory. The *Sun-Times* had backed winners before, but this was a clean sweep.

In New York *PM* did not back the winner, because *PM* was no longer in existence. When Ralph Ingersoll returned from the war in 1946, he hoped to persuade Field that *PM* ought to become even more special—that it could be saved by the recruitment of talent, real literary talent, on the level of *The New Yorker*'s, well paid and given a free hand. But John P. Lewis, who had edited the paper in Ingersoll's absence, insisted that it become less special—that with the admission of advertising, *PM* would succeed. Field, deeply committed in Chicago and ever more conscious of profit and loss, sided with Lewis, and after a few months Ingersoll left *PM*. He also left Field's orbit, and the two, though they remained friends, saw each other only rarely from then on.

Whether or not Ingersoll was right, Lewis was wrong. Advertisers never solved *PM*'s problems, chiefly because they refused to advertise in *PM*. Revenue went up, but only slightly; and meanwhile costs were rising fast, without a gain in circulation. By early 1948 it was obvious that *PM* was on its last legs.

But Field was not the only one who thought that New York would profit by a good liberal newspaper (or vice versa), and when a very unusual and capable man came to him with a proposal for *PM* he listened carefully. The man was a well-known lawyer named Bartley C. Crum, and his credentials were ideally varied. Originally from San Francisco, he had been a junior partner of John Francis Neylan, Hearst's personal attorney and right-hand man. Close observation of San Francisco's general strike in the summer of 1934 (the greatest general strike in this country's history) had inclined him to a liberal view; he had later served on Roosevelt's first Fair Employment Practices Commission, and had been a good Democrat until 1940, when he became Wendell Willkie's West Coast campaign manager. In 1946, when Prime Minister Attlee and Foreign Minister Bevin despaired of an equitable solution to the problem of Palestine, they established an Anglo-American commission to report on it; Crum was a member, and it was on the commission's report—flatly recommending partition—that the United Nations based its resolutions of 1947, which led to the State of Israel. In sum, Crum was a prominent liberal with a record of achievement. He was also a practicing Roman Catholic, which, if he became the publisher of a liberal newspaper, might exempt him from some of the indignities that had been heaped upon Ingersoll and *PM*. He was energetic, positive, thoroughly likable—altogether just the kind of black Irishman who might drive a liberal newspaper to the heights.

He proposed that he take over *PM*, change its name, bring in his own personnel, canvass for advertising, and make every effort to show a profit. Field was sympathetic. He asked Leon Shimkin to run a financial survey of the project. Shimkin did so, approved, and reported his qualified optimism. Changing the name and management would soften the resistance to *PM* that was now chronic among advertisers; would permit changes in format and policy without an appearance of desperate compromise; and would dramatize the newspaper's struggle for existence.

Field accepted Crum's proposition, and in June of 1948 Crum became the publisher of the New York *Star* (he ran it as *PM* for a few transitional weeks). His editor was Joseph Barnes, who had been a correspondent for the New York *Herald Tribune,* and then its foreign editor; he had also been an official in the Office of War Information. It was Barnes and Gardner Cowles, Jr., who had been invited by Wendell Willkie to go around the world with him in 1942, on the trip that produced *One World,* Willkie's phenomenally successful essay in internationalism. Barnes and Willkie, like Crum and Willkie, had remained close friends until the latter's death in 1944.*

---

* In 1952 Barnes wrote the definitive political biography of Willkie.

In late summer the business management of the *Star* was entrusted to Shimkin, who set about building a circulation based on habit and not on momentary idealism. He used standard devices like multivolume premium encyclopedias, and by fall he had proved that circulation could indeed be built—but at a slow and dangerously expensive rate. (It went up by 35,000 in six months, but the rate of increase kept dropping.) And he was not at all sure that even with a larger circulation advertisers would support the newspaper. The big advertisers saw no need for another outlet; many still resented *PM* and shifted that resentment to the *Star*. As autumn wore on, Shimkin lost his optimism: he concluded that it would take ten years, and ten million dollars, to make the *Star* twinkle; and even then the answer would be maybe. He recommended cutting losses.

"I think the *Star* was making progress toward a successful changeover," A. J. Liebling wrote later, "though the process resembled changing clothes under water." Barnes agreed: "What Liebling didn't know," he commented, "was that it *felt* like changing clothes under water." The *Star* made contributions to society, chief among them a drop in the price of milk in the New York area and a rise in the fortunes of its art editor and cartoonist, Walt Kelly, whose "Pogo" made his first newspaper appearance in that newspaper ("One-man log-rolling," Kelly said years later, "is infinitely more efficient") and went on to international success. During the election campaign of 1948 Kelly's caricatures of Dewey as a soulless adding-machine candidate attracted national attention. The *Star* supported Harry Truman unequivocally—to the dismay, and even fury, of many of its readers. The late Richard Lauterbach once estimated that 90 per cent of the readers inherited from *PM* voted for Henry Wallace in 1948; and the mail that poured in would have supported an even higher estimate. Wallace's candidacy was certainly the *Star*'s greatest immediate problem: New York's left wing deserted the newspaper wholesale. The *Star* might have made up for their defection by a noisy, all-out prediction of Truman's victory; but its staff was not that confident. Liebling told the sad story:

> I shall always be saddened by the thought that I saw Mr. Crum miss a signal that, had he heeded it, might have sent the *Star*'s circulation up to a quarter of a million almost overnight. I am not in a position to blame him,

because I missed it, too. I was in the Biltmore bar with a couple of *Star* men on the evening of the Thursday before election, when President Truman was making his last campaign tour of the city. The President, of course, was staying at the Biltmore, which houses Democratic National Headquarters. Crum came down from the Presidential suite and said, "The old boy is crazy. He thinks he's going to win. He's standing there under the shower telling everybody that he'll sweep the country." I laughed with the others. If, guided by some mystic light, Crum had believed and ordered the *Star* to headline the flat, unique prediction that the President would win, he would have sold more, rather than fewer, papers during the days remaining before election. And after Election Day the *Star* would have been famous from coast to coast. Crum was rooting for Truman. But he didn't believe the feedbox tip. It's a wonderful example of how you get to believe what you read in the opposition newspapers.

The *Star* was doomed. Good newspapermen and respectable liberals, starting fresh, had failed. Last-minute attempts at salvage were futile. David Dubinsky and Jacob Potofsky were approached, and asked if they would help to transform the *Star* into an out-and-out labor newspaper; they declined. The unions refused to moderate their demands; the *Star*'s 408 employees were expendable. Its last three editions appeared on January 27, 1949, and Marshall Field was out of journalism in New York.

Field had backed the *Star* by taking a chattel mortgage on the building and presses, in return for which he advanced operating money. (Crum and Barnes and a few others added their own capital, and lost it all.) When the newspaper folded, the mortgaged properties were placed in the hands of brokers. The presses were shortly sold to a newspaper in Pennsylvania; the building remained unsold for many months, and long after the *Star* had burned out it was sold to Ted Thackrey, who wanted to publish his own tabloid, the New York *Compass*. In the telescoping processes of folklore, the *Compass* came to be thought of as the successor to the *Star*. It was not; there was never the slightest connection.

So ended Marshall Field's liberal experiment in New York. Liebling's epitaph of *PM* and the *Star* was stylish and educational:

One of the good things about *PM* was that it was different from any other New York paper, and the differences were irreconcilable. You couldn't imagine it, or the *Star*, merging with any other paper. Also, it was pure in heart. It sometimes seemed to me to make virtue unnecessarily repulsive by publishing pictures of buck-toothed ballad singers and knobby-kneed rhythmic dancers and interior shots of neglected mental wards in distant states, and it occasionally occurred to me that the space thus employed could have been used for news stories. The injustices it whacked away at were genuine enough, but an awful lot of whacks seemed to fall on the same injustices. A girl to whom I gave a subscription to *PM* in 1946 asked me after a time, "Doesn't *anybody* have any trouble except the Jews and the colored people?" When you read it steadily for a while, you got the impression that you were reading the publication of some such large order as the Lonely Hearts or the American Treehound Association, whose members shared a lot of interests that you didn't.. . . .

. . . By 1945 . . . it always seemed the same. Also, it had gathered about a hundred thousand readers, who loved it exactly as it was. One hundred thousand was an awkward number, because it was half of what *PM* needed to pay its way. It was too many to throw away but not enough to make the paper go. *PM* couldn't get the second hundred thousand unless it changed; it couldn't change without losing a substantial number of the first hundred thousand.

It was the paradox that plagued all liberal publications: they were read by people who didn't need them, and there just weren't enough such people.

4

Field's reputation and political credit fluctuated through these years, but his personality hardly changed. He remained generous and considerate; he continued to make the major decisions and to leave the working decisions to those who did the work; he was still punctual about appointments and punctilious about bread-and-butter notes. He worked five days most weeks, often five and a half; he took long vacations. He smoked cigarettes heavily, drank moderately, ate well. He hunted quail at Chelsea and tended his farm at Caumsett. The Coast Guard returned *Corisande II* when the war ended; it was in rotten shape, and Field was ready to abandon it, but the family, particularly Ruth and Phyllis, liked the old boat, and they overhauled it instead. It was not as much used as formerly; Field had almost become a Chicagoan.

He still spent much of the summer at Caumsett. In 1948 his sister

Gwendolyn, Lady Edmondstone, came to America with her three
eldest children (they were ten, seven, and three). They all stayed at
Caumsett; Field met them at the dock and drove them off to the
estate. "He took so much trouble to make us happy," Lady Edmondstone wrote later. "He and Ruth let us do just as we liked at
Caumsett and gave us a wonderful time. Also, with rationing still
in force [in England], they gave us everything we wanted in food
and clothes to take home. Marshall was always such a reliable, com-
forting personality, and I always felt he would help me in any way
if I needed it. . . . I only feel so sad that I did not see more of him."

The anecdotes, the minutiae, the mosaic of his daily life, centered
on his office in Chicago, and on his staff. He was still unable to believe how much loyalty he had generated in dozens of his employees;
he liked them, and rejoiced in the presence of so many congenial
people, but that infernal modesty forbade him to admit that they
cared equally for him, and he was unconscionably delighted at any
evidence of their affection. One of his most enjoyable friendships
at work was with Carmine Pascouchi, who became assistant city
circulation manager for the *Sun-Times:* it was a friendship that consisted of constant raillery and chaffing, grins and laughter, and it
warmed Field, who always responded even to a "Happy Birthday"
with a rather astonished pleasure.

But his own loyalty and affection were always in evidence. When
Harry Baker, the *Sun*'s circulation manager, arrived in Washington for a newspaper convention and found no rooms available, he
told the manager of the Statler that Field would not be along until
morning, and asked to use his room for the night. Field arrived at
six the next morning, was informed by a flustered manager that the
room was in use, and answered, "Oh. Well, don't disturb him yet.
Let him get a night's sleep. I'll have some coffee down here, and
would you bring me all the morning papers?" He sat in an alcove
reading and smoking until eight o'clock, at which time he called
upstairs to ask if Baker would mind his coming up now. Baker had
often been happy that he did not work for Colonel McCormick, or
for Hearst; he was perhaps never happier than at that moment.

In 1943 Field hired Miss Charlotte Hagemann, who was his
secretary in Chicago from then on. She had applied for an opening
as Silliman Evans's secretary, but Evans was in a hurry, and she had

wanted to give proper notice to her old employer and take a short vacation before starting. Evans could not wait; she left her old position anyway. Three weeks later the *Sun* called; would she see Marshall Field? She would. Hospitably, he rose as she entered the office, and shook hands cordially. When the terms were settled and he was showing her out he said, "Miss Hagemann, I look forward to many years of happy association." And when he discovered sometime later that she had been receiving an unjustifiably smaller salary than many of the other secretaries, he did not simply offer a raise; he apologized formally.

To such an employer loyalty and affection were inevitable. In 1944 Miss Hagemann witnessed a possibly unparalleled example of both, when two boys about eleven and twelve, one the son of an employee on military leave, came and asked to speak to Field—because the father of the one had said so often that "Mr. Field was a wonderful man." Field buzzed just then and asked what the boys wanted; he laughed happily and said, "By all means bring them on in." The three conversed; the young gentlemen departed with expressions of amity; and Field discovered then what they had told Miss Hagemann: "We just came from the *Herald-American* and they gave us free passes for the movies, but if we could see Mr. Field we'd rather do that."

In time Miss Hagemann, like Miss Heller in New York earlier, came to know his likes and dislikes, his generosity and its limits. She often interpreted him to those who came in search of money, either for themselves or for causes. Many refused to take no for an answer until Field's irritation became obvious, but perhaps that was his own fault: one gentleman who had come to see him several times stopped in the outer office to ask Miss Hagemann, "When Mr. Field says no, does he mean it?" She asked, "Did he definitely use the word no?" The gentleman said, "Yes. But he was so very gentle and polite that I couldn't be sure he meant it." Miss Hagemann smiled: "He did."

There were also, and unavoidably, crackpots. One college boy wrote a sincere, impassioned letter about the need for money to complete his education; Field took him seriously, and an exchange of letters followed. Field finally offered $900, and asked how the young man would like it paid. The suppliant wrote back: "You

can't really think I'd have taken up your time for a mere $900."
Field said, "Miss Hagemann, there is nothing mere about $900."
Reading further, he discovered that the student's ambitions sub-
sumed a wide range of projects, for which one million dollars would
be required. The correspondence ended shortly.

With serious critics, on the other hand, he was *courtoisie* personified. When he received this letter:

In your paper there are doll dresses and presidents. On one side there are
doll dresses on the other side there are presidents in the same place. I wish
you would stop it.

Patty Biggs

he answered:

Dear Patty:

I am so sorry that the doll cut-outs were in the same place in the paper
as the president pictures, but you will notice that they have been changed
since you wrote that very nice letter to us. Thank you so much for your
suggestion.

His consideration was sometimes more than a matter of gracious
manners. The periodic staff reductions always pained him, and he
was careful to speak to as many as he could of those who had been
let out. After the *Sun* and the *Times* merged, the surplus personnel
were summoned to a meeting, and the weary word went around that
they were to be offered the consolation of a group photograph; instead of which Field greeted them, spoke very sadly about what was
happening to them, promised them help in finding new jobs, and
shook everyone's hand.*

Sometimes his loyalty was to people, and sometimes to principle.
In the winter of 1945–6 he acquired the first of two radio stations,
WJJD in Chicago (the other was WSAI in Cincinnati; much later,
in 1955–6, Field Enterprises bought KOIN in Portland and KJR in
Seattle, but they were all sold off shortly afterward). At the end of
February, 1946, he received a letter reading in part:

As one who admires your newspaper and the principles for which it stands
may I express my regret that your purchase of station WJJD has not resulted

---

* In Britain that is called "the golden handshake," and it is not easy to admire
under any circumstances. The point here is not that it was marvelous to be fired by
Marshall Field, but that his consideration was unfailing. Not many employers
would have bothered.

in the establishment for that station of a policy which could be respected and applauded by independent liberals.

One expected an interim period when because of contractual obligations, the policies of the previous owner(s) would continue. One hoped that eventually the frequency would air considerably less piety and more politics, that Mr. Utley would return as Air Editor of the Chicago Sun. One did not, ever, expect that William J. Grace * would be permitted time in which to attempt to revive what one had hoped to be a very dead corpse.

The whole question of one's intentions is re-opened by this scheduling of an America First mouthpiece by a station which should be a powerful instrument against fascism. No one quarrels with an objective presentation of news or comment. One would not wish to read a paper or listen to a station which consults a Liberal's Index before making a statement, but the "objectivity" which permits a movement such as America First to use that station's time to undermine not the Democratic party (which is admissible and at times even desirable) but democracy itself, is a sordid force—even wryly amusing—the use of a democratic outlet by a fascist group whose known intention is to destroy it.

This posed an old question—does freedom of speech extend to those who would deny it to others—and Field answered as a liberal. If he were to suppress Grace, he would himself be one of those who denied free speech to others, and would therefore, by his correspondent's logic, lose his own right to it. He did not attempt to close that vicious circle, but wrote:

. . . I think I am probably as antagonistic to him as you are. However, I do not feel that a radio station has any right, provided the material used is not in itself libelous or defamatory, to become a censor for the view of anybody who is willing to pay for the time.

I believe you will find that WJJD has increased enormously its public service programs, and has had many constructive programs on the subject of civil liberties, race relations, etc.

The dilemma was still a dilemma, but Field stuck by his liberalism, and that too was a necessary loyalty.

Sometimes it was no dilemma. If Field admitted reactionary opinion on principle, he welcomed liberal opinion with delight; but he welcomed facts even more warmly. Herman Kogan, who had joined

---

* No connection with the Rev. William H. Grace of Appleton, Wisconsin (p. 322).

the *Sun* in 1942, went out to cover a rally of Gerald L. K. Smith's antediluvian enthusiasts, presided over by the man himself; noting the presence of various representatives of the free press, Smith challenged them to "go back and tell the truth." Jim Mulroy, the managing editor, was holding the presses for Kogan's story, which gave the latter something like twenty-five minutes to run it off; he told the truth in a fine, honest story. Mulroy was appalled at its sharpness, but the space was open and the presses were ready; the story ran. Next morning Kogan and Mulroy received notes from Field congratulating them on the coverage, and Mulroy was expansive: "We really did a job," he told Kogan.

In November of that year Field survived an almost farcical gentleman's disagreement with Generoso Pope, publisher of the Italian-American *Il Progresso* in New York City. Pope was prominent in local politics, and *PM* had lashed out at him for sundry high misdemeanors. On November 15 he wrote to Field:

> *PM* has attacked me; I have in my possession material charging you with close and active relationship with Italian fascism and its outlets in the United States during the prewar years. Knowing you as I do, I have not indulged in publicizing it in my own newspaper, *Il Progresso*.

Field answered, on the 26th.

> I have always refrained from interfering with the editorial policy of *PM*. However, I have forwarded your letter to the editor. May I say that you are at perfect liberty to say anything you care to about me at any time, provided it is not libelous, and I should like to disabuse you of any idea that any such threat would influence the editors of *PM* or of any paper with which I was connected in any way.

Pope had made the common mistake of assuming that Field controlled *PM*'s policies. The material in his possession was almost surely an account of Field, Glore's participation in various Italian bond issues in the late 1920s and early 1930s, with an added bit of spice: Field had received, in 1932, a decoration from the Italian government, and had thenceforth been entitled to call himself a Commendatore in some meaningless order. (He had thought once of sending back the bit of ribbon, and had been unable to find it.) He knew, of course, that the American financial community, in which he had performed prominently, had been politically myopic (and that elements of it had been downright sinister), but he also knew that the myopia had been general (afflicting the Federal government, for example), and he had never wasted time in apologies. His whole life after 1936 was a refutation of Pope's dire hints. In July, 1947, Field received another foreign decoration, this one from England: the King's Medal for Service in the Cause of Freedom, given him primarily for his work in evacuating the children of Europe. He was pleased to have it, but never claimed importance for it; it had been awarded to many others as an official thank you, and was not an acknowledgment of personal valor or sacrifice.

Back in 1944, on October 3, Field had made a speech at the first annual dinner of the Capital Press Club, an organization founded by the rapidly growing Negro press corps in Washington when it discovered that Negroes were unwelcome at the "National" Press Club.* He addressed himself bluntly to segregation: in the armed forces, in defense work, in news media. After a review of specific Negro contributions, including the 93d Division's fight against the Japanese in the South Pacific, the Negro units in Normandy, and the supply troops at Anzio, who had been "as much under fire as though they had been exchanging hand grenades with the Nazis," he came home again:

I want to touch on a very sore point in connection with Negroes in uniform. The discriminations and indignities to which Negro soldiers and sailors have been subjected not only rankle deeply in the hearts of all Negro Americans, but are a source of shame and concern to many white Americans. I do not know, frankly, whether we should castigate the Army more or civilian Americans more. Negro soldiers have found they could get only limited transportation from camp to town; when they got there they could find only limited recreation, housing and entertainment facilities. If they got into difficulties—as who might not under those circumstances—Negro soldiers have too often found that wearing a uniform was no protection against police brutality. . . .

Americans generally don't know these things. . . . Many white Americans have no idea even of the number of Negroes in the Armed Forces, let alone

---

* Which belied the assumption that reporters and editors were always liberal and only their employers prejudiced. After the war, however, the National Press Club was the first club in Washington to break the color line.

what their role has been. The bulk of news stories in the daily press about Negroes is not connected with the war. Even now Negro crime stories are more frequent than Negro soldier stories. There are exceptions to this newspaper treatment. I wonder how many of you noticed the episode from "Terry and the Pirates" in which Terry was flying from India to China. On the way he passed by the point at which Negro combat engineers are building the Ledo road and fighting off Japanese patrols. Milton Caniff's drawing showed the Negro engineers. There was no comment, and no tag-line, but it was plain to everyone that these were Negro troops. This is the sort of thing that is needed.

A number of nationally circulated magazines have carried stories about Negroes recently, some with pictures. But none has attempted an over-all assessment of Negro contributions to the war; and few have dealt with Negroes as war-workers.

After the 99th Fighter Group brought down twelve Focke-Wolfs (eight in one day) the newsreels carried the story. Up to this time there had been no combat or serious soldier shots in the newsreels since the beginning of the war.

But the Negro press was itself segregated, and therefore limited:

There is now a newsreel devoted to Negro subjects and there are a good many well-established Negro magazines. Radio programs directed primarily to Negro audiences have mainly a religious and musical content. The shortage of Negro news on the radio is not made up in Negro news programs.

In other words, Negro news is segregated just as much as any other aspect of Negro life. The news channels which reach white Americans contain practically no reference to Negro contributions to the war. No matter how good a job the Negro media do they cannot fill this gap unaided, since Negroes read both white and Negro papers, but white Americans read only white papers.

The segregation of Negro news lends weight to Gunnar Myrdal's judgment that "to get publicity is of the highest strategic importance to the Negro people." We all know that the race problem is a problem of the mind. Publicity and information alone will not lead us to a solution of the American dilemma, but they are the necessary first steps to a solution.

Parochialism on both sides was the enemy:

If the Negro press is to lead opinion, its columns should not stop short at urging Negro participation in America's war job; or in discussing the fate of the people of the Caribbean, of India and the colonial problems of Africa and the East Indies. Wherever the struggle for freedom goes on—

the struggle for political and economic rights and opportunities, whether at home or abroad, black or white, on the farm or in the factory—that struggle should have news value for the readers of the Negro press.

In short, the Negro press has all the rights of a minority, protest press. But it has the responsibilities that go with those rights. In the narrowest sense those responsibilities require that the Negro press should follow the ordinary canons of good journalism—to tell the whole story accurately. In the widest sense those responsibilities require that the Negro press should inform its reading public about the issues of democracy abroad as well as at home. The masses of people everywhere are engaged in a struggle to broaden the base of economic opportunity and political rights and to secure the fundamental freedoms of free speech and worship. This is the true meaning of democracy. The fight to win it abroad cannot be separated from the fight to win it at home. Let the white press tell its readers more about the fight at home; let the Negro press tell its readers more about the fight to win it abroad.

These are interests we have in common. Protest is not the exclusive property of the minority press.

The speech was handsomely received. When the Club invited him to speak, Field was extremely sensible of the honor. But he had not trimmed his sails to anyone's wind: the subject chosen, he said precisely what he would have at any gathering, and if there were cynics in the audience when he had finished, they did not come forward. Field always remembered the speech as one of his best, and the occasion as heartening—relatively free of the cant that ordinarily marred discussions of race and society.

That evening—and Field's willingness to compliment one of the Colonel's properties—also led to a professional coup for Field. One of the guests wrote to Milton Caniff afterward, relaying Field's praise, and Caniff wrote Field to thank him. A letter or two over the next year maintained contact, and when the two men met in the fall of 1945 they were already friends. They were brought together by Smith Davis, a dealer in newspaper properties who had met Field through Charles Cushing and had advised him occasionally. Davis knew that Caniff was not altogether happy with the Chicago Tribune-New York Daily News Syndicate; he also knew that Caniff's contract ran out in 1947. Davis's intention was more to help Field and Caniff (and strangely enough the Hearst syndicate, King Features) than it was to discomfit the *Tribune,* though he doubtless enjoyed doing both. During the annual convention of the American Society of Newspaper Publishers Caniff was invited to the *Sun*'s suite at the Waldorf, in New York, where he found Davis. After a few minutes' chat Davis got right to business: "Milt, how'd you like to do a new strip for Marshall Field?" Very much, Caniff answered; and the two proceeded to Field's apartment, where Field and Charles Cushing awaited them. The conversation there was a model of brevity. Field asked if Caniff would really like to switch; Caniff said he would. Field asked on what terms; Caniff answered, "Total ownership and total control." Field said all right. They shook hands.

There was more to it than a change of venue. Caniff took this altogether speculative step knowing that he would have to leave behind him forever "Terry and the Pirates," one of the world's half-dozen most successful comic strips. But with the Tribune Syndicate Caniff had no proprietary interest in his own strip, though the pay was good; and he had never felt altogether free of editorial pressures, though he ignored them brazenly. The Hearst people in Chicago were waging their own guerrilla war with McCormick, and Davis had proposed that King Features, the largest syndicate in the country, distribute the new strip. He knew that Caniff would hardly prefer Hearst to McCormick, but would agree to the distribution arrangements in his delight at working for Field. The result was a contract with Field, and a subcontract between Field and King Features. At contract time Caniff asked if Field would mind signing the document himself, rather than delegating the signature to a subordinate; Field was charmed, and most flattered that anyone would so value his autograph.

"Steve Canyon," the new strip, made its debut on January 13, 1947, and was an immediate success, shortly becoming one of the most widely read comic strips in the world. The friendship between Field and Caniff endured. Based on a deep mutual respect, it nevertheless had its frivolous aspects. In the early promotional stages Field was asked to pose with an assortment of Caniff's models; the ladies were pretty, and he complied with great good nature. Some time afterward, when the Caniffs were at his Park Avenue flat, Field asked the cartoonist's opinion of the paintings on the walls.

Caniff, a highly talented, cultured, and intelligent man, was altogether fazed. "What can you say," he asked later, "when a man shows you Renoir and Gauguin and Monet and asks you what you think of them? 'Interesting'? 'Good brushwork'? Finally I just said, 'Wow.' "

Twice Field visited Alaska, and even those vacations were turned to later political account. In the late summer of 1948 he and his stepson Bobby Phipps and George Richardson went after Dall sheep and grizzlies in the Yukon country, near Mt. Wrangell; the following year they flew to Lake George on the Alaska Peninsula for mountain goats and Kodiak bears. "There was a considerable entourage on each occasion," Richardson wrote later: a pack train the first year, and the aircraft and crew the second. "To all these helpers he was 'Marshall.'. . . I am sure he never had a happier two months." To Bobby Phipps, at fifteen and sixteen, the expeditions were indescribably adventurous. The hunt was successful both years, and when the bearskins were being converted into rugs Field made a characteristic remark: asked if the mouths should be open or shut, he said, "Closed, I think. We don't want to frighten the little girls," Phyllis and Fiona.

On March 30, 1948, the *Sun-Times* had run an editorial "For the 49th and 50th States," and in the summer of 1949 Field joined the Alaska Statehood Committee at the request of Territorial Governor Ernest Gruening. The latter wrote to him in the spring of 1950 to report on committee hearings and the progress of a bill for statehood. "In your state," Gruening wrote,

> Paul Douglas is strongly in favor of statehood, but Scott Lucas, curiously enough, is anything but enthusiastic despite the fact that the Democratic platform contained a specific pledge for "immediate statehood" and President Truman is doing his utmost to get favorable action. A letter from you to Scott Lucas, urging him to take an active part in helping to get the bill on the floor and then passed, will I know be helpful.

Field promptly dashed off a note to his Senator:

> The last two summers I have been up to Alaska on hunting trips and got to know a great many people up there in Anchorage. After talking with several of them, I have become quite a crusader for the statehood of Alaska.

I really think that people up there are entitled to it and will make a go of it.
. . . You may or may not have noticed that we have taken a pretty strong
editorial position here on this subject, and we all feel the same about it.

If Field had ever been accused of behind-the-scenes politicking
because of those letters, he would have had a perfect, if rueful,
answer: Lucas failed of re-election in 1950, and Alaska became a
state only nine years later.

Field made one more major speech in the 1940s, this one the
principal address at the commencement exercises of Roosevelt College in June, 1949. It bore similarities to previous speeches—the
diffidence of the older generation, the quotation from Jefferson, the
favorable review of the New Deal—but its burden was the threat of
stagnation through fear. In 1933 the only thing we had had to fear
was fear itself, and since then we had learned to be confident, generous, avid of life and ideas; but a new danger was rising, and it
was that of which he warned the graduates:

. . . We are in danger of yielding to a psychology of fear that can be more
demoralizing than the greatest threat of physical force.

There is the pervading fear of communism, for example, a fear that is
daily being compounded into hysterical attacks upon all nonconformists,
whether they are Communists or not. . . .

But why should we dissipate our energies in unworthy fear and suspicion?
Who would dare to assert that our American system of human liberty cannot
prove vastly superior to any other system, not only on the strength of its
past record but also on the basis of any clear analysis of its future potential?

Instead of careful analysis we have expensive witch hunts that implicate
not only the avowed Communists but thousands of others whose only visible
crime is independent thinking about the problems facing society today. Instead of clear thinking, we have irresponsible statements whose only result
must be to convince the leaders of the Russian state that we welcome a
contest of war-mongering with them.

. . . We have succumbed to a new element in our national thinking. And
that element is fear, a fear that has made us supersensitive in our foreign
relations and not sensitive enough to our own ability to provide responsible
world leadership.

It will be a terrible thing if we yield completely to this kind of thinking.
Already there is evidence in Washington and other places that we are con-
doning a philosophy of guilt by association. We are no longer content to

hunt for witches. We are now seeking out those who have been associated even remotely with radical or liberal thinking. And we are imputing to them all the unproved crimes for which we condemn the twentieth-century witches themselves.

This was said in 1949, before Sen. Joseph McCarthy, for example, had exacerbated national fears. President Truman had initiated a loyalty program in March, 1947, and it was being conducted *con brio,* largely by Democrats. The "faceless informer" was filling FBI files with astonishing tidbits: not only that So-and-So gave an ambulance to Spain, but also that Another had one day stepped out onto the porch to pick up his Sunday paper *stark naked,* and that Guess Who was a subscriber to the *New Republic.** Field contended that we were not actually so spineless and brainless as to be corrupted by variety, which, even to the most extreme radical point, was essential to democracy; still more, that conformity and fear were the forerunners of despair, of an abdication of freedom. He associated the tremors and palpitations with our delusions about the atom bomb: that there was "a secret," that we could maintain a monopoly of power, that attendance at a film the scenario of which had been written by a man who had voted Communist in 1932, or even 1948, would open the gates to traitors and spies. There *were* spies, and always had been, on all sides of all international quarrels. But since Justice Holmes's famous decision for a unanimous Supreme Court in 1919, all levels of government had accepted the doctrine of "clear and present danger"—no one had a right to yell "Fire!" in a crowded theater, but up to that point, the point of overt incitement, no man could be punished for belief or advocacy. Now, however, loyalty boards were assuming that anyone who associated with Communists, or who was accused, often by simple allegation with no evidence, of left-wing sympathies, was directly aiding and abetting traitors, and was therefore a danger to the state. The law of the land—the classic, authoritative interpretation of the scope of the First Amendment—had been replaced by the controlled, steely-eyed hysteria of petty officials.

Furthermore, Field said, we seemed to have given up on free enterprise even as we persecuted its critics.

---

* These sounded like hopeless exaggerations; but they were on the record.

Perhaps we are too close to recent history to understand how our economic system has been strengthened during the past sixteen years. Perhaps we do not yet appreciate how many safeguards we now have against the abuses and the inequities which nearly stalled our economic machinery during the late twenties.

The important thing is that we have them and that they are working to stabilize our economic system. They have not only been written into legislation; they have also become a part of our social fabric.

Who today would want to revive the abuses of child labor? Who would want to abolish the machinery of the Securities and Exchange Commission? Or the Federal Deposit Insurance Corporation? Or the vitally important Government credit agencies? Or the common-sense policy of reciprocal world trade?

. . . If we are honest we will concede that during the past ten years we have transacted a tremendous amount of business with relatively little effort. There is still a lot of business to be done in this country but from now on we are going to have to think and plan and work quite a bit more. These are hard facts for graduates of every class of 1949. But they are not necessarily unpleasant facts. The opportunities for important work were never greater. The rewards can be ample.

The title of Field's address was "The American Potential for Greatness," and the disparagement of that potential worried him:

We have always tended to underestimate our capacity for greatness. We have let ourselves be sidetracked by many petty considerations until, in some period of crisis, we have proved again and again our ability and power to rise to unexpected heights. . . .

America has the potential strength to wipe out every slum, to provide a decent education for every child, combat ill-health, and to provide equal opportunities for men and women of all races, creeds, and colors.

Our potential for greatness will not be reached until we have met those challenges.

Those are jobs worthy of our mettle and our resources. Instead, we see our great strength being dissipated daily in time-consuming non-constructive activities.

We have let red-baiting achieve almost the dignity of a profession in which petty men and women devote their entire energies to proving guilt by association.

We see the fundamental question of civil rights—human rights—become a partisan political issue in Congress and in some of our state Legislatures.

We see courageous men and women in business and the professions shrinking from the assumption of public responsibilities to avoid being smeared as subversive or disloyal.

We see an America in which, for the first time,* people are becoming afraid to think objectively and to speak frankly in the great liberal tradition of the Nation.

The cost of this kind of hysteria comes high. It costs time, money, and effort to set up "thought police" anywhere in the world. We could have built a great many schools with the appropriations that have been voted to loyalty investigating committees in America during the past decade.

Our fears and our hysteria are costing us dearly in terms of the ammunition they provide those nations which are opposed to our system of government. In a very real sense we are paying for the propaganda ammunition of our critics.

The whole speech was a reaction to the first two years of a new national mood. If Field had hoped it would do any good, he was disappointed. Over the next four or five years the twin contagions of fear and guilt poisoned the air; hypocrites and perjurers became national heroes. Many good men, some in high place, did nothing; for a time a handful of writers and political cartoonists were the only voices for sanity. The loyalty oath became a national disease; the Bill of Rights was temporarily superseded by superpatriotic bombast; semiliterate joiners intimidated library boards and universities. Some foreigners assumed that the United States was about to go fascist; others, that it had already gone crazy. In 1945 American prestige stood at a historic high; by 1954, at an abysmal low. Within the United States the same might have been said of liberalism, and Field was deeply concerned at what appeared to be a national tragedy.

But his life was soon to take another sharp turn; shortly he would do his fighting as an individual, and not as a publisher.

5

When Marshall, Jr., came back from the war he had to choose between the law and journalism; the choice was easy. Field had always assumed that Marshall would join him at the *Sun*. When

---

* Here he forgot Thaddeus Stevens and A. Mitchell Palmer.

Benton asked him, during the dark, debtful months of 1943, why he didn't cut his losses and run, Field reminded him that the newspaper was a family affair. Marshall, Jr., was an officer in the corporation (he was even part owner of *PM,* and put up with a lot of ribbing for it), and one of Field's goals was to keep the newspaper alive until Marshall could return and train himself to take it over.

Marshall did just that, starting in 1946 on the tailgate of a delivery truck. The classic story was that on his first day he showed up in dungarees and an old sweater, and found the driver and loaders in white shirts and bow ties. That was apocryphal. They knew who he was, of course, but as he said later, "If the driver moderated his language because of me, I'd like to have heard him when I wasn't there." He progressed in traditional fashion through the various departments of the newspaper, spiraling upward as he went. By early 1950 he had reached the front office. (He wrote later, "The distance between tailgate and driver's seat is shorter if you own the truck.")

The relationship between the two Fields was not ordinary. They shared a strong sense of family prestige—their political disagreements, for example, were far transcended by their being Marshall Field *père et fils.* In 1950 the father was fifty-seven, the son thirty-four; but if the son had been in the newspaper business for only four years, the father had been in it for only nine, and lacked the lifetime of journalistic experience and hegemony that Hearst, say, could bring to bear on a parallel situation. Increasingly the two Fields conferred as equals in the office. The son's university education and the father's political education had been almost simultaneous, in the late 1930s. The father had chosen, from several major interests, to focus on publishing; the son had come out of the Navy with no great body of affiliations and commitments to distract him from his development as a publisher, and was a newspaperman from his first professional day. The father was a confirmed liberal, who wanted his newspaper to make money in spite of (preferably, of course, *because* of) its liberalism; the son was a more conservative man, basically a Republican (though he supported Stevenson in the Illinois gubernatorial race in 1948), to whom a more conservative, and consequently more profitable, newspaper represented a step forward and not a compromise.

All the makings of melodrama were present, but no melodrama resulted. The staff of the *Sun-Times* knew that there were differences between the two men, and that the son was on his way up; they also knew that when Marshall took over there would be a change in editorial policy. Through 1949 and 1950 change was in the air, but it was peaceful and inevitable change, not power struggle and not revolution. Field had known that the newspaper would be in Marshall's hands before long. In 1950 the time arrived.

In the summer of that year Field spent a few weeks at a dude ranch in Wyoming with his wife, the younger children (Phyllis, Fiona, and Bobby), Ruthie Pruyn, Mrs. Field's niece, and Jeannie Lincoln, a friend of the children. He enjoyed the rest, the rejection of all business worries, and the outdoor life. He was relaxing more, as Marshall took firmer charge of the newspaper. He had also been thoroughly relaxed on both trips to Alaska, knowing that the newspaper was in good hands. He spent more time at Caumsett, and at Chelsea, with friends. The first time he asked Russ Stewart, his managing editor, down to Chelsea to hunt, he urged the pleasures of the trip and asked, "When can you come down? When can you get away?" Stewart answered with a straight face, "Any time my boss lets me," and Field seemed momentarily embarrassed. He was not at all embarrassed when they got to Carolina; as the two were riding through the meadows he dropped back to tell Stewart that there was a general rule on his properties: no tipping. Stewart smiled: "It's a good rule if you can make it stick." Field was not amused: "It damned well better stick," he said gravely; and Stewart realized that the friendly diffidence of Field-at-the-office had become the manorial assurance of Field-at-home.

His vacations were good for him. He had been tiring more easily since about 1947, and an old injury to his back had bothered him occasionally. (He had been thrown from a polo pony in the late 1920s. His daughter Barbara saw him fall, thought he was dead, and wept unconsolably.) Already, by 1950, he had begun to withdraw slightly from his work—just the gentle easing-up of a man who has spent ten years fighting and who finds it relaxing to delegate responsibilities. A wise son maketh a glad father, according to Proverbs, and Field could be happy in his son's competence: Marshall enjoyed the respect earned by a good boss, without the scorn usually earned by the boss's son. A few strong liberals on the staff wondered about the future, but no one could deny that Marshall was saving money, increasing revenue, and running the newspaper closer to the black every week. There was no conflict between father and son: Field was mightily pleased at the figures, and the editorial policies were still a liberal consensus.

Field had discussed the transfer of power for some months, with both his son and Louis Weiss. Originally he had felt that Marshall, Jr., should step in as publisher. But in the late summer of 1950 Marshall visited his father at Caumsett and the two men talked a whole afternoon and evening (Weiss joined them for part of the time). Marshall contended that he would function more effectively with undivided authority—both financial and editorial management; Field agreed, and within a few weeks Marshall Field, Jr., was the editor and publisher of the Chicago *Sun-Times*.

At first glance Field's decision to relinquish control of the newspaper seems a sad and frustrating paradox. He had supported liberal journalism unstintingly and now, when liberalism was in partial eclipse, when the *Sun-Times* was nearly in the black, when he had become a knowing and effective publisher, he withdrew. He had fought hard for ten years and now, it seemed, he was quitting. Of course it was not so simple.

Liberalism had suffered a great jolt in 1948, perhaps the natural result of President Truman's relatively conservative administration. A large and articulate segment of the American left—ranging from Communists to bitterly anti-Communist liberals—had felt and expressed serious concern at the President's loyalty program, at our unilateral actions in foreign affairs, and at the mounting violence of Republican attacks on the administration and on private citizens. Those who felt that the answer was a bold step further left, chiefly in foreign affairs and civil liberties, looked to Henry Wallace for help, though many dropped off when it became apparent that Communists were doing all they could to annex him and his party. (Strom Thurmond, on the Dixiecrat right wing, stood for those who felt that the drift toward conservatism should become a rush to reaction; most Republicans were far more moderate.) The split among liberals was sharp, and Truman's victory was taken, correctly, as a sign that the country had no wish to give up the social gains of the previous fifteen years, but a very strong wish to retrench, flavored by a powerful nostalgia for the good old days of self-reliance and Perdicaris-alive-or-Raisuli-dead; the country was tired of trouble and enjoying its postwar prosperity.

Under the circumstances it was natural that some of Field's friends, and a few of his editorial personnel, should jump to the conclusion that in relinquishing the newspaper he was drifting with the times, or yielding politely to the centrist mood. True, if Roosevelt or Britain had needed his help, or if he had known that a man like Adlai Stevenson was to be the Democratic presidential candidate in 1952, he might have hung on in order to participate personally. As it was, he knew he would be criticized for stepping down—he had discussed all aspects of the move at great length with Louis Weiss; but he also knew, and so did his intimates, that politics had nothing to do with his decision. It was an intensely personal decision, made by a father and not by a public figure, and it was unfortunate that its political consequences obscured his deeper motives.

We tend to see public figures as symbols and not as people, and when they are rich we relegate them to worlds not our own, worlds of downy luxury or posh eccentricities or vaulting ambition, and not a world of sights and smells and tastes and emotions. But like millions of other men Marshall Field exulted in the sight of green hills and the smell of salt air and the taste of cold beer on a hot day —and loved his son, flesh of his flesh, deeply, as his son loved him. Marshall had grown up in his own time and his own way, and differed from his father; the love between them was not less for that. Marshall was a more conservative man. He was more energetic and more ambitious. In a technical sense he was a better newspaperman, and he had only five years less experience than his father. He was more definitely a Chicagoan. His life was considerably less complicated, at the time, by philanthropies and directorships. He was closer to the newer, younger men in the newspaper's executive offices, who were beginning to run a tighter corporation. He was more willing, temperamentally and philosophically, to assume power; more and more often moments of doubt, suspended decisions, were referred to him and resolved by him. And Field knew that even in deep personal sense his son felt ready: Marshall's first marriage had not worked out, but he was married again now, and happily; psychologically too he was in a state of commencement, of embarkation.

Field acquiesced. His lingering resistance to the abdication was quelled by the knowledge that this transfer of power had been one of his own goals; by his lifelong adherence to the principle that power must accompany responsibility; by his awareness that Marshall was a tougher and harder-working publisher than he; perhaps too by the prospect of repose, leisure, more time for public service and philanthropy; and certainly by the satisfying knowledge that Marshall—whatever their political differences—was a man of competence. (There was also a more personal reason. The years of irregular commuting—now to Chicago, now to New York—had not been easy. Neither Field nor his wife liked being alone half the week; increasingly upset at the separation, they had come close to quarreling several times. They took consolation in the thought that they resented separation, and not propinquity; and they were vastly happier after Field had stepped down and returned to New York.)

Field knew that there would be changes in policy, and that liberal newspapermen would be sorry to see him release his hold. But he believed—wished, hoped—that the responsibilities of managing a metropolitan newspaper, and probably a second newspaper later on, would gradually make a liberal of his son: intelligence and responsibility joined were, he thought, bound to produce liberal attitudes. That hope was simple and trusting, even naïve; it was also unjustified; but it was a measure at once of his love for his son and of his political faith. And if Field felt that his son's conservatism had sprung in any degree from the necessary and natural rivalry between a father and a son, he might also have felt that his withdrawal would relieve his son of that particular pressure: with full responsibility, the younger man would be free to act and not to react. But Marshall remained a conservative, and the newspaper, nominally "independent," reflected his views. Field often disagreed with its editorial position (he was *very* sad two years later, when the *Sun-Times* jumped all guns in declaring for Eisenhower), but never interfered with its management.

Field's love for his son never diminished; he never ceased respecting Marshall as a man and as a publisher. He was very sensitive to a facet of his son easily overlooked by outsiders: the younger man was much like his great-grandfather, the first Marshall Field. Twenty years old when his father became a liberal, Marshall had been deeply rooted in the older family traditions; he had carried through his early years and into his maturity the old-fashioned, rather than the new, ideas of propriety and rectitude. The two might disagree flatly on issues; but Field, who had always admired his grandfather, could neither deny nor resent Marshall's resemblance to him.

But he did miss the newspaper. He missed being a publisher, and he missed the old days of flamboyant liberalism. More than once he wished he could dictate an editorial blast at some piece of public foolishness, and more than once he thought the *Sun-Times* wrong. But he stood by his son. Liberals might wonder, might call this a falling away, a defection from the tradition of liberal ideals in which the newspaper had been founded; so it was, and if Field was now criticized by friends instead of enemies, said to have made a mistake, let them down, he could only accept the criticism. But the paper had been founded in another tradition, too, of which his liberal friends knew little: the tradition of the great family, of continuity, of primogeniture. A Field newspaper in Chicago was destined from its first moment to be someday published by Marshall, Jr. If Field had, as some said, shirked a responsibility to American liberalism, he had been faithful to another, more personal and ultimately stronger. As he was a liberal before he was a Democrat, so he was a father before he was a liberal.

On October 1, 1950, Marshall Field, Jr., became publisher of the Chicago *Sun-Times*. Marshall Field, Sr., continued in full control of Field Enterprises, Inc., which shortly became one of the most prosperous privately owned corporations in the world.

CHAPTER TEN

The studies of philosophy and eloquence are congenial to a popular state, which encourages the freedom of inquiry and submits only to the force of persuasion.

—GIBBON on Athens, c. 1780

The policy of repression of ideas cannot work and never has worked. The alternative to it is the long, difficult road of education. To this the American people have been committed. It requires patience and tolerance, even in the face of intense provocation. It requires faith in the principles and practices of democracy, faith that when the citizen understands all forms of government he will prefer democracy and that he will be a better citizen if he is convinced than he would be if he were coerced.

—ROBERT MAYNARD HUTCHINS,
Statement to the Subversive Activities
Commission of the Illinois State
Legislature, 1949

IN NOVEMBER, 1950, Louis Weiss died of a heart attack at the age of fifty-six. Weiss had understood Marshall Field better than anyone outside the family: his intellectual curiosity, liberal humanism, and compassionate understanding had not only commended him to Field but also enabled him to comprehend Field. He had sensed that Field's breeding was more important than its luxurious setting implied; that Field shared with his grandfather a great sense of obligation and was trying—as his grandfather had tried—to be a man of his times; but that the times had changed radically and were, after 1918, difficult for a rich man with a social conscience. The world of Marshall Field I had expected certain things of him; it was a world of Tennysonian nobility, and as late as 1913 Theodore Roosevelt could write to Edward Grey, "There is something to be said for government by a great aristocracy which has furnished leaders to the nation in peace and war for generations; even a democrat like myself must admit this." But the world of Marshall Field III was quite different, and Weiss knew that Field, inheriting money and position in a world which demanded of them only taxes and respectability, would have to create his own obligations to society through his own experience in that society. When Field's social energies had once been released, it was Weiss more than any man who guided him.

But Weiss was not just a traffic cop. His own profession, his own philanthropies, kept him busy; if he had not been a hardworking liberal Field would have been less amenable to his guidance. But Weiss declined to impose any of his own obligations on Field, for which the latter was grateful. Hans Simons, president of the New School for Social Research, of which Weiss was chairman of the board, wrote later about Field, "Our first contact was strange because I made it against the injunction of . . . Weiss, who wanted to 'protect' Marshall. Our cooperation was slow in developing. . . ." Field was delighted to know Simons; Weiss's injunction was here simply an extension of habit, the habit of fending off the importunate who wanted to reach Field through him. Even his law firm was circumspect, and Field was considered a client of Louis Weiss, and not of Paul, Weiss, Rifkind, Wharton and Garrison. Weiss had urged Field to certain actions—child welfare, the purchase of the *Times*—but had restrained him from others, and Field had relied heavily on both his judgment and his discretion. The trust was both cause and effect of the deep affection that bound them.*

A friend is long a-getting, and soon lost. Weiss's death meant a great loss of companionship and common purpose. Coming when it did, a month after Field stepped down at the *Sun-Times,* it meant an additional weariness, a diminution of the energy that had sustained Field through so many campaigns. Weiss died poor—he left some shares (which he had borrowed money in order to buy) in a thriving apple-juice company, and not much else—and his death impoverished Field. He had offered insight, energy, and affection,

---

* Many of Field's upper-class friends refused to believe that he and Weiss were so close. Possibly it did not seem "right" that Field's closest friend and adviser should be a liberal Jewish lawyer.

and if a friend is another self, as the Romans used to say, then Field must have felt a melancholy emptiness—and an intimation of his own mortality.

Weiss's death left a vacancy for chairman of the board of the New School, and Field was invited to fill it. He accepted immediately; it was his personal memorial to Weiss. He knew the school by reputation—serious, urban, advanced; and he served it with his customary quiet distinction, revealing in time, as Simons put it, "his gift for the simple and straightforward analysis of a situation and the soft-spoken but firm proposal for its solution, which was always conciliatory though never surrendering a principled position." He was less volatile and more diffident than Weiss, but he supplied much of the same unyielding liberal simplicity. And he was by now no amateur. He had fifteen years' experience in university matters, and "social research" was in a sense what he had been supporting and doing for the same period.

It was in 1951 that he was invited to become a trustee of Sarah Lawrence College, in Bronxville, New York—an invitation that led to another chapter of controversy later on. His links with the college had been Lloyd Garrison, Weiss's law partner, and the late Edwin Embree. Garrison's link had been Harold Taylor, the college's young and famous president, an old friend and tennis rival at the University of Wisconsin in the 1930s. Taylor had come to Sarah Lawrence in 1945 and had requested that Garrison be added to the board. Other board members included Catherine Drinker Bowen, Field's old friend Harrison Tweed (who was chairman), Agnes de Mille, and the urbane and cultured Boston lawyer Charles Curtis.

William Van Duzer Lawrence, the college's founder, had made his fortune in the drug business in Canada, after which he had moved to Michigan, and then to the East, where he bought up stretches of farmland in Bronxville, New York, a rural area in the 1920s. He and Mrs. Lawrence spent their winters in Florida. Mrs. Lawrence was interested in helping Negro women, and she aided Mary McLeod Bethune—with time, money, and advice—in establishing Bethune-Cookman College. It was, as Dr. Taylor remarked later, "all very paternalistic; but thank God such people existed at the time." Mrs. Lawrence developed a natural interest in the rights of women and in their education, an interest shared by her husband. In May 1924, with the counsel and encouragement of Dr. Henry Noble MacCracken, the president of Vassar College, Lawrence began planning a new college for women. He had intended originally to provide in his will for its establishment, but when Mrs. Lawrence died in May of 1926 he decided to begin work immediately; the college, a memorial to her, was chartered in that year. Just a year later, when construction was about to start, he too died; the work went on, and the college opened in October 1928. MacCracken, who had worked with Lawrence on all the original plans, had also seen the construction through, and had been active in raising funds. He served as chairman of the board from 1926 to 1936, and during the early years he visited the campus regularly, holding himself constantly available for meetings and consultation.

On Thanksgiving Day, 1929, Constance Warren became president of the college; she had been at the head of Pine Manor College in Massachusetts, and she was an admirable educator. She reformed here, transformed there; strengthened the curriculum, expanded the library, and invited people like William Schuman, Jacques Barzun, Max Lerner, and Horace Gregory to join the faculty. The academic world took startled notice, and contributed a steady flow of active, progressive, and distinguished teachers. When Taylor took over on August 1, 1945, Sarah Lawrence was probably the most exciting women's college in the country.

Field had known about Sarah Lawrence, from common report and from his friend Edwin Embree, who had been on the board since 1944. As chief executive of the Rosenwald Fund Embree had spent most of his professional life helping Negroes; he had a strong personal interest in writers and painters, and had backed Langston Hughes, for example, in his early efforts. Embree had died in February of 1950, before Field left Chicago and before Louis Weiss died; Field had called Taylor then to propose a memorial, suggesting that the Rosenwald family would also contribute. What, he asked, would be the most constructive sort of gift? Taylor answered immediately: a scholarship fund for Negro girls who would go out later as teachers, social workers, and writers. Field offered $10,000 on the spot, and urged Taylor to mention it when he spoke to the

Rosenwalds. Ultimately twenty-five or thirty girls took advantage of those scholarships, and almost all of them went on to do independent work of real value.

When Field came east again and it was obvious that he intended to devote his free time to education, child welfare, and philanthropies, Taylor asked Tweed to consider offering him a place on the board. Tweed agreed that the association would be gratifying to all. Field's name would add luster and vitality to the board, and would induce other philanthropists to take notice of the college. Sarah Lawrence was a school of which Field could approve thoroughly. It existed in order to educate; its teachers were excellent, some brilliant; it was liberal, and did not conceive of education as training for examinations or as an accumulation of minutiae in a social vacuum.

Field accepted with pleasure. Taylor warned him that there were immediate problems: buildings, salaries, and scholarships. The trusteeship was not honorific. Field was delighted to hear it, and on November 8, 1951, he took office, shortly becoming chairman of the Scholarship Committee and a member of the Academic Freedom Committee.

The Child Welfare League of America fulfilled several functions, most of them a mystery to the general public. It was an accrediting organization for the whole field of child welfare, establishing standards and recommending improvements in administration much as the Amateur Athletic Union did in sports or the American Association of University Professors in teaching. It also published books and pamphlets on welfare, foster parentage, psychiatric treatment and so forth; and contracted to produce special surveys and studies for interested communities and for other agencies. For its accreditation and services other agencies paid it annual dues, which amounted to about a third of its income; another third derived from its earnings in research and publication; another third from contributions. Its executives and board comprised some forty citizens from all over the country. The League was not only one of the largest organizations in the field, but also one of the furthest advanced, using modern techniques to implement modern ideas, and carrying its battles to legislative halls as well as slums.

In 1951 the board decided that the League's president should be a layman, not immersed in specific projects, who would have the time, the wit, and the presence to represent the organization to the public and to other groups. Field's name was proposed, not because he was rich and famous (though neither quality was a drawback), but because he was educated in welfare and would, if he accepted, not shirk the job. (It would require, the board estimated, about 10 per cent of his time.)

The suggestion was approved, but only after debate. The League received grants from foundations, among them the Field Foundation; would Field's presence embarrass either organization? The board's representatives met with Field, who agreed that there would be no problem of interest or favoritism, or of his exercising undue, if unintended, influence on the League's policies because he represented a source of money.

He accepted not only with pleasure, but with something like relief. Child welfare was his permanent concern, and not a philanthropy in which he had momentarily dabbled. He had maintained directorships or office in half a dozen welfare organizations (including Hull House in Chicago); the U.S. Committee was still in existence, and he was still its president; and he had, over the years, served on a variety of committees and government commissions, some *ad hoc* and some permanent, e.g., the New York City Committee on Child Welfare and the National Citizens Committee of the White House Conference on Children in a Democracy, of which he was chairman. But when he left the *Sun-Times* there was no one welfare organization to which any significant share of his energies was committed, and he saw, as did the board, that the Child Welfare League was perfect for him: a spearhead organization with great authority in the profession, with some influence on legislation, and with a continuing effect on other organizations, so that its accomplishments were ultimately multiplied out of all proportion to its size and resources.

The presidency was not primarily a fund-raising job; which was as well, because Field disliked fund raising. He disliked canvassing his wealthy friends for contributions. He distrusted financial backing that had to be renewed by constant solicitation; he was reluctant to inflict upon his friends a choice between contribution and embarrassment; and he always avoided situations in which his own prestige or friendship imposed a special obligation on others. When fund raising did become necessary he always asked advice and often hesitated to act upon it. He refused, for example, to approach the manufacturers who supplied his own corporations. He knew that a great part of fund raising was precisely that sort of polite, unresisted blackmail—and he deplored it as unscrupulous.

His contribution as president was in work. His primary responsibility was to broaden the base of the League's financing. (His own financial contributions were modest and appropriate.) The temptation to rely on the Field Foundation was formally resisted: money previously granted was tied up in research projects, and during Field's tenure no new Field Foundation projects were placed on the agenda. Once more, he felt that too much support from him, or from his interests, would subvert an organization—if he withdrew or lost interest or resigned over a matter of principle, the League would be left without a solid income.

The suggestion that no Field Foundation projects be permitted to confuse the relationship had come from Joseph H. Reid, who had joined the League in 1950 and who became its executive director in 1953. Reid had come east from the Ryther Child Center in Seattle, which had benefited by several grants from the Field Foundation. Field had met him in the mid-1940s during an informal swing around the country to inspect recipients of Foundation grants. From 1952 on the two saw each other at least once a week. Reid, like so many others, felt at first that Field was preoccupied, somewhat vague; but shortly afterward changed his view entirely. "At first," Reid said, "it was hard to say whether he was very bright or just an average fellow with good instincts. Then—after a very short time— his knowledge and intelligence became obvious. But he was never predictable—he reacted to situations in his own way. Sometimes that was almost annoying: you had something all figured out, and you came to him with it, and he came up with an entirely fresh personal reaction to it, and you had to go away and rethink the notion. But he was invariably cordial—more than that, he was kind, and he was friendly."

Reid saw him really angry only once. The Children's Aid Society, an old and rich organization suffering temporarily from complacency, had refused to pay its dues to the League on the simple but assailable ground that the Society was the best in the business. They offered instead to train people. Field wrote them an indignant letter saying that fifty years previously their statement might have been true, but that if exemptions were to be allowed on the basis of an organization's present contribution to the country, the Society would be well down on the list.

Reid got to know Field well, and observed with a wondering eye some of the trifling contradictions in his character. Field could emerge from a meeting at which millions had been bandied about, and turn back to be sure that the lights were switched off. He liked his staff to be parsimonious with office supplies, and he always considered salary hikes carefully. But on broad issues there was never any question of economy or conservatism. Where a substantial social advance was at stake he went all out; when Federal funds were needed for day-care help he hammered at the issue in speeches and letters, though he was innately so gracious that it usually took a spectacular challenge to rouse him to anything like ferocity. In his speeches, or presentations to the board, he sometimes argued as though he had been briefed, speaking almost mechanically; that was most true when the burden of his talk consisted of facts and figures. But in personal conversation or informal discussions he was always warm and often funny. He wrote good speeches but had little confidence in his own composition, and always asked someone else to look over his work. Knowing how much more impressive he was when he spoke extemporaneously, Reid once hid his copy of an address, and Field was forced to speak informally; he was fluent, witty, and very effective—altogether so successful that he forgave Reid instantly.

The "entirely fresh, personal reaction" was not a matter of arbitrary or capricious statements. Field was a reader, and what he read he thought about. Worried over the spread of institutional care for preschool children (of which he disapproved; foster homes were what he advocated), he studied reports from England, the United States, and South America. He found no reason to change his stand. Studying maternal deprivation, he wanted a book of several hundred pages prepared for the World Health Organization by Dr. John Bowlby of London; offered an abridgment, he rejected it in favor of the full volume, in which were the graphs and statistics he would have to quote. And when studies were made on salaries in social work and child welfare, Field offered an unusual insight. Those salaries were low, as they had always been, and the League proposed to publish its studies as a salutary rebuke to the profession. Field thought it inadvisable. "People tend to strike averages," he said. "They will with these figures, and the average isn't high. The study would probably depress salaries—anybody making more than the average would be told not to complain, and starting salaries might go even lower. If you want to publish figures on the upper twenty-five per cent, fine. That might improve matters."

On May 1, 1952, Field delivered an address at a regional conference of child welfare workers in Long Beach, California. He offered a brief survey of progress since the 1930s, a survey that must have afforded him personal satisfaction—he was to some extent catching up with the whole effort in welfare after a decade in which he had been primarily a publisher. The changes themselves were gratifying: not only the specifics, like a sharp drop in the maternal death rate ("Former scourges of our adult population that swept unhappy orphans into asylums of 'early penitentiary architecture' have disappeared before the advance of medicine") with a consequently sharp diminution in the number of orphans, but also the trends. As living conditions improved it ceased to be so often necessary to separate children from their parents for "the long-outmoded reason of poverty alone"; and it became possible to improve psychiatric services (". . . Nancy, living in a too long neglected boarding home, who . . . must take cruel and unusual punishment for overeating and other symptoms that cry out for expert understanding and treatment").

Field also noted the shift toward public responsibility: in the past few years "there was a shrinkage of twelve per cent in the number of children being cared for by private voluntary agencies. In those same years, the numbers cared for by government agencies rose seventeen per cent. . . . We know that government agencies are now bearing at least sixty-three per cent of the cost of services to children. Clearly, those who attack the increasing role of public agencies must be prepared to give heed to the role of the private agencies and consider how they are to be supported financially."

He noted that many private agencies simply surrendered to their financial problems by limiting their work, a course that would eventually eliminate private agencies altogether; and he proposed that those agencies concentrate instead on difficult cases, specialized problems, and experimentation. He reserved to the private agencies another function, and his comment might have been a surprise to those who assumed—as many did, and how mistakenly!—that a liberal was a man who wanted the government to do everything: "Who but the boards and staffs of private agencies are equipped with the knowledge to criticize fairly and constructively the work of public agencies, and, just as important, to spring to their defense when they are ignorantly or unfairly attacked?" And he pointed out that when governments justified their own welfare agencies, the justification was considered propaganda; it was the private agencies that could "select the facts appropriate for telling; select the people who should be hearing them, and proceed to learn the best way to tell them."

It was a speech in the most uncompromising vein, implying (where it did not state) that welfare as a whole was a moral obligation of the community and that attacks upon the principle of welfare were regressions to what the speaker hoped was a dead age of selfishness. ("And yet, we are seeing today open attacks upon these principles and waves of agitation for a return to archaic methods . . . political intrusion, in the fight against adequate public appropriations.") Yet more than one listener, including Reid, noted that the speaker was quite conservative in manner, dress, financial outlook, and social behavior.

2

No longer a publisher, Field was still a wealthy and influential American businessman. If some of his business friends lamented his immersion in liberal social action, some of his liberal associates wondered at his steadfast insistence on free enterprise and sound business practice. Both the lament and the wonder reflected the difficulty of fixing upon a category for Field, of assigning him a series of compatible adjectives that would classify him in the American political taxonomy. The difficulty arose not because he was some sort of Renaissance man, or a cultural chameleon, or a sage with deep and obscure motivations, but because he was a rare bird in American life, a rich liberal, a millionaire Mill. He could talk intelligently about Mill and Bentham and Locke, and not many rich men could; it almost seemed as though he had skipped directly from them and Jefferson to the New Deal, and perhaps when his enemies called him a traitor to his class, or un-American, they meant only that he had rejected the clamorous revisionism of Spencer and Sumner, Grant and McKinley, in favor of the more pristine and honorable traditions of genuine humanism.

"Patrician in taste, radical in outlook" is the British phrase, and even as he approached sixty an understanding of his British formation remained essential to an understanding of the man. He had, as his cousin Ronald Tree saw clearly, imbibed completely the old British tolerance for the radical and the eccentric, for Keir Hardie or Holman Hunt, for homely Gibbon and handsome Byron, for Bernard Shaw in his Jaegers or Winston Churchill in his overalls or the Pearly King in his nacreous toggery. It was a tradition of tolerance that transcended faction, and that imposed an obligation: to take one's own observations and to make up one's own mind.*
(It was stronger in the upper and lower classes; the middle classes not only revere, but define, respectability.) Of course to accept variety, still more to approve of it, was to run the risk of a wild eclecticism, of haring off after faddish idols, skipping about from vegetarianism to free love to fanatic nationalism and so on, and on, and on. Field was spared that futility by a real simplicity, the trait so often called *naïveté* by his critics and even his friends. He was tolerant, and he was democratic, and what was complicated about that? To the British tradition he had assimilated an American tradition, that of Jane Addams, of the populists, of a century and a half from Shays' Rebellion to the New Deal—that "the people" were the best arbiters of their own destiny; the more economic

---

* That made it an honorable but risky tradition, and during a television appearance in the early 1950s an interviewer said to Field, "You seem to have gone through life with your neck out." Like most of us, Field was not as quick on his feet as he might have wished, and returned only a polite murmur: "Well, I suppose so." Again like most of us, he thought of a very logical and effective answer when it was too late, and could have kicked himself for missing it: "Isn't that what a neck's for?"

democracy, the better; if we had to support governments, they had better make that democracy their business.

The two traditions had combined to produce a political libertarian in the guise of a perfect gentleman. Field's asking Russ Stewart, "When can you get away?" was of a piece with his concern for civil liberties or sick children. It never occurred to him that he might order a subordinate to take a few days off and visit Chelsea, just as it did not occur to him that he could silence William J. Grace by buying WJJD. Child welfare and minority rights and the AP case had a common root: Field's conviction that without economic life and political liberty the pursuit of happiness was an empty, deliberately deceptive phrase. He was restating, in his own beliefs and projects, Oliver Wendell Holmes's insistence that the function of law, and therefore of government, was to establish "the equality of position between the parties in which liberty . . . begins"—and without which justice was impossible. If in biological and economic fact equality was an illusion, in political fact it had to be made reality; the alternative was a chaotic world of pure power. Field's deepest emphasis was on *equity*—even-handed dealing; that which is fair and right—which in modern society took the form of utter tolerance within the law and utter equality before the law. Perhaps his simplicity was best defined as a total commitment to equity. When Harry Phipps was about sixteen he and his mother were discussing the contrast between Field's usual warm affection and the occasional withering rebuke he was capable of. "He can really take your hair off," Harry said; "but every time he does it, it's because I'm hurting someone else."

Tolerance, democracy, fair play. The words had an embarrassing, oratorical ring. But they were not rhetoric. They were what centuries of men had groped toward, and millions died for, and they were not yet ours.

By 1952 the hunt for subversives was a national sport and a national disgrace. It was a political hare-and-hounds in which the hare was anything with long ears and the hounds were whoever bayed loudest. Charged by liberals with destroying freedom in the name of freedom, the inquisitors answered that they were not punishing, merely exposing. But they created a climate of opinion in which heterodox views were equated with treason—absolutely and perfectly the antithesis to the climate Field had labored for. From the initial loyalty legislation in 1947, through the bitter tragedy of the Korean War, to the Army-McCarthy hearings in the summer of 1954, an expanding wave of accusation, guilt by association, perjury pro and perjury con, confession-and-conversion, and vigilante action engulfed government, education, the arts and sciences, and eventually the private citizen in his private business. The carnival crossed political lines, but because the Democrats had been in power since 1932, the Republicans profited: allowing a few of their number to do the dirty work, they acquiesced in the charge that the Democratic party was Communistic and traitorous. Even Gen. George Catlett Marshall, a public servant of whom any nation in any era could have been intensely proud, was attacked as a tool of the international conspiracy; and so frightening was the political hysteria that General Eisenhower, a moderate and a gentleman, campaigning in Wisconsin in 1952, was persuaded by his advisers —against his will and to his later regret—to delete from a speech a blunt and admirable statement of loyalty to and friendship for Marshall. Lesser lights than Marshall had virtually no chance of real public vindication.

To analyze the Grand Guignol here would be impossible; to rehearse its details, tedious. China had much to do with it. So did the New Deal, and it often took on the aspect of a belated but massive attack on Franklin Roosevelt. The New Deal was said to have scattered seeds of treason, and an old lie was revived as a diffuse implication: that Roosevelt had indeed been a Kerensky, surrounded by little Lenins and Stalins, and that if it had not been for the sleepless vigilance of the right kind of American we would long have been sold to Moscow at a kopek a head.

The country was relieved of mass lunacy by a few brave figures who spoke out in public;* by, oddly enough, a solid streak of

---

* E.g., Field's old friend William Benton, who, as senator from Connecticut, on September 28, 1951 (Field's birthday, by coincidence), delivered a scathing and minutely documented attack on the public, professional, and business ethics of Senator McCarthy, including blunt charges of perjury, acceptance of money for the use of influence, the repeated breaking of his pledged word, and flagitious and deliberate slander. The charges were never refuted or even effectively rebutted, though the Senate did not act for three years. Herbert L. Block of the Washington *Post* and Dan Fitzpatrick of the St. Louis *Post-Dispatch,* both of whom Field admired greatly, never faltered in their outspoken denunciation of the dangerous and divisive nonsense; some of their cartoons on the subject became classics.

skeptical conservatism in the American public, large segments of which simply refused, after a time, to believe that where there was so much smoke there wasn't someone with a smoke machine; by a small but significant part of the American press; and, in a frivolous manner of speaking, by the old Liberty League itself—by an inherent paradox of the post-New Deal world.

The New Deal had drawn almost every American into the political workings of his country. Millions of them, in and out of office, shared a direct, participating interest in the processes and goals of society. And even the politically indifferent carried Social Security cards or consulted the county farm agent or joined unions or profited by an expanded Public Health Service. But the New Deal's goals were left of the traditional American center, and reactionaries, as well as many conservatives, called it Communist. The average politically active citizen, however, approved of the New Deal.* So when he ran into Communists, even in the government, he was neither frightened nor terribly surprised: the Liberty League and other such groups, including many congressmen, had told him he would, and had implied that where he found Social Security, collective bargaining, racial tolerance, and a militant desire for social justice he would also find Communists. Seeing nothing wrong with Social Security and so forth, he saw nothing dangerous in the existence, or even the company, of American Communists. Their noisiest detractors, after all, seemed to be Hitler and Father Coughlin and William Dudley Pelley; not a savory bunch.

There were many exceptions, of course. There were some to whom the word "Communist" was synonymous with "devil." There were others, more thoughtful, who had been revolted by the purge trials in 1937–8; many of these were confirmed liberals, a breed that did not lightly acquiesce in the subordination of liberty and justice to the "truths" of the state or of tradition. The Nazi-Soviet pact of 1939 was a stupendous shock, and disenchanted millions more. When Hitler turned on Russia, and when America entered the war, there was a reflux of sentiment; *The New York Times* quoted Capt. Eddie Rickenbacker in 1943 as saying, "If they keep going on as they are you'll find Russia coming out of this war the greatest

---

* Unless four consecutive elections were fraudulent.

democracy in the world." * Field himself, who admired the strength of the Russian people, and their obdurate resistance to the invader, had never shown the slightest enthusiasm for American communism; on the contrary, he had deplored our inability to make democracy work so well that a Communist party could survive only as a fossilized symbol of innocuous desuetude.

But there remained innumerable good Americans, doubtless including Field, who had at one time or another associated with Communists—at work, in legitimate organizations with limited goals, at parties or folk-song festivals or in school or in local elections. By an irony of the New Deal period, the more desperately a man fought for economic and social justice, the more likely he was to have been in contact with Communists—and the more likely he was to have been a liberal. But people of many political complexions had been involved. These people did not wake up one morning to find that their former friends, associates, or acquaintances were taboo and must be strung up immediately; slowly, from 1945 to 1950, it was borne in upon them by the Americanists that they had committed an unpardonable sin in associating with Communists. And these citizens were no longer young fire-eaters, avid of experience, full of curiosity and vinegar; they were settled, with homes and children, civil servants or professors or newspapermen or grocers or actors or whatever, with a position in the community and a mortgage payment due. By the time they awoke to the consequences being forced upon them by vengeful or panicky inquisitors, it was too late to offer the reasonable and unexceptionable answer: "Of course I knew Communists. Anybody in government, or a university, or journalism or the theater or the labor movement—even lumberjacks and merchant seamen—in the 1930s was bound to meet one somewhere." By 1950 that sort of statement could lose a man his job. The alternative was frightened silence; and if the fear or disillusionment were sufficiently acute, one could join the inquisitors.

But if all that was true, the inquisition would necessarily be endless. If A was a Communist, and B had ever associated with him, then B was a security risk—and all of B's friends had to be investi-

---

* He was never accused of being a dupe, or of spreading subversive propaganda.

gated. But B's friends had their own friends. . . . A fanatical genealogist of the subversive could, in time, trace half of America to a reputed Communist, and then trace the other half to the first half. Which is an exaggeration; but not by much. Soon enough the only good Americans would be those who had joined the swelling chorus of delators.

It never reached that point, of course. It reached General Marshall, and Prof. J. Robert Oppenheimer; ultimately, through a perfectly logical extension of the original dementia, it reached President Eisenhower. Along the way the investigations made life miserable for a large number of innocent idealists. They deprived good men of jobs, standing in the community, credit with their government; some, of physical liberty. They made heroes of perjurers and villains of honorable men. Democrats who fought back were charged with partisan blindness; liberals, with complicity. Out of the various committee hearings came more convictions for contempt than indictments for subversion; hundreds of thousands of Americans lived (and would from then on) with the knowledge that their pasts, reported with dubious reliability, reposed in FBI dossiers; but only a few dozen people were found to have broken a law. (It became necessary for the experts to point out that for each working Communist there were ten, or fifty, or a hundred sympathizers ready to rise in the night when the rocket went up; which figure one accepted depended on which expert one consulted.)

After 1955 the clamor subsided, though loyalty checks and oaths seemed to have been woven permanently into the national fabric. After all the furor, acrimony, time, money, energy, and bitterness, no one noticed that the result had been appallingly meager. Up to 1950 the Congress had enacted only one lone piece of legislation recommended by the House Un-American Activities Committee— and that was promptly declared unconstitutional; it had been aimed not at subversion but at three individuals, who were not only never convicted, but never even accused, of a legal offense. Many people thought specific results were unimportant; the main thing was that the country had been "alerted to the Communist danger"—as if the American people had not been alerted by a century of tradition, by Truman and Churchill and the American press, by books and magazines and radio commentators and traveling lecturers! Or as if the fifth column was about to take over Indianapolis! Even in the early 1930s, at the peak of Communist numbers, respectability, and influence, the beneficent reforms of the New Deal and the natural skepticism of Americans had combined to preclude any slightest possibility that the Communist party would dominate one or another branch of government or business or culture. Half a dozen unions had at one time or another been under the control of Communists, including the powerful New York City chapter of the Newspaper Guild; much of the difficult, viciously opposed, tooth-and-claw organizing of major unions like the United Auto Workers and the United Mine Workers was doubtless done by Communists; there had been a few Communist newspapers and magazines, many mass meetings and rallies sponsored by the party—and the United States stood, foursquare, free and prosperous and the hope of the Western world. If the menace had really been what the committees and commissions and friendly neighborhood Torquemadas said it was, then the American people had resisted it with unparalleled fidelity and courage.

In the end, when President Eisenhower was unmasked, the character of the witch hunts became more obvious. A minute fraction of the monumental effort had been directed at real subversion. There had been some genuine and justified abomination of the hypocrisy and ruthlessness within the Communist party—Negroes, for example, were often tactical symbols and not human beings (an argument rarely stressed by the Southern patriots), and Communists had denounced and expelled each other with cold hatred in kangaroo courts (a phrase much disliked by investigators). But the objects of most of the hearings and warnings and road-company melodrama—of most of the grand, sustained effort to prove that a major conspiracy was rampant and that the watchdogs were all that stood between us and compulsory borscht—were not Communists at all but assorted loose characters like democrats and idealists and integrationists and pacifists and socialists.

Because there were dangers after all. The dangers were higher taxes, expanded welfare programs, disarmament, socialized medicine, immigration by inferior breeds, the defeat of entrenched politicians, modern art, psychoanalysis, atheism. At some point in the 1940s and 1950s each of those (among other items like juvenile delinquency, free love, and foreign movies) was equated with procommunism, if not by a Congressional committee then by an amateur organization in the same field. Increasingly the anti-Communist movement became a haven for racists, religious and sexual bigots, opponents of foreign aid, tax haters, union haters, medieval scholastics, and rascally opportunists (how many elected officials rode it to victory!)—while reasonable conservatives and subdued liberals sweated to solve the real problem of emerging communism in Africa and South America and Asia, and often failed because to reject a reactionary leader abroad was to court political annihilation at home.

There had been one grave internal danger that no committee investigated: the deliberate suppression of free thought by harassment, officially endorsed slander, local social pressure, arbitrary police action, and vigilante blackmail, all suddenly hallowed by what Gibbon called "the pernicious maxim that, where much is alleged, something must be true." Private patriots took their cue from Congress, and small-scale investigation became a new industry; local "Americanism" committees set themselves up as judges of teachers, books, films, and neighborhood morality. The ex-corporals were on the march, and one of them might make it all the way. And it was fun: ten tin-pot fuehrers could frighten a school board out of its bookish dignity; or demand that a college president account for his private opinions; or clean out the local library; or buy themselves funny hats and hold maneuvers.

We were the best hope of democracy—and we had responded to the challenge by investigating, calumniating, and suppressing democracy at home; by reducing a historical battle centuries old to the political prejudices and opportunism of a surrealistic twenty-year period; by yielding without struggle to a hysteria born of ignorance —ignorance of history, ignorance of science, ignorance of a free man's worth; by surrendering the world's oldest and greatest republic to a pompous regiment of bigots.

Field met the issue several times, but only by proxy, except for one appearance in Washington in late 1952. He was left alone because there was not much a committee could, or wanted to, do to him. *PM* was dead; the *Sun-Times* was respectable. Field was too obviously not a subversive, and if his associates were suspect it was easier to call them up than to attack them through a man of such wealth and position; even in the good old days of *PM* and the AP case and the Danaher amendment no one had presumed to associate Field with active subversion.

The same was not true of *PM*'s staff, though when Albert Deutsch was called to Washington in May, 1945, it was by the House Veterans Committee and on an issue apparently unconnected with the Communist menace. Still, Mississippi's John Rankin was the committee's moving spirit, and he must have relished the encounter. Deutsch had been exposing incompetence and mismanagement in veterans' hospitals, and on the 18th had refused flatly to name "about five" Veterans Administration officials who gave him information. That was a hallowed point of journalistic honor, in the breach of which no one would ever be able to trust a reporter's discretion. Deutsch was threatened with a citation for contempt; the committee voted it, 13-5. Representative Huber, Republican of Ohio, had dissented vigorously, saying, "I take the position that the committee is supposed to be investigating veterans' facilities and not newspapermen." He was quite right, but he was overruled. That evening Deutsch called Field in New York; what did Field think of his stand? "You've got to do what you think is right," Field said. Deutsch agreed, somewhat relieved; he would continue contumacious. "By the way," Field added, "what's your favorite food?" Momentarily baffled by the irrelevancy, Deutsch finally answered, "Chocolate cake." "All right," Field said. "If they send you to jail I'll be there every day with a chocolate cake." To that note of low comedy was added another on May 22, when various members of the committee announced, without elaboration, "The Deutsch case is dead."

But those were the good old days. Five years later there was little inclination to joke; there were simply too many victims, and there was no way of knowing who was next. (It was in 1948, incidentally, that J. Parnell Thomas, Republican chairman of the House Un-American Activities Committee, said publicly to Rankin, "We have been unearthing your New Dealers for two years, and for eight years before that," and Rankin replied, with equal elegance, "I know the Senate is busy now nagging the white people of the South, and all of the FEPC, and all this Communistic bunk," an exchange that summed up the committee with precision and brevity.) By 1952 Senator McCarthy had replaced the Bill of Rights, and we were probably closer than anyone dreamed to some system of permanent loyalty registration.* Perhaps worst of all, President Truman had relieved Gen. Douglas MacArthur of his command in Korea, and MacArthur had returned to a triumph unequaled since Diocletian's,† amid mutterings that Truman should be impeached.

At a meeting of *PM*'s stockholders in 1940 Field had met Lillian Hellman. As a playwright she was already distinguished by *The Children's Hour* and *The Little Foxes;* in 1941 she added *The Watch on the Rhine.* A brilliant and serious talent, obviously; more, a sharp critical sense and a detestation of hypocrisy. It was she who stated bluntly that the prepublication dummies of *PM* were "a mess —badly written, no stance, cute and unprofessional," which did not conduce to warmth and good cheer in the executive offices. Her subsequent comment that she thought the newspaper was doomed was even more dismaying, but she had never been famous for ingratiating optimism. As a backer Field, who could ignore the fulminations of outraged right-wingers, was more thoughtful when *PM*'s friends weighed in with blunt complaints, but was prepared for a long period of experiment and revision. Neither he nor Miss Hellman was a constant visitor to *PM*'s offices, and their friendship grew slowly out of other interests: politics in the broadest sense, and the theater. Field did not invest in plays; if he had become known as an angel he would have drowned in scripts, whether or not every newspaperman had one tucked away. Mrs. Field invested now and

---

* Such a system was suggested in *The Nation* by Arthur Miller, in a sharply ironic "Modest Proposal." It was much too close to reality to have been as funny as Swift's, but it was grimly effective. Many poor souls took it seriously, and approved.

† There were even gladiators; a fistfight was reported in New York; a welcome relief from the panegyrics. That General MacArthur failed politically was an encouraging comment on American political stability—as though the people knew, 'way down deep, that their government could be trusted, but had to blow off their accumulated political steam in a brief orgy of hero worship. Field, who most certainly did not venerate MacArthur, had noted nevertheless that the General achieved a program of land reform and encouragement of labor unions in Japan that was radical, to say the least, and that effectively inhibited the growth of a serious Japanese Communist party. The lesson was lost on the General's fans, including those in Congress, who persisted in favoring reactionary governments as "bulwarks" against communism. It is possible that history will have its little joke, and prove the General a rather Heliogabalan military commander but a talented, conscientious, and liberal civil administrator.

then, but never heavily, and in only one or two of Miss Hellman's plays.

Their friendship was quite formal at first. Field's gentlemanly reserve was part of that; so was his great respect for Miss Hellman's art, a respect he would have expressed not in direct compliments but in a slightly shy admiration easily confounded with formality. His reserve lessened over the years, but never quite disappeared. It diminished sharply in the summer of 1944, at Union Station in Chicago. Miss Hellman was off to visit the war in Russia, by way of Alaska and a Russian flight from Fairbanks. The first leg of her trip was by train to Chicago. She ran into Field on the train. He bought her dinner and they played gin rummy; a car was to meet him in Chicago, and he offered Miss Hellman and her secretary a lift. When they got off the train there were no porters in sight, so he picked up her bag, in which were many small bottles of various medicines. The bag promptly fell open, and a small pharmacy of assorted pills, all colors, shapes, and sizes, skittered and bobbled across the concrete platform. Any lingering notion of Field as a stuffed shirt was permanently dispelled by the sight of a millionaire-publisher-and-former-noted-sportsman down on all fours pouncing on vitamins, roaring with laughter, and trapping aspirin like a schoolboy in the finals of a marbles tournament.

After the war the Fields and Miss Hellman saw one another socially for an occasional dinner in the city or weekend at Caumsett. There was liberal agreement among them; they worried harmoniously about peace and politics, the United Nations, the American press, and Miss Hellman's reviews. *Another Part of the Forest,* in 1946, was a great hit. One or two of her plays were weak, as she wrote later, because she tried to do too much at once, but her successes "evidenced," as critics and reference works noted, tight construction, skillful dialogue, and "an illuminating sense of socio-historic forces."

In 1952 Miss Hellman acquired other worries: in May she was subpoenaed by a House committee chaired by Rep. John S. Wood of Georgia, and was summoned to Washington, like anybody who was anybody, to testify about her Un-American Activities, some of which doubtless related to her "illuminating sense of socio-historic forces" in, for example, the American South, and others of which derived from the work, associations, and attitudes she had shared with thousands of intellectuals in the 1930s and 1940s.

She reverted to an old tradition. Once upon a time Congressional committees had simply excused witnesses who announced beforehand that they would decline to testify on one or another constitutional ground, usually the Fifth Amendment. (That was *la belle époque*. The witnesses were usually ranking businessmen, public servants, and gangsters, and the purposes of the investigations were legislative and not punitive.) Miss Hellman wrote to Representative Wood, on May 19:

. . . I am ready and willing to testify before the representatives of our government as to my own opinions and my own actions, regardless of any risks or consequences to myself.

But I am advised by counsel that if I answer the committee's questions about myself, I must also answer questions about other people and that if I refuse to do so I can be cited for contempt. My counsel tells me that if I answer questions about myself, I will have waived my rights under the Fifth Amendment and could be forced legally to answer questions about others.

This is very difficult for a layman to understand. But there is one principle that I do understand: I am not willing, now or in the future, to bring bad trouble to people who, in my past association with them, were completely innocent of any talk or any action that was disloyal or subversive.

I do not like subversion or disloyalty in any form, and if I had ever seen any I would have considered it my duty to have reported it to the proper authorities. But to hurt innocent people whom I knew many years ago in order to save myself is, to me, inhuman and indecent and dishonorable.

I cannot and will not cut my conscience to fit this year's fashions, even though I long ago came to the conclusion that I was not a political person and could have no comfortable place in any political group.

. . . I am prepared to waive the privilege against self-incrimination and to tell you anything you wish to know about my views or actions, if your committee will agree to refrain from asking me to name other people. If the committee is unwilling to give me this assurance, I will be forced to plead the privilege of the Fifth Amendment at the hearing.

The committee announced that it would not allow witnesses to set the conditions of inquiry, implying strongly that it was not Miss Hellman's thoughts or activities they were interested in, but the names with which she might embellish their proscription lists. Miss

Hellman declined to associate herself with the "friendly witnesses" whose convenient memories had become notorious; she pleaded the privilege of the Fifth Amendment, and that was that.

At least one of the committee's possible objectives had been attained: Miss Hellman had exposed herself to public contumely. (Committee members often said that their purpose was "to present the facts and let the people judge"; when "defendants" pointed out that they were not permitted to present witnesses, or often documents, in their own behalf, they were informed that the committee was "not a court.") The Fifth Amendment had once been a Constitutional safeguard of which Americans were proud: it was the republican answer to the Inquisition, the Star Chamber, the rack and thumbscrew. But in the investigations of "subversion"—so comfortably vague, ranging from an attempted assassination to membership in a bookshop—a hodgepodge of misdeeds was lumped together indiscriminately; so was a hodgepodge of procedures; so was a hodgepodge of punishments. Publicity was a great punishment; and through publicity the Fifth Amendment became, in the early 1950s, tantamount to an admission of guilt.* Of course there were Communists among those who invoked it; it was unlikely that even a committee as inept as the House Un-American Activities Committee could fail to call in several party members. But there were also scores of perfectly good citizens who had known—or once been—Communists, socialists, radicals, New Dealers, and who were recalcitrant because they refused to drag before the indiscriminate Congressional floodlights others they believed as innocent of subversive intent as they themselves were, or because they refused to make it harder for the next witness to take the same position.

At any rate Miss Hellman returned to New York quite depressed, and not at all sure that she would be hearing again from many old friends. She let herself into her apartment, and found the hallway blocked by what she later called "two of the prettiest plants in the history of the floral business." One was from Ruth Field, the other from Marshall Field; and Miss Hellman discovered later that neither had consulted the other. There were also two telephone

---

* It was virtually re-legitimized a few years later, when suspected racketeers and allegedly crooked businessmen invoked it. The egoist is folk hero; the altruist, traitor.

messages, one from Marshall, one from Ruth, urging an immediate weekend of recuperation at Caumsett. It was friendship when friendship mattered.

In the midst of that feverish period there was a national election. Field supported Adlai Stevenson with warm enthusiasm. He liked General Eisenhower, whom he had approached on behalf of the Democrats in 1948; but Stevenson was very much Field's kind of man. They were good friends, and had celebrated what Field might have considered a joint triumph in 1948. Stevenson was intelligent, cultured, honest; his liberalism was ingrained and not donned and doffed with changes in the political weather. He even shared Field's affection for England.* His views on domestic and foreign policy coincided largely with Field's, though it was certain that as President he would have had to make compromises with Congress (e.g., in the areas of loyalty procedure, foreign aid, and defense spending) that Field would have regretted. But any President would have that problem, and Field preferred to see Stevenson solve it.

The *Sun-Times,* under Marshall, Jr., came out for Eisenhower in January of 1952, long before either convention. That was criticized as premature, but there was a logic behind it. Marshall was a Republican, and the newspaper was middle-of-the-road, but beyond those facts, a good many political centrists, ranging from mild conservatives to mild liberals, were offering the argument that the Democrats were prisoners of their past, and that the barbarous excesses of name calling and witch hunting, the divisions within the public and within Congress, could be reduced and with luck eliminated only by a vastly popular moderate Republican President. The argument was not profound, but it was supported by other arguments: that the Democrats had been in too long, and that it would do them good to let someone else take some of the responsibility for the mess the world was in; that the Korean War was a fatal stalemate; that the country needed a period of calm, conserv-

---

* Addressing an Anglo-American group in London during a time of strained relations between the two countries, he had once said, near the end of his talk, "I do not believe that there can be any permanent hostility between two peoples who, when they fall in love, have recourse to the same poets." Not precisely a hardheaded political sentiment, but it was the sort of thing that charmed Field.

ative government in order to recover from the sometimes flamboyant reactions of an embattled and maligned Democratic party; and even—such was the power of wishful thinking—that Eisenhower would bring tax cuts and a reduction in the national debt. All things being equal, the *Sun-Times* would have supported Eisenhower on grounds of party and personality; but there was a strong feeling that as usual all things were not equal, and that there was much to be gained in freshness and vigor from a change of administration.

Marshall Field disagreed, and he broke into print again with a letter to the editor of the *Sun-Times* which must stand as a classic in polite diffidence. It was not even a "guest editorial"; he would not have imposed to that extent on the working management of the newspaper. It appeared on October 9. The salutation ("Dear Marsh") and the close ("With my best love, Dad") were omitted in the published version.

From Marshall Field Sr.

Mr. Marshall Field Jr.
Editor and Publisher
The CHICAGO SUN-TIMES
Chicago, Illinois

This is written to you as the editor of the SUN-TIMES.

When the editorial leadership of the paper was turned over to you, I was certain that you would assume an independent and direct attitude, and this you have done.

Your support of Gen. Eisenhower in this presidential campaign I both understand and respect.

However, in the minds of many, my position in this campaign is confused with yours, and I am sure that both you and I are equally anxious to clear this up.

I have always had a great admiration for the general, and was delighted to see him nominated at the Republican convention. I had hoped he might lead the liberal element of the Republican party into the ascendancy, and that whoever won the election, this country could look forward to furthering the social gains that have been made in the last 20 years.

As the campaign proceeds, I develop stronger and stronger doubts that he will be able to accomplish this.

On the other hand, Adlai Stevenson has made his position entirely clear, and I find myself in complete agreement with his aims, and more and more convinced that the country needs a statesman of his caliber, supported by

Democratic control of Congress. I can see no prospect of the Republican
Party, even under the leadership of Gen. Eisenhower, accomplishing the
objectives that we so much desire for the American people.

This letter is, of course, in no way intended as an effort to influence your
attitude. But I did wish to clear up the confusion which I know exists, and
I am certain that you respect my independence as I admire yours.

MARSHALL FIELD

The diffidence was surely unique. Owners of major American newspapers are notoriously autocratic and domineering, and any but
Field would probably have asked his son to take a leave of absence
for the duration of the campaign—as Field might easily have done
if he had been another sort of man. But he had given Marshall, Jr.,
responsibility for the *Sun-Times;* he would not—as he never did—
go back on a commitment; and it was unthinkable to him that his
son, bearing responsibility, should be denied commensurate authority. So that letter was the full extent of Marshall Field's exercise of
influence, or manipulation of the press, in favor of his friend and
choice Adlai Stevenson. He made campaign contributions, and both
he and Mrs. Field exerted themselves as private citizens, but the election was hopeless for the Democrats. Eisenhower swept into office,
dragging large numbers of Republicans behind him, and the country
did settle into a period of relative calm, if not, in some areas, outright
torpor. It remained to be seen whether the new regime would restore
manners and morals to the discussion of political loyalty.

Before the year was out Marshall Field was himself in Washington, testifying before a committee: the Select Committee to Investigate Tax-Exempt Foundations and Comparable Organizations. It
was

authorized and directed to conduct a full and complete investigation and
study of educational and philanthropic foundations and other comparable
organizations which are exempt from Federal income taxation to determine
which such foundations and organizations are using their resources for purposes other than the purposes for which they were established, and especially
to determine which such foundations and organizations are using their resources for un-American and subversive activities or for purposes not in
the interest or tradition of the United States.

Well. Comfortably vague terms, again. To a Southerner, for example, a grant in race relations would render a foundation suspect; if it was not out-and-out subversive, or even if he admitted that it was in the interest of the country, he could certainly claim for his constituency that it was not in the American tradition. Was the New Deal in the American tradition? Few Republicans thought so, and many Democrats were inclined to doubt it, except in election years. Was a study of socialized medicine subversive? Not in itself; but its conclusions might be. Those, however, were simple questions. The committee's tortuous logic led to far more baroque possibilities; e.g., was a perfectly sound grant subversive if made by a foundation one or more of whose board members had belonged at any time to an organization then or later cited by the House Un-American Activities Committee or the Attorney General? The scope and conclusions of the inquiry were limited only by the beliefs and preferences of the inquirers.

The committee's chairman was Rep. Eugene Cox of Georgia. Other Democrats were Brooks Hays of Arkansas, Aimé Forand of Rhode Island, and Donald O'Toole of New York; Republicans were Richard Simpson of Pennsylvania, Angier Goodwin of Massachusetts, and B. Carroll Reece of Tennessee. It was a lame-duck committee, sitting in November and December of 1952, after Eisenhower's election; when it reconvened in 1953 its composition had altered and Reece was its chairman.

Field and Max Hahn sat together at the hearing. Field did most of the talking; the Foundation's executive director interrupted occasionally with facts and figures. Most of the questioning was done by Harold M. Keele, the committee's general counsel. Field first identified himself, discussed his other enterprises briefly, and stated that the Field Foundation's assets were between eleven and twelve million dollars. In answer to a question about the "general nature" of the Foundation's activities, he read his own introduction to the first annual report. There followed a perfectly reasonable discussion of the role of foundations in our society, during which Field plumped for total independence but deplored the foundations' distrust of one another and failure to cooperate more openly.

Keele then asked about five of the Field Foundation's grants: $2,500 to Open Road, Inc.; $1,000 to the People's Institute of Applied Religion; two grants to the Southern Conference for Human

Welfare; and $1,250 to the American Council of the Institute of Pacific Relations. The first was dismissed quickly; the organization was a sort of travel agency for the academic world, arranging trips and tours, originally recommended by many college presidents, and any political overtones had sounded long after the date of the grant. The second was slightly more complicated; the Institute had asked for $4,000 to promote "tolerance and active brotherhood" among "impoverished rural citizens in the South," i.e., small farmers and sharecroppers, white and colored. That had a nasty ring to the Southerners present. Field pointed out that the applications had been supported by the Presbyterian Church and the Unitarian Committee. Keele went on to the next grant. The Field Foundation had given the Conference $2,500 in 1942 and $5,000 in 1945. The first had helped to defray the expenses of a conference in Nashville, and the application had been accompanied by, among other communications, "a letter from the White House signed by the President saying he thought this was a good thing." The objective had been to work out ways and means of mobilizing Southern manpower for the war effort. That explained, Field questioned the proscription:

Mr. Keele. They are cited at page 104 of the House un-American Activities Guide to Subversive Organizations. It probably was not cited at that time [1945].

Mr. Field. As I remember it, they protested that, and I rather think they were relieved from that allegation. I think at some later date they protested it.

Mr. Keele. We were checking on that this morning. I think they did protest it, but I believe it stands.

Keele then went on to his *pièce de résistance,* the Institute of Pacific Relations. Among the Institute's sponsors and staff were certainly some left-wingers; also middle-of-the-roaders and right-wingers. One of its board members, Alfred Kohlberg, had charged in the mid-1940s that it was functioning as a source of Communist propaganda on the Far East; its board, a respectable and representative body, had rejected his demand for an investigation (of some 2,000 members, only 66 voted aye), and he had carried the fight to Congress and the public. Any organization interested in Asia, with the exception of militant partisans of Chiang Kai-shek, was suspect during the decade after the war, and the Institute admitted a wider diversity of opinion than most. The Field Foundation's grant had helped to pay for an international conference of the Institute at Mont Tremblant, Quebec, on December 14, 1943, when the enemy was momentarily Japan. The list of sponsors and personnel was impressive, and Field pointed out that in 1943 the I.P.R. was "looked upon as an excellent educational institution . . . probably knowing more about the East than any other institution." The Institute had more recently been under heavier fire; it was an ideal scapegoat for frustrated Americans, citizens of a nonimperialistic democracy who could not understand why, unless there had been treason, the millions of Asia had been unwilling or unable to embrace the virtues and benefits of life as lived in Elm City, U.S.A. In 1950 the attacks on it had culminated in the famous, and fortunately unsuccessful, Congressional lynching of Prof. Owen Lattimore, in which both allegations and tactics touched a historic low in political morality; echoes of that bitter farce were still loud. In 1943, when the Foundation made its grant, Lattimore was on leave from his work as political adviser to Chiang Kai-shek, who had shortly before refused to accept his resignation, writing to President Roosevelt, among other compliments:

Mr. Lattimore has fully measured up to our expectations and has entirely justified your choice. You unerringly detected the right man to select to act as a counselor at a time when decisions which will affect the whole world for generations to come are in the balance. . . . His absolute integrity is manifest in everything that he does or says, and I never have the slightest doubt that any suggestion that he may make is based upon a genuine desire to assist China to the utmost of his power.

That had not impressed Senator McCarthy, who had alleged that Lattimore was the "top Russian espionage agent in the United States," and had staked his reputation and integrity, neither of which was as yet perfectly defined, on the truth of the charge. A Senate Foreign Relations Subcommittee, in its majority report, found the charges utterly baseless, but they had been trumpeted so loudly in the press and, unfortunately, from more than one pulpit, that very strong prejudice lingered. Field was being very gently tarred with the same tired old brush. Consider the sequence: an organization had been attacked on apparently flimsy pretexts; one of its members had been slandered, and thoroughly vindicated; and Marshall Field was being asked to justify a grant made to it nine years previously, before any of the baseless attacks. His defense of the Foundation was hardly a defense at all, because he did not see why a defense was required; he simply reminded Keele of the Institute's high repute when the grant was made, and Keele was satisfied; not much of an edifice could be raised on a cornerstone of fantasy.

Then the committee got to what Field had known was inevitable: character analysis of some of the Foundation's directors.* The first questions were about Dr. Channing Tobias, which was not unexpected: he was a Negro leader and had belonged to many organizations judged dangerous at one time or another. Field spoke of him as a thoroughly honest gentleman, adding, "all his advice . . . shows the greatest wisdom and consideration and, furthermore, he saved us from a lot of very foolish grants, I think, in race relations, which didn't really have any validity."

The questioner then went on to Field himself: had his name not appeared on the letterhead of the American Committee for Yugoslav Relief, on August 6, 1945? † Yes, it had. The organization had been represented to him by reliable people as a legitimate relief organization; its one purpose at the time was the collection of old clothes for ravaged Yugoslavia. Had his name not appeared on the letterhead of the Chicago Council of the National Council of American-Soviet Friendship on September 17,†† 1951? Yes. It had appeared without his knowledge or permission; he had asked the organization to desist, and it had complied. Field was never asked what he thought of the programs of these organizations.

The questioning shifted to Judge Justine Polier. She had been a member of several organizations reprobated by the Attorney General, including the National Lawyers Guild, which, being a haven for those who chafed within the starchy confines of the American Bar Association, would naturally harbor a large component of rad-

---

* Rep. Brooks Hays of Arkansas had publicly deplored much of the irrelevant foolishness of these hearings, had stood up to defend the liberal outlook, and took no part in any personal attacks.

† Hiroshima Day.

†† Constitution Day. On May 16, 1963, the Federal courts finally ruled that the Council had not been subversive, or a Communist front, after all.

icals and freethinkers, and probably a few Communists too. Field answered:

> Well, Judge Polier has been a judge of the Court of Domestic Relations in New York for over fifteen years. I have actually sat in her court and listened to the way she handles children, and I really think that perhaps she is . . . among the greatest experts on children's courts in the country. . . . She has written a book on it which is very widely quoted.
>
> I have always found her the most charming person, the most understanding person about children, of anybody I knew. Furthermore, I have dined at her house and she has dined at mine, and I would never have had the slightest—I *wouldn't* have the slightest—hesitation in saying that she has never by any intimation shown communistic leanings.

There followed a somewhat technical discussion of grants and of the funneling of foundation money, in the course of which Field said that he thought no grants should be made, or old grants continued, to organizations which were, or came to be, overtly subversive of the government. By that he understood the classic Holmesian definition of subversive—the man falsely shouting fire in a theater and causing panic. If asked Zechariah Chafee's interesting question—"How about the man who gets up in a theater between the acts and informs the audience honestly, but perhaps mistakenly, that the fire exits are too few or locked?"—Field would have replied firmly that such a man was within his rights. His was not a violent or heroic resistance to the committees; there were others far more outspoken in their testimony. He detested their intolerance and their timorous partiality; but however foolish and unnecessary their charades, they were legitimately constituted and had legitimate precedent; it was up to Congress to regulate them, and up to the people to vote themselves a decent Congress. Field, relatively immune himself, reacted rather by a well-bred and slightly weary tolerance of the inevitable coupled with a firm refusal to acquiesce, even by implication, in ignorant criticism of his friends and beliefs.

When the committee finished its work in 1953 it issued a report. Like most such committee reports, it led to much righteous homily and no legislation. Prominent among its conclusions was the complaint that few foundations supported pro-American projects.

Race relations? Child welfare? Education? Full employment?

Care of the handicapped? Mental health? Art museums and concerts? Grants to poets? The Boy Scouts? Hospitals and universities
and youth gang projects? The East Harlem Protestant Parish and
the Catholic Interracial Council of Chicago and the American Jewish Congress and the YMCA and the YWCA? Labor-management
studies? Decent pay for teachers? Scientific conferences? Seminars
in American studies?

Not pro-American. What the committee wanted was essay contests, papier-mâché reconstructions of Valley Forge, studies of the
economic philosophy of Calvin Coolidge, dissertations on the destruction of liberty by the New Deal, and illustrated biographies of
Theodore Bilbo and Merwyn K. Hart. That, as near as anyone
could make out, was what the Americanists stood for.

It was not what Field stood for.

Field's next brush with the Capitoline geese was in March of
1953, when the Senate Subcommittee on Internal Security called up
twelve members of the Sarah Lawrence faculty to determine more
precisely what subversion had been accomplished by their pernicious habit of independent thought. Popularly, or unpopularly,
known as the Jenner Committee, the subcommittee was chaired by
William Jenner, Republican, Indiana, a man of notorious patriotism
whose investigations brought him much public attention. The teachers were by no means helpless and befuddled. Sarah Lawrence was
liberal, integrated, not at all hesitant to explore controversial social
issues. (Field had returned home from the campus one evening and
reported to his children that he had spent part of the day listening
to a class try to define a conservative. "By God, they couldn't," he
said. "And in the end neither could I.") Attacks upon the school
had swollen to a fortissimo in 1951, inspiring a statement in January, 1952, from President Taylor and Chairman of the Board Harrison Tweed, which read in part:

Until very recently Sarah Lawrence has been spared the kind of attacks
on freedom in education which have occurred at many other institutions.
Elsewhere the demand has been made that certain speakers be barred from
the campus, that textbooks be screened, that loyalty oaths be imposed, or
that faculty members be investigated.

At Sarah Lawrence such questions have not come up. No one inside the

College has ever suggested that we should have less freedom than we do, nor have we had any threats or accusations from outside the College.

However, during the past two months we have had such attacks. They have come from the usual sources. One was a newspaper article in the Hearst press; another came from *Counterattack*, whose publisher also issues *Red Channels;* to add to the variety, on the same day as the *Counterattack* issue, the Communist Party *Daily Worker* denounced us for alleged discrimination against Negro students on a College-sponsored trip to the TVA; another attack appeared in a circular issued by Mr. Allen Zoll listing faculty members with "subversive connections" teaching in women's colleges, including Wellesley, Smith, Mount Holyoke and Sarah Lawrence; another appeared in an article by Mr. Louis Budenz in the November issue of the *American Legion Magazine* which attempted to throw suspicion of "harboring subversives" at 15 colleges and universities, among them Harvard, Cornell, Amherst, Columbia, Pittsburgh, New York University, California, Chicago and Sarah Lawrence.

Early in November, the Americanism Committee of the Westchester County Legion, no doubt stimulated by Mr. Budenz' article, asked to talk to the President. . . . The names of three faculty members (one of whom has been at the College since it opened in 1928, another with ten years of service) out of 71 members of the teaching staff were brought into the discussion by the visitors. They were informed that the persons mentioned were good and honest teachers who enjoyed the confidence and respect of their students, their colleagues, the President and the Board of Trustees. The discussion was frank, and it became clear that the visitors felt that college presidents should dictate the political beliefs and activities of students and faculty, as against the College view that students and faculty are free to act and to speak for themselves.

The Commander of the Bronxville Post of the American Legion then entered the situation, and wrote a letter which demanded, under threat of the "fullest publicity," that the President give an "official" answer to questions relating to possible communist party membership or sympathy on the part of Sarah Lawrence faculty members.

The Board of Trustees had held its fall meeting on November 8, 1951: it was the day on which Field took office as a trustee. That meeting had authorized a committee to compose a statement of policy, which was quoted within the larger statement:

An educational institution must teach its students to think for themselves by giving them the knowledge on which to base judgments. The teaching faculty of Sarah Lawrence College is responsible for the development in students of intellectual independence and maturity. In carrying out this responsibility faculty members are expected to deal candidly and honestly with controversial questions. Teachers who meet the test of candor, honesty, and scholarly integrity may not be deprived of any rights they hold as citizens of this country, including the right to belong to any legal political organization of their own choosing.

It is a principle accepted by the Faculty, the President, and Trustees alike that there is to be no indoctrination of students with a political, philosophical or religious dogma. No person, therefore, who takes his intellectual orders from an outside authority, whether communist or any other, could be given or could retain the responsibility of membership in the Sarah Lawrence faculty.

"Communist or any other." That included the busybodies who were making all the fuss, though the hint was lost on them. The larger statement then continued:

. . . It is an essential part of good educational policy that a college ask for no orthodoxy in its teachers as to religion, politics, or philosophical theory. If it were otherwise, teaching would be done not by the faculty but by the governing board of the institution. . . .

It is in this refusal to exact an oath or to cross-examine the teacher as to political belief or to spy upon his political activities that the educator differs from the outsider who wishes to investigate college faculties. The latter fails to understand the necessity that the teacher be free to have and to express his own ideas, and that the teacher is not a person hired to follow certain rules and to advocate certain economic or political dogmas.

As everyone who has attended Sarah Lawrence College already knows, the idea that a member of the faculty should take intellectual or political dictation from any quarter is alien to everything Sarah Lawrence stands for. Prejudiced or politically inspired teaching would quickly reveal itself, and would be rejected by the students and by the whole College.

At its spring meeting the board approved that stand, after a moment that Dr. Taylor would never forget. He had reported the latest demands of the Legion, still fulminating, and asked for the opinion of the board. They all knew that his own inclination was toward a flat rejection of such juvenile meddling, but there was a long moment of silence when he had finished; and it was suddenly clear that the board was waiting for Marshall Field to speak—a new boy on the board but a veteran of many such conflicts (and a member of

two posts, and the Society of Founders, of the American Legion).
He did speak, quietly but with a distinct note of annoyance and
exasperation: "Oh, tell them 'Nonsense,'" he said. "I'm sure we
have more important things to do."

The hearings of the Jenner Committee were held a year later. The
issue, as always in such investigations, was not whether the teaching
was biased (or, at other times, the film shown or the music played
or the ballet danced; the investigators were hardly qualified for that
sort of judgment), but whether the teacher's private convictions
were heterodox as measured against the new orthodoxy. To assume
that the committee was looking for Communists would be to give
that body more credit than it merited; it was, like so many of its
counterparts, simply looking for anything left of center that it could
make loud noises about. If it turned up a real Communist, that was
a windfall; and if he was a teacher of old Icelandic, whose private
views remained without pertinence to his work, that made no difference. But Communists were rare; much more common in all
colleges were our old friends, the reliable villains: "premature anti-
fascists" (as if all Americans should not have been permanent anti-
fascists), articulate New Dealers, and so forth. Sometimes there
were ex-Communists who had quit the party and become liberals.
That was sinful. Those who had quit the party and become conservatives were solid citizens; if they had become vigorously reactionary,
they were heroes.

President Taylor was in a sensitive position. He knew that his
teachers were good; their right to their beliefs had therefore to be
defended to the utmost. But that defense required the support of
a stubborn board, or at least of the majority of a stubborn board.
No one, Taylor realized gratefully, was more stubborn than Field.
"He had fundamental, intuitive convictions about how a college
should be run, and they were flatly liberal. There was no guff in
him, and he disliked rhetoric. He was direct and simple, and often
made decisions on a personal basis—he consulted those intuitions."
Taylor felt that as president he should have discretionary powers
over the fate of faculty members in political trouble; and Field
backed him up. (It was reminiscent of Robert Hutchins's need for
authority over the University of Chicago. At one point only Field
and Sewell Avery, the archconservative, stood behind him—Field

because he approved so fully of Hutchins as a man, Avery because he disliked restrictions on the power of executives. At Sarah Lawrence Field amalgamated those reasons.)

The board had adopted the policy statement unanimously, but it was not unanimous in deciding individual cases, and Taylor was not sentimentalized into a great liberal hero. No one was sure for several years that the universities would survive the political attacks, that superpatriotic legislation would not transform them into cafeterias of dull orthodoxy. Many institutions, big ones like Harvard and small ones like Sarah Lawrence, fought it out on the lines drawn by Socrates; others, like the University of California and many publicly supported colleges, could offer only token resistance to the bureaucracies that governed them. Some of Sarah Lawrence's board members feared the loss of reputation and credit, the undoing of a quarter century's good work, and were not persuaded that a handful of teachers was worth the risk of destruction.

Taylor was sure, and so was Field, and the college did survive. Mainly because the board, even divided, stood behind the decisions of a majority, but also because another paradox had crept into the illogic of investigations. Too many men and institutions and ideas had been condemned. The public had first been too willing to accept an unsubstantiated charge as equivalent to a verdict of guilty, and now there was a reaction, in the press, in magazines, in discussions, even in the streets: if General Marshall and the Protestant clergy were subversive, maybe the Founding Fathers were too, maybe the committees' version of Americanism was not quite accurate; maybe, in short, there was something fishy going on. A creeping cynicism was abroad in the land. McCarthy was parodied, satire was revived, at the most solemn moments of national peril someone giggled. To Field that giggle was a sign of returning national health, and capped his deep satisfaction at serving on the Board at Sarah Lawrence in its most perilous years.

At a meeting of its executive committee at the Coffee House Club in New York City, late in 1953 when the attackers had been repelled and the board could relax for a time, a toast was raised to Marshall Field. He improvised an acknowledgment, in the course of which he said, "I've spent many years on many boards, and this is the best of them all because everybody lets me do my own thinking. On other boards I'm briefed to death before each meeting. But that's in the spirit of Sarah Lawrence, and I'm glad we kept that spirit alive." He then assigned the credit to Taylor, in a pledge of friendship and support; he himself, he insisted, was just another board member.

He was, as Taylor said later, sweet, generous, loyal, and as tough as they come in matters of principle. When Harrison Tweed left the board in 1954 Taylor suggested to Field that he take the chair, and make Sarah Lawrence a central part of his life: all his major interests were reflected there. That was not quite accurate. Field Enterprises was still a major interest, and so was active work in child welfare. Field declined. He had too much still to do.

3

In the summer of 1953 Field took another long and very pleasant vacation: he and Ruth and the younger children packed up and went off to Europe for several weeks. Field caught up with a few old friends whom he had seen rarely, if at all, since 1936. He dined with Rudolph de Trafford, a delightful occasion for two friends of forty years' standing. De Trafford had always felt that Field became a liberal democrat out of the simple desire to help the underdog, but now, after so many years, he sensed a deeper motive: Field said that injustice was a "self-aggravating condition," and had to be fought always and everywhere. The two discussed Adlai Stevenson and President Eisenhower; European politics, the economic situation; they gossiped and reminisced. Field's political views were not at all startling in England, and no need to go back to the Whigs, either: there were Labour peers in Lords, and British wits would shortly remind us that "we have two parties in England; the Labour party, which you Americans call socialist, and the Conservative party, which you Americans call socialist." An American liberal, however staunch and however patrician, was nothing remarkable.

Field also spent some time with his old friend Oliver Lyttelton, who was then Secretary of State for the Colonies and had his hands full, what with Malaya, the emerging African nations, British Guiana, and particularly, that year, Kenya. Lyttelton thought Field seemed quite tired. The two were in a very small venture together, and at one point Field said, "You take care of it, will you?" That was quite uncharacteristic; Lyttelton had previously found him always interested and decisive. They talked world politics and families and trade. They reminisced about Trinity College and Caumsett and President Roosevelt, whom Lyttelton had known—and had once found in a very testy mood because of some criticism in *PM*. He reminded Field of an old anecdote—Field had forgotten—and they laughed together over it: as a director of the Guaranty Trust Company, from 1920 to 1933, Field had once been asked to guarantee personally a transaction involving some $2,000,000; he had listened carefully, and refused: "My fee as a director is one gold piece for each meeting. I do not consider that a businesslike percentage." When the two parted Lyttelton experienced a moment of even more than his usual strong affection for the United States, when he reflected that it could produce Marshall Field's kind of man.

Family also visited family; the Fields and the Edmondstones met in London. It was Field's first meeting with his sister Gwendolyn since her visit to Caumsett in 1948. It was also a meeting of many children: there were five young Edmondstones by then.

The weeks on the Continent were pure fun. Field had always liked museums, and visited as many as he could, displaying a preference for—though he never collected—the Dutch and Flemish masters. The family traveled mostly by car, seeing France, Austria, and Italy, and passing through Germany. At an inn in Austria, reeking of cabbage, fiddlers, dark beer, and distilled *Gemütlichkeit,* a local roisterer rebuked Field, who was not dancing. Field said he was wearing his unmusical shoes. The Austrian offered to swap shoes with him; it was done; Field danced. The joke, however, was on the Austrian, whose feet were size 10; Field's shoes were size 8.

Throughout the trip their emotions were the usual careless delights of Americans touring Europe, and their conversation was the ordinary happy chatter of tourists. As at home, the dinner table was not a rostrum, and Field dropped the weight of his political and philanthropic burdens when he was relaxing with his wife and children. Now and then, to be sure, he took a half hour to explain the state of the world, or animadverted briefly on the history of a town.

(When he did that at home he was likely to be interrupted by an underage daughter asking if she could smoke a cigarette—the answer was no, but she could puff on his pipe—or challenging him to a game of Chinese checkers.) At any rate the trip through Europe was neither a Grand Tour nor a seminar; it was a pleasant, slow, comfortable tour, and it was a real vacation for Field, who was a tired man.

They had always been an informal bunch at home. With two generations of children Field had enjoyed far longer than most men that strange, warm, lovely, antic confusion that children bring to a home. Even his friends shared that confusion; the children were rarely banished from daytime activities. In the 1940s Charles Cushing had suffered a disastrous series of defeats at Chinese checkers; he hied himself to an expert, polished up his game, returned grimly to Caumsett, and lost three in a row to the girls. Howard Seitz of Paul, Weiss was Field's impeccably groomed personal attorney, but when he came out to Caumsett one Sunday he found himself outside after luncheon playing kick-the-can. Field gave himself wholly to play, or to sport, with his children and never burdened them with his own cares; but when they had cares of their own he was always there.

He was severe when he took Bobby and Harry to the Bronx Zoo in 1938 and Bobby wanted to see the monkey house but Harry couldn't stand the smell; Field said, "Harry, the trouble with you is you're overcivilized. If I can take it you can. Let's go." But a dozen years later, when Bobby went through a painful period of doubt—college going badly, worries about the future and his usefulness, values badly shaken up—Field said, "Bobby, do exactly what you want. Don't let others tell you what you *ought* to be doing. Dig ditches if you feel like it. Don't worry about 'living up' to anything. I'll be behind you," which was precisely what the boy needed to hear. (Years later, reading Witter Bynner's translation of Lao-tzu, Bobby found this passage, and thought it perfect for Field:

> A leader is best
> When people hardly know that he exists,
> Not so good when people obey and acclaim him,
> Worst when they despise him.

'Fail to honor people,
They fail to honor you';
But of a good leader, who talks little,
When his work is done, his aim fulfilled,
They will all say, 'We did this ourselves.')

The informality, and Field's natural fatherliness, kept his interest in his children at a constantly high level, and his love for smaller children made him a conscientious and happy grandfather. After 1950, when he had more time for them, he became mildly patri-archal—not with the benevolent, silver-haired majesty of fairy tales, but with the active concern of a man whose affections ran deep and who had seen, in his work, broken homes and starving children. Twice divorced himself, he had stood close with help and sympathy when Barbara's first marriage was dissolved in 1941, and when Marshall, Jr.'s, ended in 1947. His first concern was always for the grandchildren.

Bettine, the youngest child of his first marriage, had been divorced from Dr. McChesney Goodall. She was married again in Frederik-sted, Virgin Islands, on December 26 (there called "Christmas Second Day"), 1951, to Eldridge Bruce, a man she had known for some time, and with whom she had worked for Henry Wallace dur-ing the Presidential campaign of 1948. It was a lovely tropical wed-ding, performed by a local official ("like a justice of the peace . . . a lovely dark-faced man with many wrinkles and kind eyes") at the home of Mr. and Mrs. Stanley Coulter, good friends of the bride. The guests were Julia and Joseph Higgs (he was a doctor in Hun-tington, Long Island, and delivered their first baby two years later) and Penelope Draper, who had been Bettine's closest friend since early childhood.

A social note of little consequence; in a reasonable society it would have been just another divorce and remarriage. But ours is a society not always reasonable, and the marriage, which proved to be a great success, was, when it was announced six months later, momentarily a *gros scandale:* Eldridge Bruce was a Negro, and his mother had been Bettine's daughter's nurse in the Goodall establish-ment.

Field did not care about Bruce's color or social standing. He did care about the painful position of a mixed couple in American society. If Bruce had been some sort of folk hero, distinguished and famous in the arts or sciences, society would not have cared so much; but Bruce was simply a rather handsome, rather intelligent, highly personable young man, a college graduate, with no special claim to public adulation. Field liked him. (There were some who did not believe that. A variety of spurious "inside stories" on his reaction made the rounds: he felt guilty because he thought Bettine had done it to vindicate her father's social views; he really disliked Bruce; his own "latent prejudice" had come out strongly after the wedding; etc., etc. These were monstrous and unforgivable lies. They were accurate reflections of the gossips' feelings, but not of Marshall Field's.) He knew that Bettine would not be permitted custody of her first child, Bettine Marshall Goodall (the Goodalls were Virginians, and it would have been unnatural of them not to be appalled), and said sadly to a friend on the train to Chicago, "I'd hoped there would be at least one generation of Field children that would never know loneliness." Realizing that mother and daughter would be separated, and feeling as deeply as he did about children, he might, if he had known beforehand, have asked Bettine to defer the marriage. But the secret had been kept even from him. When it became public he felt sadness for the child, but no disapproval of the marriage: he wished the couple only happiness. Perhaps inevitably, the Bruces removed to London in 1953, and a few years later to France. They were happy.

4

Field's physical condition had always been good. He had worked hard, and occasionally even overworked for a few weeks at a time, but he had never been subjected to years of ceaseless, debilitating effort, and his long vacations as much as his sporting activities had always replenished him. His teeth and eyes were good, his muscle tone excellent; he suffered no orthopedic problems, no arthritis, not even unusually severe colds. He endured an occasional backache from that old fall at polo, but his periodic checkups were uneventful—though the doctors had always taken watchful note of a minimal flutter, or fibrillation, of the heart. It was all that remained of his early rheumatic fever; it was not dangerous. It was just something that needed looking at, or listening to, once a year.

But in early 1954 he experienced an unusual lassitude, a complete lack of energy. He entered the Johns Hopkins Hospital for examination. The doctors were thorough. The old fibrillation was still present, and still not dangerous. But a routine X ray revealed a small spot, about two centimeters by three, on one lung. As it turned out, the spot was not tubercular; it proved to be cancerous, but completely encapsulated. Surgery was performed in May by Dr. William F. Reinhoff, Jr.

The malignancy was successfully removed, and Field was home in a month. As a patient he had displayed his customary consideration, never accepting so much as a glass of water from a nurse's aide without a please and a thank-you. He might have been excused a breach of manners. The comforts that money could buy were limited in a hospital: private rooms and a radio or television and modern equipment were not reserved to the very rich; barring those, and leaving aside the horrors of some public hospitals, there was little difference within an institution between one patient and the next. The differences were physical: Field with cancer of the lung was, medically speaking, poorer than the man in the next room with a broken leg. It was the perfect opportunity for testiness, self-pity, and arrogance—of which he displayed absolutely none. When Milton Caniff called Mrs. Field from San Francisco to ask after him, Field was astonished at so much consideration and overjoyed at the compliment—though he had made innumerable such calls, and paid innumerable hospital bills for others.* If his gentleness seemed unusual to the staff, it was not so to those who knew him. And perhaps here an ingrained sense of *noblesse oblige,* so inadequate as an explanation of his public courage and integrity, revealed itself in pure form: when the bill for a good life was tendered, one paid without whining.

He was, for the moment, lucky. He was weak and tired (sixty is not the best age for major surgery) but he had come out of it well,

---

* Field received many letters while in hospital, and they were not all friendly; the gist of some was "I hope you don't come out of it." Mrs. Field censored those at the time; such gratuitous invective was horrifying.

and he had an inestimable advantage in his convalescence: leisure. He used that leisure well, regaining his strength at Chelsea and Caumsett.

Later that year Field met a brilliant young Colombian diplomat named Hernando Samper, who served with the United Nations as Andrew Cordier's aide and who became one of Dag Hammarskjöld's three immediate assistants. Samper and Phyllis Field fell in love, and Samper proposed marriage. Field acceded to the marriage—which took place on June 11, 1955—though he did not believe that Phyllis, at the age of eighteen, was altogether ready to leave college and marry of man of thirty-four. If he had not liked and respected Samper so much he might have disapproved. Still, he was tired, and had been sick, and unquestionably felt satisfaction and relief at the knowledge that Samper would cherish and take care of his daughter. But his reservations may have been justified; the marriage ended after only two or three years.

Field gave up none of his offices, directorships, or trusteeships, though he missed more than one board meeting; and if he did no heavy work, he sloughed no responsibilities—he read reports, wrote out comments, and behaved generally as though he had suffered nothing worse than a boil. In March he had inaugurated "The President's Letter," a long report to members of the Child Welfare League, which he proposed to repeat every few months; the second letter, of four and a half single-spaced pages, went out on August first. He referred to his absence:

It was a source of deep regret to me that I was unable to attend the Annual Meeting as well as having to absent myself from the League Board meeting in June. A bit of surgery, from which happily I can report I'm almost fully recovered, prevented my attending.

"Almost fully recovered." But the pace of his life had slowed sharply, and it would never really quicken again. When his friends later talked about that summer, and the years following, they invariably remembered that "he looked tired," and "tended to take it easy."

5

He certainly had no worries with Field Enterprises, which was more
than ever a going concern. The *Sun-Times* was in the black. Pocket
Books and Simon and Schuster were steadily profitable and expanding; so was Functional Music, Inc., an acquisition of the 1950s
which piped music into offices (brisk tunes during hours of normal
fatigue; less obtrusive music during peak work hours) and other
public places, possibly including mass-production chicken houses.
The Quarrie Corporation, with the World Book Encyclopedia
(which became Field Enterprises Educational Corporation), had
acted with rigorous logic on a repeatedly confirmed observation:
the more calls made, the more encyclopedias sold. Its sales staff had
been vastly expanded, and its sales had consequently spiraled to
sensational heights. Minor enterprises like the Hudson Press and
the Delta Manufacturing Company were long gone. *Parade* was
booming. By 1950 its circulation had passed 5,000,000; by 1954
it stood at 6,500,000, which represented some fifty newspapers;
advertising sales for that year totaled almost $11,000,000. (By
1958, when *Parade* was sold to John Hay Whitney, its circulation
was 8,600,000 in sixty-one newspapers, and its advertising revenue
was almost $24,000,000.)

Much of the prosperity was due to new, more aggressive, generally younger management. *Parade,* for example, had been reorgan-
ized at the beginning of 1946, and placed under the firm direction
of Arthur H. Motley ("Red" Motley except on the most official
documents). "Heavy, sensible budget cutting ensued," in the words
of a later report. New marketing techniques were developed. Editorial content grew more serious, shifting from frivolity and cheese-
cake to current events of importance; the ratio of pictures to text
dropped from 75:25 to 35:65. Advertisers approved and responded,
and by the fall of 1947 *Parade* was permanently in the black. It was
being printed in four separate plants, and when it bought the roto-
gravure plant of Triangle Publications it was able to print half its
pages in four colors without delay. Even television, which not only
subverted readers but also engorged large chunks of advertising
money, failed to slow the supplement's growth. Field had held the
controlling interest personally until 1949, though for conversational

purposes *Parade* was considered part of Field Enterprises; in November of that year the interest was formally transferred to the parent corporation. Motley and Charles Cushing had guided a very spindly journalistic child to a flourishing maturity. As usual, Field had exercised no editorial control but had kept a close watch on the supplement's financial health. (He did interfere once. The interference was not characteristic; its purpose was. He asked Motley to kill an article about Margaret Truman that he found snide. Motley complied without hesitation, and 600,000 copies of *Parade* were scrapped.)

Motley was not close to Field's political and philanthropic life, and formed various judgments largely through an uncomplicated business association. "He was the most honest man I ever knew," Motley said later. "I suppose conservatives—I'm one of them—would like to claim him for their own, but he was a liberal, all right, though he was very conservative in his personal economics. But that meant—and this is important—that if he was willing to risk several million dollars on an idea, he thought the idea was worth more than money. Most of his ideas were. I'm not sure how he felt about government in business, but I know he wanted more humanity in both. I didn't think of him as a crusading liberal; I admired him for his day-to-day virtues. He was a damned fine human being, and if he'd lost every penny he wouldn't have changed."

In Chicago too there was new executive talent. Richard Finnegan and Russ Stewart had come into the newspaper end in 1947. Carl Weitzel remained Field Enterprises' treasurer. John Wharton, in New York, was its general counsel. Assorted newspapermen and executives found the atmosphere of progress and expansion congenial, and the roster accumulated a number of respected names—Thomas Reynolds, Larry Fanning, Emmet Dedmon, Herman Kogan. In the business and advisory offices new talents brought new methods and energy to the organization, merging smoothly with the old-time editorial men like Milburn Akers. There was L. B. Sizer, for example, who came to Field Enterprises after a successful career in advertising (with N. W. Ayer in Philadelphia) and merchandising (with Marshall Field and Company), and who as a general assistant to the publisher was never quite sure how his position should *really* be defined, quoted Pericles easily, and did not hesitate to call Plutarch "an old gossip." Or Will Munnecke, who had been controller of Marshall Field and Company's retail store from 1933 to the end of the war, had left the store to become a vice-president (on the business end) of the University of Chicago and secretary of its board, had shifted to the Encyclopædia Britannica, revamping the management of the Great Books, and in January, 1951, had become business manager of the *Sun-Times*. From these and others of his new executives, Field was happy to draw one inescapable conclusion: the more generally intelligent, the better-read, the better-traveled, his executives, the better businessmen they proved. He could take pride in Field Enterprises—newspapers, encyclopedias, *Parade,* book publishing, radio stations, even a little music. The conformity of rich and respectable corporations in an affluent and stable society was natural, but a country was educated by its publishing empires and would in time evolve its own ideas. That was part of Field's faith, and was why he insisted on competition; the thought delighted him and often irritated his competitors. Believing that education was ultimately a force for liberalism, he could justly have claimed that Field Enterprises, made successful by him, by his son, by the talented management finally acquired, was the most valuable asset he had offered the country.

He had begun to think of a permanent home for Field Enterprises—particularly the newspapers—almost before he incorporated them, and to discuss it in the late 1940s. Nothing was done immediately. In the early years *PM* and *Parade* were shaky; the book publishers had their own home; what form Field Enterprises might take in five years was hardly predictable. Besides, the two newspapers were losing a lot of money, and heavy building investment could wait.

It waited. It was talked about at board meetings until it became a running fantasy. "It was discussed," John Wharton said, "only to afford a relaxing opportunity to invent new and wilder reasons why it shouldn't be built." After Weiss's death, when Wharton became general counsel and corporate prosperity looked like a good bet, the talk became more serious. Marshall, Jr., was in favor of construction; Wharton thought the time had come, and Carl Weitzel agreed. They all realized that in addition to its physical advantages a new building would be excellent public relations, showing Chicago that the Fields were there to stay, and inspiring civic pride. At a directors' meeting in 1952 Wharton announced blandly that he thought the corporation should adopt a fiscal policy that would permit construction of the new building. For a moment it was the old joke: "Dear, dear, what ideas John has!" Field said. But Wharton was not fooling this time. Weitzel backed the suggestion; the two Fields talked it over; in March the decision was made. The board approved construction of dock facilities at the site (on the northern side of the Chicago River Canal at Wabash Avenue), and authorized preliminary planning. The architects got to work and made estimates. Before the ground was broken in 1955 they were back to announce that the estimates had been low by three million dollars; but the commitment to build was firm.

The building was planned and built to house two newspapers. That elusive second newspaper was still a goal, even more desired by Marshall, Jr., than by Field. Most cities had two newspapers at best, and with luck they were competitors. Chicago could afford four, New York seven. Ideally no two of them would be under the same management, and the metropolitan reader would have a Lucullan choice; but the reality was other. In Chicago at least one of the four, the *Herald-American,* was financially flabby; in New York at least three were. When a struggling newspaper changed hands, a new owner had to pump new money into it. But when it merged with an existing newspaper it became part of a profitable enterprise, generally making it even more profitable shortly because the cost of running two newspapers under one ownership is not twice the cost of running one. Money could be saved on staff, presses, distribution, and on ground rent, which is a considerable item. The tendency was, in short, toward mergers for economic reasons. The Fields could gamble on acquiring an afternoon paper at some time in the next five or ten years.*

---

* It was a bit over three years. In January, 1959, Field Enterprises acquired the Chicago *Daily News* from John S. Knight. It was a major newspaper with a loyal following and its own staff of foreign correspondents—a rare luxury in American journalism. The sale price was $24,000,000, considerably more than Field would have had to pay fifteen years before. But the property had grown; by 1959 it included so much real estate, which was sold off, that in the end the net cost to Field Enterprises was slightly under $4,000,000; a financial coup. The newspaper itself had been in the black all along, but under Knight's management it had run down, quality being sacrificed to profits. When Marshall Field, Jr., took over he not only

Field delivered a brief address at a luncheon before the ground-breaking ceremony on November 16, 1955. (L. B. Sizer had collaborated in writing it, but it lacked a quote from the Greeks.) The luncheon was at the Palmer House, Mayor Daley was present, and Field's satisfaction was great. The ceremony was like dozens of others in dozens of cities; every time a plant went up some executive scooped out a spadeful of dirt and grinned for the cameras. But this was a moment of culmination for Field. He had, long before, consciously set himself against the grain of his social class, against the tide of his early life as a sportsman. In twenty years of wearying and expensive effort he had created a successful corporation that embodied much of what he considered socially useful and politically moral, and he was about to give it a permanent home. Officially a resident of New York, he probably felt more like a Chicagoan on that afternoon than ever in his life. He spoke vigorously and emotionally, but slowly. In a couple of paragraphs he rehearsed the history of his newspaper; then:

> It has been a cause of great satisfaction to me that this newspaper [enlisted] the active interest of my son Marshall; although I had no thought of directly influencing my son toward this end. He has always exhibited a mind and a will of his own that strongly remind me of my grandfather who began our family affairs here in Chicago.
>
> As many of you know, my grandfather was a man of determined mind and unswerving purpose. So, I believe, is my son. And I know that whatever choice of a career he made had to be wholly his own. Happily, returning from wartime service, he responded strongly to the challenge of a newspaper's exacting demands. Furthermore, and to my great pleasure, he evidenced a strong attachment to Chicago as a place to make his home. . . .
>
> I have only one injunction for Marshall and his associates, and that is to honor the original dream by always jealously keeping the paper's freedom and intellectual integrity. The Chicago *Sun-Times* was organized on the platform that it would stand up for and say what it believed, regardless of consequences. Today I myself do not always agree with its viewpoints—but I recognize the freedom of its publisher and editors as the essence of the

---

restored its vigor, but improved it beyond anything Knight had dreamed of. Meanwhile the Tribune Corporation had bought Chicago's *American*, so Chicago became a two-family newspaper city. The Field newspapers were of course more liberal than the McCormick newspapers, and went immediately about the business of catching up with them in circulation, advertising, and profits—a real vindication, on one level, for Marshall Field.

Sun-Times' success. I respect it, and will always do anything in my power to help defend it.

He closed with good wishes for the future, and after lunch he broke the ground.

6

Child welfare remained Field's first obligation; he clung tighter to children as he grew older. Even the old U.S. Committee for the Care of European Children claimed his attention. It was dissolved in the summer of 1953 and Field, who was still its president, issued invitations to a final grand party in honor of its executive director, Miss M. Ingeborg Olsen. Joseph Reid of the Child Welfare League, noting the occasion but not aware of Field's direct involvement, said, "They'll have a lot of office furniture to get rid of. We need it." Field said, "I had a bit to do with them. Maybe we can get it. Why don't you go ask them?" Reid did, wondered at the smiles, and of course got the furniture.

Field continued to speak and write for the Child Welfare League. His "President's Letter" appeared every few months, and he appeared at regional conferences all over the country. In April, 1954, just before his operation, he addressed the Southern Regional Conference in Jacksonville, Florida:

We must know what we believe and why we believe it. . . . We must believe that *all* children have the right to a home, a real home, not a shanty on a South African rooftop—or on a Carolina mudflat, either. We must believe that *all* children have the right to good health—the right to proper food, pure water, the latest immunization against disease, protection against hookworm and pellagra, and hospitalization when they require it. . . . They must have the right to be loved and accepted for what they are—physically, intellectually, temperamentally—accepted by their parents, their peers, and their community. Children have the right to be so nurtured that they grow up with a belief in the essential goodness of people. . . .

. . . Why is it that, with so much known about the basic needs of children, we fall so short of meeting them?

Some of the fault, surely, is not ours. You cannot have calm, serene parents, teachers—or social workers—in times like today, which are clouded by uncertainty, suspicion, and unrest. It is hard to create an island of security in an ocean of insecurity. . . .

. . . Some towns still use jails as temporary shelters for children—60,000 innocent children are lodged in jails today. Those communities don't know what a terrible thing they are doing.

. . . They lack the imagination to see that there, but for the grace of God, go they or their children. . . .

Now one of the most important truths of our time is that the community has a responsibility toward those of its citizens who cannot be responsible for themselves. But how many of our citizens know the extent of their responsibilities? . . . How many know what still needs to be done—and why?

. . . Our concern is with a commodity whose lack no nation can long survive—healthy, happy, well-adjusted children.

In February, 1955, he addressed the same organization, this time in Charleston, South Carolina:

. . . I kept thinking of that satirical suggestion of Bernard Shaw's for the "improvement" of child care. Children, he said, should be "hunted or shot during certain months of the year," so that they could be fed and preserved the rest of the time, "as generously and carefully as pheasants now are."

Facetious? Bitter? Yes. Farfetched? Not really. Not when you recall that only last year it was testified at one of our own Congressional hearings that we spend more on migratory birds than on services to the children of migrant farm workers.

And in March, 1956, he addressed the New England Regional Conference in Boston:

There are many reasons offered for the cutbacks. The most common is illegitimacy. Welfare board after welfare board has become obsessed with the idea that women are having babies in order to make money on [the Aid to Dependent Children program]—and obviously this must not be encouraged. You may have to starve the children in order to improve the morals of the mothers—but first things first. The press has been quick to report the dreadful fact of illegitimacy in ADC. It has not been as quick to supply corroborative figures. The average ADC grant is now $21 a month per child—in Southern areas where the cry of illegitimacy is shrillest, the average grant is closer to $10 a month. I have seen no budget that would allow one to bring up a child on $2.50 to $5 a week and still make a profit, but I suppose it *is* possible.

We may make mistakes but what is better, "grandeur with a few flaws or mediocrity that is impeccable"? I think we are past the era of "impeccable mediocrity."

His speeches were crowded with references to administrative and political problems, to new techniques, to the grim need for public education in welfare; he was often severe about the uncritical adoption of new methods or standards, warning repeatedly that good intentions were not enough. In his last President's Letter he was critical of the Child Welfare League itself: "The League's face has been red for many years over the fact that its own constitution is not consistent with what it advises local agencies to have."

In 1956 he took Joseph Reid to visit with Mrs. Anna Rosenberg, the former Assistant Secretary of Defense, who had established herself in public and industrial relations. She had proposed to Field a series of annual awards for work in social welfare, to be called the Marshall Field awards, and to be presented to individuals and organizations of unusual courage, imagination, or effectiveness. Mrs. Rosenberg's feeling was that a certain panache—fanfare, wide publicity—would interest the public and invite its support. Reid argued that to the professionals such commotion, and its cost, would be excessive for the results, and might alienate a public already amused rather than impressed by the intramural backslapping of so many charitable organizations. Child welfare was not charity; it was partially supported by philanthropy, but it was also a concern of Federal, state, and local government; statuettes and champagne dinners (symbolically speaking) raised more eyebrows than money. Reid suspected that Field enjoyed hearing him argue with Mrs. Rosenberg, though his manner remained grave and decorous. The final decision was to go ahead with the awards; as it turned out, they were given only once.

Public relations had come late to Field's life. His "public image" was of little concern to him; he was a gentleman, and he believed what he believed, and that was that. But some of his friends felt that his public service was not over, and that he might, given the proper push and perhaps a change of national administration, go on to some of the "higher" functions for which he was qualified. Perhaps an ambassadorship, or a high place on the World Bank, or—and this suggestion was most interesting—a seat in the Cabinet as Secretary of Health, Education and Welfare. But politics being the art of the possible, of compromise and maneuver and promise and reward, it was not at all certain that so gentle a man could have attained high appointive office. He remained a contributing Democrat, and a firm partisan of Adlai Stevenson: it was pleasant for his friends to speculate on Marshall Field's future if the Democrats came back in 1956.

But he was tired. In March of 1955 he had taken a vacation in Barbados, where Ronald Tree was living. He vegetated quietly, soaking up sun and sipping cool drinks, trying to relax; but he was bored and restless, and glad to get home. Tree thought his cousin weary, more abstracted than ever. That summer, though, Field perked up a bit. He was not really well and often suffered inordinate fatigue, but Dark Harbor, Maine, in summer was what the doctor might have ordered, and there were moments of fun and forgetfulness. In the fall his vitality ebbed again. He saw friends and tended to business, but his energy came in spurts. Even when he seemed to be having a good time his intimates suspected that he was politely forcing himself to laugh.

He was honored once again, on December 16, when the University of Chicago conferred upon him its highest nonacademic award, the Rosenberger Medal. The citation read:

> In recognition of his profound concern for children in this country and abroad and his manifold contribution to their welfare, his encouragement of men and women exploring and ministering in psychiatry, his persistent efforts to improve relations among the races, his unswerving belief that "freedom is more than a word."

Field entered 1956 with only one serious problem, but that of overriding importance: his health.

CHAPTER ELEVEN

One's sense of honor is the only thing that does not grow old, and the last pleasure when one is worn out with age is not, as some say, making money, but having the respect of one's fellow men.

—PERICLES *to the Athenians,* 430 B.C.

Every age creates its own aristocracy.

—STRINGFELLOW BARR,
in conversation, 1955

IN 1956 MARSHALL FIELD WAS AN EXTREMELY HANDSOME MAN. His hair was silvering, his complexion was healthy and tan, his carriage and gait were dignified. His hazel eyes had softened and warmed with the years and his face had acquired a gravity, almost a melancholy, that made his sudden bright smile all the more striking. A sense of repose was growing in him. Not that he had "fought the good fight and could rest on his laurels," or any such old-soldier sentiment; but he could look back at twenty years of solid altruistic accomplishment—twenty years in which he had contributed a liberal dose of yeast to the ferment of American society. He could remember the rickety orphans of 1936, and look about him at child welfare work on a national scale, steadily gaining dignity and respect and public support. He could remember the first explosive days of *PM* and the *Sun,* and look at the *Sun-Times* with the gratifying and probably amusing knowledge that its weskit-respectable editorial policies would have been considered visionary in 1940. He could remember the explosive reaction when Henry Wallace predicted jobs for 60,000,000, and look at the most prosperous country in the world employing 65,000,000. He could remember the end of free enterprise with the Wagner Act, and read every day that another great corporation had achieved the best year in its history. It was not a bad retrospect, and the prospect was even better. He had given up some of his directorships, and looked forward to increased work in child welfare and education. (Marshall, Jr., had succeeded him on the board at Marshall Field and Company and at the University of Chicago, where Field remained an honorary trustee.) He would have more time for Fiona and Harry and Bobby—not to mention more grandsons and granddaughters from his married children. He could sail and swim at Caumsett, shoot at Chelsea, enjoy the theater and concerts and museums in New York, perhaps travel again, and revisit England.

On June 7 he delivered a commencement address at Sarah Lawrence College. Later that month he suffered a dizzy spell; then another; then one so severe that he lost consciousness. The neurologists found nothing. He was advised to rest as much as possible. He did, and felt fairly healthy all summer; but fatigue set in quickly, and he often grew abnormally sleepy. His mind remained alert; he shared the excitement of the political conventions and campaign; worked for Stevenson in his personal circles; spent much time seeing old friends.

But in September the discomfort returned, and then a sharp attack of dizziness and fatigue, and a real fuzziness of mind. Marshall, Jr., returned from a trip to Hawaii and was much perturbed by his father's condition and appearance. For a time the doctors thought the attack might have been a slight stroke, and recommended absolute rest. The Fields retired to Caumsett, where they were shortly joined by Hernando and Phyllis Samper, who moved in to keep him company and take care of him. Barbara was a neighbor on Long Island and visited often; the Sampers were cheerful and encouraging; summer turned to fall, and Field relaxed in the sun, the salt air, the changing colors.

He had never been conscientious about doctors' orders; vigorous and confident most of his life, he had tended to pooh-pooh suggestions that he go easy, or stop smoking, or diet. (After the operation in 1954 he had quit smoking, but only for a few days. When he resumed, though, he did cut down.) But this time he was strict with himself. Naturally he wanted to get well, but he had an added reason: he had immersed himself wholeheartedly in Adlai Stevenson's election campaign, and wanted badly to swing back into the lists. He never got his wish. The family did not deceive themselves; they knew it was cancer of the brain, and advanced. They also knew that there was almost no hope for him—none, really, barring a miracle. But they kept their fears and anxieties from him. His mind seemed to be wandering more and more. And then, in late September and early October, his eyes began to fail.

It was a tragic development. The trouble was pressure on the brain, and waiting would be futile—even under the best of care and even at Caumsett, which he loved and which the doctors knew was the most comfortable and restful place for him. He might go blind while he was still alert, and live through days or weeks of dark fear. His personal physicians, Dr. Crispin Cooke of Long Island and Dr. Charles Poindexter of New York, called in Dr. Bronson S. Ray of New York, who confirmed the diagnosis and recommended an immediate operation to remove the pressure.

Field entered New York Hospital on October 17. He spent three or four days undergoing supplementary tests and resting. The family knew more about his critical condition than he did, and insisted on being near him; but their presence—all of them, visibly worried— might have alarmed him. Harry Phipps wanted to fly in from Paris, and Ruth warned him that his sudden appearance, after an absence of six months, might frighten Field; he solved the problem by wiring that he was returning to take care of her until Field was out of the hospital. Bobby was in the Army, and ready to apply for compassionate leave; at Ruth's suggestion he held off until after the operation. It was obvious that Field would not recover, but it was impossible to say how long he might live: perhaps days, perhaps months. Fiona returned to Radcliffe. Bettine was in France, bedridden by a slipped disk and pregnant; she had letters from Barbara and from Phyllis, who also kept in close touch with her by telephone, warning her that Field's condition was extremely grave; but she herself was immobilized.

Field was optimistic, and more worried about the coming election than about himself. The natural assumption was that the *Sun-Times* would announce for Eisenhower, but with the election only three weeks off the newspaper had not yet made its formal declaration, and Field never abandoned the slim hope of a conversion. In 1952 the newspaper had been committed to Eisenhower even before Stevenson was nominated, but in 1956 it was not, to Field's mind, thus morally committed; Marshall, Jr., had, after all, supported Stevenson for governor of Illinois in 1948, and Field had been hoping all along that responsibility would make a liberal of his son. Wishful thinking, yes; but he never lost hope.

And he was never to know that the hope was disappointed. The editorial declaration for Eisenhower appeared after the operation, and by Election Day Field was in a coma, and never learned that his great friend Adlai Stevenson had been defeated again. Marshall, Jr., came to New York, of course. Very early on the morning of the operation, when Field was awakened to be prepared, he heard his son's voice in the hallway and brightened immediately, saying, "Why, the old boy's here! How nice!"

The operation, performed by Dr. Ray, was a success in that it did relieve the pressure on the brain, and Field's sight was saved. But the doctors' worst fears about the cancer itself were confirmed: it had become massive. (They discovered later that it had also metastasized in other systems of the body.) There was no possibility of permanent surgical relief. The best they could hope for was time.

But Field never really recovered after the operation. He regained consciousness; he was lucid for periods, then lost the thread of the conversation, then slept. For a week he remained conscious and occasionally alert. His children saw him as often as possible. There was little doubt now that his last days were upon him.

On about the first of November he failed to recognize his daughters; for the next day or two only his wife could reach him, and even she for only a few seconds at a time. His mind wandered wildly in time and space; disconnected thoughts fought for expression.

It was the pattern of cancer of the brain: from the oppressed recesses of the mind come images, fragments of conversation, flashing and turbulent echoes of the past. Yet within the terrible confusion is a bright lucidity: the memories and ideas are clear, the details vivid.

Slowly the confusion won out, the lucidity dimmed. For three days they fought as he dozed, awoke, dozed again. He may have relived much of his past, answering questions decades old, chatting with friends long dead, sinking back and back with each dream. Last summer in Maine, shimmering blue sea and friendly sun; Senate committees and Sarah Lawrence, the University of Chicago, wind and gray cloud over Lake Michigan; the war ended and Marshall safe; Roosevelt dead; the *Sun*'s first day, crowds in the streets, a letter from the President; the quail at Chelsea, whirring out of the brush, a double!; "Marshall, what are you doing in that nest of radicals?" and noisy little *PM* on its makeshift racks; La Guardia at the zoo; Louis Weiss, rumpled, agitated, thousands of sick and loveless children; those funny, reliable people in Trollope, unchanging old friends; his marriage to Ruth, for good, they knew it surely; stretches of green dipping to the Sound in a sharp November afternoon; pheasants, a clean shot, the *coup du roi!;* stacks of bonds, cables from Europe; the real prewar stuff, just off the boat from Canada; a German command post going up in smoke; Henry dead; the boisterous horseplay when Marshall was born, my flesh; his mother gone, Albertine, the *grande dame;* the Atlantic crossing with his first love; King's Chapel, the chestnut stallions, the ruby port and the beautiful green Backs along the Cam, punting in May; the wan fire in his chill room at Eton, "Field major, will you construe?" and the long turfy meadows at Cadland rolling to the sea; "Why can't I see my father?" and the pony cart and little Henry and baby Gwendolyn, and Chicago, and a fierce, tender old man whose name he bore.

On Thursday, November 8, 1956, at five in the morning, after two days of deep coma, Marshall Field III died.

2

The public religious services were held at St. James Episcopal Church* in New York and St. James Cathedral, also Episcopal, in Chicago. His pallbearers and ushers included close political and business associates, and also old personal friends who had been no part of his public life. In New York they were Ronald Tree, Charles Cushing, James Warburg, Edward M. M. Warburg, Frederick R.

---

* Toward the very end Msgr. Wilders, in attendance at the hospital, had signified his desire to perform the last rites of the Roman Catholic Church despite Field's long neglect of formal religion; and the family acquiesced.

Moseley, Jr., Henry Parish II, Wolcott Blair, Thomas K. Finletter, John Wharton, Dr. Charles Breed, Carl Weitzel, George Richardson, John Lincoln, and Russell Forgan. In Chicago they were Joseph Carroll, Hughston McBain, Donald McKellar, John Pirie, Jr., Leonard Reiser, George Richardson, Adlai Stevenson, Russ Stewart, Carl Weitzel, and George Young. He was buried in the family plot at Graceland Cemetery in Chicago.

His mourners ranged from the most rarefied strata of high society to the most anonymous depths of the underprivileged. Hundreds of wires and letters came to Ruth Field, to the Foundation, to the newspaper: a deluge in the first weeks, still a trickle three months later. They were from friends, political figures, newspapermen, professors, publishers, welfare groups, corporations, cultural and religious organizations, doctors and lawyers, bridge players, hunting companions, horsy clubs, socialites, hospitals, assorted intellectuals, and dozens of small groups of Mexicans and Negroes and Puerto Ricans; the Elks and Rotary and the American Legion and the Suffolk Obedience Training Club; Eleanor Roosevelt and John D. Rockefeller, Jr.; the Piping Rock Club of Locust Valley and Jacob Potofsky of the Amalgamated Clothing Workers; Hull House in Chicago and the Society for the Preservation of Long Island Antiquities; the Boy Scouts of America and Robert Moses; Francis Cardinal Spellman and Anna Freud; the Salvation Army and the NAACP; the American Public Welfare Association and the Chicago Racquet Club; hundreds more. The Community Service Organization of Oakland, California, one of many in the West and Southwest devoted to community action and full integration for Mexicans, got his name wrong and wrote its letter to "Mrs. Betty Fields," but the sentiment was right: "We . . . are saddened at the passing away of such a great man as Mr. Fields. . . . We thank you Mrs. Fields for everything as we said before we are sorry to lose such a great person. We are sure his generosity will be eternally rewarded." Every group, every individual who wrote seemed to find in Field the virtues most prized by the writer. Y. C. James Yen recalled his "great idealism and Christian humility." The Decalogue Society of Lawyers remembered that after bestowing upon him its Award of Merit it had gone on to honor similarly Wendell Willkie,

Rabbi Wise, Bishop Sheil, Adlai Stevenson, Harry Truman, and Albert Einstein. Cole Porter wrote:

Dear Mrs. Field:—

I used to know Marshall years ago and have always thought of him as everything nice and delightful in this world.

I send you my deep sympathy.

James Warburg was more personal:

If ever a man was finally given inner peace, serenity, and happiness, that man was Marshall after he was married to you.

Hughston McBain remembered the family tradition:

He was a worthy member of a distinguished American family, and our sympathies go out to his survivors. He not only acted as an able steward to his inheritance and to the family traditions, but he added to them his own keenness of mind and independence of action.

He was a fine man, and this city, his associates and friends here, mourn his death. Like his grandfather, Mr. Field was a leader in the civic and cultural life of Chicago, and it was characteristic of him that this leadership and his contributions were virtually unknown to the public generally. He preferred the personal satisfaction of this service to any public recognition for himself.

A resolution of the City Council of Chicago acknowledged his special contributions to the city in housing, construction, education and freedom of the press and radio, as well as his "broad humanitarian philanthropies." Senators Douglas, Kefauver, and Neuberger wrote or wired Mrs. Field; other senators made statements, and so did governors and congressmen and mayors, and James Farley and Averell Harriman, Stanley Isaacs and Newbold Morris. Even the Associated Press let bygones be bygones: "We mourn the loss of Marshall Field, whose constructive and effective idealism contributed immensely to our times." Unknown mourners wrote spontaneously for no ascertainable reason other than human sympathy; one was a specialist 2d class with the 10th Infantry Division in Europe. The gratitude was not only for Field's example and good works. Serge Obolensky wrote to Mrs. Field:

I just want to tell you how deeply I feel for you in your great sorrow. Although I seldom saw Marshall lately I always had a deep affection for

him. He was the first American I met when he played polo for Cambridge
in 1914 and I played on the Oxford team against him.

He was one of the kindest and most considerate men I have ever known
and I will always cherish his memory.

Speaking not only for himself but for many who might never have
known that Marshall Field played a part in their lives, Dr. Channing Tobias wrote:

Marshall was a prince; in fact, he is a prince, for as long as interest in the
poor lives, he will live. This sad morning I can only repeat what has been said
many times over. He used money to make men rather than men to make
money.

Letters came from Leona Baumgartner, commissioner of health in
New York City, and Judge Polier, and Mrs. Crystal Potter, once
assistant commissioner of welfare; from Carolinians who had
hunted quail with him at Chelsea; from Adopt-A-Child ("An Interracial, Interfaith Program to Find Permanent Homes for Negro and
Puerto Rican Children") and the Commercial Club of Chicago;
from Americans for Democratic Action and the Metropolitan Club
in Washington, D.C.; from the National Urban League, which
helped distressed Negroes at home, and the St. George's Society of
New York, which helped distressed Britons abroad. Rudolph de
Trafford wrote from England; Harold Taylor from Bronxville; John
Pirie from Chicago; Roland Redmond from the Metropolitan Mu-
seum of Art; Arthur M. Schlesinger, Jr., from Cambridge; Edward
R. Murrow from just around the corner. Letters came from Topeka
and Nashville, Memphis and Jacksonville, Philadelphia and Los
Angeles, Brussels and Paris, Anchorage, Kentucky and Flint, Mich-
igan. R. E. A. Drummond, Maldwin's nephew, wrote to "Aunt
Ruth" from Gizo, British Solomon Islands Protectorate, Western
Pacific; Turner Catledge wrote from Times Square. John R. Crawford and Sam Fry, Jr., who had sat across bridge tables from him,
wrote; B. Jay Becker expressed the sorrow of the Regency Club.
Glore, Forgan and Company gave $5,000 to the Child Welfare
League in his memory. Thomas F. Reynolds, managing editor of
the *Sun-Times,* told Mrs. Field a story she had never heard:

On the day that the national convention opened in Chicago in 1944, I
was writing the lead story for the old Sun. In the midst of this production,

I received an urgent call from Mrs. Reynolds, who had my daughter, then three years old, in Omaha visiting her grandmother.

My daughter had been hit by an automobile and the situation was difficult, to say the least. On that occasion, [Field] left his office and came over to the Hilton Hotel to assure me that I could do anything I wanted to make sure that the little girl was all right. As it turned out, the child was not badly injured and she is now a beautiful girl of sixteen. But in that moment of crisis, Marshall Field told me that I could leave the assignment and fly out to Omaha, and that I need have no worry about medical bills.

He had previously written, "I have been in the newspaper business for almost thirty years. During that time I worked from Seattle through Washington, Atlanta, and down to Miami. But never in my experience did I ever encounter a man who was quite equal to Marshall Field."

Dozens of resolutions arrived, passed by settlement houses and welfare groups and gentlemen's clubs, psychiatric services and citizens' committees and the Academy of American Poets and the staff of *Parade*. Of course, *de mortuis nil nisi bonum;* of course, many of the writers had reason to be politely grateful. But these were not bread-and-butter notes, or form letters. Something of Field's character, will, personal courage—of his presence—came through each letter. Carl Sandburg wrote to James Warburg later, "I had an admiration and an affection for him that grew and deepened with every year," and that seemed also true of people who had never met him, who had only heard about him or read his speeches or had a note from him.

On the night of the day he died the Philharmonic-Symphony Orchestra gave a concert at Carnegie Hall. Howard Taubman's review in the next day's *Times* began:

The Philharmonic-Symphony Orchestra began its program at Carnegie Hall last night by paying a tribute to Marshall Field 3d. Dimitri Mitropoulos conducted the affecting Bach aria after the Chorale-Prelude, "O Mensch, bewein' dein' Suende gross."

Mr. Field had served the Philharmonic-Symphony Society for twenty-seven years as member of the Board, president and chairman. If there had been time to rearrange the program, the Society might well have devoted a greater share of it to Mr. Field's memory.

In a black-bordered announcement inserted into the program, the Society expressed its indebtedness to Mr. Field's "farsighted leadership, his strong belief in the essential role of music in the community, his fidelity to the interests of the Society, and his constant generosity."

Marshall Field deserved Bach.

The press took full and properly reverential notice of Field's death. Disputes, public or private, had no place on the obituary page. Even his Will, admitted to probate on December 10, was reported with respect, and with none of the fanfare and sensationalism that so often accompanied the transfer of great fortunes. It was not a complex document, barring the surveyor's precise description of Caumsett. His dependents had been well provided for by separate previous arrangements. The Field Foundation was left considerable property and securities. Servants and employees were remembered generously. Daumier's painting *"L'Amateur d'Estampes"* was left to the Art Institute of Chicago. The bulk of the Estate was left to Marshall, Jr., to whom certain interests had been transferred during Field's lifetime.

Field Enterprises was passed on intact, and in a manner reminiscent of the arrangements made half a century before by Marshall Field I. Its preferred stock was left to the Field Foundation,* but its common stock—all of it—had already been placed in trust. Marshall, Jr., during his own lifetime, was to be the sole beneficiary of that trust, after which Field Enterprises would, still intact, be left to his two sons. (This arrangement alone, much more ramified than it would seem, and described by one lawyer as "brilliant," should have been enough to exonerate Field of those silly charges that he was a "bad businessman.") And what Field had foreseen came about: Field Enterprises burgeoned. In less than ten years—with the addition in 1959 of the Chicago *Daily News* and the Manistique Pulp and Paper Company of Manistique, Michigan; with the *Sun-Times* very profitable; with the Quarrie Corporation (Field Enterprises Educational Corporation) *netting* more each year than its original purchase price; and with *Parade* expanding so rapidly that when it was sold in 1959 (primarily to raise capital for the purchase of the *Daily News*) its sale price was larger than all the losses sus-

---

* Of which Adlai Stevenson shortly became president.

tained by the Chicago *Sun* and *Sun-Times*—*Field Enterprises was one of the two most prosperous privately owned corporations in the United States.* That was a smashing posthumous vindication of Field—of his judgment, his business abilities, and his courage and persistence through the years when he was considered a fuzzy-minded and extravagant radical, instead of the pragmatic liberal he was.

He would not have been astonished that the myth died hard, but he would certainly have been amazed by the respectful attention paid him in his death. In addition to innumerable obituary notices, sixty-odd newspapers all over the country ran news stories—and thirty-nine of them unbent to the point of composing favorable editorials. Even the *Chicago Tribune* bowed its editorial head in a brief paragraph. The *Sun-Times* ended a two-column statement of grief, "A free and honest newspaper is the best guarantee that the people have against corruption, oppression and tyranny—the very forces against which Mr. Field selflessly fought in his battle to make ours a better world."

Of all the tributes and summations, Field himself would most have appreciated two. The first appeared in the *Yearbook of the Century Association* in 1957. That Association was quite different from his other clubs: the criterion for membership was intellectual achievement. (And the classic anecdote was of the old clubman who, hearing that, exploded, "Achievement? *Achievement?* What sort of standard is that?") The brief biography ended:

He began to take an interest in good works and liberal causes, and in the expression of his own ideas in newspapers that he established or bought control of. When the witch-hunters got after Hutchins, President of Chicago University, Field supported him. He put up . . . money to establish *PM*, the first daily paper to be established in New York in sixteen years. With the encouragement of President Roosevelt, he started the Chicago *Sun;* and its first issue came out three days before Pearl Harbor. The *Sun* from its birth was locked in mortal combat with the isolationist *Tribune*, owned and directed by Colonel McCormick, and no quarter was expected or given.

From here in Field had a good time. The people he used to play polo with and who used to come and shoot his pheasants now referred to him as a traitor to his class, but he couldn't have cared less. He worked hard at the things that interested him: the Metropolitan Museum of Art, the Metropolitan Opera, the Philharmonic-Symphony, and the never ending battle with the Chicago *Tribune*.

He matured late; but once past his salad days, there was nothing the matter with his head. He knew Europe, and had no patience with the delusion of a Fortress America or the idea that the United States could stand apart and alone in a frenzied world. He was not only a cultivated, civilized person; he was a man, generous and true, willing to fight for the right as he saw it.

And he would have treasured an editorial in the *Christian Century*, a magazine that spoke for liberal Protestantism in the United States. Accepting this accolade, he might for once have admitted that he was proud of himself:

MEN WITH DIFFERENT MOUNTAINS

When Marshall Field III died in New York on the morning of November 8, editors and commentators found themselves offering a curious variant on that most American legend: the cherished story of the boy who conquers poverty and rises to significant achievement. In the case of Marshall Field, it was necessary to say that a man had conquered riches and risen to significant achievement. In his youth it seemed that Mr. Field would be distinguished only by the amount of money he had inherited. Then something happened. He became a man of conscience and courage, a citizen who would take risks and face criticism for the sake of unpopular causes. His was a very great victory over the pressures and temptations to live a life of caution, of comfort and conformity. It was a victory exemplary to other men and to their institutions. For organizations as well as individuals are handicapped today by the same pressures and temptations incident to inherited wealth. Churches, universities, business firms, communities, the nation itself—all must struggle now against the inertia of their fatness, and that is a fight that is the harder because the goads of self-discipline never sting like the whips of necessity. How fantastic all this would sound to the late Charles Johnson, president of Fisk University, dead a few days before Marshall Field. Hemmed in from birth by privations close around and prejudice beyond, he yet persevered to become an internationally acclaimed educator, sociologist, mediator and UNESCO leader. None of his achievements may be more lustrous than the latest—that orderly integration of Nashville schools toward which he had worked so long. No property or power ever insulated Dr. Johnson from the demanding realities and clamoring necessities of his day. Two men, much mourned. Two kinds of challenge, equally met. One stature of achievement.

3

The achievement was easier to define than the man. Field was, indeed, patrician in taste and radical in outlook. He urged all men, and required none, to share his beliefs; and he assumed the obligation of speaking out for any man's right to his own beliefs. He addressed himself to issues, and rarely to philosophy; yet his greatest achievement may have been not his enterprises, not his newspapers, not his liberation from the prejudices and superiorities of money, birth and breeding, but his constant effort—and encouragement of others to the same effort—to create a climate in which all men could live at something like their full potential. Though he never held office, that effort made him a more genuinely political man than most of his contemporaries. He cherished the individual. But he knew that any two individuals composed a political system, and that what two hundred million individuals had to say to one another, and to do with one another, and to accomplish together, was precisely what American politics was all about.

Field was born to take a place among the defenders of ancient prejudice, and to safeguard the traditions of his class by resuscitating moribund traditions; instead of which he transcended class by taking seriously the American dream. Not the egotist's nineteenth-century dream of wealth and power, Horatio Alger and the boss's daughter and the Presidency; but the altruist's eighteenth-century dream of a world in which every man owed respect to every other man's life, liberty, and pursuit of happiness. Far from advocating a world of approved attitudes, Field not only consented to variety, but insisted upon it; and because he defended the existence of the momentarily opprobrious, his critics found it easy to identify him with it and to deprive him of respectability and credit. Those critics, who claimed moral superiority for their own beliefs, would—and often did—suppress others in the name of those beliefs; and they were unwilling to acknowledge that those who must suppress forfeit all claim to morality and reveal themselves as the instruments and advocates of naked, amoral force. They were not really republicans; they were nostalgic oligarchs. "A monarchy," Fisher Ames said in the House of Representatives in 1795, "is a merchantman which sails well, but will sometimes strike on a rock, and go to the bottom; a republic is a raft which will never sink, but then your feet are always in the water." Field was born to the quarterdeck, preferred the more crowded and lively raft, and got very wet feet. He may have been among the last of a strange and wonderful line, the line of patrician liberals, perhaps stemming from Pericles, certainly passing through Beaumarchais and Jefferson and the great British Whigs. Patricians, like everyone else, are being assimilated; Field's kind of fortune will not often be passed on again. And those who are lucky enough to be even moderately rich will never again find it easy to abjure social responsibility—high taxes, if nothing else, will see to that.

That said, the genuine modern liberal continues to defy precise definition. He is, ideally, the antidoctrine man—with the one transcendent exception that, inhabiting a complex and hazardous world, he believes in the good sense of educated men. People believed for centuries, with Rousseau, that "natural" man was good—simple, innocent, trustworthy. But they found it much harder to admit that an educated, urban, altruistic man could be good; and they still do. Today's liberals are said to have "lost their roots." But the roots of modern man are not so natural: they are largely urban, industrial, technological, organizational. It is hard for the modern liberal to state his beliefs. He lacks a tested array of dogmas. He wanders, armed in his one fundamental belief, through a contemporary forest of new techniques and shifting relationships. He must make judgments constantly ("The TVA is a good thing"), but when he exalts his judgments to general, overriding principles ("All public ownership is a good thing") he becomes by so much less a liberal, and often a pseudoliberal, bringing disgrace and bitterness to the others. He joins with most of mankind in certain permanent condemnations ("Segregation is a bad thing"); his difficulty lies in explaining what he is *for,* because his desires must alter as the human condition alters. He must constantly adapt his means and ends to the new needs of humanity, and that means a full and unashamed acceptance of ethical relativism, with only man as the constant—which is, to conservatives, a sinister and sinful doctrine. Conservatives have appropriated and glorified traditional morality and religion, which proved inadequate to the liberal; and the liberal has created nothing comparable—*can* create nothing comparable, and remain true to his one belief—to substitute for them. He can offer no Decalogue, no hallowed inventory of eternal verities, and is obliged to fall back on loose words like decency and unselfishness. He can only say, hoping to be understood, that his concern for his fellow man underlies *all* morality. His qualities are easier to state than his beliefs: he has courage, some pride in his species, honor, and a sense of humor. That last is important: without it a man is a puritan, whatever his beliefs.

Marshall Field had all those qualities. He was not a "great" man; we have had many of those, and they are often not worth their keep. He was a good man, which is rarer. "Marshall never did a mean thing," a friend wrote after his death, "never did a cheap thing, or a cowardly thing; never hurt those who could not defend themselves, never asked favors (though he could accept them), and was never frightened away from the pursuit of his ideals."

Every age creates its own aristocracy. Marshall Field was born into one, rejected it, and helped create another and a better. He saw the difference between what the world was and what it might be. He was brave enough to try to improve it, not because some implacable moral imperative drove him on, but because he felt affection and pride for the race of man. He cared.

Acknowledgments

The immediate family of Marshall Field III were unfailingly hospitable and frank, and I wish I could thank them more elaborately: Mrs. Marshall Field, in New York; Mr. and Mrs. Marshall Field, Jr., in Chicago; Mrs. Barbara Field Benziger, in New York; Mr. and Mrs. Eldridge Bruce (Bettine Field), in France; Mr. and Mrs. R. E. A. Drummond (Phyllis Field) in London; Mrs. Fiona Field Rust, in Washington, D.C.; Mr. Robert Phipps and the late Harry Phipps, in New York. Field's sister Gwendolyn, Lady Edmondstone, took the time and trouble to write letters from Scotland. Mr. Stanley Field, in Chicago, gave me important help; so did Mr. Clifford Rodman. Perhaps, considering the kind of book this is, my debt to them will be best illuminated by the grateful note that though each of them saw Field in a different way, none even hinted that I should conform to any but my own view of the man and his world.

In England many people helped me to reconstruct Field's early years: Mrs. Nancy Lancaster, Henry Field's widow; Mrs. Audrey Pleydell-Bouverie; Oliver Lyttelton, Viscount Chandos; Rudolph de Trafford; Dr. J. R. G. Bradfield, Dr. R. Robson, and the late Sir Dennis Robertson at Trinity College, Cambridge; Mr. P. S. H. Lawrence at Eton.

In Chicago Miss Charlotte Hagemann, who had been Field's secretary there, gave me valuable and constant help. Others were Mrs. Kathryn Lewis and Messrs. Milburn P. Akers, Saul Alinsky, James Brown IV, Emmett Dedmon, Raymond Keegan, Herman Kogan, Hughston McBain, Will Munnecke, L. B. Sizer, Russ Stewart, Robert Straus, Carl Weitzel, and George Young; Dr. Edward Sparling; and Archbishop Bernard J. Sheil.

Robert Lasch, of the St. Louis *Post-Dispatch,* and Aubrey Williams, of Montgomery, Alabama, gave me important help.

In New York many gave freely of their time and thought: Miss Gesine Heller, who had been Field's secretary there; Miss Lillian

Hellman; Judge Justine Polier; Mrs. Dudley Schoales; Mrs. Diego Suarez; Mrs. Louis Weiss; and Messrs. Joseph Barnes, William Benton, Turner Catledge, Milton Caniff, Russell Forgan, Max Hahn, Ralph Ingersoll, Ben Kocivar, Nathan Levin, Arthur Motley, Eugene Rachlis, Joseph Reid, Hernando Samper, M. Lincoln Schuster, Howard Seitz, Leon Shimkin, Carl Stern, Adlai Stevenson, Harold Taylor, Ronald Tree, James P. Warburg, James Wechsler, and John Wharton; Dr. David Denker of Rutgers; Dr. Charles Poindexter; and Judge Samuel Silverman.

There were many others who helped, by correspondence, casual reminiscence, offhand remarks, provocative insights and questions, points of fact. No one but me, however, is responsible for the opinions, interpretations, and attitudes in this book.

Notes

These are few and brief. Most casual quotations and accounts of current events were taken from newspaper files, and to list every such reference seemed fussy and overmeticulous. The more strictly biographical material came almost entirely from personal interviews, private correspondence, and the Field files in New York and Chicago.

There is no bibliography. References to Field are available in standard indexes (*Periodical Literature, The New York Times,* the card catalogue) in larger libraries. And a bibliography of the social-political background would have been so general as to be useless. I was cavalier about classic texts, like the histories of wealthy American families, from which I derived nothing of value. Field was discussed directly in two books noted below, which were helpful; but my approach to his life was quite different from that of either.

Many speeches and writings, by various people, are quoted in this book. They were set down precisely as composed, errors and all, without emendation; I did not use the invidious "[*sic*]," feeling that fidelity and flow were more valuable than grammatical accuracy.

CHAPTER ONE

17. Baxter (1615–1691) was a minister, and the excerpt is from his *Christian Directory,* a thoroughgoing guide to moral and ethical behavior for the layman, more detailed and less unctuous than its modern "inspirational" counterparts.

17. The Tawney is of course R. H. Tawney, *Religion and the Rise of Capitalism,* Harcourt, Brace & Company, Inc., New York, 1926.

18. Mumford's quotations are in *The Brown Decades,* of which I used the 1955 edition, Dover Publications, Inc., New York.

19. On the genealogy John Tebbel, in *The Marshall Fields,* E. P. Dutton & Co., Inc., New York, 1947, wrote, "According to Burke's *Landed Gentry,* the family name was originally De la Feld and its possessors lived in Alsace, near the Vosges Mountains and not far from Colmar, where they ruled over lands and castles from the Château de la Feld. The first of the

clan to migrate into England was Hubertus de la Feld, who arrived with the avid band of land seekers accompanying the Conqueror."

20. The remark in the footnote was made by Stanley Field to Wayne Andrews when the latter was doing his remarkably thorough research for a very interesting book called *Battle for Chicago* (Harcourt, Brace & Company, Inc., New York, 1946). Mr. Field later made approximately the same comment to me. Andrews is one of the two or three secondary sources I referred to with pleasure and profit, and this chapter owes a great deal to his book, including the half-dozen very short unattributed quotes. I refrained from thanking him for each, not (to paraphrase Dr. Johnson) that I might appropriate his labors or usurp his honors, but that I might spare a perpetual repetition by one general acknowledgment. He deserves thanks for a delightful survey of Chicago's first century and for pulling together many statements made, in speech or in writing, by Marshall Field I which had to be dug out of relatively obscure sources. Most of the quotes in this chapter are available to anyone, but their existence and sources were brought to my attention by Andrews's book. I have been warned, by those who know, that secondary sources are infra dig., that acknowledging them will secure me a reputation not for honesty but for laziness, and that most writers paraphrase instead, a form of larceny that makes the literary world go round. But I used very few such; I did paraphrase; I acknowledge gratefully. Gibbon (to go from small beer to vintage champagne) preferred Ammianus, but did not hesitate to use Tillemont, Muratori, etc.

33. A very good discussion of Social Darwinism is Richard Hofstadter's *Social Darwinism in American Thought, 1860–1915,* University of Pennsylvania Press, Philadelphia, 1944, which is copyright by the American Historical Association. These quotations on this and the following page are from that book.

39. The extract is from Mumford, *op. cit.*

50. A tumultuous account of Chicago's seamier side at the turn of the century is in *Lords of the Levee,* by Lloyd Wendt and Herman Kogan (Bobbs-Merrill Company, New York, 1943).

CHAPTER TWO

64. The note on Sir Lawrence Jones's autobiographies is the only reference note in the text proper; which I intend as a further compliment and expression of gratitude.

75. Field was here exaggerating for effect. He was capable of driving a car, and had piloted airplanes. He may have meant that he was no mechanic.

CHAPTER FOUR

122. Mr. Gifford's testimony was quoted from the record by Arthur M. Schlesinger, Jr., in *The Crisis of the Old Order* (Volume I of *The Age of Roosevelt*), Houghton Mifflin Company, Boston, 1957. The other incredibilia in this section were dug out of newspapers.

131. The decision is in 67 Fed. 2d 876 (2d Cir. 1933).

145. Schlesinger quoted Johnson, Tugwell, and Lippmann in *The Coming of the New Deal* (Volume II of *The Age of Roosevelt*), Houghton Mifflin Company, Boston, 1949.

CHAPTER FIVE

176. The extracts and quotations on the European refugee children are from *Transplanted Children*, by Kathryn Close, printed by the U.S. Committee.

CHAPTER SIX

217. "No good history of *PM* has been written." Dr. David Denker, now assistant to the president of Rutgers University, wrote a thesis on *PM* in 1951 but delayed its expansion and publication until the passage of time, and the cooling of emotions, might offer a better perspective. It should appear as a book in 1964, and promises to be interesting. Writing a history of *PM* consists in great part of reconciling the vastly different personal accounts of its backers, advisers, and staff, and is reminiscent of the fable about the four blind men and the elephant.

217. All quotations from Marshall Field's *Freedom Is More Than a Word* are printed with the kind permission of the University of Chicago Press, which published that book in 1945.

CHAPTER SEVEN

279. The extract is from *The Lowering Clouds, 1939–1941*, Volume III of *The Secret Diary of Harold L. Ickes*, Simon and Schuster, Inc., New York, 1954.

CHAPTER EIGHT

352. Brown's summation appeared in *The Social Service Review*, June, 1957.

CHAPTER NINE

401. A. J. Liebling's piece on *PM* and the *Star* first appeared in *The New Yorker* on February 18, 1949, and was reprinted in *The Press*, Ballantine Books, New York, 1961. Earlier studies of the press by Liebling were *Mink and Red Herring* and *The Wayward Pressman*.

INDEX

About the Author

STEPHEN BECKER, a distinguished writer and translator, has given two years to this book, his first biography. His first novel, *The Season of the Stranger,* was a Harper Find prize winner in 1951, and was followed by *Shanghai Incident* in 1955 and *Juice* in 1959. He has also written *Comic Art in America.* Among his translations from French have been *The Colors of the Day* by Romain Gary, *Faraway* by André Dhôtel, and *The Last of the Just* by André Schwarz-Bart.

A graduate of Harvard, Mr. Becker also studied in France and at Yenching University in Peking.